OREGON POLITICS AND GOVERNMENT

*Politics and Governments
of the American States*

General Editor

John Kincaid
Robert B. and Helen S. Meyner
Professor of Government and
Public Service, Lafayette College

Founding Editor

Daniel J. Elazar

Published by the University of
Nebraska Press in association
with the Center for the Study
of Federalism at the Robert B.
and Helen S. Meyner Center
for the Study of State and Local
Government, Lafayette College

EDITED BY RICHARD A. CLUCAS,
MARK HENKELS, AND BRENT S. STEEL

Oregon
Politics and
Government

PROGRESSIVES VERSUS CONSERVATIVE POPULISTS

UNIVERSITY OF NEBRASKA PRESS
LINCOLN AND LONDON

⊗

Library of Congress
Cataloging-in-Publication Data
Oregon politics and government :
progressives versus conservative
populists / [edited by] Richard A. Clucas,
Mark Henkels, and Brent S. Steel.
p.   cm.—(Politics and governments of
the American states)
Includes bibliographical references and index.
ISBN 0-8032-1531-2 (cl. : alk. paper)—
ISBN 0-8032-6436-4 (pbk. : alk. paper)
1. Oregon—Politics and government.
I. Clucas, Richard A.   II. Henkels, Mark, 1958– .
III. Steel, Brent.   IV. Series.
JK9016.074   2005
320.9795—dc22
2004027407

Printed by Edwards Brothers, Inc.

CONTENTS

ILLUSTRATIONS

Acknowledgments

This book represents the collaborative effort of fourteen political scientists and one sociologist from across the state of Oregon. Although some of us eventually took on a more active role in the development of the book, the project would not have succeeded without the willingness of the contributors both to share their ideas about Oregon and to work with us as they put together their individual chapters.

We do not have enough space to thank everyone who helped contribute to the book in one way or another. But there are several individuals who helped us or one of the chapter authors, and we would like to give them special thanks. These individuals offered invaluable advice, tracked down data, read through rough drafts of chapters, provided editorial assistance, or simply offered much-appreciated inspiration.

Our thanks go to Judy Hall, Secretary of the Senate; John W. Lindback, Elections Division director; Fred Neal, campaign finance manager, Elections Division; Scott Tighe, former operations manager, Elections Division; Richard Townsend, former executive director, Oregon League of Cities; Bob Cantine, executive director, Association of Oregon Counties; Kelly Freels, budget manager, Department of Administrative Services; Rob Larson, director of policy and research, Department of Education; Morgan Holm, news director, Oregon Public Broadcasting; Virginia Breen, director of radio, Oregon Public Broadcasting; Floyd McKay, author and former Oregon journalist; David B. Harrell, Legislative Administration; Deborah Murdock, assistant to the president for Government Relations, Portland State University; Gordon Dodds, Professor Emeritus, Portland State University; former state senator Ron Cease; Karen Arabas, Willamette University; Carolyn Long, Washington State University Vancouver; Jerry Bieberle; Peter Grundfossen;

Ellen Lowe; Jane Blume; Carmel Finley; Jessica Pearse; Shayla Sharp; and Valentina Fomenko.

We also want to express particular thanks to Clive Thomas at the University of Alaska Southeast for providing continuous advice on how to edit a volume such as this. We may not have always followed his suggestions perfectly, but his insights were always helpful and he was quite prescient in recognizing the problems we would confront.

Finally, we want to thank our supporters at home—Beth, Marcella, and Becky—for their understanding and patience.

OREGON POLITICS AND GOVERNMENT

CHAPTER ONE

A State Divided

Richard A. Clucas and Mark Henkels

Every state has its own political character, but at times Oregon seems especially unusual. The word that might best describe politics in the Beaver State is schizophrenic. The state is driven by two different visions of government and politics. Many state residents desire an active government that rationally seeks to solve societal problems; other residents want a smaller government, one that keeps taxes low, produces few regulations, and protects traditional social values. Sometimes Oregonians are proud of their state's innovative and pragmatic government policies; at other times, voters want to tear down those policies. The divide between these two visions permeates the state's political landscape, from small local debates over development issues to high-profile battles over statewide ballot initiatives.

To understand Oregon it is essential to appreciate these two visions because they play such a central role in the state's politics. We start this introduction to Oregon politics by exploring the historical roots, philosophies, and importance of both perspectives. One view is rooted in the state's "progressive" heritage; the other is rooted in "conservative populism." We then discuss the character of the state's political geography and its constitution. These two factors also significantly structure the state's government and politics.

PROGRESSIVES AND CONSERVATIVE POPULISTS

Contemporary Oregon government and politics remains strongly influenced by the Progressive and Populist movements that arose more than one hundred years ago. Although many of the original concerns of these movements have lost significance, their underlying values remain potent and help explain the ideological division between the modern progressives and conservative populists in Oregon politics.

The Progressive movement (1890–1920) embraced a variety of different and often conflicting goals. Underneath the varying goals two concerns motivated most Progressive reformers. The first was a desire to reduce the economic and political power of corporate interests. Certainly, this desire helped spur Progressive leaders to champion the initiative and referendum, or what became known as the "Oregon System."[1] These procedures were seen as ways to wrest power from the dominant influence of business and corrupt politicians and return it to the people.

Second, the Progressives believed that government should be a positive force in society, one that helps further the common good. Among other things, Progressives advocated that expert officials control government policies. It was this desire for government by experts that led Progressives to advocate civil-service reform and changes in municipal governments, including the introduction of the commission system of government in Portland. Although the "Progressives" were to disappear as a distinct force in Oregon politics by 1920, their belief that an open, activist, and pragmatic government could lead the way to a better, more "modern," society remains influential.[2] Throughout this book, we use the term "progressive" to identify the ideas, policies, individuals, and groups that follow this latter strain of Progressive thought. Progressives, as we use the term, promote the active use of government power to solve societal ills. They support the promotion of experts in government, the use of rational problem solving, and the adoption of innovative policy solutions.

Progressives of the early 1900s sometimes overlapped and sometimes were in conflict with another reform movement—Populism. The early Populist movement was based in agricultural areas where farmers and others believed that their well-being was controlled by powerful outside forces, particularly the railroads and banks.[3] Seeing the underlying political problem to be the power of the corporate elite, the early Populists sought government policies that supported the interests of farmers and the working class. There was a natural alliance between Populists and Progressives in their early days because both sought to give political power more directly to citizens. The Populist movement in Oregon peaked in the 1880s and 1890s, when supporters helped elect a Populist governor (Sylvester Pennoyer) and several state legislators. Like Progressivism, Populism as a formal movement faded early in the twentieth century; yet its core belief remains a potent political force.

Today, the term "populism" is commonly used to describe political movements premised on the belief that powerful elites prevent the common people from acquiring what is rightfully theirs. The appeal of this idea goes beyond the rural communities and small businessmen of the original Populist Party, or what was called the People's Party in Oregon. Contemporary populists hold a variety of different and often conflicting goals. Populists can be roughly divided into two groups: liberal populists and conservative populists.

Liberal populism and conservative populism are both "populist" because they identify an elite that must be fought to promote what advocates see as the true will of the people. Yet they focus on different elites, public values, and issues. Liberal populists (sometimes referred to as "progressive populists") see the will of the people as being denied by the influence of large corporations and a wealthy elite. Accordingly, they advocate government programs that advance the political power and material interests of the less wealthy.[4]

Although occasionally recognizing problems connected to corporate power, conservative populists believe that the core problem of modern politics is how government agencies, politicians, and an elitist media interfere with the popular will. They fear that these groups hinder private economic choice, the effectiveness of the market, and the public's ability to promote broadly shared conservative social values. Thus, conservative populists seek to restrict the size of government and to rely more on the free market. There is one area where conservative populists do promote an active government: social regulation. While criticizing the liberal social values presented in the media and academia, conservative populists often support government regulations that promote their view of appropriate personal behavior. Thus, conservative populists often advocate government intervention that promotes "traditional family values" and inhibits such activities as abortion and homosexuality.

In this book we use the term "conservative populist" to refer to the ideas, policies, individuals, and groups that want to reduce taxes and limit the role of government in most social and economic contexts, except where the government may serve to promote traditional values.

In many works examining American politics today, authors tend to focus on the split between "liberals" and "conservatives." We could have used those terms in describing Oregon's politics, for in truth the conflict in Oregon does reflect a split between those two groups. However, both of those terms incorporate a wide variety of groups as well as diverse and sometimes contradictory political ideas. We chose the terms "progressives" and "conservative populists" to give a more precise and historically appropriate description of Oregon politics. We use the term progressive, in large part, because of its historical roots in the state. The state's image has long been associated with progressivism, and the term is still used by many to describe Oregon. We wanted to capture that history. We have also used the term in order to emphasize the tie to the Progressive movement's support for government by experts, rational problem solving, and innovation. The term "liberalism" does not convey that particular tie.

We chose the term "conservative populism" because we want to emphasize the strong concern that many Oregonians have for protecting the rights, interests, and values of the people from an overly intrusive government and a morally divergent intellectual and media elite. The plain term "conservative" misses the significance of the anti-elitist nature of this movement.

THE MODERN CONTEXT

The terms "progressive" and "conservative populist" are crude categories for complex movements and sets of values. The two terms certainly do not capture the full character of Oregon politics. Not all liberals in the state are progressives. Not all conservatives are populists. Not all the conflict is between progressives and conservative populists. As several of the chapters point out, Oregon has initiative activists and opponents to free trade who champion liberal populist values. There are also traditional conservatives, who value a healthy economic environment more than a conservative social climate. Yet much of Oregon's political conflict reflects the collision of the progressives' strong support for an active government and the conservative populists' general desire to limit government. This conflict is found in most states and in national politics, but in Oregon it is so prominent that we argue that it is the defining characteristic of the state's politics today.

Certainly, progressivism has long played a significant role in Oregon politics. Historically, the state built a reputation for progressivism through its adoption of a variety of innovative policies. At the beginning of the twentieth century, Oregon was a leader in the Progressive movement, championing such reforms as the initiative and referendum, the recall of public officials, the direct primary, the direct election of U.S. senators, and women's suffrage. Since then the state has asserted public control over ocean beaches, imposed strict land-use laws, created one of the nation's only regional governments (the Portland region's Metropolitan Service District, or "Metro"), experimented with universal health care coverage (Oregon Health Plan), passed the first bill requiring a deposit on beverage containers (the "bottle bill"), and introduced Vote by Mail.

Recently, one of the state's newer progressive policies received national attention for its achievements. In 1989 the state created the Oregon Progress Board. The board's mission was to create a benchmark system to measure Oregon's social conditions and to clarify goals in many areas of policy. Through the benchmark system, Oregonians and their officials can determine whether their government is fulfilling its goals. In 2002 the John F. Kennedy School of Government at Harvard University recognized this effort as one of the top fifteen outstanding examples of innovation in state or local government in the past fifteen years.[5] Another more recent progressive policy has captured even more attention, however. Since adopted by voters in 1994, the state's physician-assisted suicide law has been the continuous target of opponents in Congress and the White House, who would like to see it blocked.

Despite this lengthy list of accomplishments, Oregon's progressive image is not entirely accurate. There are two problems with this perception. First, the actual impact of many of the state's progressive programs often fall short of their advocates' hopes. For example, the adoption of the bottle bill greatly increased the recycling of cans and bottles, but more than twenty other states still have a higher overall recycling rate than Oregon.[6]

Second, and more important, the state has another side to it, namely, strong support for conservative populist ideals. In recent years conservative populists, like progressives, have enjoyed some success in pursuing their own innovative legislation and shaping the state's political agenda. The most visible way that conservative populists have been able to articulate their vision is through the initiative process. During the past fifteen years or more, several conservative populist leaders have turned to the initiative to pursue their goals. If one counts the total number of victories by these conservative leaders, one finds that their success rate is not much different from that of progressive activists. Yet many of their proposals have been at the forefront of political debate in Oregon, and some very important ones have become law. These include ballot initiatives reducing taxes (Measures 5 and 47), controlling government takings (Measure 7), stiffening penalties on criminals (Measure 11), and imposing legislative term limits (Measure 3). Conservative populist proposals have also enjoyed greater support in the state legislature in recent years, ever since the Republican Party took control of both houses in 1995 for the first time in four decades. But even beyond the initiative process and state legislative politics, the ideals of conservative populists are often heard in a variety of political debates in Oregon, including on such diverse topics as the building of a home in the Columbia River Gorge (chapter 3), the selection of state court judges (chapter 11), and the character of public education (chapter 17). Thus, conservative populism cannot be ignored if one is to capture Oregon politics accurately.

Given their different visions, it is not surprising that these two groups are frequently in conflict with each other, setting the stage for some of the most important political fights in Oregon today. In the chapters that follow, we describe a variety of ways in which progressives and conservative populists, and the conflicts between them, shape Oregon politics. The next section, however, presents two case studies that illustrate the importance of both sides in defining Oregon politics. These specific issues are illuminating because they are often held up as examples of Oregon's progressive policies. In reality the politics surrounding them is more complex and their current status has been strongly shaped by conservative populist activism. The two examples are land-use planning and the Oregon Health Plan.

LAND-USE AND HEALTH CARE CASES
The Ecotopia *Legacy and Measure 7*

Oregon's reputation as a pioneer in environmental protection developed in the early and mid-1970s when Republican governor Tom McCall promoted novel concepts such as the bottle bill, universal land-use planning, and open public beaches. McCall's strong advocacy inspired many who felt Oregon was at the forefront of a new social model. State leaders dubbed the state's emerging environmental ethic as the "Oregon Story." In 1975 the spirit of Oregon's environmental movement was so influential that it provided the setting for an influential utopian novel, *Ecotopia*. Authored by Ernest Callenbach, the novel describes a world in which the Pacific Northwest has become a separate nation built around the principle of ecological balance.[7]

Oregon's public was never as completely committed to McCall's environmental activism as later media generalizations depict. Both the adoption and the implementation of the environmental policies of the early 1970s were hard fought, reflecting Oregon's deep splits regarding economic and social priorities. In truth Oregon's economic dependence on the timber industry has often meant that its environmental reputation has exceeded its environmental practices (see chapter 14). Still, the Ecotopia image captured how many viewed Oregon's progressive environmental record in the 1970s. Even today many progressive environmentalists believe that the region's commitment to environmental values may allow the state to develop in closer harmony with the natural environment than is true elsewhere.[8]

The early and mid-1970s were heady times for progressive environmentalists, but since that time state environmental policy battles have been more in defense of the McCall legacy than with pushing these goals further. The ongoing skirmishes over land-use planning and other environmental regulations reached a critical point in the November 2000 general election, when Oregonians passed Measure 7 with a 53 percent majority. Although the Oregon Supreme Court ruled Measure 7 to be unconstitutional on the grounds that it amended more than one section of the constitution in a single ballot measure, the values and political movement that led to its passage demonstrate the forcefulness of conservative populism in Oregon.

Measure 7 was a ballot initiative that would have required state and local governments to compensate property owners when public regulations restrict the use of private property and lower its value. Existing provisions in the state and federal constitutions recognize the citizen's right to "just compensation" when the government takes property, but Measure 7 was categorically more specific and rigid about when and how the government should compensate owners. The law did not forbid state and local regulations regulating property use. The crucial aspect of Measure 7 was its possible costs.

Clearly Oregon's existing land-use planning and other environmental regulations would be inoperable if state and local governments had to compensate owners for the full loss of value due to regulations. For example, state Attorney General Hardy Meyers determined that governments would have to compensate not only landowners when land-use laws prevent them from subdividing their land, but also store owners who have to set aside part of their sites to provide for bottle and can returns under the bottle bill. Estimates of the possible costs of Measure 7 to state and local governments ranged up to well over $5 billion.[9] Property rights advocates argued that this number is inflated and that such compensation is only fair because the public benefits from the owner's loss. They feel that the government should never reduce property values without giving owners the "just compensation" required by their interpretation of the Oregon and United States constitutions.

All parties agreed that Measure 7 would have crippled Oregon's progressive environmental policies. Oregon would have been transformed from being foremost in the control over land-use to a leader in "property rights" protection.[10] Although progressives may have breathed a sigh of relief with the court ruling, their environmental policies are far from secure. The primary sponsors of Measure 7 and their California allies in the Pacific Legal

Foundation have pledged a "redoubled effort to reclaim property rights for Oregonians."[11]

Oregon Health Plan

The state's recent efforts to ensure adequate health care for all Oregonians also reflect the state's divided character. In 1989 the state adopted the Oregon Health Plan, which promised to be the first state program in the nation to provide nearly universal health care. Designed by John Kitzhaber, then president of the state Senate, the plan was intended to expand health care coverage in two principal ways. First, the plan broadened the state's Medicaid program to cover more low-income citizens by stipulating what would be covered. In other words, the plan sought to help more people by rationing services. Second, the legislation required private employers to provide health care coverage at least comparable to the state's basic package.[12]

Combined, these proposed changes put Oregon in the forefront of health care reform by promising to close the major gap in health insurance, namely, coverage for the working poor. The program never developed as envisioned. In the 1990 election Oregon voters provided conservative populists a decisive victory by adopting Measure 5. Measure 5 strictly limits property taxes and requires the state to compensate school districts for the lost revenue.

Between 1990 and 1996 the state's share of public school (K–12) funding rose from about 28 percent to 66 percent, dramatically squeezing the state funds available to implement the Oregon Health Plan and other progressive programs. This budget pressure was enhanced further by passage of even stricter property tax controls through Measure 50 in 1997. The Oregon Legislative Revenue Office estimated that the state would have to spend $2 billion per year in the 2001–2002 budget cycle to compensate local school districts for property tax losses due to Measures 5 and 50, thereby removing that much from the pool of money available for programs such as the Oregon Health Plan.[13] The economic downturn that started in 2000 forced a continuation of health care cuts, as it severely reduced state revenue. In order to protect state programs, the legislature voted to raise income taxes at the end of the 2003 session. However, the defeat of Measure 30 in February 2004 overturned the tax increase, forcing cuts in government services. As a result, some 30,000 people were expected to lose coverage, bringing the number of non-Medicaid recipients served by the plan down to 24,000 in 2004 from a high of 120,000 in the mid-1990s.[14] In 1995 the state legislature removed the other leg of the Oregon Health Plan by rescinding the employer mandate. Although Oregon still possesses a unique system of rationed health care insurance, budget constraints and the 1995 changes in the plan make universal health care a distant vision.

Oregon's ideological heritage provides part of the explanation for why there is a split between progressives and conservative populists, but the divide also reflects trends influencing politics across America today. Oregon, like the nation, is sharply divided geographically. Conflicts between Portland's interests and values and those of the rest of the states have long haunted Oregon politics. Urban residents are the most supportive of progressive ideals, and rural residents tend to support conservative populism. As in many parts of the country, the suburbs have become the battleground between the two visions.

The political differences arise in part from economic and demographic variation. The most urban part of the state is the Willamette Valley, especially between the Portland metropolitan area and Salem. This is Oregon's most economically diverse and densely populated region, with more than 70 percent of the state's residents. During the 1990s the valley saw the largest job growth rate of any part of the state.[15] Portland itself is the most racially and ethnically diverse community in the state, with a population of almost 8 percent black and another 10 percent who are Asian, Pacific Islander, Latino, American Indian, or Native Alaskan.

Eastern Oregon is the most rural area of the state. Unlike the Willamette Valley, the eastern side of the state has a narrow economic base, with a strong dependence on agriculture and forest-product industries. Historically, many of the coastal and southwestern communities have also had narrower economic bases, focused on fisheries and timber. The diversity and high-tech nature of the Willamette Valley's economy fostered considerable job growth in recent decades, whereas communities dependent on natural resources faced harder times as their industries adjusted to declining harvests and tougher regulations.

There has always been a tension between the Portland area and the rural areas of the state. Until the 1930s Portland was strongly Republican, and the rural areas supported Democrats, a situation now reversed.[16] The distribution of votes in the 2000 presidential election makes it clear that important differences between urban and rural, and east and west remain. As was true across the nation, the urban areas of the Willamette Valley strongly supported Democrat Al Gore; the more rural areas of the state supported Republican

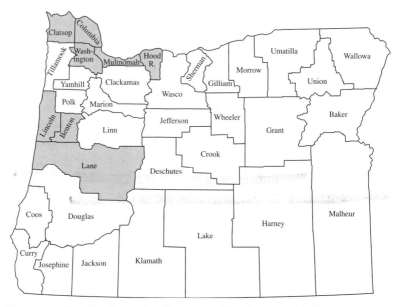

Figure 1.1. Counties Supporting Democratic Vice President Al Gore in the 2000 Presidential Election

George W. Bush. Figure 1.1 gives a rough sense of this distribution, showing much of Gore's support coming from Lane and Benton counties in the southern part of the Willamette Valley, and Multnomah and Washington counties in the northern part.

Recent ballot-measure battles show the differences between these regions more clearly. Votes on these measures show that general attitudes in more urban areas of the Willamette Valley differ considerably from those held by voters in the eastern and southern parts of the state. This was true, for example, in the November 2000 election when there were twenty-six measures on the ballot. These measures focused on a wide variety of issues, including taxation, gay rights, gun control, animal rights, health care funding for the poor, and the rights of unions to organize.

On almost all twenty-six measures, the residents of Multnomah, Lane, and Benton counties either cast the highest percentage of votes in favor of each measure or the lowest percentage. Such eastern Oregon counties as Malheur, Lake, Grant, Wallowa, Crook, and Harney were consistently at the other extreme. In other words, when the urban voters were most likely to favor a measure, the eastern counties were the least likely to support it. When

Table 1.1. Percent of Voter Support for Four Measures on 2000 Ballot

Region	Measure 97 Pro–Animal Rights (Progressive)	Measure 5 Pro–Gun Control (Progressive)	Measure 9 Restrict Gay Advocacy in Schools (Conservative Populist)	Measure 88 Cut Taxes (Conservative Populist)
Portland (Multnomah)	53.6	75.5	32.8	42.4
University counties (Benton, Lane)	46.8	66.2	41.2	42.2
Portland suburbs (Clackamas, Washington)	42.1	66.8	46.4	55.1
North Coast (Clatsop, Columbia, Tillamook, Lincoln)	37.2	57.4	47.5	51.4
Mid–Williamette Valley (Marion, Polk, Linn, Yamhill)	35.6	58.1	53.6	52.9
Southern Oregon (Douglas, Josephine, Jackson, Coos, Curry)	36.9	50.1	57.3	54.5
Eastern Oregon (18 counties)	28.1	46.5	57.4	55.3
Statewide total	41.1	61.7	47.1	50.5

urban voters opposed a measure, the eastern counties provided the greatest support.

These regional differences can be seen in table 1.1, which shows the popular vote on four measures on the November 2000 ballot. Measure 97 was an animal rights initiative that sought to limit the use of animal traps. Measure 5 sought to extend background checks on gun sales. Measure 9 called for a ban on public school instruction promoting homosexuality. Measure 88, the only legislative referral of the four, sought to increase the maximum state tax deduction for federal income taxes paid. The table lists the counties in each region. Lane and Benton counties are identified as "university counties" because they are the homes of the University of Oregon and Oregon State. Despite the diverse content, the pattern of voting on these measures remains quite consistent. These regional voting patterns are discussed more fully in chapter 4.

Certainly, not all the political conflict in Oregon reflects the divide between progressive ideals and conservative populist ones, as will be seen in other chapters. There are times too when there can be considerable agreement throughout Oregon. For example, the vote in 2000 on Measure 94, which would have overturned the state's strict sentencing law, demonstrates some shared values across Oregon. Even though the voters in Multnomah and the university counties were the most supportive of Measure 94, and eastern county voters were the most opposed, the measure was defeated soundly in every county. In a wide variety of areas, however, the division between progressivism and conservative populism plays a fundamental role in shaping Oregon politics.

THE STATE CONSTITUTION

Along with the split between progressives and conservative populists and with geographical differences, state law also plays a fundamental role in shaping Oregon's political system. The most important law in shaping the formal structure of Oregon government and politics is the Oregon Constitution. The constitution is the state's highest law. When there is conflict between the constitution and a state or local law, the constitution takes precedence because it is the highest expression of the people's sovereign will. Oregon's constitution is one of the oldest in the nation. It was approved by Oregon voters in 1857 and took effect when the state entered the Union on February 14, 1859. The original constitution still provides the foundation for the state's governance.[17]

The drafters of Oregon's basic constitution did not believe in reinventing the wheel. They basically borrowed from constitutions in the states of the upper Mississippi valley that they knew well. Gordon Dodds states that the Oregon Constitution was "hardly innovative in any respect."[18] The original constitution thus reflected the concerns of immigrants from the agrarian states and had elements reflecting the social tensions that would lead to the rise of Populism. For example, there was much concern that the state should regulate banking and corporations to protect farmers from unbridled market forces. The prejudices of the time were reflected in the section stating, "No Negro, Chinaman, or Mulatto shall have the right to vote." Otherwise, the design of the government basically followed what had become traditional in America: a balance of power between three branches of government, citizen rights similar to those granted in the federal constitution, and limitations on the size and scope of state and local governments.

The distinctiveness of Oregon's constitution arises from the 228 constitutional amendments that have been adopted through ballot measures since 1902, some of which have been reversed by the courts or later ballot measures.[19] The Oregon System makes it comparatively easy to place measures on the ballot and enables both progressive and conservative reformers to inject their policies into the heart of the government. Amendments to the Oregon Constitution often are minor matters, such as altering the rules for municipal bonding in specific jurisdictions or establishing specific regulatory commissions. Some changes have powerful impacts on policy, such as tax reforms and alterations in the rules for the initiative process. Since its original adoption, the constitution has grown from 11,200 to an estimated 49,326 words.[20]

The constitution performs three important functions: it lays out the general structure of the government, it protects citizen rights and liberties, and it establishes the rules for how it can be revised.

Government Structure

Oregon's basic governmental structure has never been altered and resembles the federal government's designs, with some important differences. As with the federal government, the state constitution divides power among three branches of government: legislative, executive, and judicial (see figure 1.2). The constitution also provides for two houses in the legislature (House of Representatives and Senate), and it establishes the relationship between the state and its local governments.

One of the major differences between the state and the nation's govern-

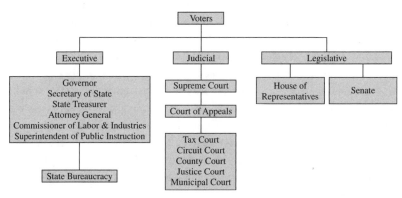

Figure 1.2. Government Structure

ment is that the executive power in Oregon is divided among several office holders. In Washington DC, the president is the chief executive, overseeing the entire federal administration. The Oregon Constitution, however, establishes six executive offices, each with its own powers and responsibilities. The governor is the chief executive, but Oregon also has a secretary of state, a treasurer, an attorney general, a commissioner of labor and industries, and a superintendent of public instruction—each of whom is elected independently.

Another difference is that there is no state office equivalent to the vice president. The secretary of state assumes the governor's office if there is a vacancy, but the secretary of state is more independent and has a longer list of formal duties than the vice president. In addition, state court judges are elected by the people rather than being appointed as they are in the federal judiciary. Finally, the legislature is known as the Legislative Assembly, not the Congress.

Rights and Liberties

The first article of the Oregon Constitution is the state's Bill of Rights. Like the national Bill of Rights, the state's Bill of Rights serves to protect the civil rights and liberties of citizens. Although similar, the Oregon Bill of Rights and the national one have some differences. As in the United States Constitution, the state constitution guarantees some of the nation's most cherished rights and liberties. Among other provisions, it protects Oregonians' freedom of religion, speech, and press, and it protects individuals from being subject to unreasonable searches or being tried twice for the same offence.

The state Bill of Rights, however, goes beyond the United States Constitution in protecting the rights and liberties of state citizens. State governments cannot deny people the rights spelled out in the U.S. Constitution, but they can guarantee more extensive rights. One area in which Oregon provides greater protection than the U.S. Constitution is in freedom of speech. The Oregon Constitution has a very strong statement protecting Oregonians' rights to express their opinions freely. The constitution states that there shall be no law passed restricting the right to speak "on any subject whatsoever." Even though a large segment of the Oregon population supports this protection, some Oregon citizens criticize the free speech rule for limiting the government's ability to regulate the adult entertainment industry and pornography. The clause has also made it more difficult for the state to regulate campaign finance.[21]

Amending the Constitution

State constitutions, and Oregon's particularly, differ from the federal constitution also in the ease and frequency of their amendment. Three different methods can be used to amend the wording of Oregon's constitution. The first method is that the state legislature can place a proposed constitutional amendment on the ballot for voters to accept or reject, or what is called a "legislative referral." A majority of members of both state houses must vote for the amendment for it to go to the voters. If a majority of the voters who cast a ballot approve, the amendment becomes part of the constitution.[22]

The second method is through the initiative process. This method, described more fully in chapter 5, enables citizens to place amendments directly on the ballot themselves. To get their proposal on the ballot, amendment supporters must gather signatures from approximately a hundred thousand voters. Once on the ballot, an amendment needs to receive a majority of the votes cast on the measure for it to be added to the constitution.

The state constitution also allows the legislature to call for a statewide convention to amend the constitution if state voters approve such a convention. There has not been a state constitutional convention since 1857.

Just as with the federal constitution, changes in how the words of the state constitution are interpreted may be as important as changes in the words themselves. The legislature, governor, attorney general, and others in the executive branch often influence how the constitution is interpreted, but the Oregon Supreme Court has the ultimate authority in determining what the constitution means. The supreme court's use of that authority has had important consequences for state politics. For example, the court ruled in 1998 that the clause allowing initiatives to amend only one part of the constitution should be interpreted to mean a single ballot measure can change only one very narrow part of the constitution.[23] The court's ruling, as explained more precisely in chapters five and eleven, has resulted in several voter-approved initiatives to be struck down. As powerful as the court's interpretative role can be, the ease by which Oregon's constitution can be amended through referrals and initiatives ensures that interpretations that are publicly unacceptable can be countered by amending the constitution relatively quickly.

THE NEW OREGON STORY

Oregonians tend to be very proud of their state. One particular source of this pride is the perception that "things are different here," that somehow Oregon pursues a unique course of history. This perception is frequently conveyed in state histories and in the biographies of state leaders.[24] Oregon is often seen as being a policy innovator and the home of maverick politicians. State political leaders and political commentators emphasize this uniqueness by attaching Oregon's name to state programs; thus, we have the Oregon System, the Oregon Health Plan, and the Oregon Story. The notion that there is something special about Oregon politics has, in many ways, become a part of Oregon political lore.

One cannot help but believe the reason many Oregonians feel the state is different is because of the way the state's progressive heritage has often been romanticized, which is understandable, for it is this heritage that has frequently brought the state national attention. Yet if Oregon is indeed special today, it is not because the state is a progressive one. Certainly, the state has an important progressive side to it, one that has historical roots. Yet Oregon also has a very strong attachment to conservative populism. Despite the lore, Oregon today is a divided state, one in which two different sets of ideals compete to influence state policies. The conflict is not seen on every issue or in every political campaign, but it is surely the dominant feature of Oregon politics. In the chapters that follow, the authors describe the structure of Oregon government as it is laid out in the constitution and state law, and they frequently discuss the importance of geography in shaping the state's politics. But more than anything else, the book tries to explain how this split between progressives and conservative populists shapes the different aspects of the state's politics—for this split is, in many ways, the Oregon Story today.

CHAPTER TWO

Place, People

Joe Bowersox

There are many myths about Oregon: myths of its discovery and "conquest," of its first peoples, and of the history and character of its later inhabitants. An important characteristic of myths is that they may have little to do with reality. Instead, they often tend to be based at best on half-truths.

One such myth concerns the role of religiously motivated immigrants in the formative years of the Oregon Territory. Jason Lee, Marcus Whitman, and the other Protestant missionaries who left the Northeast to found the first Protestant missions in the region beginning in 1834 are often credited for creating a consciously moralistic regional political culture. Indeed, many of the pathbreaking political developments in Oregon have been associated with the distinctly moralistic appeals and righteous wrath of would-be reformers, from the late-nineteenth-century and early-twentieth-century crusades for the initiative and referendum and other "good government" reforms, to battles over innovative environmental laws of the 1970s and more recent conflicts over tax reform, campaign financing, abortion, health care, and assisted suicide. For many, the politics and culture of Oregon are defined by its moralism.

Daniel J. Elazar's classic study of American political culture provides some qualified support for this vision of Oregon. Elazar argues that the political culture of Oregon was shaped by the early predominance of immigrants from the northeastern United States, who brought with them a highly moralistic political culture emphasizing a "strong commitment to communitarianism" and "good government." This commitment, he wrote, could be seen "by the degree to which it promotes the public good and in terms of honesty, selflessness, and commitment to the public welfare of those who govern." Elazar juxtaposes such a moralistic political culture to "traditionalistic" and "individualistic" cultures, the former associated with the deferential, class- and race-based politics of the Old South, the latter with the spoils and patronage politics of Huey Long's Louisiana or the urban political machines of the mid-twentieth century. For many casual observers, Elazar's typology clearly explains Oregon's progressive politics, linking it politically and culturally with historical progressive strongholds like California and Wisconsin. But Elazar himself notes other elements in Oregon's political culture, including a healthy dose of individualism.[1]

George Wilkes, an explorer of the Oregon Territory who popularized his experiences in order to rally American support for annexation in the face of British territorial claims, constructed another myth about Oregon. In 1845 Wilkes wrote, "We are a new people, in a new era, acting on new principles, and working out a new and grand problem for the benefit of mankind." Arguing against those who would counsel against the overextension of empire, Wilkes continued, "There is too much of this knuckling to precedent and old opinion. We can benefit by the experience of a past age, without becoming the hereditary bondsmen of their ideas . . . without presenting the absurd spectacle, of a people claiming to be free, who have absolutely signed away freedom's main component in the liberty of the mind."[2] Wilkes's visionary rhetoric thus exemplifies another common myth of Oregon as politically populist and independent, and is enshrined in the state motto, "She flies with her own wings."

Like all myths, certain aspects of these two images *are* accurate. As we shall see, certain moralistic traits have been common in Oregon politics. Nevertheless, Oregon's political culture and political history could just as easily be described as suffering from the corruption and paternalism associated with Elazar's individualistic or traditionalistic political cultures. Oregon also has been prone to borrowing heavily from "old" political ideas like the rights of states, nativism, and racism. The purpose of this chapter is to explore Oregon's political culture and history, examining some trends, their origins, and their broader implications, and thus encouraging readers to separate myth from reality.

OREGON: THE LAND AND CLIMATE

If there is one thing that unites the experiences of the inhabitants of Oregon both prior to and after European settlement, it is the importance of the land itself. The boundaries of Oregon encompass a diverse array of features, spanning from the Coast Range in the west to the Wallowa Mountains and Hells Canyon in the east, the Columbia River Basin to the north, and the Siskiyou mountain range to the south. Indeed, some two hundred million years ago, Oregon was simply a bunch of disparate geologic features strewn across the Pacific Ocean on a collision course with the West Coast of the North American tectonic plate, in what is now western Idaho and northeastern Washington. Over the next 140 million years or so, the Wallowa, Elkhorn, Greenhorn, Strawberry, Aldrich, Ochoco, and Klamath mountains piled up on the North American plate's edge, while a chain of marine volcanoes formed a loose archipelago that would be the base of the Oregon Coast Range. Teaming with marine life, the seaway between the archipelago and the plate's edge was slowly dispelled by the uplifting of the Willamette Valley (beginning some fifty million years ago), the volcanic formation of the Cascade Range (starting some forty million years ago), and the lava flows of the Columbia/Deschutes Plateau (six to seventeen million years ago). While human habitation began possibly some forty to sixty thousand years before the present, the geographic mosaic of Oregon continued to change, with the castrophic Missoula floods (fifteen thousand to twelve thousand years before the present), to eruptions like those forming Crater Lake through the destruction of Mount Mazama some sixty-nine hundred years ago.[3]

Located astride the forty-fifth parallel and hence halfway between the equator and the North Pole, Oregon has a temperature largely controlled by the moderate amount of solar energy it receives. Oceanic currents further moderate the temperature, and orographic precipitation dictates regional climatic differences across the state. This in turn has virtually dictated both vegetation patterns and human and nonhuman habitation throughout Oregon's history, with the most populous areas being west of the Cascades, and sparse population on the arid leeward side.[4] This east-west climatic divide is also the single most important cause of the economic, and hence social and political, divisions of the state. The water-rich west has been more conducive to settlement and to intensified agricultural production, industrial development, and urbanization. The dry and sparsely populated east has remained dependent on dry-crop farming, livestock raising, and mineral and timber extraction, except in places where state and federally subsidized water projects have allowed intensification of agricultural production and some industrialization, such as in the Columbia, Umatilla, and Klamath river basins. These economic patterns, shaped by climate and geography, have in turn affected Oregon politics, exemplified by eastside residents' customary apathy to environmental initiatives—often sponsored by westside activists and politicians—that would disrupt historical land and water-use patterns.

PEOPLE AND POLITICS

First Peoples

Another common myth of Oregon and the West generally implies that the region, prior to European settlement, was only sparsely inhabited by Native Americans and that these Native Americans possessed little sophistication. Russian and Spanish explorers along the Northwest coast described small flotillas of seventy-foot-long solid cedar canoes holding fifty warriors. Similarly, during a voyage in 1788, Robert Gray found the Oregon coast heavily populated. Indeed, experts now believe that prior to European settlement, Native Americans lived along the coast with densities reaching twenty-five persons per square mile, and approximately eighty thousand lived in the Willamette Valley and along the Columbia River, foreshadowing contemporary habitation patterns.[5] With the exception of the small familial bands traversing the southeastern portion of the state, most tribes in Oregon were rather prosperous, well organized, and well armed; commerce among tribes was advanced, with "marketplaces" like Celilo Falls and the Dalles oftentimes hosting several thousand Native American traders from across the Northwest, exchanging salmon, shellfish, horses, animal skins, seashells, copper, drift iron, and war prisoners. Conflict and cooperation among people were facilitated by the Chinook trading language, soon picked up by the first Europeans interested in developing their own trading relations with local Native Americans.

European Designs

While Russian, Spanish, Portuguese, and French explorers pursued the fabled Northwest Passage and economic gain in the region, only Britain and later the United States established a permanent, nonindigenous presence in the area. Spain began exploring the region north of California in the 1540s, and English privateers, including Francis Drake, were active off the Oregon coast pursuing Spanish ships in the late 1500s. But after an encounter between British commander James Colnett and Spanish personnel at Nootka Bay on Vancouver Island in 1789, Spain abandoned all claims to the Northwest in 1795.[6] The American explorer Captain Robert Gray became the first to pilot a vessel over the bar into the Columbia River, in 1792, establishing the first American claim to the region. Meriweather Lewis' and William Clark's famous expedition, culminating in their journey down the Snake and Columbia rivers and their establishment of Fort Clatsop on the Oregon coast in 1806, further enhanced American claims.

English and American competition over the Northwest intensified in 1811, when German-born American John Jacob Astor established Fort Astoria for his Pacific Fur Company at the mouth of the Columbia, seeking to challenge the British North West Company (NWC). During the War of 1812 Britain captured Fort Astoria, and Astor reluctantly sold the remaining assets of his company to NWC that same year. Thus, between 1813 and 1843, except for occasional merchant ships and short-lived trading ventures by Nathaniel Wyeth (1832–1834) and Captain Benjamin de Bonneville (1832–1835), there was little American presence in Oregon.[7]

Early Politics, Early Alternatives

From 1812 until the early 1840s, the only permanent "political" presence in Oregon besides the loose social organization of the larger Native American groups was the British fur-trading interests of the North West Company and the Hudson's Bay Company (HBC). Competition and private warfare became so intense and deadly between the two companies that the British parliament forced a merger of the two rivals under the name of the Hudson's Bay Company in 1821. Parliament also extended a twenty-one year trading monopoly to the company and gave it full civil and criminal jurisdiction over British subjects within the Northwestern territories. In 1824 Dr. John McLoughlin (1784–1857) was chosen to be chief factor (administrator) of the Columbia District, which included all of Oregon. In 1825 McLoughlin moved his headquarters from Astoria to Fort Vancouver, on the north bank of the Columbia, east of the confluence with the Willamette.

Until the formation of the provisional government at Champoeg in 1843, McLoughlin was the undisputed authority in the Oregon Country. Officially, neither British subjects nor the few Americans in the region could establish a formal political authority in the area without violating the 1818 treaty of joint occupation. But through the 1830s there really was not much to govern. Until the arrival of Methodist missionary Jason Lee and four others at Fort Vancouver in 1834, all nonnative settlers were former HBC employees (mostly French Canadians) who had settled on small farms and intermarried with women from various tribes. Until 1840 American settlers were a definite minority. In fact, even with the arrival of more missionaries and laypersons, by the beginning of 1842 there were only about 140 American settlers in Oregon, and the members of the "Missionary Party" in their midst were the only ones pushing for U.S. hegemony over the territory. Many, if not most, of the nonnative population still believed other alternatives, including an independent nation, were possible.

While Lee's "mission to the Indians" was a dismal evangelistic and financial failure (the only missionaries that had some success with Native Americans in the Northwest were Catholic priests, who tended to live and travel among them), it served as an impetus for American migration to Oregon. During the 1830s and 1840s immigrant-borne diseases devastated indigenous populations, though Native Americans continued to outnumber settlers until the 1860s. Furthermore, these new arrivals refused to learn native languages, yet occupied the lands. Hence, some scholars suggest that by the 1840s the Methodist mission had little to do with evangelism and was simply a front for Americanization. Indeed, prior to 1844 various members and agents of the Methodist mission in Oregon had been clandestinely lobbying Washington to abrogate the treaties with Britain and establish American political authority in the region.[8]

Popular myths of the Champoeg meeting of May 2, 1843, which led to the formation of a provisional government, often describe it as an event at which moralistic Methodists and American patriots "saved Oregon" from Britain and the Hudson's Bay Company.[9] But much of this is patriotic retrospective. The actual events that led to the provisional government of 1843 were much more mundane. Since 1835 various meetings of both American settlers and British subjects were held to establish elements of political authority and to find solutions for local problems (such as a criminal court to prosecute theft, selection of a justice of the peace, settlement of an estate , and wolf eradication).[10] Furthermore, the actual vote at Champoeg, fifty-two in favor of "organization" and fifty against, simply endorsed drafting of "organic" laws, and vested executive and legislative powers into committees, not persons. In fact, the resolution prohibited election of a governor. Taxes were also outlawed, to avoid the appearance of a permanent government. Various accounts of contemporaries suggest that until 1846 (when a treaty between the United States and Britain established the permanent international boundary at the forty-ninth parallel) even many Americans living in Oregon favored an independent state—an early indication of Oregon's populist tendencies.[11]

Statehood and State's Rights

Oregon's original executive in the provisional government was actually a three-person committee—a structure that would be proposed again by Progressive reformers at the beginning of the twentieth century. In 1845 this executive committee was replaced by a provisional governor (George Abernathy, 1845–1849), and following the passage of the Oregon Territory Act by Congress in 1848, General Joseph Lane became the first territorial governor, in March 1849. In 1859 Oregon (with its present political boundaries) became the thirty-third state in the Union.

At the outbreak of the Civil War in 1861, Oregon's place in the Union was rather ambiguous. In 1857, while ratifying the state constitution, voters prohibited slavery within Oregon's borders (75 percent to 25 percent) but also excluded free blacks (89 percent to 11 percent). In the 1860 presidential election, Oregon's Joseph Lane, an outspoken proponent of allowing slavery in Oregon, was the vice presidential candidate on John C. Breckenridge's pro-slavery, pro–states' rights Southern Democrat ticket. In the November election in Oregon, Abraham Lincoln barely edged out the Breckenridge/Lane ticket by 270 votes (5,344 to 5,074), with Stephen Douglas garnering 4,131 votes. In fact, Oregon was the only Northern state to give Breckenridge a larger vote than Douglas. In 1861 and 1862 Southern sympathizers and pro-slavery forces repeatedly tried to get the state to switch sides, declare itself an independent Pacific Republic, or at least refuse to raise troops for the Union cause. Oregon's first state governor, pro-slavery Democrat John Whiteaker, denounced the war in 1862, the same year federal forces shut down several Oregon newspapers that agitated for the Southern cause. Ultimately, few Oregon troops were sent east to fight; instead they were kept in Oregon for fear of insurrection or Native American uprisings. Throughout the war Oregon politics walked a fine line between loyalty to the Union and popular support for states' rights, another indication of the state's continued tendency toward conservative populism.[12]

LESSONS ON POPULISM AND PROGRESSIVISM, 1870–1922

In post–Civil War Oregon, Democrats and Republicans enjoyed a fairly competitive environment, oftentimes with one party winning the presidential vote and the other winning state offices. This pattern held until the early twentieth century. Election results tended to reflect local concerns and political personalities rather than national party ideologies. Thus, a close look at the politics after the Civil War displays some unique and characteristically Oregonian proclivities.

Between 1849 and 1862 the Democratic Party dominated state and local elections via a robust, Salem-based political machine called "the Clique." Fueled by the spoils system, the Clique's politics was anything but moralistic.

After suffering some electoral setbacks during the Civil War, the Clique returned to relative dominance in 1866, playing to states' rights, Populist xenophobia, and practical policy innovation. Such was the mix exemplified by Clique politico Lafayette Grover. Educated at Bowdoin College, Grover became Oregon's first U.S. representative in 1859 (for sixteen days) and then governor in 1870. Grover opposed the Civil War and favored the exclusion of "undesirable" foreigners (mainly Chinese and Japanese laborers). Nevertheless, he promoted fish conservation and the construction of fish ladders, acquired state lands, and encouraged (with state bonds) the creation of the Willamette Falls canal (a national engineering marvel when completed in 1873). Hence, Grover represents a curious yet uniquely Oregonian blend of conservative populist demagoguery and progressive policy innovation.

Another exemplar of early Oregon politics was Harvard-trained lawyer, publisher, and lumber baron Sylvester Pennoyer. Elected governor as a Democrat in 1886, he was reelected as a Democratic Populist in 1890. Though a man of aristocratic tastes and significant wealth, he promoted labor unions, nationalization of the railroads, creation of a state boys' home, a soldiers' home, free municipal boarding houses for the unemployed, a graduated income tax, William Jennings Bryan's free silver currency policy, and Chinese exclusion. With Pennoyer's leadership, Populists and sympathetic Democrats won a majority of legislative seats in 1892 and 1894, but because of internal divisions they were unable to achieve much of a legislative record against a more coherent Republican minority.[13]

As indicated by the success of Pennoyer, Populist reform movements gained ground in Oregon politics after the Civil War. In the 1870s Oregon farmers formed the Independent Party, which had considerable electoral success in the state races of 1874, running, as it did, against the inordinate political and economic power of the railroads and playing to nativist xenophobia. During the 1880s farmers linked up with labor activists and prohibitionists and formed an Oregon chapter of the Farmers' Alliance and Industrial Union, to yet again do battle with the railroads, other monopolies, and the liquor trade. In the wake of the 1888 presidential election, in which Benjamin Harrison defeated Grover Cleveland amid charges of election fraud, the alliance secured passage of a state secret-ballot bill in 1891, which Pennoyer gladly signed into law. This severely curtailed the power of the railroads in the state legislature.[14]

As the Progressive reform movement emerged in Oregon during the 1890s, it displayed a decidedly Populist orientation. While some of the traditional staples of Progressivism's "good government" reform package (such as the nonpartisan city-manager form and increased voter qualification requirements) were adopted, reformers like William S. U'Ren and Jonathan Bourne labored to increase the substantive impact of the average voter. U'Ren's Direct Legislation League (renamed the Peoples Power League in 1905) popularized the Swiss model of initiative and referendum in the United States—eventually securing for it the moniker of the "Oregon System" even though it was not official law in Oregon until 1902 (two years after it had been adopted in South Dakota and Utah).[15] Bourne and U'Ren also persuaded the legislature to require legislative candidates to publicly declare whether they would select a U.S. senator who won a preferential election; Bourne then became the first U.S. senator chosen by the legislature under this system in 1906. Bourne became president of the National Progressive Republican League in 1911, only to be defeated in his 1912 reelection bid by traditional Republicans upset with his radical reform ideas and his campaigning for third-party presidential candidate Teddy Roosevelt over incumbent president William Howard Taft.[16]

Between 1902 and 1922 U'Ren used the initiative process to promote such radical (and often more Populist than Progressive) reforms as a single tax, direct primaries, proportional representation, women's suffrage, single legislative and gubernatorial terms, popular election of the president of the Senate and speaker of the House, and even the formation of a unicameral legislature. During this period more traditional Progressives in both major parties focused on worker safety, minimum-wage and maximum-hour laws, and the proper stewardship of public lands and natural resources. Progressive Democratic governor George Chamberlain (1903–1909) and his state land agent, Oswald West, went after corrupt public land deals involving common school lands and the newly created federal forest reserves. During West's single term as governor (1911–1915), Oregon beaches were declared part of the state highway system (protecting them from private development until passage of the Oregon Beach Bill in 1967). West established the Bureau of Forestry (today's Department of Forestry), Office of the State Forester, and the Fish and Game Commission (currently the Oregon Fish and Wildlife Commission). He also pushed for women's suffrage (finally achieved via the initiative in 1912), minimum-wage laws, and state prohibition (passed by initiative in 1914).

Thus, tendencies often individually associated with the late-nineteenth-century and twentieth-century Populist and Progressive movements have been part and parcel of Oregon politics from the beginning, and they have often been in apparent conflict. After World War I such paradoxes continued to find expression in Oregon. During the 1920s the Ku Klux Klan used the machinery of direct primaries to elect a governor and a sympathetic legislature that would eventually bar aliens from owning land. The Klan also used the initiative to pass a law banning private (predominantly Roman Catholic) schools. Yet in 1930 Oregon voters would elect Julius Meier, a politically progressive—and Jewish—Independent, as governor.[17]

OREGON AFTER WORLD WAR II
Increasing Diversity

Prior to World War II, most new arrivals to Oregon came not because of beliefs but for jobs, and the typical new Oregonian was not necessarily a white, Protestant Yankee. During the nineteenth and early twentieth centuries, Scandinavian and German loggers from Michigan and Wisconsin migrated in vast groups to places like Coos Bay, to cut and mill the virgin forests. Swiss and German migrants settled in Tillamook and Portland to work in the dairy industry. Basque and Irish shepherds were recruited to tend flocks in eastern and southern Oregon, and Chinese, Japanese, and African American laborers sought economic security and suffered political persecution while building railroads and developing service trades, farms, and orchards.

World War II and its aftermath provided further impetus for new arrivals. More than twenty thousand African Americans came to Portland and the Willamette Valley during the war to work in defense-related industries. Although many had left by the end of the 1940s, those who remained indelibly altered the social, economic, and political landscape of Oregon. World War II fostered revolutionary changes in Oregon agriculture, including growing reliance on Latino migrant laborers in fields and processing plants. By war's end more than fifteen thousand *braceros* (federally contracted migrant workers) were working in Oregon.[18] Though the *bracero* program was phased out after the war, the need for labor was not, prompting continued migration from Mexico, Central America, and South America. By the 1950s permanent Latino communities were integral parts of the Willamette, Umatilla, and Klamath river valleys. The 1960s and 1970s saw the emergence of Latinos as a vital economic, political, and cultural force in Oregon.[19] Today, Latinos are the largest non-Caucasian ethnic group in the state, constituting approximately 275,000 individuals, or 8 percent of the total population. The largest concentrations of Latinos are in Washington, Multnomah, and Marion counties.[20]

Table 2.1. Demographic Characteristics of Oregon and the United States, 2000

	Oregon	*United States*
Population in 2000	3,421,339	281,421,906
Percent population change, 1990–2000	20.4%	13.1%
Percent white	86.6%	75.1%
Black or African American	1.6%	12.3%
Native/Alaskan Native	1.3%	0.9%
Asian	3.0%	3.6%
Hispanic/Latino	8.0%	12.5%

Source: U.S. Census Bureau, "Census 2000 Data for the State of Oregon," General Demographic Characteristics, file OP-1, 2004, http://www.census.gov/census2000/states/or.html.

More recent international events have also changed Oregon's demographic landscape. The country's military involvement in Southeast Asia in the 1960s and 1970s spurred large waves of refugees to the United States, including Oregon, which now boasts vibrant Vietnamese and Hmong communities. The collapse of the Soviet Union initiated a second wave of Russian and Ukrainian immigration to Oregon in the 1990s, as newer arrivals joined established ethnic communities in Woodburn and other Willamette Valley towns founded by immigrants earlier in century, many of them having fled due to religious persecution. Despite these migrations, which have increased Oregon's diversity, the state remains more homogeneous than the nation as a whole (see table 2.1).

Oregon's Changing Postwar Economy

The hundred years prior to World War II saw Oregon's economy dominated by agriculture, mining, and beginning in the 1880s, other extractive industries like timber, wood products, and fishing. From the Great Depression through World War II, government construction and work projects dominated the economy, supplemented by the emergence of some heavy industry (such as aluminum production) and—with the outbreak of war—shipbuilding. In the postwar era Oregon's economy temporarily shifted back to traditional strengths in wood products and agriculture. Since the 1970s, however, Oregon's economy has become increasingly diversified, with high-tech industries and agriculture vying for predominance. Faced with increased foreign and domestic competition, the costs of modernization, and constraints on publicly subsidized supplies of timber, the wood products sector continues to lag behind.

Politics in the Postwar Era

As the war years stimulated economic and demographic change, they reshaped the political landscape as well. Despite the successes of Democrats like Chamberlain and West and like Independent Meier at the beginning of the Depression, a socially and politically conservative Republican Party dominated state elections for the first half of the twentieth century. But the 1940s saw the rise of popular liberal candidates in both parties, such as socially liberal Republicans Wayne Morse (who as a U.S. senator made history in the 1950s by switching to the Democratic Party), Mark Hatfield, and Tom McCall, and economically liberal Democrats Richard Neuberger and Edith Green. As a state legislator in the early 1950s, Hatfield (governor, 1959–1967; U.S. senator, 1967–1997) pioneered the fight to repeal Oregon's racial segregation laws affecting accommodations, public facilities, restaurants, and land purchases. As Oregon's Democratic U.S. senators in the 1950s, Morse and Neuberger promoted public works and conservation projects, and Edith Green, representing Oregon's third congressional district, worked on education, labor, and women's issues.

As governor (1967–1975) Tom McCall exemplified a socially liberal and rather bipartisan era in Oregon politics. In an era of unprecedented economic prosperity, both Democrats and Republicans advocated quality-of-life innovations in the public arena, ranging from school reforms to innovative environmental and labor legislation. McCall himself championed a nationally renowned cleanup of the Willamette River and secured, with Republican and Democratic legislative support, four national environmental firsts: public ownership of Oregon's beaches; sweeping environmental reforms, which were codified in the state's Forest Practices Act; a bottle deposit bill; and passage of a comprehensive land-use planning act. In pursuit of preserving Oregon's quality of life, McCall even placed signs at Oregon's borders reading, "Welcome to Oregon. We Hope You Enjoy Your Visit," and personally clarified the intent: "Come visit us again and again. . . . But for heaven's sake, don't come here to live." Yet as the regional economy soured in the 1980s, a fellow Republican governor, Victor Atiyeh, would remove the signs, which he claimed exemplified an elitist, high-tax, antigrowth, antibusiness mentality that threatened preservation of the state's quality of life far more than a few more immigrants.[21]

The political dynamics that have ensued in recent decades continue to display conflict over the meaning of Oregon, and the conflict has emerged as one pitting largely urban liberal "progressives" advocating the McCall era's quality-of-life politics against predominantly rural residents who are more economically and socially conservative. On one hand largely urban and suburban voters and legislators have supported landmark legislation over the last thirty years, such as 1971's Bottle Deposit Bill, 1973's Senate Bill 100 (establishing comprehensive land-use planning), and 1994's initiative approving physician-assisted suicide. On the other hand, predominantly rural voters passed Measure 5 in 1990, severely limiting property taxes, and Measure 7 in 2000, which required compensation for any regulatory action that reduced the value of private property.[22] Oregon's gubernatorial race of 1998 pitted progressive incumbent Dr. John Kitzhaber against conservative tax activist Bill Sizemore. The 2002 race to succeed Kitzhaber illustrated the continuing war for the political soul of the state, as liberal Democratic supreme court Justice Ted Kulongoski squeezed by conservative Republican Kevin Mannix by fewer than thirty-four thousand votes. The results of the election demonstrate the deep divide in the state between rural and urban, conservative and liberal constituencies, and the race turned on economic and social issues like taxation, abortion, school reform, and environmental regulation.

Indeed, one does not have to look far in Oregon politics to catch glimpses of Oregon's divided political culture. As this chapter has illustrated, there is no single story or comprehensive myth of Oregon nor a shared common vision of what Oregon should be. Rather, individualism and moralism, populism and progressivism, agrarianism and urbanism remain in dynamic tension.

CHAPTER THREE

Oregon in the Nation and the World

Richard A. Clucas and Melody Rose

When Oregon voters cast their ballots in the November 8, 1994, election, they thrust the state into the federal spotlight. On the ballot was a proposal to allow physicians to help terminally ill patients commit suicide. The proposal was Ballot Measure 16, the Death with Dignity Act. The battle over the measure was closely fought. On one side was the Right to Die organization, led by a man whose ill wife had committed suicide several years before by taking sleeping pills and placing a plastic bag over her head. On the other side was a coalition of groups, many from the religious right but others representing disabled and senior citizens. The opponents poured some $2 million into the race to defeat the initiative, but when the final votes were counted, the supporters had won with a touch more than 50 percent of the vote. By passing the measure, Oregon became the first state in the nation to legalize physician-assisted suicide. In so doing, the state, as it has on other occasions in the past, helped spark a nationwide debate on a critical political issue.[1]

While the battle over assisted suicide did not end after the vote, the general election was a pivotal event. Oregon's decision to legalize physician-assisted suicide sparked an intense battle between the state and federal government over a seemingly simple question: Which government shall determine the state's policy on assisted suicide? Although the question appears to be a simple one, the answer is not. Mired in issues of constitutional law, morality, and political ideology, the fight between nation and state to control assisted suicide can be read as a matter of federalism theory, a perennial struggle between state and federal power. As we shall see in the pages that follow, the question of who should decide is a serious issue in Oregon politics, and it applies not just to assisted suicide but also to a number of major policy debates in the state.

This chapter investigates the practice of federalism, or the relationship of Oregon's state government to the federal government. We describe trends in American federalism overall and how Oregon fits within those trends. The debate in Oregon over assisted suicide is valuable to examine because it provides an insightful example of the conflict that has characterized the state's relationship with the federal government in many areas in recent years. The debate illuminates the impact that the federal government can and does have in Oregon.

To be sure, Oregon politics is affected not only by the actions of the federal government but also by the state's relationship with other states and other nations. With its borders facing California, Washington, and Idaho, the state must find ways to work with its neighbors to address problems that transcend state lines. With a large part of its economy driven by exports and a vocal segment of its population opposed to free trade, the state must also be concerned about foreign relations.

In recent years some of the most intense political battles have surrounded issues dealing with Oregon's relationship to the rest of the nation and the world. This chapter describes several of these battles and explains how Oregon politics is affected by the broader political world. The chapter also highlights how the battle lines over many of these issues are often drawn between progressives on one side and conservative populists on the other.

TRENDS IN FEDERALISM

To understand Oregon's place in the nation and the world, it is helpful to begin by examining the changing character of federal-state relations in general, since the state's relationship with the federal government has generally followed the broader trends that have swept across the nation. When the nation was founded, there was a fairly clear separation between the roles of the federal and state governments, with the federal government focusing primarily on economic coordination and federal security, and the states focusing on such domestic policy concerns as safety, public health, and welfare. Still, it was apparent from the nation's birth that the relationship between the federal government and the states would not be an easy one. As some predicted, the federal and state governments struggled with one another for power, eventually blurring the distribution of powers and responsibilities.

One scholar described the change to a more complex pattern of federalism by using an analogy of a cake. In the past, he wrote, the distribution of power was like a layer cake; today it is more like a marble cake.[2]

Within the U.S. Constitution, the precise roles and responsibilities of the two governments are not clearly laid out, which has allowed the distribution of powers to shift over time. The Great Depression was a major turning point in federal-state relations, since it led to a greater concentration of power at the federal level than ever before. In that period, people turned to the federal government for relief from the financial devastation of the Depression. The federal government responded by creating an unprecedented array of poverty programs and public works projects. During President Lyndon B. Johnson's presidency in the 1960s, the federal government became even more powerful, expanding the programs created in the 1930s, adding new ones, and directing more money to subnational governments. Beginning in the late 1960s and into the 1970s, the federal government expanded its efforts to regulate state activities through an increased use of preemptions, direct orders, and the placement of conditions on federal funds. To be sure, there are some policy areas that the states have controlled with only moderate federal intervention. For instance, the federal government historically has played only a marginal role in education, providing a small amount of funding and focusing on a few specialized policy concerns, such as equal access and special education. Still, overall, our nation's history reveals a centralization of power over time.

Over the last three decades, however, there has been a movement to strengthen the role and power of the states relative to the central government. At least two different forces have helped lead this movement. On one hand, there has been an effort nationwide to transfer some of the federal government's responsibilities back to the states, or what is called "devolution." Some argued that federal power, especially during the Johnson administration, had become too dominant. As a result the federal government has ceded some powers back to the states. One example is poverty policy, where we have seen a shift toward greater state control and responsibility. The Personal Responsibility and Work Opportunity Reconciliation Act of 1996 is perhaps the most frequently cited example of the recent efforts to devolve power to the states. The act gives the states greater discretion in handling welfare than was true of its predecessor, Aid to Families with Dependent Children.

Changes in the state governments themselves have also been important in improving the intergovernmental position of the states over the past three decades. The state governments have become stronger and better able to govern than in the past, which has allowed them to become more assertive in reclaiming their place at the federalism table. In the 1950s and 1960s, and again in the 1970s, there was a concerted effort to strengthen the power of state executives. In the 1970s and 1980s many states moved to strengthen, or professionalize, their legislatures.

Because of these efforts to modernize state governments, the states have emerged as more important players in intergovernmental relations than they have been for several decades.

THE SIGNIFICANCE OF THESE TRENDS FOR OREGON

Oregon's relationship with the federal government over time has generally followed these broader trends, though some interactions have been shaped by Oregon's particular political character. Initially, federal involvement in the state was minimal, but as the federal government became more involved in domestic matters during the Great Depression, Oregon saw the impact of this change.

Most Oregon historians argue that the single most important political issue in Oregon during the 1930s was the question of who would control the power generated by federal dams, especially the newly proposed Bonneville Dam along the Columbia River. From the early 1930s to the end of World War II, state leaders continuously fought over whether the power would be held in private or public hands. In addition, a variety of the federal works projects initiated in the 1930s, including the Works Progress Administration and the Civilian Conservation Corps, played a very important role in helping to strengthen the state's infrastructure. Among other projects, these programs led to the building of numerous roads and buildings across the state, several important bridges along the coast, and Timberline Lodge at Mount Hood. The federal government also established new rules regulating the use of federal lands by ranchers, setting restrictions on the use of these lands in Oregon for grazing. Moreover, the federal government's efforts to underwrite public housing beginning in the 1930s, along with its more active efforts to regulate interest rates, have been credited with helping to strengthen the state's timber industry and its overall economy by building demand for new housing.[3]

After World War II and into the 1960s, an active federal government continued to help expand Oregon's infrastructure. Of particular importance, the federal government helped underwrite the costs of three new dams on the Columbia River, two on the Snake River and many others on smaller rivers throughout Oregon. These dams provided electricity, irrigation, flood control, and recreation, which helped the state's economic development. The government also provided money for public housing, including the creation of the ill-fated Vanport community along the Columbia, which was destroyed in the Memorial Day floods of 1948. The Federal-Aid Highway Act of 1956 helped cover the cost of building Oregon's two interstate freeways.

The expansion of federal regulations in the 1960s and 1970s has played an important role in shaping Oregon politics. Perhaps none of the federal laws and regulations enacted during that period were more significant to Oregon than the Endangered Species Act of 1973. The act has frequently been a target of harsh criticism among many Oregonians, who see the law as a threat to local economies. Yet others praise it for protecting the environment. Also important were the Clean Air Act of 1970 and the Clean Water Act of 1972, which caused governments in Oregon to impose new demands on industries, ranchers, automobile users, and others to meet the requirements in these laws.

More recently, the movement to devolve power has also been important in defining Oregon politics. One of the most visible ways that Oregon leaders have responded to devolution is by seeking waivers to federal government rules so that the state can create its own programs. One example of this is the Oregon Health Plan. The Oregon Health Plan was created between the late 1980s and the mid-1990s to provide universal health care to Oregon residents. To implement the plan, the state needed a waiver from the federal government on how it administered the state's Medicaid program because the plan called for rationing treatment. When President Bill Clinton granted the waiver, it was considered a milestone in federal-state relations, marking one of the first of many waivers granted by the federal government in the 1990s to give states greater flexibility in how they administer federal programs.[4] The state has also pursued similar types of waivers in administering welfare (The Oregon Option) and addressing environmental issues (The Oregon Agreement).[5]

As in other states, Oregon has taken steps to improve the government's performance. In the 1950s the legislature created both the Legislative Counsel Committee and the Legislative Fiscal Office to provide legislators with greater legal and policy expertise. Later, the state capitol building was expanded, providing better facilities for legislators and staff. In the late 1960s and early 1970s, the state took a series of steps to reorganize the executive branch so it would work more effectively. The state eliminated several departments, created others, and moved to concentrate power in the governor's office. In the early 1990s the state established a set of performance goals (Oregon Benchmarks) to help improve government performance. It also created the Oregon Progress Board to monitor the state's progress in meeting those goals.

FEDERAL POWER REMAINS

Despite these gains for the states and Oregon, the federal government continues to play a prominent role in shaping state politics. When the federal government wants to exert itself over the states, it remains in a strong position to do so. More important, the federal government has continued to exercise its power over the states in many areas despite the talk about devolution and the strengthening of state governments.

One important way in which the federal government impacts state politics is through the use of mandates, which are federal laws requiring states to perform a particular task or service. On occasion, when Congress approves a mandate, it will not provide funding, or at least sufficient funding, for the states to accomplish the new task. State leaders frequently criticize these unfunded or underfunded mandates because they force the states to redirect funds from other programs to meet federal demands.

Congress has passed several mandates in recent years that have reshaped the direction of state policy and put new stress on the state budget. These include laws to improve education (No Child Left Behind Act of 2001), to reform election procedures (Help America Vote Act of 2002), and to protect against terrorism (homeland security).

Some mandates place greater burdens on the state than others. For example, the No Child Left Behind Act is considered one of the most extensive federal mandates in recent years, both in its reach and its potential cost. It is also considered to be the federal government's largest expansion of power ever over the traditionally state-controlled area of education. The central goal of the act is to improve K–12 education by making schools more accountable. The act requires states to regularly test student performance and then to take firm steps to fix schools that perform poorly. Yet the eleven-hundred-page law is very complex and detailed. As of 2003 education officials were still assessing the potential impact of the act on Oregon's education system and the state budget. Among other consequences, the state will have to develop a more sophisticated data-collection system to track the schools and develop policies on how to treat those that are not performing adequately. As for costs, the law's impact on Oregon may be great. Studies in other states suggest that the act may force state education budgets to increase by as much as 35 percent, with the federal government covering only a fraction of that amount.[6]

Other mandates are not as costly. For example, efforts to bring the state up to compliance with the Help America Vote Act were expected to add just under $1.2 million to Oregon's 2003–2005 budget, with the federal government providing an additional $2.5 million.[7] Yet combined, the presence of these less costly mandates still places significant demands on the state, both in creating new duties for the state and in absorbing funds that could be spent elsewhere.

Along with mandates, the federal government influences state politics through the power of the purse. The federal government frequently shapes state action by making federal funds available for particular activities. For example, the federal government's efforts to improve homeland security include some direct mandates, such as a requirement that community water systems be assessed for their vulnerability.[8] Yet the federal government has also relied extensively on grants to encourage states to strengthen security. In 2003 Oregon was slated to receive more than $30 million in homeland security grants from the federal government. Federal money was being used by the state for planning and training, and for the administration of public safety efforts.[9]

The federal government directs a considerable amount of money to Oregon each year. During the 2001 fiscal year the federal government channeled more than $18 billion to individuals, groups, and government organizations in the state. This included more than $4 billion in direct aid or grants for such programs as child nutrition, food stamps, state and private forestry, education, Medicaid, and highways. Although this funding is important to the state, the total dollar amount of funds flowing to Oregon from the federal government is relatively small, at least when compared with other states. Overall, Oregon was ranked forty-second in the nation in 2001 for the total amount of federal funds received on a per capita basis.[10]

Despite this low ranking, Oregonians have seen federal funds flow to some particularly important projects over the past decade. One benefit the state enjoyed until recently was that its senior U.S. senator, Mark Hatfield, was the chair of the Senate Appropriations Committee. It has been estimated that Hatfield was able to channel more than $405 million to the state over a five-year period in the early 1990s, an amount that led him to receive a federal award for providing pork. Hatfield's efforts were particularly beneficial to higher education and research, including helping to fund several major research centers at Oregon Health Sciences University.[11]

Of course, federal money rarely comes without strings attached. Many grants often feature "conditions," which are requirements that recipients must abide by in order to receive the money. In years past, Congress has used conditions attached to federal grants to force states to reduce speed limits and raise the legal drinking age.

There are other resources the federal government can use to influence Oregon's politics. Preemptions, for example, are federal laws that preempt or supercede state laws. The federal government has enacted more than 275 preemptions during the past three decades.[12]

It is also worth remembering that the federal government owns more than 52 percent of the land in Oregon; hence, it has direct control over a large portion of the state. For many Oregonians, this means that government rules on the use of federal lands for timber harvesting, ranching, and mining are of great concern. In addition, the federal government alone has the constitutional authority to work with the nine federally recognized tribes in the state.

THE BATTLE OVER DEATH WITH DIGNITY

In Oregon many of the federal government's actions generate little public attention. In some cases, such as when the government provides funding for a new research center or to help underwrite a local program, the government's actions produce a good deal of praise. Yet there are several high-profile issues in which the federal government's involvement has played a critical role and has been the focus of intense debate. The fight over assisted suicide is one of these. Yet we could also talk about recent efforts in Congress to ban Vote by Mail or decisions by the U.S. Fish and Wildlife Service to add Oregon animals to the endangered species list.

The fight over assisted suicide is particularly valuable to study because it has probably generated more debate in the state over federal-state relations than any other recent issue, except perhaps for federal environmental law, especially the Endangered Species Act. Environmental issues are so impor-tant that we take them up separately below. The battle over assisted suicide is also valuable to examine because it, like many of the other actions that have led to debate over federal-state relations in Oregon, reveals the split between progressives and conservative populists in the state. To be sure, the reason that many of these federalism concerns move from generating little debate to becoming high-profile topics is that they do touch upon this split.

Oregon voters passed the Death with Dignity Act through initiative on November 8, 1994, by 51 percent in favor, 49 percent opposed. Immediately upon implementation, opponents challenged the law's legality, claiming among other things that the law breached the U.S. Constitution's equal protection clause. After several years of legal challenges and court proceedings, the law was upheld by the United States Court of Appeals for the Ninth Circuit and implemented on October 27, 1997. The law is the first of its kind, allowing physicians to assist terminally ill patients who wish to end their lives. The law expressly prohibits euthanasia, however, and contains a number of provisions to protect the patient.

Despite these protections, many Oregonians continued to oppose the law, fearing that it would diminish respect for life or that it would negatively impact end-of-life care and pain management. Two conservative populist organizations in particular, Oregon Right to Life and the Oregon Catholic Conference, continued to fight assisted suicide through the legislature even as the law took effect. In February 1997, Oregon's Catholic Conference approached the state legislature with policy options designed either to undermine or repeal the Death with Dignity Act. These efforts resulted in passage of HB 2954, which offered Oregonians the opportunity to overturn the act. Both chambers passed the measure as a referral to the voters, a move that did not offer the governor an opportunity to sign or veto. Ballot Measure 51, if passed, would have overturned the earlier vote on Death with Dignity, but on November 4, 1997, Oregonians preserved the law, this time by the much wider margin of 60 percent to 40 percent.

The vote on the two Death with Dignity ballot measures followed the geographical patterns that shape much of the politics in Oregon. Table 3.1 indicates the level of support for both ballot measures by region. In both cases strongest support for legalizing assisted suicide is found in the state's more progressive urban regions: Portland, the university counties, the Portland suburbs, and the North Coast. On Measure 51, all regions of the state voted to uphold the law. Conversely, the strongest opposition to the practice was found in the state's more rural regions, where conservative populism is more prominent.

The Federal Government Responds

Death with Dignity can be seen as a victory for progressive forces in Oregon. Yet opposition to the law from across the nation inspired the

Table 3.1.   Percent of Voter Support for Death with Dignity

Region	Ballot Measure 16 (1994)	Ballot Measure 51 (1997)
Portland	56.9	65.6
University counties	55.1	63.6
Portland suburbs	51.8	59.4
North Coast	55.1	64.0
Mid–Willamette Valley	44.5	53.7
Southern Oregon	49.7	58.2
Eastern Oregon	46.0	56.2

federal government to become involved. Initially, the effort to overturn the law was led by several conservative members of the U.S. Congress, who were morally opposed to assisted suicide. On November 5, 1997, the day after Oregonians rejected Measure 51, Senator Orrin Hatch (R-UT) and Representative Henry Hyde (R-IL) argued that Oregon's physicians would run afoul of the federal Controlled Substances Act (CSA) if they prescribed life-ending pharmaceuticals. Hatch and Hyde maintained that the federal Drug Enforcement Agency (DEA) had advised them that physicians could not lawfully prescribe controlled substances for the purposes of hastening death under the CSA rules.[13] As these federal actors began seeking to overturn Oregon's law, the supporters of assisted suicide argued that this was not an issue in which the federal government should be involved. Rather, they argued, the choice of who should set this policy should be left to the state.

Attorney General Janet Reno, after having investigated the DEA's claims, issued a statement on June 5, 1998, that the DEA did not have the authority to punish Oregon doctors under the Controlled Substances Act. In response to Reno's ruling, Representative Hyde introduced the Legal Drug Abuse Prevention Act of 1998 (HR 4006) in the House that same day. The act was designed to amend the CSA in order to give the DEA the powers of investigation and enforcement over Oregon's physician-assisted suicide practices. Several days later, Senator Don Nickles (R-OK) introduced a companion bill in the Senate (S 2151). Still, the bill was not brought to the floor of either chamber before the end of the session in October, and the practice of assisted suicide continued in Oregon.

The state of Oregon and the federal government were clearly struggling over the fate of the law by early 1999. In July 1999 Nickles and Hyde sponsored and introduced the Pain Relief Promotion Act (PRPA), reigniting the issue of assisted suicide on Capitol Hill. The bill would make it a federal crime for a physician to prescribe a controlled drug for the purpose of assisted suicide. By the end of that October, the House passed the bill safely by a margin of 271 to 156, over the objections of all five Oregon representatives, clearing the way for Senate consideration. As in many aspects of federal-state relations, the state was not without some power to respond to this congressional challenge. In this case, a threat to filibuster the act by Senator Ron Wyden (D-OR) prevented passage in the Senate.

The effort to overturn Oregon's Death with Dignity Act soon shifted from the Congress to the White House. There are two reasons for this shift. First, the 2000 election made passage of the PRPA less likely in the Senate, where a new, razor-thin Democratic majority would inevitably turn a floor debate of assisted suicide into a high-profile filibuster. Most senators, regardless of their position on assisted suicide, would seek to avoid the intransigence of a filibuster, leaving the issue behind. Second, the election delivered opponents of Death with Dignity a powerful new weapon in the battle over assisted suicide: the new conservative administration could look for *nonlegislative* ways to undermine Death with Dignity.

The new strategy came from the U.S. attorney general's office. While his predecessor had refused to use federal means to undermine this state-crafted policy, the new attorney general took a different tack. On November 6, 2001, Attorney General John Ashcroft issued a ruling ordering the DEA to prosecute pharmacists and physicians who, through the prescription of lethal doses of narcotics, "hasten death." In effect, his directive reversed his predecessor's position, opening the way for direct federal intervention in Oregon's use of assisted suicide. Not taking this action lightly, Oregon Attorney General Hardy Myers filed suit in federal court the next day, asking the federal court to overturn the Ashcroft ruling, citing the state's right to regulate end-of-life decisions.

In April 2002 U.S. District Court judge Robert E. Jones upheld the Oregon law, arguing that the federal government lacked authority to intervene in this policy arena. Unwilling to let the issue rest with the Jones ruling, Attorney General Ashcroft filed an appeal on May 24, 2002, taking the issue next to the federal appeals court. On May 26, 2004, a three-judge panel for the United States Court of Appeals for the Ninth Circuit ruled that Ashcroft did not have the legal authority to prosecute physicians who prescribe a lethal dose of medication under the Death with Dignity Act. Three months later, the twenty-five active judges on the appeals court voted to deny a rehearing. As of late August 2004, the U.S. Justice Department had not made a decision as to whether it would appeal the ruling to the U.S. Supreme Court.

It would be folly to hazard a guess at the outcome of the Death with Dignity debate. But the outcome will have serious consequences for the citizens of Oregon, particularly those facing agonizing end-of-life decisions. At the end of 2003 the Oregon Department of Human Services reported that 171 Oregonians had lawfully ended their lives through physician-assisted suicide. If the state's position is upheld, Oregonians meeting the state's requirements will continue to exercise physician-assisted suicide. If not, then terminally ill patients will not be legally given this option.

The more relevant concern for this chapter is not the fate of the law per se but what the battle over assisted suicide reveals about Oregon politics and federal-state relations. Death with Dignity is important, in part, because it has generated one of the most prominent federalism debates in the state in recent years. Yet it is also important because it shows that Oregon politics is not just shaped by local or statewide concerns; the federal government also plays a significant role in political outcomes in the state despite the prominent talk about devolution. When there is sufficient concern, federal actors can try to determine state policies through Congress, the White House, and the courts. Often the federal government never becomes involved. But in this case, as in many others, federal actors decided to interject themselves in what had been a state policy debate. When they did so, the battle over assisted suicide moved beyond the state and into our nation's capitol. Ultimately, the fate of assisted suicide will not be decided by the state but by one specific federal actor: the U.S. Supreme Court.

FEDERAL ENVIRONMENTAL LAWS

The battle over Death with Dignity is unusual in one regard. In this case it was the progressive supporters of Death with Dignity who were arguing that the question of assisted suicide should be left to the states, and conservative populists were less opposed to federal intervention. In general, the conservative populists in Oregon are the ones who are more frequently opposed to an active federal government. The more rural regions of the states, as well as small towns, tend to show stronger support for letting the state or local government decide policy issues that are now often decided by the federal government. Part of the reason for the conservative populists' opposition to an active federal government is based on their ideals about the appropriate role of the government in society. Yet some of this opposition also reflects local experiences with the federal government. For at least two decades, many rural Oregonians have been unhappy with federal environmental laws, which they see as a threat to local jobs and economies. The problem, these opponents argue, is that the environmental laws have put severe restrictions on the use of natural resources, causing a loss of jobs and an increase in economic problems for the local communities that depend on agriculture, timber, fisheries, and other industries for their survival.

Many rural Oregonians have been particularly dissatisfied with the Endangered Species Act. The act emerged as one of the most important political issues in the state in July 1990, when the U.S. Fish and Wildlife Service listed the northern spotted owl as an endangered species. The listing forced the federal government to place stronger restrictions on timber harvesting on federal land. The listing also meant that private landowners would have to take steps to avoid harming the owls. These steps included restricting the harvesting of timber within seventy acres of where owls nest or are active.

Initial state estimates projected that the listing would result in the loss of sixty-four hundred jobs in the timber industry and another nine thousand jobs elsewhere.[14] Although the ultimate economic impact of the listing is disputed, many rural residents certainly blame the act for causing a decline in the state's timber industry and for the economic problems confronting many local communities throughout the 1990s. Environmentalists, on the other hand, have been supportive of the act for protecting threatened species.

More recently, the act has been at the center of a major political fight in the Klamath Basin in southern Oregon. In the 1980s the Fish and Wildlife Service listed two types of suckerfish in Upper Klamath Lake and salmon in the Klamath River (an outlet of Klamath Lake) as endangered species. Throughout the 1990s the listing repeatedly led to battles between environmentalists, Indian tribes, farmers, and commercial fishers over protecting the species. The environmentalists and the Klamath Indians repeatedly sought to limit the draining of water from the lake in order to protect the fish. The farmers and commercial fishers sought to keep a sufficient flow of water out of the lake to support farming and protect salmon fishing. The battle intensified in 2001 when the U.S. Bureau of Reclamation decided to shut off all the water from the lake to downstream farms to protect the species from a worsening drought. The action met with considerable protest from farmers and local communities. At the height of the conflict, a group of farmers illegally used a crowbar to force open the main irrigation canal, allowing water to flow to the farms.[15] The issue arose again in late 2002 when more than thirty-four thousand salmon in the Klamath River died unexpectedly when water levels dropped and water temperature rose too high for the salmon to survive.

The deaths led the U.S. Bureau of Reclamation to release more water down northern California's Trinity River, a tributary of the Klamath, in 2003 and 2004 to keep water levels high enough to protect the fish.

Despite the opposition one finds in rural areas toward these federal laws, Oregon has not generally confronted the same level of antigovernment extremism that some other western states have encountered over federal land-use rules. There has been some support for what is called the "county supremacy" movement, but it has not developed the same acceptance in the state as it has elsewhere. Supporters of the county supremacy movement challenge federal authority over public lands, claiming that they should be under local control. In total, six counties in Oregon, all more rural ones, have passed resolutions or ordinances claiming local ownership over federal land.[16] Perhaps more telling about Oregon politics, however, is that the county board in Klamath Falls voted down a county supremacy measure at the height of the water battle in 2001.

The rural areas are not alone, however, in feeling the effects of these federal environmental laws. In 2000 the Federal Marine Fisheries Service issued a list of new rules to protect fourteen different stocks of endangered salmon, including ones that run through the heart of Portland and the Willamette Valley. The rules place restrictions on a variety of private and public activities, including the use of pesticides, the building of new housing, and the maintenance of city streets.[17] Moreover, the federal government has also taken actions that have been strongly opposed by environmentalists. One recent example of this was the passage of the salvage-logging rider, a short amendment that was tacked onto an emergency appropriations bill in 1995. The rider eased environmental restrictions on timber harvests and made it easier for the government to sell timber to logging companies.

WORKING WITH OTHER STATES

Along with the federal government, other states also play a role in shaping Oregon politics. Because many public policy issues transcend state lines, Oregon political leaders often have to work with the leaders of other states, particularly neighboring ones, to address mutual concerns. In general, there are two primary ways in which Oregon works with other states. One is through an interstate compact in which two or more states work out a formal agreement on how to work together on a particular issue. The compact is much like a business contract, establishing the terms of the agreement among the participants. In cases where the compact touches on federal concerns, the compact must receive congressional approval. The second way in which Oregon works with other states is simply through more informal joint efforts.

As of 1998 Oregon was a partner in twenty-six major interstate compacts. These included ones dealing with such issues as the treatment of mentally retarded patients, the sharing of forest fire-fighting units, the provision of library services, the transportation of nuclear waste, the eradication of agricultural pests, and the handling of traffic violations for nonresidents.[18]

Most of Oregon's interstate compacts do not receive much public attention, but a few have been the center of political debate. One that has received particular attention in recent years is the Columbia River Gorge Compact, which was approved by Oregon, Washington, and the U.S. Congress in 1987. The compact included the creation of the Columbia River Gorge Commission to oversee the development of the land contained within the Columbia River Gorge Federal Scenic Area. The commission entered the political spotlight in 2001 when it ruled that a new house, which had been built in a site overlooking the gorge in Washington, had to be torn down because it was too large, violating the scenic area's development rules and the terms of the building permit. The owners of the house sued, arguing that the commission did not have the authority to force them to remove the home. The conflict became a major duel between property rights advocates, who supported the homeowners, and environmentalists. The case was ultimately decided by the Washington Supreme Court, which ruled that the gorge commission had indeed overstepped its authority in demanding the removal of the home. Yet the environmentalists did not entirely lose the battle, because the homeowners were still required to redesign the home so it was less visible from the gorge.[19]

State leaders also pursue less formal methods to work with the leaders of other states to address mutual concerns. These efforts are sometimes accomplished through the formation of formal groups, such as the Western Governors' Association. For example, Oregon is a member of the Western States Water Council, which tries to coordinate efforts among eighteen western states in the management of water resources. The council provides a means for these states to cooperate on water policy, which is frequently a major political concern in the region. Instead of working through an ongoing group such as the water council, the cooperation can be more ad hoc. For example, Portland State University and Washington State University Vancouver sponsored two conferences in the late 1990s to examine problems confronting the Portland metropolitan area, which incorporates parts of both states. The conference brought together nearly three hundred state leaders, including both governors, to talk about such issues as transportation, growth management, the environment, and education.

Oregon politics is affected by international concerns as well. In general, the most important international issues in Oregon in recent years have revolved around trade. Trade is particularly important because Oregon's economy depends heavily on foreign exports. A 2001 report by the Oregon Economic and Community Development Commission placed Oregon within the top ten states in both exports per capita and the state's dependence on exports. In total, the commission reported that one in five manufacturing jobs in Oregon were related to international business and trade.[20] By far, the two largest exports from the state are semiconductors and wheat. These two goods accounted for about 20 percent and 9 percent, respectively, of the total value of state exports.[21] Because trade is so important to both the rural and urban areas of the state, most elected officials in Oregon tend to support free trade. There are some exceptions. The most outspoken opponent of free trade among the state's elected officials is U.S. representative Peter DeFazio, who represents the southern portion of the Willamette Valley. DeFazio has criticized U.S. free trade policy for harming workers and the environment.

Even though most elected officials tend to support free trade, not everyone in the state agrees. In recent years the state has begun to see a growing number of political demonstrations against free trade in general, and the World Trade Organization in particular. The state's free trade opponents became particularly mobilized after a 1999 demonstration in Seattle against the World Trade Organization. That protest brought thousands of activists to Seattle. Since 1999 Oregon has witnessed several smaller protests in Portland and other communities, including a May Day protest in 2002 that attracted over a thousand participants.

The debate over international trade in Oregon is unusual in the sense that it does not split along the traditional line of progressives versus conservative populists. Because exports are important to both the urban and rural communities, there tends to be support within all regions for free trade. What makes the opposition to free trade of particular interest is that it represents a more populist side of progressivism than is seen in many aspects of the state's politics today. As was discussed in the first chapter, liberal populists have historically been concerned about using government to overcome the social ills created by corporations. In Oregon today, however, the state's progressive leaders rarely talk about the will of the people being denied by large corporations and a wealthy elite. Yet it is a concern about the power of corporations and business that underlies the protests against free trade and the World Trade Organization. Thus, the protesters and their supporters represent a different type of progressive or liberal than is typical within the state.

Much of Oregon politics today is dominated by local and state-specific concerns. This domination can be seen by looking at the issues that come up in one chapter after another in this book. Repeatedly, we talk about such issues as school funding, state land-use policies, property taxes, the bottle bill, and growth. Yet Oregon's politics is not entirely homegrown. The state exists within a broader political system and an interconnected world. The federal government frequently plays an important role in major political issues in the state, whether it is over education reform, assisted suicide, or in simply providing funding to important state programs. The state frequently works with other states to address mutual problems or concerns. International issues, especially trade, are also important.

In this chapter we have tried to explain Oregon's political position in relationship to the nation and the world. There are two particularly important lessons to draw from this discussion. One is that the debate over federalism, or which level of government should decide major policy issues, plays a central role in many important political battles in Oregon today. The second is that much of the political fighting that goes on in the state over federalism and over the state's role in the broader world, reflects the divide between progressives and conservative populists. Certainly, this is not true in all policy areas, as is evident in the broad support statewide for free trade. Yet on issues dealing with assisted suicide, federal environmental laws, and the oversight of the Columbia River Gorge, the progressive activists routinely line up against the conservative populist activists. In other words, Oregon's position within the nation and the world still often reflects its homegrown character: it is split between two different sets of political ideals.

CHAPTER FOUR

Parties and Elections

E. D. Dover

The laws relating to nearly all aspects of elections in Oregon derive from progressive values. Many of the state's most important election laws were enacted during the height of the Progressive Movement in the early twentieth century. The Progressives were particularly worried about the influence of political parties in state politics, believing that parties were inherently threatening to democracy and that they were dominated by corrupt politicians. The Progressives' view of parties was shaped by their belief that a unifying and singular public interest can be attained simply by removing the corrupting influences of politics. The idea that voters could legitimately disagree with one another over such significant matters as the purposes of government and the preferred directions of society was an alien concept to many Progressives. Moreover, many reformers saw little merit in the idea that political disagreements could be voiced through responsible political parties in ways that might strengthen democracy.

Driven to seek change, Progressives enacted several important laws to improve elections, primarily by weakening political parties. Among these laws were the adoption of primary elections, the initiative, and referenda. Progressives also championed the direct election of U.S. senators and the use of nonpartisan elections for many local and statewide offices.

As a consequence of these reforms, two distinguishing features today mark Oregon elections. One is the existence of weak political parties with candidate-centered campaigns. The other is a strong reliance on the use of direct democracy to enact laws. This chapter provides an overview of parties and elections in Oregon politics, with particular attention devoted to the Progressive influence on candidate elections. Chapter 5 examines direct democracy.

Although the Progressive reforms of the early twentieth century severely weakened parties, they did not eliminate parties altogether. Today, political parties continue to play an important role in structuring elections. To understand electoral politics in Oregon, it is helpful to look first at the role played by parties. From there we can then examine the character of the election system.

POLITICAL PARTIES: AN INTRODUCTION

Political parties are nongovernmental institutions that attempt to take control of government by contesting elections. Parties are nongovernmental in that they are private entities (despite the central role they play in elections). They are institutions in the sense that they are composed of committees, officers, and individual members whose actions are defined and often limited by state law. Their ultimate goal is to win enough elections to take control of the institutions of government. The formal party organizations do not actually govern, however, for they are much too weak. A party cannot force a governor to act as it wishes. However, a governor may be strong enough to force a party to act as he wishes.

Oregon has a competitive two-party system today. This means that two major parties—the Republicans and Democrats—have enough supporters that both have realistic chances of winning a majority of elected offices. Why are there two major parties in Oregon? Why not one or three? Part of the answer involves the state's electoral system. Duverger's Rule, named after the French political scientist who formulated it during the 1950s, attributes the existence of two-party systems to two different and independent features of election law: single-member districts and plurality voting.[1] The presence of both features virtually guarantees that a two-party system will dominate elections. The absence of either one provides incentives for minor parties to compete on more equal grounds with major parties.

A single-member district refers to an election in which the voters cast ballots for only one candidate for a specific office. This is what Oregon uses today, for example, in legislative and gubernatorial elections. In contrast is the multiple-member district, in which voters elect more than one candidate from the same district for the same office. Some school boards and city councils use these types of elections. For most of the state's history, some members of the Legislative Assembly were also elected from multimember districts. The legislature voted to end the use of multimember districts, however, during the 1971 special session.

Under a system of plurality voting, the candidate who receives the largest number of votes wins the election, even if the number does not equal a majority of the votes cast. For example, Democrat Barbara Roberts was elected governor in 1990 with 45 percent of the vote.[2] The alternative to plurality voting is majority voting. Under majority voting, a candidate needs to receive more than 50 percent of the votes to win. If no candidate receives a majority, then a second election takes place between the two candidates who received the most votes in the first election.

Part of the reason, then, that Oregon has two major parties is that the elections for all major offices in Oregon are conducted through single-member districts and plurality voting. The major offices include those of the two U.S. senators, the five members of the U.S. House of Representatives, the governor, all ninety members of the legislature, numerous mayors, and hundreds of other local officials. But the type of electoral system is only part of the explanation. The structure of the state's current party system also reflects the system's history.

HISTORY OF OREGON PARTIES

Oregon has not always had a competitive two-party system. In fact, for much of Oregon's history, one party tended to dominate the state's politics. From the end of the nineteenth century to the 1950s, most state voters considered themselves Republicans, and the Republican Party controlled most of the state's elected offices.

The emergence of the Republican Party as the dominant party began in the 1880s, and is considered to have been triggered by an influx of migrants from Michigan, Minnesota, and Wisconsin, as well as immigrants from several northern European countries.[3] Until the 1880s the Democratic Party had controlled most of the state's politics. The influx of new residents changed the balance of support within the state, giving Republicans an advantage. By the turn of the century, the Republican advantage had turned into dominance.

In his study of Oregon political parties, Robert Burton found that Republican Party registration levels were two to three times as large as Democratic Party registration levels from 1900 into the 1930s. During the Great Depression of the 1930s, the Republican Party's registration levels fell, but the rate continued to exceed that of the Democratic Party. The Democrats did not regain majority status until the 1950s.[4]

With the large registration advantage, the Republicans generally dominated elections. The party's advantage can be seen in figures 4.1 and 4.2, which show the partisan distribution of House and Senate seats from 1901 to

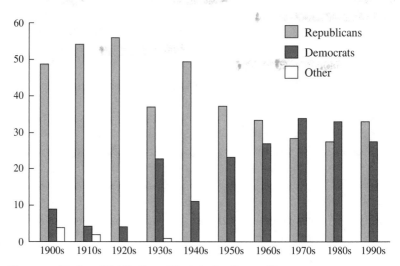

Figure 4.1. Partisan Distribution of Seats in the Oregon House

1999 by decade. As the figures make clear, the Democrats rarely controlled more than a handful of seats during the first three decades of the twentieth century. Moreover, it was not until the 1970s that the Democrats were able to gain continuous control over the legislature for more than one or two sessions at a time. The Republican Party's advantage can also be seen in statewide elections. From the mid-1890s to 1953, only four Democrats were elected to the offices of secretary of state, treasurer, attorney general, commissioner of labor and industries, and superintendent of public instruction.[5]

The main exception to this rule was that Democratic candidates were able to win the governor's race in five different elections during that same period. Why were the Democrats able to gain control of the state's most important office during those elections despite having a large disadvantage in registration? Oregon historians have generally attributed the party's success to two main factors. One was the presence of factional conflict within the Republican Party, splitting the party between progressive reformers and more conservative members who opposed change. The other was the tendency of Democratic gubernatorial candidates to deemphasize partisanship in their campaigns. With the Republican Party split, the Democratic Party candidates, using nonpartisan rhetoric, would reach out to progressive Republicans to build a winning coalition. It was through such bipartisan

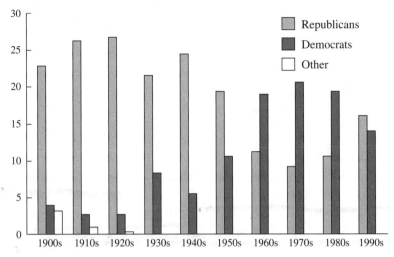

Figure 4.2. Partisan Distribution of Seats in the Oregon Senate

coalitions that two of Oregon's most important progressive reformers were elected to office: George Chamberlain (1903–1909) and Oswald West (1911–1915). The building of these coalitions and the use of the nonpartisan rhetoric also helped establish the state's reputation for political independence.[6]

Beginning in the 1930s, however, the Republican Party's dominance began to diminish. From 1930 to 1940 the Republican lead in voter registration declined from almost three times the Democratic Party's figure to almost even.[7] Since the mid-1950s the Democrats have led in registration, although the numbers are fairly close, as described below. The Republican Party also began to see a decline in its dominance of elections. The Democrats gained control of the House of Representatives in the 1935 and 1937 sessions before falling back into minority status. In the 1958 election the Democrats gained control of both houses for the first time in the twentieth century. The party also began to elect members to the other statewide offices besides the governorship.

What brought about the resurgence of the Democratic Party? Again, historians tend to attribute the change to demographic trends, particularly an influx of workers to the state during World War II, which bolstered Democratic registration. Many of the migrants were drawn to Portland to work in the shipyards, making the city and surrounding communities particularly vital to the reemergence of the Democratic Party. Yet counties throughout the state also saw a rise in Democratic registration after the war.[8] As a result of these demographic trends and the strengthening of the Democratic Party, the state now has a competitive two-party system.

The closeness between the two parties was apparent in the 2002 election. In the gubernatorial race, Democrat Ted Kulongoski defeated Republican Kevin Mannix by fewer than thirty-four thousand votes. The Libertarian candidate in the race, Tom Cox, received more than fifty-six thousand votes. The election also produced an evenly divided state Senate for the first time since the 1957 session, with the Democrats and Republicans both capturing fifteen seats.

Even though Oregon can be categorized as a competitive two-party system, it differs from many other states because of the particularly loose ties that Oregonians have to political parties. Oregon, of course, is not the only state with loose party ties. In recent years many voters nationwide have been unwilling to identify themselves with one of the two major political parties and have been more likely to split their votes among candidates from different parties. Oregon voters, however, tend to be among the more independent in the nation. Overall, almost one-quarter of Oregon voters are frequently registered as Independents, which is higher than the nation's average. Moreover, many state voters have been reluctant to support the major party candidates in recent presidential elections. In 1992 Ross Perot won 24 percent of the vote in the state, which was higher than the 19 percent he received nationwide. In the 2000 election Ralph Nader's campaign as the Pacific Green Party candidate initially generated considerable support in Oregon, though Nader ultimately received only 5 percent of the votes in the state, which was less than he received in ten other states. The vote probably would have been higher, however, if not for a concerted effort by several prominent progressive groups to get voters to abandon Nader for Democrat Al Gore. These groups warned progressive voters that supporting Nader could lead to a Bush win in Oregon.[9]

Despite the large number of Oregonian voters who declare themselves to be Independent today, and despite the examples from these two presidential elections, the state has not been particularly supportive of third-party candidates in years past. Since the 1940s only one third-party candidate has been elected to the Legislative Assembly. Since the turn of the last century, fewer than three dozen third-party candidates have been elected. During that same time there were no Independent candidates elected to a statewide office, with one important exception. In 1930 the factionalism within the

Republican Party led one of the state's leading Republicans, Julius Meier, to run an Independent campaign for governor. Meier entered the race only after the party's progressive nominee died and after the Republican Party leaders chose a candidate who was opposed to progressive ideals as the party's replacement. Supported by both progressive Republicans and Democrats, Meier beat both of the two major party candidates.[10] This was an unusual election, however. Third-party candidates historically have not done well in the state.

MAJOR AND MINOR PARTIES

Oregon law categorizes parties as being either major or minor. This distinction is important because it affects the ability of parties to put their candidates' names on the ballot, or what is called "ballot access." Holding major status assures a party that its candidates' names will be printed on the ballots in all the partisan races for state or federal office.

The laws governing party status were revised during the 2001 legislative session. As of January 2002 a party qualifies for major status if at least 5 percent of the voters in the state are registered as members of that party by 275 days before the primary election. To maintain major party status, a party must continue to meet this same registration requirement before each primary election. Reaching this number is not difficult for the two major parties. In 2000 about 39 percent of Oregon's registered voters were Democrats and 36 percent were Republicans.[11]

The laws have historically been harsher on minor parties. In order to gain ballot access, a minor party must gather signatures from registered voters in the electoral district in which it wants to run candidates. The total number of signatures needed is determined by the number of votes cast in the district in the last gubernatorial election. The number of signatures gathered must be greater than 1.5 percent of the total votes cast in the district for all the gubernatorial candidates combined. As a result, a minor party must gather more than seventeen thousand signatures to gain ballot access in statewide elections. To gain access in specific legislative or congressional districts, the number is smaller.

Once established, a minor party can retain its status through one of two ways. The first way is that one of the party's candidates must receive at least 1 percent of the votes cast in the electoral district for all the candidates for any single statewide partisan office. In addition, the party's membership must also remain over one-tenth of 1 percent of the total votes cast for all candidates for governor in the most recent gubernatorial election. This registration requirement must be met between the day after the primary election and ninety days before the general election. A second way a party can maintain minor party status is if 0.5 percent of the state voters are registered as party members at any time between the primary election and ninety days before the general election. This alternative allows a minor political party to maintain its status but not have to run candidates at the general election.

The requirements for minor parties have often been prohibitive, especially if the parties wanted to compete in statewide campaigns. In order to succeed, the parties had to devote considerable time and money solely to trying to retain ballot access. Major parties do not have this problem.

Despite these obstacles, several minor parties did win statewide access to the 2002 ballot because of their performances in the 2000 election. The Pacific Green Party qualified in both the presidential and secretary of state elections. The Libertarian Party qualified in the elections for secretary of state, state treasurer, and attorney general. The Reform Party qualified in the treasurer race, as did the Constitution Party. The Socialist Party received enough votes to place candidates on the ballot in the third and fourth congressional districts.

PARTY ORGANIZATION

Along with setting the rules on ballot access, the state regulates the organizational structure and membership requirements of political parties. State law requires major parties to operate through a set of committees. The primary decision-making authority for each party is a "central committee" in each of the state's thirty-six counties. Each committee is composed of representatives from every one of a county's precincts. Precincts are geographic districts that are created by counties to facilitate balloting. Each precinct contains no more than five thousand voters. Party members in each of a county's precincts choose one male and one female representative to the county central committee for every five hundred party members in the precinct. These representatives then elect the officers of the county central committee and determine its agenda. The central committee oversees the party's activities within each county, handling such traditional chores as recruiting candidates, raising campaign money, and observing ballot counting. The central committee also elects the county's delegates to the state central committee.

The state central committee performs the same roles at the state level that county central committees do locally. The state central committee is composed of a minimum of two delegates from each county, with the larger counties receiving additional delegates. As at the local level, the county delegations must include an equal number of male and female representatives. The state party organizations also hold regular conventions to handle a variety of political matters, including the selection of delegates to national committees and nominating conventions.

A distinguishing feature of this organizational pattern is a lack of vertical and horizontal authority among the different committees and officials. State committees or officers cannot order a county committee to act as they wish. In addition, committees in any county have the right to act independently from committees in other counties. In Oregon, as with most other states, the county committees are considered to be the most powerful, yet even they cannot exert much authority over committee members. Political scientists call a pattern of this nature a *stratarchy* and distinguish it from a *hierarchy*.[12] A hierarchy places authority in the roles of specific offices, whereas a stratarchy does not. The power in a hierarchy exists at the top of the structure, and the power in a stratarchy is diffused through all levels of the organization.

Minor parties rarely operate through county-based structures. Instead, they usually grant direct authority to their state conventions and leaders.

PARTY MEMBERSHIP TODAY

As in other aspects of Oregon politics, the party system today is strongly influenced by the split between progressives and conservative populists. This can be seen in the members of the two major parties. Voters who are liberal, female, members of labor unions, or racial minorities tend to favor the Democratic Party. Voters who are conservative, male, business or farm owners, and white are likely to be Republicans. The members of the state Democratic Party generally support progressive governmental actions that regulate corporate interests and encourage social and economic equality. Republicans, on the other hand, are more likely to support conservative populist efforts to limit the power of government over economic activities and property. They also tend to support greater regulation of personal and moral behavior.

Democrats tend to dominate in the larger urban counties, particularly Multnomah, and in the western part of the state. Republicans attract many of their members from smaller and more rural counties in southern and eastern Oregon. These differences can be seen in figure 4.3, which shows the

Figure 4.3. Counties with a Majority of Registered Democrats

counties in which a majority of voters are registered Democrats. The figure is noteworthy because it shows how closely the voting patterns resemble those described in chapter 1.

Overall, there were 1,885,917 registered voters in Oregon in June 2004. Of those, 736,709 (39 percent) were Democrats, 683,381 (36 percent) were Republican, and 64,479 (3 percent) were members of minority parties. A very large number of Oregonians, 401,348 (21 percent), have registered to vote as nonaffiliated or independent.[13]

ELECTION RULES

Many of the most important laws governing elections in Oregon were enacted in the early part of the twentieth century as part of the Progressive Movement. None of these reforms, however, may have been more important than the introduction of direct primary elections in 1904. Prior to the use of the direct primary, the party organizations selected the candidates. The primary election removed the power of choosing nominees away from the party organization and gave it to voters. The result, as described more fully below, was the eventual decline in the power of political parties and the rise of candidate-centered campaigns. Not all the major laws affecting elections were enacted during the early 1900s. In the 1990s Oregon voters passed ballot measures authorizing the use of all-mail ballot elections (Vote by Mail) and establishing legislative term limits.

Types of Elections

Perhaps the most important value in joining a party is the ability to participate in selecting that party's candidates. Republican and Democratic nominees for the state's partisan political offices are chosen in the primary election, which is held on the third Tuesday in May of even-numbered years. The most important partisan state offices are governor, secretary of state, state treasurer, attorney general, and the Oregon Legislative Assembly. Minor parties nominate their candidates for these offices through state conventions.

In addition to selecting party nominees for these partisan offices, the primary election is used to select two final candidates in each nonpartisan race. The leading nonpartisan offices include the superintendent of public instruction, commissioner of the Bureau of Labor and Industries, various judgeships, and most positions in local governments. In these nonpartisan elections, every voter can participate; the franchise is not limited to party members. In general, the two candidates who receive the most votes in the primary election face off against each other in the general election. If a candidate receives a majority of the votes cast in the primary, however, he or she is automatically elected and a second vote is not taken. This happened in 1998 when incumbent Jack Roberts won every county and a majority of the total vote in his bid for a second term as commissioner of the Bureau of Labor and Industries. In contrast, sixteen candidates competed for superintendent of public instruction that year. Stan Bunn and Margaret Carter were nominated after finishing in first and second place with 24 percent and 18 percent of the vote respectively.[14]

The main activity that takes place in the general election is the final selection of who will serve. As described above, all of the major state offices are selected in single-member districts with plurality voting. The general election occurs on the first Tuesday after the first Monday in November of every even-numbered year.

The offices that are voted on in each election year follow a pattern, depending on whether the nation is electing a president. During presidential election years, voters cast ballots for the secretary of state, state treasurer, and attorney general. In nonpresidential election years, voters select the governor, commissioner of the Bureau of Labor and Industries, and superintendent of public instruction. All the seats in the state House of Representatives, and half of the Senate, come up for election every two years.

Vote by Mail

One of the distinct aspects of Oregon's election system is its reliance on voting through the mail rather than in voting booths. In Oregon this practice is called Vote by Mail. Elsewhere, it is often referred to as all-mail-ballot elections. Oregon is not the only government to use the U.S. mail for voting. All states allow some citizens to vote through the mail using absentee ballots. What makes Vote by Mail different, however, is that it requires all voters to cast their ballots through the mail. Although some local governments across the nation have tried all-mail-ballot elections, Oregon was the first state to use this approach for a higher office. Oregon has also used mail ballots far more extensively than any other state. Oregon first used Vote by Mail for a statewide election in 1993. In 1998 Oregon voters overwhelmingly approved Measure 60, which requires the use of Vote by Mail for all state and federal elections.[15] The measure passed with almost 70 percent of the voters supporting it.

Under Vote by Mail, ballots are printed by the election officials and sent to voters approximately two weeks before the election. Voters must then return the ballots to the county clerk in the county in which they live by eight o'clock in the evening on election night. If a voter is unable to return the ballot by mail before the deadline, the voter can return it in person.

The use of Vote by Mail is popular among Oregon voters, yet it is not without critics. In particular, some argue that the use of Vote by Mail increases the potential for voter fraud and coercion because voters no longer cast their ballots in secret. Opponents also criticize Vote by Mail for abandoning what they view as an important civic ritual—going to a polling place on Election Day. The secretary of state, as well as Vote by Mail supporters, counter that there have been only minor reports of fraud or coercion. The state protects against voting fraud by requiring voters to sign the envelope in which they return their ballots. The signatures are then verified against a master list. Supporters also dismiss the argument that Vote by Mail harms an important civic ritual, arguing that its benefits in making voting easier and increasing turnout are more important. Initial scholarly studies on Vote by Mail provide evidence that its use has indeed increased turnout.[16]

Campaign Finance

There are some national laws relating to campaign finance, but they apply only to presidential and congressional elections. Among the most important of these laws are the amendments to the Federal Election Campaign Act (FECA) that were adopted in 1974, limiting the amount of money that individuals, political action committees (PACs), and parties can contribute to candidates.[17] There are no comparable laws for state elections in Oregon, which means that candidates can spend as much money as they can raise. Candidates for state office are, however, required to file regular campaign contribution and spending reports.

Campaigns are often very expensive. In recent years the amount of money spent on elections has risen dramatically, especially in state legislative races. In 1998 the total amount spent by all legislative candidates combined reached a record high of $11.6 million. Two years later the total was close to $14 million.[18] In one Senate race that year, and in another in 2002, the two leading candidates spent almost $1 million combined. In general, the races for statewide office have also grown in cost, with the exception of the 1998 gubernatorial race. The most expensive gubernatorial election came in 1990, when the two major party candidates spent a total of $5.6 million combined. However, in 1998 incumbent governor John Kitzhaber and his opponent, Bill Sizemore, spent less than $2 million.[19]

Candidates spend most of their money on advertising. They use various media, such as television, radio, direct mail, and newspapers to reach voters. In general, candidates for statewide office tend to rely more on television than do those seeking to join the legislature. Legislative candidates tend to concentrate more of their funds on direct mail. Candidates for all offices also frequently purchase advertisements in the "Oregon Voters' Guide," the state's official guide to the measures and candidates appearing on the ballot. The guide is published by the secretary of state's office and is then distributed free through the mail to all voters.

Term Limits

In 1992 Oregon voters adopted Measure 3, a constitutional amendment limiting the number of terms that individuals can serve in both the executive and legislative branches. Under Measure 3 individuals could serve only eight years in each statewide office, six years in the state House, and eight years in the state Senate. The measure also limited the total number of years that an individual could serve in House and Senate combined to twelve. The law was considered one of the strictest in the nation.

In January 2002, however, the state supreme court overturned the term limits law, ruling that because Measure 3 changed more than one part of the state constitution, it violated state rules on constitutional amendments (see chapter 5). The problem with Measure 3 was that it not only placed limits on state legislators but included restrictions on federal officeholders as well. The ruling, however, may not mean the end of term limits. Anticipating that the court might throw out the law, term limits advocates had already filed a new initiative within a few days of the court's ruling.[20]

THE POLITICS OF OREGON ELECTIONS

All Oregon elections are dominated by candidate-centered campaigns. That is, candidates seek office as individuals rather than as representatives of political parties. The candidates develop their own personal issues, recruit their own advisors and staff, raise most of their own campaign finances, direct their own marketing efforts, and attempt to sell themselves as tribunes of the people. Rarely do they try to link themselves to a political party, except in the most general sense. Rather than asking voters to support them because they are good Republicans or Democrats, candidates ask voters to view them as individuals and neighbors.

The prominence of candidate-centered campaigns is one of the important legacies of the Progressive Movement. With the passage of the direct primary and other reforms, party organizations became less important in state elections. As the party organizations declined, candidate-centered campaigns emerged over time in their place. The direct primary was particularly important in opening the door to candidate-centered campaigns because it meant that candidates no longer needed to appeal to party leaders in order to become nominated; they could just reach out to voters.

The rise of candidate-centered campaigns has had important effects on electoral politics. Among other consequences, the campaigns appear to have helped incumbents. In almost all elections the most frequent electoral result is a victory by the incumbent officeholder. Incumbents do well because they have more opportunities to create public identities. Because they are better known, incumbents are often the strongest players in candidate-centered campaigns.

Despite the importance that individual candidates now play in campaigns,

Table 4.1.   Party Membership by Region, Oregon House of Representatives, 2001

Region	Democratic seats	Republican seats
Portland	11	1
University counties	6	0
Portland suburbs	7	5
North Coast	2	1
Mid–Willamette Valley	0	10
Southern Oregon	2	7
Eastern Oregon	0	8
Total	28	32

there are some underlying partisan trends that resurface occasionally and contribute to close electoral outcomes. These trends derive, in large part, from the split within the state between progressives and conservative populists. Democrats receive most of their votes from the former, and Republicans do better among the conservative populists. One election that strongly reflected this split was the 2000 presidential race, which was described in chapter 1.[21]

The distribution of votes in that race closely parallels voter registration trends (figure 4.3) and the vote in nearly every close statewide election. Democratic candidates usually dominate Portland, the counties of the north coast, and the Willamette Valley communities of Eugene, Springfield, and Corvallis. Republicans win most elections in southern and eastern Oregon, and are stronger than the Democrats in the rural mid–Willamette Valley. The Portland suburbs in Clackamas and Washington counties are divided about evenly between Republicans and Democrats; hence, they often decide the outcomes of close elections. The basic pattern of urban areas supporting Democrats and rural areas supporting Republicans is a nationwide phenomenon but is most pronounced in the West. Congressional, regional, and local elections also follow this pattern, as do state legislative races. For example, this same pattern can be seen in the distribution of seats in the Oregon House of Representatives. Table 4.1 shows the regional distribution of House seats by party following the 2000 election. The counties in each region are the same as those in table 1.1.

Once dominated by the Republican Party, Oregon elections are today conducted in the context of a competitive two-party system and a political culture divided between progressivism and conservative populism. The power of the two parties, however, is fairly weak because of the antiparty electoral laws that were enacted during the early decades of the twentieth century. These laws helped bring about a reliance on candidate-centered campaigns as the primary method of selecting elected officials. In addition, many voters do not belong to either major party. Instead, they are nonpartisans or members of eight minor parties that have ballot access in all or parts of the state.

Despite the weakness of the party organizations, political parties continue to play an important role in Oregon elections. Moreover, the split between progressives and conservative populists plays a major role in shaping the character of the party system. Not all Democrats are progressives nor are all Republicans conservative populists. But clearly, this split between the two sides of Oregon politics plays a critical role in state elections.

CHAPTER FIVE

Direct Democracy

Richard J. Ellis

Distrust of state legislatures runs deep in the United States, but citizens must generally act through their legislatures, no matter how much they may distrust them. They can keep a watchful eye, join interest groups, attend hearings, write letters or e-mail messages to their representatives, even vote them out of office or protest on the streets, but the job of writing and passing public policy lies with the elected officials, not the citizens. In twenty-four states, however, citizens have the power to bypass the legislature and enact legislation directly. In all but a few of these twenty-four states, citizens also have the power to force a popular vote on laws passed by the legislature. These twin instruments of direct democracy are known respectively as the initiative and the referendum.[1]

Although the initiative and referendum are often lumped together, their implications for the political system are significantly different. By enabling citizens to force a public vote on recently enacted legislation, the referendum adds an additional check to the normal legislative process. Legislators are still writing the laws and governors are still signing the laws. The referendum just adds one more veto point to the process. The initiative, in contrast, is not an additional check but an alternative law-making process. Through the initiative process, citizens can enact laws with little or no involvement of elected officials. The initiative thus poses a qualitatively different challenge to representative democracy than does the referendum.

HOW THE PROCESS WORKS

The state manual explaining the operation of the initiative and referendum processes is more than fifty pages long, but its essential features can be readily summarized. To qualify an initiative for the ballot, an initiative's sponsors must first file the full text of their proposed law with the elections division in the secretary of state's office. The elections division then forwards the initiative proposal to the attorney general, who prepares a title for the ballot, which explains the initiative's content and potential effect. The secretary of state also reviews the proposed initiative petition to make sure it complies with the procedural requirements of the state constitution.

Once the proposal has received a ballot title and passed this review, the sponsors can then collect signatures from registered voters. The total number of signatures required to reach the ballot depends on the type of initiative. There are two types of initiatives in Oregon: the *statutory initiative* and the *constitutional initiative*. A statutory initiative seeks to create a new state law (statute) or revise an existing one. A constitutional initiative seeks to amend the state constitution. To qualify a statutory initiative, the sponsors must obtain signatures equal to 6 percent of the turnout in the previous gubernatorial election; for constitutional initiatives, supporters must gather 8 percent. Oregonians have up to two years to gather the signatures for an initiative petition, and unlike in many states there are no restrictions on where the signatures may be gathered within the state.

When the sponsors have collected enough signatures, they submit their petitions to the elections division, which then verifies the validity of the signatures. Initiative sponsors routinely try to submit more signatures than is required in order to ensure they have enough valid ones. If there are enough valid signatures, the elections division will then place the proposal on the next statewide general election ballot. To become law, initiatives must receive more than 50 percent of the votes cast.

To qualify a referendum, the referendum sponsors must file a copy of their proposed referendum petition with the elections division within ninety days of the end of the legislative session in which the law was enacted. If the proposed petition complies with state regulations, the elections division then will notify the sponsors that they can begin collecting signatures. The signature threshold is lower for a referendum, but the time allowed to gather signatures is much shorter. To qualify for the ballot, the referendum sponsors must obtain signatures equal to 4 percent of the turnout in the previous gubernatorial election, but they are allowed only ninety days to gather these signatures. For a referendum to pass and thus overturn the legislature's action, it must receive more than 50 percent of the vote.

THE OREGON SYSTEM

No state has used the initiative and referendum more often than Oregon. Since the first initiative election in 1904, Oregonians have voted on more than three hundred initiatives and sixty popular referenda. Only California comes close to matching Oregon's record of activity. Although not the first state to adopt the statewide initiative and referendum (that distinction goes to South Dakota), Oregon was the first to use these new mechanisms of democracy. Oregon's pioneering role in the use of the initiative and referendum was widely recognized in the early twentieth century; indeed, the initiative and referendum were often referred to as the "Oregon System." Political reformers hailed the state as the nation's "political experiment station." Between 1904 and 1908 Oregonians voted on twenty-three initiatives and passed seventeen. In contrast, only two statutory initiatives qualified for the ballot in the rest of country during this period, and both were defeated.

What made the nation take notice of Oregon was not only the quantity of initiatives but also the innovative uses of direct legislation. Among the earliest initiatives passed by Oregon voters were some of the most important reforms of the Progressive Movement. Laws and amendments were enacted that opened up the primary process, instructed state legislators to select the people's choice for U.S. senator, enabled voters to recall public officials, expanded the initiative process to cities, and established the Corrupt Practices Act. Observers came away from Oregon persuaded that they had glimpsed the future. Here at last, many thought, was a mechanism to defeat the power of the political bosses and organized wealth. It was from out of these landmark laws that Oregon's reputation as a progressive state first emerged.

States that did not yet have the initiative and referendum rushed to get it. By 1918 nineteen states had adopted the initiative and referendum. Although Oregon's early experience helped spark national enthusiasm for direct democracy, within the state the euphoria was short lived. When twenty-five initiatives qualified for the ballot in 1910 and twenty-eight in 1912, many Oregonians began to question the wisdom of direct legislation. Even erstwhile supporters criticized the initiative's overuse and abuse. The state's special interest groups quickly learned to use the initiative and referendum to advance their own interests. Because there was no requirement that an initiative campaign reveal to the public how much money they had received and from what sources, groups were often able to conceal their involvement. Until 1913 the secretary of state was not even required to record who had filed the petition for an initiative, and so the public often did not know which interests were sponsoring, let alone bankrolling, an initiative.

The less-regulated political environment of the early twentieth century meant that fraud and corruption were widespread in the circulation of petitions. The most infamous case was a popular referendum in 1912 that aimed to overturn the legislature's appropriation for the University of Oregon. The circuit court that heard the case concluded that over 60 percent of the thirteen thousand signatures gathered for the referendum were fraudulent. Even the defendants conceded that about 30 percent of the signatures had either been forged or fabricated. It is difficult to determine how typical or pervasive such corruption was because under a 1907 law, petitions were verified by the signed affidavit of the circulators. The large number of initiatives combined with stories of fraud and abuse soon cooled voters' enthusiasm for direct legislation. Of the fifty-three statewide initiatives on the Oregon ballot in 1910 and 1912, only sixteen passed. In the following election, in 1914, voters rejected all but two of the nineteen initiatives on the ballot. After 1914 initiative use in Oregon declined precipitously. Between 1920 and 1969 Oregonians voted on fewer initiatives than in the five general elections between 1906 and 1914. Even more striking, the twenty-three initiatives passed during the five decades and twenty-five general elections stretching from the 1920s through the 1960s is less than the number of initiatives passed in the three general elections between 1906 and 1910. In the 1920s and 1930s less than one in five initiatives succeeded, and during the 1960s not a single initiative passed and only seven qualified for the ballot.

Since reaching its nadir in the 1960s, initiative use in Oregon has climbed steeply in each of the subsequent decades (see figure 5.1). In the 1980s and 1990s Oregonians approved more initiatives than in the previous six decades combined. The recent revolution in initiative use reached its apex in 2000, when a modern record of eighteen initiatives qualified for the ballot. In that one election, Oregonians voted on more initiatives than they did in the twenty-year period between 1956 and 1975.

While initiative use has increased dramatically in Oregon over the last several decades, use of the popular referendum has generally declined (see figure 5.2). Referenda have never been as common as initiatives, but in the first half of the twentieth century, they were a regular and important feature of the political landscape. Between 1904 and 1952 forty-seven referenda were voted on; in contrast, during the next half century (1953–2002) only thirteen referenda reached the ballot. There has been some tentative evidence recently that the referendum may be staging a minicomeback. Two referenda

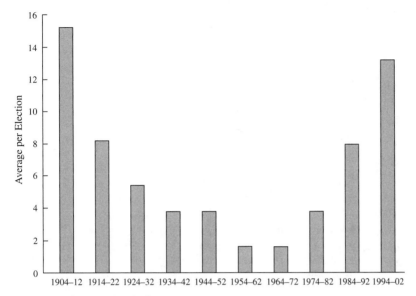

Figure 5.1. Initiative Use in Oregon, 1904–2002

qualified in 2000, which is only the second time since 1952 that there has been more than one referendum in a single year. For the most part, however, the story of direct democracy in modern Oregon is the tale of the initiative process.

SUPPLY-SIDE POLITICS

Why does Oregon have so many initiatives compared to other initiative states? In 2000 almost one-quarter of the nation's statewide initiatives were in Oregon. In 2002 the absolute number of initiatives in Oregon declined precipitously (to seven), but Oregon still qualified more initiatives than any other state. Why, moreover, has initiative use increased so dramatically in Oregon (as well as in the nation) over the past several decades?

Initiative activists often explain the increase in initiative use by pointing to voters' distrust of politicians or to the ineffective performance of government. However, citizens in Oregon are not more alienated from government or distrustful of politicians than voters in low-use initiative states like Idaho or Ohio. The record number of initiatives in 2000, moreover, came at a time when voters' distrust of government was not notably high by modern standards. Nor can the explanation be attributed to poor legislative performance.

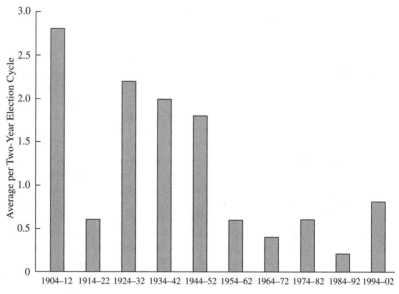

Figure 5.2. Referendum Use in Oregon, 1904–2002

The Oregon legislature is not any more ineffective or unresponsive than the legislatures in Wyoming or Oklahoma, where the initiative continues to be used infrequently.

Part of the explanation for why Oregon has more initiatives than other states is that it is relatively easy to qualify an initiative in Oregon. If Oregon required, as Wyoming does, that petitioners gather signatures equal to at least 15 percent of the total number of votes cast in the preceding general election, initiative use would decline substantially. Also important is the absence of a geographic distribution requirement that requires signatures to be gathered in a certain number of counties or legislative districts across the state. None of the top six initiative states in the 1980s and 1990s had a geographic requirement. In contrast, all but a handful of the states in the bottom half of initiative use have some form of geographic requirement.

Legal rules and procedural hurdles account for much of the difference among states in initiative use, but they also leave much unexplained. On paper it is easier to qualify an initiative in South Dakota than in Oregon; yet Oregonians have used the initiative process more than six times as often as voters in South Dakota. In California, petitioners have only 150 days to gather signatures for initiative petitions, which is among the most restrictive circulation periods in the nation. However, California typically has far more initiatives on the ballot than other states, including states that allow petitioners several years to gather signatures. Nor can signature requirements explain why Arizona, which has a relatively high requirement (10 percent for statutory initiatives and 15 percent for constitutional initiatives), has seen far more initiatives than many states with much lower signature thresholds.

What separates Oregon from most other initiative states is less its signature requirements than its bevy of experienced initiative activists who are skilled at using direct legislation to serve their political ends. Initiative use in Oregon has become institutionalized, driven not by the demands of the public but by the activists and professionals who supply the initiatives.

In the 1990s the most accomplished initiative user in the state and per-haps in the nation was Bill Sizemore. Since becoming head of Oregon Taxpayers United in 1993, Sizemore has been responsible for well over a dozen initiatives, including some of the most important conservative ballot measures. He has championed initiatives that have sought to cut property and income taxes, reduce public employees' pensions, curtail the power of labor unions, abolish Portland's regional government, block the expansion of Portland's commuter railway, and link teacher pay to performance. In 2000 Sizemore sponsored six of the eighteen initiatives on the ballot. Contributing to Sizemore's success was that he turned the initiative process into a lucrative business. In 1997 Sizemore established his own signature-gathering firm, I&R Petition Services, Inc. Through this business, Sizemore was able not only to introduce his own initiatives but also to qualify them. In addition, he was able to sell his services to other chief petitioners.

Sizemore is only the most prominent of a network of energetic conser-vative initiative activists in the state. Lon Mabon and the Oregon Citizens Alliance qualified three antigay initiatives in the late 1980s and early 1990s and came close to qualifying several more in the mid and late 1990s. In 2000 Mabon and the alliance were able to place Measure 9 on the ballot, which unsuccessfully tried to ban the teaching of homosexuality in schools. Don McIntyre, one of the fathers of Oregon's landmark 1990 tax limitation initiative (Measure 5), is another conservative activist who has qualified initiatives in many elections, including a measure (Measure 8) that would have placed a lid on state spending in 2000 (it was defeated) and another in 2002 that would have changed the way that the state supreme court and appeals court justices are elected (also defeated). Ruth Bendl has been instrumental in qualifying conservative proposals as well. In 2000 Bendl coordinated the signature-gathering drive for Measure 8, and in the mid-

1990s she worked in a similar capacity for Loren Parks, one of the leading financial supporters of conservative initiatives in Oregon, including many of Sizemore's. Together with Parks, Bendl played a pivotal role in qualifying nearly half of the sixteen initiatives on the 1996 ballot as well as several on the 1994 ballot.

Activists and groups on the left have also frequently used the initiative to pursue their agenda. Perhaps the most persistent has been Lloyd Marbet, a fixture of Oregon initiative politics since the mid-1980s, when he led three separate initiative campaigns to close the Trojan nuclear power plant along the Columbia River. Marbet has also sponsored initiatives to force the cleanup of radioactive wastes and to stop Portland General Electric from earning profits from the mothballed Trojan plant. In 2002 his effort to qualify a campaign finance reform initiative fell about ten thousand signatures short of making the ballot. Marbet, like many users of the initiative on the left, is more of a liberal populist than a progressive.

Environmental groups in the state have also periodically supplied initiatives. In 1998, for instance, the Nature Conservancy spearheaded Measure 66, which allotted 15 percent of state lottery money to salmon and parks. In 1996 the Oregon Natural Desert Association sponsored the Clean Streams Initiative. This measure (Measure 38) was widely seen as too extreme and was handily defeated at the polls, a fate that befell a number of other environmental initiatives in the 1990s, including efforts to limit the use of polystyrene in packaging (Measure 6 in 1990), restrict fish harvests (Measure 8 in 1992), restrict strip mining (Measure 14 in 1994), expand the bottle bill (Measure 37 in 1996), and limit timber harvests (Measure 64 in 1998). During the 1970s and 1980s environmentalists were often among the most vocal proponents of the initiative process, believing that environmental issues—where benefits are widely distributed and costs are narrowly concentrated—are ideally suited to the majoritarian bias of direct legislation. These recent setbacks (and similar defeats in other states, most notably like California) have arguably chastened some environmentalists' enthusiasm for the initiative, but environmental groups remain formidable players in initiative politics and will undoubtedly continue to supply initiatives in the future.

In recent years, labor unions have been the most important (and successful) supplier of progressive initiative campaigns in Oregon. Tim Nesbitt, president of the Oregon AFL-CIO, has emerged in recent years as a leader in organized labor's increased use of initiatives. Nesbitt helped direct the successful campaigns for two prolabor initiatives on the 1998 ballot: Measure 62, which included a clause granting constitutional protection to union payroll deductions, and Measure 63, which established new rules making it more difficult for antitax advocates to create "supermajority" requirements for tax increases. The latter measure required that all future initiatives that establish supermajority voting requirements be passed with the same supermajority of votes. In 2002 Nesbitt and the unions qualified two more measures, one prohibiting payment by the signature on initiative petitions, and the other increasing the minimum wage and indexing it to inflation.

"Good government" groups have also championed several initiatives in the past decade. One of the most active of these is the Oregon State Public Interest Research Group (OSPIRG), a statewide organization that is led by college and university students. OSPIRG played a leading role in the 1994 passage of Measure 9, placing restrictions on campaign finance (the measure was subsequently invalidated by the courts). OSPIRG has also pushed initiatives focusing on the environment and consumer protection. For example, OSPIRG helped champion an unsuccessful initiative (Measure 37) in 1996 to expand the state's bottle bill law. In addition to OSPIRG, Common Cause and the League of Women Voters have played leadership roles in promoting "good government" initiatives.

Paid Signature Gatherers

Some of these initiative petitioners (most notably, Lon Mabon) have relied entirely on volunteers, but the overwhelming majority of the successful initiative activists in Oregon rely on paid signature gatherers. Between 1990 and 2002 all but eight of the eighty-two initiatives on the ballot used paid signature gatherers. As recently as the early 1980s, paying people to gather signatures was illegal in Oregon, as it also was in Washington and Colorado. Oregon's long-standing ban on paid signature gatherers (the ban had been in effect since 1935) was repealed by the legislature after a 1982 court decision held that barring individuals from paying people to gather signatures unconstitutionally restricts freedom of speech.[2] That decision and a 1988 U.S. Supreme Court ruling invalidating Colorado's ban on paid signature gatherers[3] helped pave the way for the explosion of initiative activity in the 1990s. From World War II through 1982, while Oregon's ban on paid signature gatherers was in place, there were only two elections in which more than four initiatives appeared on the Oregon ballot (1948 and 1978) and never was there more than seven; after the ban's elimination, however, there has been only one election (1988) in which fewer than seven initiatives have appeared on the ballot.

Volunteer signature campaigns are difficult. They require organization, experience, and intense commitment. Little surprise that about 90 percent of volunteer-only signature drives over the past decade have failed to gather the necessary signatures. Initiative campaigns that pay for signatures have a much higher rate of success. Moreover, the amount of money it takes to secure a place on the Oregon ballot—between $100,000 to $150,000— is small enough that wealthy individuals have little difficulty purchasing a place on the ballot for their ideas. A particularly good example of a wealthy private citizen purchasing a spot on the ballot came in 1996, when Gordon Miller, a Salem eye doctor, underwrote virtually the entire cost of qualifying three initiatives he had written (Measures 35, 41, and 42). In 2002, to take a more recent example, Loren Parks single-handedly secured a place on the ballot for two initiatives (Measures 21 and 22) that would have changed the way judges are elected. Qualifying the two constitutional amendments, both of which were defeated, cost Parks $256,453, which was 99.7 percent of the total amount raised by the two qualifying campaigns.[4] In initiative politics, money may not always be a *necessary* condition for ballot access but in large enough quantities it is a *sufficient* condition.

WHY INITIATIVE SPONSORS MATTER

According to some, it does not much matter who places a measure on the ballot, or where the money comes from, because the citizens decide whether to vote yes or no. Voters have the final say, so no initiative can become law unless it represents the will of the people. Dr. Miller's three 1996 initiatives, for instance, were all soundly defeated and left no lasting impression on Oregon politics or policy.

Even allowing for the limitations of money in electoral campaigns and the good sense of Oregon voters, there are still strong reasons to be concerned about how initiatives get on the ballot and who places them there. To begin with, initiative sponsors frame how an issue is presented. As anyone familiar with polling knows, public opinion on many issues is extraordinarily sensitive to how questions are worded. For example, if you ask people whether they support spending for the "poor," their responses will be far more favorable than if they are asked about spending on "welfare." Just as the answer one gets in a poll depends on the way the question is asked, so the support an initiative receives depends in large part on the wording of the ballot title.

Supporters and critics of the initiative process agree that the wording of the ballot title is important in an initiative's success. Speaking before a legislative committee in 1999, Sizemore was asked by a state senator about his strategy of submitting multiple versions of the same initiative to the secretary of state's office. The ballot title and accompanying statements describing the effects of the measure, Sizemore explained, are "very important"; indeed they are perhaps "the sole determinant" of the vote. If the sponsors do not like the ballot title and summary drafted by the attorney general, it is simple "prudence" for them to shop for one more appealing to voters.[5]

Those who write initiatives, moreover, structure and thereby shape voter choice. Voters may prefer a particular initiative to keeping the status quo, but if given a wider range of options voters might rank that initiative near the bottom of their preferences. For instance, given a choice between A and Not-A, voters may choose A, but given a choice between A, B, and C, A might be voters' least favorite option. The power to structure the choices on the ballot thus carries with it the power to shape the vote.

A recent tax-cutting initiative illustrates this phenomenon. In 1996 Oregonians were offered Measure 47, which promised to roll back property taxes dramatically. The choice given voters was between a large rollback or no change in their taxes. There were no other options, such as for a more moderate rollback or providing rebates for low-income and fixed income property owners. So while the vote on Measure 47 (52 percent supported it) did reflect a majority's preference for lower property taxes, the precise policies that were enacted did not necessarily reflect the voters' most preferred policy.

A further reason that voters' approval of an initiative cannot erase concerns about who sponsored it is that passage of an initiative does not necessarily reflect the issue's salience to voters. For example, antitax initiatives dominated state ballots in 2000, appearing in Oregon, Alaska, California, Colorado, Massachusetts, South Dakota, and Washington, even though polls consistently showed that a large majority of voters were less concerned with reducing taxes than they were with adequately funding government services.[6] Once on the ballot, however, less salient issues can quickly become the central focus of political debate.

Finally, the presence of an initiative on the ballot can force elected officials and interest groups to play defense on issues promoted by initiative sponsors. Thus, even when initiative sponsors lose the electoral battle, they may still win the political war by controlling the agenda. In 1998, for example, Democrat incumbent governor John Kitzhaber soundly defeated Sizemore, the Republican nominee, by a two-to-one margin. Yet soon after the election, Sizemore was able to seize control over much of the agenda by qualifying a measure that would have dramatically scaled back state income taxes. In response, Kitzhaber felt compelled to challenge his defeated opponent to a series of debates over Sizemore's proposed tax cuts. Moreover, Kitzhaber dropped one of his own planned initiatives, which would have established a rainy-day fund for schools, so that he could concentrate his campaigning and fund-raising efforts on defeating Sizemore's tax proposals.

VOTING ON INITIATIVES

If there is more reason to worry about how initiatives reach the ballot than is commonly assumed, there is arguably less cause for concern about the election itself than some initiative critics believe. Many citizens worry a great deal about the role of money in deciding election outcomes, but most research has shown the role of money in initiative campaigns to be limited in important respects. Studies have consistently shown that the power of money is greatest when spent in *opposition* to an initiative and that money spent on behalf of an initiative has substantially smaller effects. Moreover, a recent study by Elizabeth Garrett and Elizabeth Gerber finds that the effects of spending on behalf of an initiative are most pronounced among initiatives that receive less of their money from a few large contributors. Interestingly, Garrett and Gerber found that this effect was not present in spending in opposition to initiatives. In fact, campaigns with more large contributors did better opposing initiatives than those campaigns that had more broad-based contributions.[7] The clear implication of this and other studies like it is that our real concern in initiative election is less that powerful, well-endowed interests will be able to push through a favored policy than that these interests will be able to halt policy change via the initiative.

Those who are most concerned about the effects of the initiative process should be the ones most resistant to the idea of limiting money in initiative elections. Far from corrupting the initiative process, special interest groups across the political spectrum play a vital role in helping voters become aware of an initiative's deleterious effects, which are often obscured by attractive ballot titles or arcane technical language. It is when powerful special interest groups mobilize against an initiative and spend large sums of money on television and radio advertisements that voters have the best chance of hearing opposing arguments and making a reasonably informed decision.

Few voters are policy wonks or political junkies. But they do not necessarily need to be in order to make informed decisions on ballot measures. As in candidate elections, voters use information shortcuts to make decisions. Although voters will only rarely understand the many ramifications of complex proposals, they can ask themselves the much simpler question: Who is for it and who is against it? The more money spent in a campaign, the more likely voters will find out which groups are behind a measure and which groups oppose the measure. So long as voters have an attitude toward those groups—whether they be labor unions or antitax groups, Democrats or Republicans, environmental organizations or pro-life groups—they can generally arrive at a reasonably informed decision.[8] Oregonians' strongly negative attitude toward Sizemore after his failed 1998 gubernatorial bid may explain why all six of his measures were defeated in 2000.

Ballots crowded with issues undoubtedly present more of a challenge to voters than a ballot with only a handful of measures. In particular, the problem with a crowded ballot is that a few issues hog the media limelight, leaving others struggling to gain public attention. In Oregon in 2000, one of the chief ballot hogs was Measure 9, which would have prohibited public schools, including community colleges, from promoting or sanctioning homosexual or bisexual behavior. Between Labor Day and Election Day, nearly 30 percent of the measure-related letters to the editor in the state's leading newspaper, the *Oregonian*, were devoted to Measure 9. Add Measure 94, the effort to repeal mandatory minimum sentences for violent offenders, and one has accounted for almost half of the letters to the editor. Throw in Sizemore's prohibition on double taxation (Measure 91) and the number exceeds 60 percent. In contrast, sixteen of the twenty-six measures (including the seven legislative referrals and one popular referendum) accounted for only about 13 percent of the letters to the editor. This makes it possible for a measure to slip through without the same level of scrutiny it would receive on a less crowded ballot.

Although crowded ballots raise legitimate concerns for the quality of voter decision making, there is also evidence that the process is self-correcting because voters seem to react to confusion by voting no. In 2000 only five of the eighteen initiatives passed, whereas in 1998, when there were only nine initiatives on the ballot, six passed. In 2002 four of seven were approved. Since the initiative's inception in 1904, there have been six elections with sixteen or more initiatives on the ballot, and the passage rate has been only 28 percent. In contrast, in the remainder of the initiative elections, the passage rate has been about 40 percent.

THE INITIATIVE GOES TO COURT

Elections are the most visible arena in which initiatives are contested, but experienced initiative activists know that the most important battleground is often the courts. During the 1980s and 1990s half of Oregon's statewide initiatives approved by voters were challenged in court, and of these half were struck down either in whole or in part.[9] Why do such a high percentage of initiatives get entangled in the courts?

Part of the answer lies in the technical and legal deficiencies of some initiatives. Although initiative proponents generally seek out legal counsel in drafting a measure, initiatives do not have to run through the institutional gauntlet of staff analyses, committee hearings, and markup sessions that helps to ferret out drafting flaws in the state legislature. More important than the legal deficiencies, however, may be the *political* deficiencies of the initiative process. In the legislature some bills skate through with virtually no serious opposition, but on contentious issues, the sort that routinely appear on initiative ballots, legislation does not normally get passed without significant concessions being made to opponents. By moderating a bill to take into account opponents' objections, the legislative process makes it less likely that these groups will seek to challenge the law in court. The winner-take-all politics of the initiative process, in contrast, encourages sore losers to take their political grievance to the courts.

The courts' importance in initiative politics has increased still further in the wake of its decision in the 1998 case *Armatta v. Kitzhaber*. In *Armatta* the court heard a challenge to Measure 40, a 1996 "victim's rights" initiative. Prior to the *Armatta* decision, the primary legal constraint on both statutory and constitutional initiatives was that they could only address one subject, or what is referred to as the single-subject rule. In the *Armatta* case the court expanded restrictions on constitutional initiatives, ruling that an individual initiative cannot offer more than one amendment to the constitution. If two or more amendments are sought, then each one must be submitted "separately" to the voters. Since Measure 40 changed five different sections of the Oregon Constitution and implicated a number of distinct constitutional rights, the court ruled that it violated the people's right to vote on different amendments separately.[10]

The court's decision opened up a new legal challenge to constitutional amendments and had an immediate impact on the secretary of state's preelection review of initiative petitions. Using the "separate-vote" test of the 1998 *Armatta* decision, the secretary of state's office rejected seven initiatives in under a year, which was roughly equal to the number of initiatives that had been turned down in the previous eight years combined. Lower courts have also begun to use the *Armatta* decision to strike down initiatives. In November 2000 the Oregon Court of Appeals relied on *Armatta* to invalidate Measure 62, a complex campaign finance measure sponsored by labor unions in 1998. A few months later a circuit judge used *Armatta* to invalidate Measure 7, a controversial initiative on the 2000 ballot that required government to compensate landowners for any government regulation that lowers property values. The supreme court also relied on *Armatta* in overturning Oregon's 1992 term limits law and in upholding the lower court's ruling on Measure 62.

Courts are often seen as the protector of minority rights, a role that seems particularly important given the majoritarian bias of direct legislation. In the *Armatta* decision, however, the court arguably advanced majority rule. The chief petitioner of Measure 40, state legislator Kevin Mannix, responded to the *Armatta* ruling by breaking the measure into seven different amendments, pushing each through the legislature and referring them to the voters in November 1999. The results of that election are a cautionary tale for those who assume that a successful initiative represents the will of the people. Three of the seven proposals that were part of the successful Measure 40— the eleven-to-one jury verdict in murder trials, the weakening of immunity law, and the prosecutor's right to insist on a jury trial—were comfortably defeated in 1999. In the case of the prosecutor's power to demand a jury trial, close to 60 percent voted in opposition. The remaining four measures passed, in all but one case by roughly the same margin as the original Measure 40. Far from depriving people of their voice, the high court had enabled people to speak more clearly and to express their preferences more accurately.

The *Armatta* decision may also create an incentive for initiative sponsors to craft initiatives as statutory changes, where the hurdle will be a lenient single-subject rule, rather than as constitutional amendments, where they face a more exacting separate-vote requirement. Hitherto the only difference between statutory and constitutional initiatives has been the slightly higher number of signatures required for the latter. The additional signatures required for a constitutional amendment are generally a small burden for a well-endowed initiative sponsor, especially when weighed against the benefit to initiative sponsors of being able to insulate their initiatives from legislative meddling. The result has been a host of lawlike initiatives, including Mannix's 1994 measure requiring prisoners to work, that have been enshrined in the Oregon Constitution. Nearly 60 percent of the initiatives that made it to the ballot between 1990 and 2000 were constitutional amendments, though many could as easily have been written as statutory changes. Some may see the *Armatta* decision as a positive step in helping to arrest the erosion of a meaningful distinction between constitutional and statutory law, but others less trusting of the legislature will likely see this as making it harder to prevent the legislature from undoing the will of the people.

The primary risk of the *Armatta* decision, and more generally of relying on the courts as a check on initiative politics, is that the check has the potential to threaten courts' legitimacy because it puts them squarely in the middle of highly volatile political disputes. When initiative advocates meet a setback in the courts, they frequently lambaste the judges for judicial arrogance, for legislating from the bench, and for thwarting the public will. Initiative sponsor Bob Tiernan was so outraged by the supreme court's invalidation of Measure 8, a 1994 initiative requiring public employees to contribute to their pension benefits, that he promptly filed an initiative to alter the rules of judicial elections. The initiative sought to overturn the state regulations restricting judges from raising money directly and from discussing decisions during campaigns. Although unsuccessful in his initiative bid, Tiernan's aim was to lift the profile of judicial races, making them more competitive and more politicized, and thereby making it easier for challengers to unseat incumbents. In 2002 two initiatives were aimed at changing judicial elections, and both were sponsored by conservatives upset at recent court rulings on initiatives. Both initiatives were defeated, though the measure promoting the election of appellate and supreme court judges by district received 49 percent of the vote.

Of particular concern to some observers is the supreme court's growing involvement in the writing of ballot titles. A ballot title consists of a fifteen-word caption, a summary of the measure, and a description of the potential results if the measure is approved or rejected. If the proponents or opponents of the measure are dissatisfied with the attorney general's ballot title, they can ask the court to review the ballot title. The court must take the case and conduct the review of the ballot title "expeditiously" so as to "ensure the orderly and timely circulation of the petition." In practice, this has meant that the court immediately moves ballot-title cases to the top of its docket. The court can either certify the ballot title as written by the attorney general or, if the title fails to "substantially comply" with statutory requirements, it can rewrite the ballot title. Over half of the ballot titles certified by the court in the late 1990s were rewritten by the court.[11]

In recent years, moreover, the number of such cases has mushroomed. Of the 146 ballot titles certified by the attorney general's office in the 1999–2000 election cycle, 92 were appealed to the court. In March and April 2000, according to the supreme court's staff attorney, the justices and staff dedicated virtually all their time to ballot-title cases.[12] More than one-fifth of the court's opinions between 1998 and 2000 related to initiative titles. Crowding the judicial docket with ballot-title cases means less time to hear other cases.

The growth of the court's ballot-title caseload is due in part to the increase in the number of different measures submitted. Far more important, however, has been the rise of ballot-title shopping and ballot-title challenges. In an effort to secure the most favorable ballot title, initiative advocates submit multiple versions of the same measure. Meanwhile, opponents of ballot measures have become increasingly savvy as well, and now routinely challenge ballot titles. Even if the challenge is unsuccessful, opponents know that it can delay the commencement of signature gathering and thus leave proponents less time to gather the required signatures. The political battle between rival ideologies and interests is thus fought out not only in the electoral arena but also in the courtroom.

THE FUTURE OF DIRECT DEMOCRACY

Oregonians generally remain strongly supportive of the initiative process. A survey taken shortly after the 2000 election found that four out of every five Oregonians believed that initiatives "enhance the democratic process in Oregon." To be sure, most acknowledge that there are problems with the process. Many complain that there are too many initiatives on the ballot, that ballot measures are often badly written, and that voters are ill-informed on ballot questions. Many also criticize the role of money in initiative politics.[13] Yet despite these concerns, voters have usually resisted efforts to make qualifying or passing initiatives more difficult. In the May 2000 primary, for example, Oregon voters soundly rejected a legislative referral that would have increased the number of signatures required to qualify a constitutional initiative, and in 1996 they rejected a proposal to add a geographic distribution requirement.

Those who wish to reform the initiative process in Oregon face two imposing obstacles: the courts and the state's political culture. The reforms that most voters readily endorse—banning paid signature gatherers and restricting funding—have been prohibited by the U.S. Supreme Court as violations of free speech rights.[14] The reforms that the courts apparently will allow—increasing signature thresholds, adding geographic requirements, and requiring supermajority votes for passage—run headlong into two powerful strains in American political culture: libertarianism and populism. Suspicion of government and faith in the people converge in a profound distrust of legislators. Given that state legislators are generally responsible for placing reform proposals on the ballot, opponents of initiative reform have little difficulty framing initiative reform as a struggle between the people and the politicians. This is a fight that legislators will almost always lose. In Oregon these strains are defining features of what others in this book have described as conservative populism, though the appeal of populism in Oregon as well as in the nation transcends political ideology.

That is not to say that the initiative process will remain unchanged. But the most consequential changes to the initiative process will most likely continue to come not from the legislature but from the courts. Eliminating the ban on paid signature gatherers was arguably the most significant change in the rules of engagement in modern initiative politics, and that change was made by the judiciary. Allowing paid signature gatherers made life easier for initiative sponsors, but courts have also changed the rules in ways that have made the lives of initiative proponents more difficult. In September 2000, for example, the Oregon Supreme Court, reversing its own decision in 1993, ruled that owners of private property, including owners of supermarkets and shopping malls, do not have to allow initiative petitioners to gather signatures on their property.[15] Most observers agree that the court's ruling, by significantly reducing the places where petitioners can gather signatures, was an important factor in the precipitous drop in the number of initiatives in 2002 and 2004 (seven and six initiatives respectively) as compared to 2000. Even though the court may be the most likely source of consequential change, initiative sponsors were handed a setback in 2002 when state voters passed an initiative banning sponsors from paying signature gatherers for each signature they obtain. If the new restriction survives the court challenge, petitioners may find that qualifying initiatives for the ballot has become more costly.

Despite this decline in initiative use and this new challenge, reports of the imminent demise of the initiative are greatly exaggerated. Predicting the future is always risky, but there are good reasons to think that heavy use of the initiative process will remain a fixture of Oregon politics for the foreseeable future. To begin with, a record-high number of initiatives were submitted and certified for circulation in Oregon in 2002, which suggests that the activists' and interest groups' enthusiasm for direct legislation is undimmed. Second, initiative use was down among all the traditionally heavy-use states (California, Colorado, Washington, and Arizona) in 2002, which suggests that election-specific factors (for instance, the depressed state of the economy and stock market, which made raising money more difficult) may have contributed to the initiative downturn. Third, despite the downturn in 2002 Oregon was still the nation's initiative leader. Fourth, the 2000 election is not a useful baseline year but rather is better understood as an aberration due to the extraordinary number of initiatives that Sizemore qualified for the ballot. If Sizemore is taken out of the equation there would have been only eleven initiatives on the 2000 ballot, which, as it happens, is exactly the same as the average number of initiatives in the 1990s. Finally, the number of initiatives in 2002 is roughly the same as the state had in 1998 (nine), 1992 (seven), and 1990 (eight), none of which were considered at the time to be years of light initiative usage. That six or seven now seems to many people to be a small number of initiatives tells us more about the centrality of the initiative in contemporary Oregon politics than it does about its imminent demise. Love them or hate them, ballots laden with initiatives supplied by activists and groups from across the ideological spectrum are likely here to stay in Oregon.

CHAPTER SIX

Interest Groups

Russ Dondero and William Lunch

Interest groups have always been in the center of American politics. In 1787 James Madison noted that a critical responsibility of a republican government is to "secure the public good and private rights against the dangers of . . . factions."[1] In Oregon, voters, initiative gurus, citizen legislators, and interest groups (and their lobbyists) all compete for influence. The general concept that the competition of interest groups determines public policy is called *pluralism*. When considering interest groups in Oregon politics, certain questions stand out. Do the values of interest groups or lobbyists differ from those of the average Oregonian? Do interest groups have less or more influence in Oregon than in other states? Does Oregon's political culture make interest group politics different here than in other states?

This chapter emphasizes lobbying and the work and influence of lobbyists, but interest groups influence public policy in many other ways. Oregon's progressive legacy arose from interest group agitation in both the legislature and in the initiative process. For conservative populists the initiative system has been the weapon of choice in recent years. Progressive groups, such as unions and environmentalists, wage a continuous battle against the supporters of conservative populism through the initiative process. The anti–property tax ballot measures, Measure 5 (1990) and Measure 50 (1997), which obligated the state to shift two billion dollars annually to K–12 education from other state programs to compensate for local tax losses, demonstrate how conservative populists powerfully affect politics inside and outside of Salem.[2] For their part, progressives have countered conservative populist successes with intense legislative lobbying and judicial appeals, as well as sponsoring their own initiatives. Ultimately, these groups are battling to establish new majorities that share their perspective. The struggle between progressivism and conservative populism is an always evolving competition between groups. This struggle takes place in the legislature, the press, the courts, and through ballot measures and party politics.

THE "THIRD" HOUSE

The terms "interest group" and "lobbyist" conjure the image of ghoulish figures lurking in the political backwaters of the state capitol to subvert the will of the people.[3] While such imagery may be fodder for the supermarket tabloids or a cynical general public, nothing could be further from the truth. Oregon's small size and tradition of open politics largely prevent such shenanigans. Lobbyists are no better or no worse than society in general. There are always some bad apples. The successful lobbyist is the one whose word is always good. The amount of information, policy ideas, and coalition building provided by interest groups and lobbyists during a legislative session is so great that the lobby is sometimes referred to as the "third house" of the legislature.[4]

Interest groups certainly seek special advantages, and lobbyists often narrowly promote their clients' interests. But in a political process as complex as the one in the Oregon legislature (and official Salem more broadly), if interest groups or lobbyists did not exist, they would have to be invented. Very few Oregonians are left out of this process, whether they know it or not. Interest groups and their lobbyists represent employers and employees in the mainstream of the state economy—small business, agri-business, timber, fisheries, and high tech. Teachers, lawyers, medical professionals, real estate agents, developers, and contractors are all represented. Public agencies have representation. Advocates for the elderly, students, and farm workers make the case for vulnerable Oregonians.

Most Oregonians have a place at the table in the state legislature, but that does not mean all are equally represented in Salem. The most influential groups have 1) full-time paid lobbyists in the capitol; 2) political action committees (PACs) that contribute to election campaigns; 3) a constituency that will mobilize quickly to pressure legislators; and 4) interests that can be addressed within the limitations of the legislature. Lobbyists and interest groups do not always seek direct gains. They also may encourage "non-decision-making," inaction that favors their interests by limiting what officials think is politically or practically possible. With the balance of power between Republicans and Democrats so close, lobbyists have a great ability to block legislation they do not like even if they cannot sell the policy changes they prefer. Lobbyists are also particularly important in times of budget cuts. Programs with weaker advocates are more vulnerable to cuts.

Oregon's independent spirit has produced political mavericks in both major parties who distinguished themselves nationally by working across party lines, including Wayne Morse, Richard Neuberger, Mark Hatfield, Bob Packwood, and Tom McCall. Political parties are traditionally weak here, a characteristic magnified by the swelling ranks of Independent voters. Bipartisanship, which was particularly strong in decades past, still has a role. Legislators routinely seek colleagues across party lines to bring closure to the legislative session. Politicians still think of themselves as Oregonians first and Democrats or Republicans second. As a result of this and of Oregon's high economic dependence on relatively few industries, Ronald Hrebner and Clive Thomas call Oregon a state where interest groups are "dominant/complementary." Their study indicates that Oregon interest groups are periodically, though not consistently, overwhelming in their influence over state politics.[5]

The relationship between parties and interest groups is neither distant nor static. Many of the groups active in Salem have strong ties to one of the major parties. Business groups generally favor Republicans, and labor groups usually ally with the Democrats. Also, term limits clearly strengthened the role of party caucuses and leaders even though the law was overturned in 2002.

A TYPOLOGY OF INTEREST GROUPS

Five types of interest groups typically lobby the Oregon legislature:

Economically Motivated Groups
Professionally Motivated Groups
Public Interest Groups
Ideological Groups
Government Agencies

Economically motivated groups are the most numerous among the three hundred or more groups represented by lobbyists in Oregon. These include a variety of trade, business, and union organizations, such as the Oregon Federation of Independent Businesses, the Farm Bureau, and the American Federation of Labor-Congress of Industrial Organizations (AFL-CIO). Their focus is usually on specific provisions that could damage their members' economic interests. Such groups have the broadest impact, day to day, on the legislative process because their economic interests require them to pay careful attention to a wide range of issues and many bills. A good example would be the regular revision of landlord-tenant laws that affect renters, legal aid attorneys, owners of multifamily dwellings, and cities or counties. Such issues rarely generate headlines, but their impact on thousands of Oregonians is profound.

Professionally motivated groups represent lawyers, doctors, nurses, teachers, and other certified or licensed professionals regulated by the state. The focus of such groups is often on "turf" struggles with competitive professions, such as physical therapists versus nurse practitioners or public versus private universities. For example, major battles regularly take place over whether those with out-of-state licenses should be allowed to practice their professions in Oregon. Prestige makes groups like the Oregon Bar Association and the Oregon Medical Association particularly influential in their fields.

Public interest groups are often self-appointed, and sometimes controversial, tribunes of "the public interest" on issues such as the environment, human resources, or public education. This category includes local affiliates of familiar national organizations, such as the Sierra Club or the American Civil Liberties Union, as well as local or state groups like the Oregon Taxpayers United or 1000 Friends of Oregon. Sometimes "public interest" groups are categorized as "ideological groups," particularly when their issue-advocacy consistently reflects a specific philosophical or value orientation, such as the socially conservative Oregon Citizen's Alliance (OCA). Ideological and public interest groups often represent grassroots activists focused on single issues like lower taxes, abortion, environmental protection, or gun control. These single-interest groups can be part of national organizations that carefully monitor particular issues throughout the country, such as Americans for Term Limits, the National Rifle Association, Right to Life, and Planned Parenthood. State affiliates of such groups have the capacity to alert members on short notice using phone banks and e-mail, and may quickly organize postcard, phone, and e-mail campaigns and rallies to pressure legislators. Other similar groups are Oregon-based, such as the OCA or the Friends of the Columbia Gorge. Public interest groups and ideological groups often grab headlines because of the emotional and volatile nature of their positions on issues such as tax cuts, restrictions on abortion or contraception, or sexual preferences. Despite the great attention their issues receive, these groups are more successful in blocking change than in creating major new policies.

Government agencies from all levels of government also prominently lobby the legislature. Agency heads regularly testify before legislative committees. They provide policy background, budget data, and other information for legislators on agency missions, activities, and needs. Agency or contract lobbyists are regular participants in the legislative process. Permanent associations like the League of Oregon Cities, the Association of Oregon Counties, and the Confederation of School Administrators enhance the influence of local governments.

Oregon's open-meeting laws give citizens relatively easy access to the legislative process. Citizens can simply show up at a public hearing and sign in to testify before a legislative committee. Lobbyists use this access with great effect. Often, hearing rooms overflow with citizen advocates taking time off from work or school to be heard. There are many constituent lobby days when hundreds of citizens rally on the capitol front steps, followed by door-to-door engagement with legislators or their staff.

More than three hundred groups have registered lobbyists at the capitol, and Oregon ranks number twenty-two in the country for the number of entities employing lobbyists.[6] According to the Center for Public Integrity, lobbyists in Oregon spent $11,212,639 in 2000, eleventh in the country. During the 1999 legislative year, they spent $18,607,678. The top five sectors in terms of the number of paid lobbyists in Salem were education, local government, insurance, health, and public sector unions.[7]

In terms of influencing the legislative process, the groups with reputations for having the greatest clout include the Associated Oregon Industries, the Oregon State Restaurant Association, the Oregon Hospital Association, the Oregon Farm Bureau, the Oregon Bar Association, the Oregon Education Association (public school teachers), the Oregon AFL-CIO, petroleum distributors and producers, high-tech firms, home builders, building trade and contractor groups, and education advocates from administrators to specific school districts. These groups resemble those that have much influence in state capitols across the country.[8] These groups are particularly successful because they are the "regulars" in day-to-day lobbying.

REPRESENTATION: INTEREST GROUPS AND THE LOBBY

Lobbyists perform three primary functions in the legislative arena: 1) disseminate information needed for crafting legislation to legislators and their staff, 2) aggregate public opinion around major issues affecting their clients, and 3) help set the political agenda by creating coalitions to support or oppose specific bills. These functions can be elaborated into seven complex tasks necessary for the functioning of the legislative process.[9] Lobbyists are, in effect, the following:

Eyes and Ears of the Public

Information Providers

Representatives of Their Clients and Constituents

Shapers of the Government Agenda

Movers of Legislation

Coalition Builders

Campaign Contributors

Interest groups—usually represented by lobbyists—act as the eyes and ears of citizens and groups unable to travel to Salem during legislative sessions, keeping them updated on key developments. Lobbyists also provide critical information and analysis to legislators. Four to five thousand bills are introduced each session, so it is impossible for legislators or their staffs to digest all the contents in a brief session of some six months every other year. Lobbying is a two-way communication process. The interest group or lobbyist both informs constituents (and hears from them) and serves as the "great" communicator to legislators within official Salem.

In a state with weak political parties, interest groups often assume roles performed by political parties in other states: aggregating issues, mobilizing voters, and providing leadership. Often, interest groups and lobbyists representing opposing positions must propose and draft legislation during the interim (the time between sessions) and, once the session begins, negotiate compromises on proposed legislation. Legislators on committees often look to lobbyists to craft compromises that will bring all affected parties to the table. The sheer number of groups active in Salem forces lobbyists to build coalitions on issues of mutual interest. In this sense, the interest group or lobbyist exercises leadership by articulating issues, setting the agenda, and reconciling differences among competing positions. The work of interest groups is rarely appreciated by those unfamiliar with the process.

Information is power. Legislators regularly depend on interest groups and lobbyists, along with agency heads, to provide information detailing the reasons for existing laws and policy and to link past to present. This was particularly true under term limits. Because legislative staff is very limited and inexperienced, lobbyists must provide critical institutional memory and information if anything is to be accomplished in abbreviated biennial sessions. The work of interest groups and lobbyists extends far beyond the legislative sessions. Lobbying never ends.

Sometimes insider strategies are not enough. Frustrated lobbyists and groups may seek to influence policy through grassroots advocacy campaigns, PACs that influence elections through political donations, and the use or threat of initiatives or referenda.

TYPES OF LOBBYISTS

There were 385 lobbyists listed as members of the Capitol Club, the association of Oregon lobbyists, during the 2001 session of the Oregon legislature, up from 300 in 1991. Of those lobbyists, 135 (35 percent) were women, compared to 85 (28 percent) ten years ago. There are only a handful of minority lobbyists in Oregon, and many key lobbyists have previous experience in the legislature.[10]

Professional lobbyists can be classified into five categories. "Independent lobbyists" are contract lobbyists who represent several varied interest groups or clients. These lobbyists may be hired by anyone who can afford them. "Corporation lobbyists" are employees assigned by their company to be its governmental relations specialist, that is, its lobbyist. "Association lobbyists" are employed by a membership association or interest group. "Governmental lobbyists" serve as legislative liaisons for units of state, regional, or local government. Finally, there are "single-issue lobbyists," who primarily represent a group with a specific philosophical, religious, or political viewpoint. In addition to the professionals, many groups and individuals work to influence legislators without being compensated financially.

Most lobbyists in Oregon represent single clients or a group of clients who have distinct or complementary interests. Representing clients with conflicting interests, while possible, is frowned upon by lobbyists. Informal sanctions among members of the lobby prevent abuses in most cases. Regulation of lobbying is governed by ethics standards created by the Capitol Club and Oregon law, which are enforced by the Government Standards and Practices Commission.[11] Self-regulation is usually more potent than legal sanctions in a profession where reputation goes a long way to determining success. Lobbyists occasionally run afoul of the law, but such cases have been very contentious, and enforcement of legal sanctions has been modest.[12] Major newspapers also do a good job covering such cases, so transparency and disclosure largely prevent abuses familiar in some other states.

How do lobbyists see their role in Oregon's political process?[13] Although there have not been any empirical surveys of Oregon lobbyists in recent years, most lobbyists in Salem will tell you that the lobbyist's role is changing. In the 1970s, before the new House and Senate wings were added to the capitol, legislators were crammed into nearby buildings and often shared offices with other legislators. Their staff usually consisted of a spouse working as a secretary. This environment fostered a good-old-boy system of insider lobbying but also provided for much formal and informal mentorship and information sharing. Now, with separate offices, each legislator has a secretary and legislative assistant during the session, and some have an intern or two.

Despite the improvement in their physical environment and staff, the increased amount of legislation means that legislators remain very dependent upon lobbyists for information. The old system of lobbying had fewer professionals, but they interacted much more intensely and socially with the legislators. Long-term Salem insiders say that the relationships between legislators and lobbyists are more complicated and impersonal today. A few lobbyists still work hard to nurture long-term and social relationships with legislators, but most lobbyists today rely on more businesslike relationships built on delivering credible information. Lobbyists play a crucial role in the process; they are the legislator's "library, the research assistant and issue manager." Even so, lobbyists must be very careful in presenting only the facts. If a lobbyist does not, the legislator "will never trust him again."[14]

Legislators do not have the time they once did. Lobbyists have to scramble to catch the legislators between hearings or daily sessions. Sometimes it takes weeks to get an appointment. So legislators need lobbyists more but also lack the time to really listen and understand the viewpoint of the lobbyists' clients. Instead of listening to lobbyists, legislators often follow ideological conceptions they developed before coming to Salem.

During legislative sessions, lobbyists provide detailed reports regularly to their clients to ensure the clients understand the atmosphere around the capitol as well as what is happening with their issues. The client is most important in strategic big-picture discussions. The clients have to let the lobbyists know what they consider important, and they have to provide background material and be available when the lobbyist needs to know how a bill might affect the organization. But sometimes lobbyists do not listen to their clients when it comes to tactical political decisions.

Most political insiders in Salem argue that term limits altered the relationship between lobbyists and legislators. As term limits forced incumbents out of office, there were fewer veteran legislators for new representatives to turn to for help. Many legislators did not seem to understand the process and key issues until early April, only three months before the legislature traditionally adjourns. In Oregon, this inexperience appears to have made legislators more dependent on caucus leadership, the Salem bureaucracy, the governor, and agency heads for information. Private lobbyists are not thought to have gained as much influence (though see chapter 16 for another perspective). Term limits seem to have increased the influence of the party leaders and caucuses particularly. In the past, bipartisan coalitions could be formed more easily because of weak party discipline. But with term limits, party loyalty has become increasingly important. There is less tolerance of political mavericks, once a hallmark of Oregon politics.

This emphasis on party loyalty has transferred to the election cycle, as party leaders try to recruit candidates they think will fit into the party caucuses. Besides following their own ideological conceptions, new legislators rely more on their caucus and leadership in deciding issues they know little about. In addition, many legislators often make judgments on complex issues simply by determining who was for the legislation and who was against it. Research by Gary Moncrief and Joel Thompson on five states other than Oregon coincides with what many say has happened in Oregon. Moncrief and Thompson's research suggests that term limits make lobbying more difficult because lobbyists devote more time to simply educating legislators. They also note that lobbyists feel that governors, agency heads, caucus staff, and interest groups have more influence over legislators than before.[15] What will happen in the future is uncertain. Term limits have been overturned, but the impact will be a factor for years to come.

DO LOBBYISTS BUY ACCESS TO LEGISLATORS?

A lobbyist's credibility is based on giving the legislator the "best" information he or she has in hand. This information is always colored by the lobbyist's interests, but that is not a problem as long as the legislator knows the lobbyist is being honest. Interest groups that try to throw their weight or money around or bring in hired guns often find that such tactics backfire. It is better to be represented in Salem by known Oregon lobbyists than by a high-powered outsider.

Some PACs, however, contribute to candidates they think will win and are not concerned with the candidate's views on the issues. They think they are buying access. What they really purchase is goodwill, which does not necessarily translate into access. Legislators are simply too busy to meet with many contributors, and if they do meet with them, it is often for only a brief exchange. Other PACs concentrate on candidates that match their clients philosophically. In this case, they are not buying access; instead they are supporting like-minded legislators. Some contributors would like not only to buy access for themselves but also to deny access to their potential opponents. This tactic is rarely successful.

Campaign contributions are a reality of this business. Election campaigns are expensive. It is not sinful for politicians to raise money, and it is not bribery to contribute to candidates. Lobbyists do not usually provide campaign contributions to buy access. One can succeed without having large PACs (or any PAC at all). Clients need to understand that they are not buying anything with a campaign contribution. They are affirming their political convictions by helping people they favor get elected.[16] One example of a group that seeks to get like-minded legislators elected is the Victory Group, headed by former House speaker Larry Campbell. The Victory Group works particularly hard to promote Republican candidates in the House.

The amount of money spent on Oregon elections is notable. According the National Institute of Money in State Politics, in the year 2000, political contributions in Oregon state elections totalled $22,002,561. Of this amount, $9,299,346 came from business-related groups and $2,092,819 came from labor sources.[17] The average amount spent in general elections for Oregon Senate seats hit a record high of $118,019 (up from the previous high of $77,005 in 1998), and average general election contributions for House race was $62,099 (up from the 1998 record of $43,528.) Spending on the November 2000 ballot measures alone amounted to $23,694,474.[18]

INTEREST GROUPS BEYOND THE CAPITOL

Interest groups also promote their goals by influencing how agencies implement policies and by using the courts to intervene in the policy process. Four specific aspects of interest group involvement in the administrative process are particularly notable: 1) participation in open hearings, particularly the rule-making process, 2) ongoing informal contacts and negotiations with agency administrators, 3) influence over appointments to boards and commissions, and 4) appeals to the legislature to reverse bureaucratic actions.

Agencies in all states must follow specific procedures when they develop the details of how they will implement legislation.[19] The process by which agencies develop specific regulations about their standards and procedures of implementing policies is called "rule making." Because of Oregon's Open Meeting Law and Administrative Procedures Act, agencies must allow for public participation in rule making and other deliberative processes. The common citizen is neither aware of nor concerned about these processes but interest groups are. Groups such as the pro-planning 1000 Friends of Oregon and the property rights advocates of Oregonians in Action constantly monitor how the state implements its land-use laws, for example, and they give testimony and file comments when they dislike the direction of a policy or specific decision.

In addition to these formal interactions, interest groups maintain constant contact with agency officials who make decisions affecting their interests. For example, public-housing advocates and builders may repeatedly contact state and local housing agencies to determine the status of general guidelines and specific projects. When groups feel agency policies wrongly hurt their interests, they may turn to the legislature or to the courts to challenge the policies. A good example from the 2001 legislature was the battle fought within the state legislature between environmentalists and natural resource users over the direction the Oregon Fish and Wildlife Agency should go with endangered species policies.[20]

A final notable way in which groups directly affect agency work is through their influence over state boards and commissions. As chapter 10 examines more closely, boards or commissions oversee many agencies. Members of these boards or commissions are appointed in very diverse ways and have diverse requirements. For example, the Real Estate Board, which reviews real estate licensing, has nine members appointed by the governor. Seven members must be in the industry; the other two are public citizens. Membership on the Land Use Board of Appeals, which considers appeals of those dissatisfied with land-use planning decisions, has three members who must be lawyers appointed by the governor and approved by the Senate. Generally, the composition requirements and appointment process ensure that professional groups, industry groups, and well-organized public interest groups are strongly represented in the administrative oversight process. The resignation in spring 2004 of former governor Neil Goldschmidt from his appointment as chair to the Board of Higher Education, resulting from the cover-up of a thirty-year-old sex scandal, cast a public light on commissions, which often do not receive much attention from the public or media.

A final critical way interest groups seek to influence Oregon laws and policies is through judicial appeals. Interest groups use the courts in a myriad of ways, but among the most important are challenges to ballot measures, the appeal of specific government policies, and suits filed to punish or cripple their political opponents. Groups have fought various conservative populist ballot measures very successfully in recent years by convincing the Oregon Supreme Court that the measures violated constitutionally protected contractual rights, contained too many separate constitutional amendments, or violated the signature collection process. Groups of all stripes have always used the courts to contest agency decisions that they perceived violated their rights. A classic example, again examined in depth in chapter 10, was the Dolan case of 1994, in which property rights advocates successfully overturned local government requirements connected to a property owner's right to develop.

Finally, interest groups sometimes attack their opponents in the courts by suing them directly for the harm they cause. SLAPP lawsuits are a common example of court-based strategies. SLAPP stands for "strategic lawsuits against public participation." The term describes situations where people are sued for comments they make in public hearings. SLAPPs have been used by developers to silence individuals and groups who oppose their projects. The developers file slander or other civil suits based on what their opponents say in public hearings. This intimidates people from participating in hearings and expressing their views because they might not be able or willing to fight the legal suit even if they could ultimately win.[21]

Progressive interests have used the courts as well. The recent success of the Oregon Education Association and the American Federation of Teachers in a case against Bill Sizemore and Oregon Taxpayers United shows this very well. The two labor unions sued Sizemore for damages caused by two antiunion measures, which they argued had gotten onto the ballot with forged signatures and the use of falsified record keeping. As a result of the suit, a jury required Sizemore's organization to pay the unions more than $2.5 million as punishment for fraudulent practices in the initiative process and the mishandling of organizational funds. This case could have long-standing implications for any group or activist that creates strong opposition through the use of the initiative.[22] It also demonstrates that no list could include all the methods groups use to influence public policy and politics because groups continually expand their range of tactics.

The yin and yang of interest group politics in Oregon follows a pattern not unlike that of many other western states affected by taxpayer revolts, sagebrush rebellions, and divided government. Recent years have been highly turbulent; there have been notable shifts among groups, some rising quickly, others falling fast. In this section we discuss the relative position of groups in Oregon but preface the rankings with a description of the force in state politics that has produced the greatest change among the constellations in the interest group firmament—initiative politics.[23]

Hooked on Initiatives: Group Strategies

A principal attraction of sponsoring initiatives is that—if successful—the sponsor need not compromise with adversaries (or allies, for that matter). Most initiatives fail, but a group that manages to pass even one major initiative can gain very significant leverage. As noted in chapter 5, the use of ballot measures surged in the 1980s, when organizations and political consulting firms sprang up to take advantage of a court ruling that legitimized professional signature gatherers. These firms guarantee that if an interest group or a wealthy individual invests the required sums, an initiative will be qualified.

The result has been an avalanche of interest-group-sponsored initiatives and, less commonly, referenda. This tool has sometimes served progressive causes, such as in 1996, when health care groups, led by hospitals and physicians (including the governor), sponsored an initiative to raise tobacco taxes to help pay for expansion of the Oregon Health Plan. Conservative populists have also used the process very effectively, such as with tax limit initiatives. Clearly the process creates policies the legislature would never consider, such as Measure 5's steep property tax cuts in 1990 and the adoption of assisted suicide legislation in 1994. Even in defeat, initiatives can force the public to examine issues the legislature may studiously avoid. For example, the Oregon Citizen's Alliance (OCA) could not get even a committee hearing for its proposal to deny legal protections to gay and lesbian citizens but managed to qualify initiatives on that issue in 1992 and 1994. Though most socially conservative initiatives fail at the ballot box, they impact public dialogue and mobilize groups and voters.

Ranking Oregon Groups

Which groups have the most influence in Oregon politics? Which ones have the least? According to Hrebner and Thomas, the most influential interests in the fifty states are 1) general business organizations, such as chambers of commerce, 2) schoolteachers' organizations, 3) utility companies and associations, 4) lawyers, 5) health care organizations, 6) insurance organizations, and 7) general local governments.[24] In the Oregon legislature, this pattern seems to hold true, but the picture changes when one goes beyond the statehouse.

In terms of overall influence on state policy, conservative populist groups, particularly Oregon Taxpayers United (OTU), are considered by political insiders to be among the most influential in Oregon, despite recent losses in 1998 and 2000. They have set the fiscal agenda for both state and local governments since Measure 5 was passed in 1990. These cuts, and initiative-based measures requiring great expenditures, transformed the legislature by forcing it to spend much of its time and political energy on meeting the requirements of initiatives rather than on undertaking new policy directions. Whether OTU maintains its influence following the recent legal defeat by the teachers' unions remains to be seen. With strong support from national antitax and business groups, the Oregon Citizens for a Sound Economy has already stepped in to replace the OTU as the lead antigovernment populist organization.[25]

In recent years business groups have been seen as runners-up in the race for political influence in Oregon, particularly Associated Oregon Industries. Despite their worries over excessive government and taxes, traditional business groups sometimes part company with the conservative populists over deeper tax cuts that threaten the state's public infrastructure, particularly education and transportation.

Groups that influence policy in their specific areas of interest constitute the next level of influence in the state. This tier is led by the health industry and law enforcement groups. The health industry was helped by former governor Kitzhaber's emphasis on the Oregon Health Plan. Law enforcement benefited from a 1994 mandatory-sentencing initiative that required a very large expansion of state prisons. Environmental groups and the emerging high-tech industry lobby also operate at about this level of influence. Environmentalists have had substantial success using the Endangered Species Act to advance salmon recovery policies, for example. In the more conservative political climate of the 1990s, environmental groups have effectively defended policies such as the bottle bill and land-use planning, though passage of Measure 7 in 2000 may signal a decline of their influence.

Government lobbies, particularly those representing K–12 public education and local governments in the Portland area, operate at the next level of influence. Though unable to reverse the loss of revenue caused by property-tax limitation measures, these groups have succeeded in mitigating the damage by laying claim to increasing fractions of the state general fund. The education lobby has stimulated parent and community support in the Portland area and some other communities, mainly in the Willamette Valley, but has not yet created a stateside majority in favor of new funding. The 46 percent to 54 percent vote on Measure 28 in January 2003, which would have temporarily increased income tax rates to fill in for declining state revenues, demonstrates that the public remains unconvinced that education merits new taxes.[26]

Beyond these major players, other groups have managed to either establish or maintain a presence in Salem. Native American tribes are now much better represented than even a decade ago, in part because of income from casinos. Public employee unions, as well as private sector unions, have enjoyed great success in the past. Since 1990 unions have found themselves on the defensive but still enjoyed success. For example, unions defeated a number of initiative measures that would have greatly hindered their ability to raise funds to support candidates or to contest hostile initiatives. However, unions have taken a more offensive approach and championed their own initiatives in recent years. Similarly, public utilities—while much weaker than a quarter-century ago—have usually been able to resist adverse proposals, such as breaching a number of dams in the Snake River to improve salmon recovery, which were advanced by environmentalists in 1999 and 2000.

Finally, there are dozens if not hundreds of second- and third-string lobbies in Salem that claim occasional victories but mainly count success as preventing hostile proposals from being adopted. For example, the Oregon Student Association (previously the Oregon Student Lobby) has repeatedly persuaded legislators to reject huge tuition increases proposed by conservatives. Similarly, the timber industry, while in decline, has nonetheless defeated a variety of strict regulatory proposals from environmentalists. The work of these groups illustrates how blocking change is a core goal for many groups in many contexts.

WINNERS AND LOSERS?

While it is fashionable to decry the role of special interests in the political process, the simple fact is that government in Oregon could not function without interest groups and their lobbyists. In Oregon lobbyists provide vital assistance to legislators, who often lack the expertise or institutional memory to understand the consequences of the thousands of bills introduced in each legislative session. This was particularly true under term limits. The saving grace is that virtually every citizen in Oregon, however rich or poor, is represented by someone who advocates for them, that is, a lobbyist, be it the Association of Oregon Industries or Ecumenical Ministries.

Although no one would claim that all are equal in the game, everyone is heard or represented to one degree or another. Today, lobbying is a very sophisticated and expensive process based on gaining access to legislators and presenting the client's point of view. The coin of the lobbyist is more in relationship building and information gathering than in cold cash. However, the money game does come into play at election time, when lobbyists and interest groups stock campaign war chests for incumbents and challengers with PAC money. But as *Oregonian* reporter Steve Suo writes, when the legislature is in session, "the majority of the money [pays for] lobbyists' salaries rather than late night bar tabs and fancy meals for legislators."[27]

If there is a bias in the process, it favors the status quo. It is always easier to kill an idea than to get it passed. This has probably been one of the most important elements helping to preserve progressive policies. As one practitioner said, lobbyists are "good ambassadors—they know the country they're visiting and they know where they come from. Effective lobbyists are consummate insiders."[28] But Oregon's tradition of reform guarantees to "insiders" and "outsiders" a comparatively open and clean government. Given Oregon's small population, politics occurs in an environment akin to an extended political family. In a place where all the insiders know your name—whether you are a politician, a lobbyist, a bureaucrat, or a journalist—it is hard to hide in the political shadows.

A final haunting question is whether Oregon's interest groups are deepening the state's political cleavages and making it harder for people of good faith to come to the table and reach a middle ground in policy development. With the easy availability of the initiative or referendum, why should groups attempt to reach compromise except over the most banal public policy areas? The fracturing of Oregon's political landscape over social, fiscal, and environmental issues indicates that Oregon's political fabric is torn. Bipartisanship is less the norm than is bickering across increasingly high ideological fences that separate rural Oregon from urban Oregon; the Portland metro area from the so-called other Oregon; the timber/agribusiness economy from the high-tech economy; young Oregonians from an increasingly aging Oregon. We are divided, as are neighboring states, along predictable ideological and demographic lines. Our interest groups play hardball to forward their agendas. In this way, things no longer look so different in Oregon.

CHAPTER SEVEN

Media

Russ Dondero, William Lunch, and Jim Moore

In 1900 Harvey Scott, the editor of the *Oregonian* newspaper, wrote nineteen editorials against a proposal to grant women the right to vote. Abigail Scott Duniway, his sister, led the fight to adopt the measure. She lost, but Progressivism won in 1912 when a people's initiative was passed to grant women suffrage.

The dialectic in Oregon politics between conservative populist and progressive values and activism was joined in that fight. As the voice of conservative opposition, the *Oregonian* and its role were not unusual. Throughout the state's colorful political history, the print and broadcast media have served the interests of progressives, conservative populists, and reformers of all types.

The media have also had an important impact on government. In 1933 and 1934, for instance, the Medford *Mail Tribune* published an influential series of articles about corruption surrounding irrigation contracts, the sheriff's department, and local officials. This progressive series won Oregon's first Pulitzer Prize.[1] The media played a critical role in politics again in 1962 when a progressive television documentary on pollution in the Willamette River changed Oregonians' views about the environment and relaunched the political career of Tom McCall, whose environmental policies became models for the nation.[2]

The media's role in Oregon politics is evolving. Some changes are visible, such as in 1992 when the formerly conservative *Oregonian* endorsed a Democrat for president for the first time since its founding in 1850. A less visible but much more significant change has been the loss of local control over commercial media outlets. In the 2000 election the vast majority of newspaper endorsements were made by corporate owners outside of

Oregon. No television stations endorsed candidates or ballot measures. And on election night one of the oldest radio stations in the western United States covered a preseason Portland Trailblazers basketball game instead of the closest presidential election in the twentieth century. That station is owned by Paul Allen, the Blazers' owner, who resides in Mercer Island, Washington. Decisions regarding Oregon's news are now made elsewhere.

Recent developments in Oregon's media parallel nationwide changes. The 1980s witnessed a decline in competition among newspapers, an increased reliance on television as a news source, and a growing emphasis of the media on news personalities and niche reporting. These trends, in turn, have led to the marginalization of coverage of state and local politics.[3] Floyd McKay, a former local television journalist and now a journalism professor at Western Washington State University, explains the problem this way: "News decisions are still made in local newsrooms, but highly influenced by corporate executives thousands of miles away, who determine budget levels and hire top managers."[4] As a result, news anchors, news sets, and coverage of state or local politics vary little across the nation.

The change in news reporting from the 1980s to mid-1990s is demonstrated by the fact that Bhagwan Shree Rajneesh, the Bob Packwood scandal, and Tonya Harding received far more attention than some major transformations in Oregon's political life. Among the issues receiving little analysis in this period were 1) the shift from a timber-based economy to a more diversified high-tech economy; 2) the rise of the Portland metro area as the economic hub of the state at the expense of the "other Oregon" beyond the I-5 corridor in the Willamette Valley; and 3) how the state's share of funding for local schools went from about 29 percent of the operating expenditures to approximately 70 percent between 1989 and 1999, and how this shift squeezed the state budget by increasing the K–12 portion of the general fund from 33 percent to 43 percent over that decade.[5]

Why and how did the role of the media become so homogenized in a state known for being different? How has this change affected the balancing between progressivism and conservative populism?

THE PRINT MEDIA IN OREGON POLITICS

A favorite story told by Oregon politicians goes something like this. The Oregon Trail pioneers reached the sign marking where one rutted wagon road headed south to the gold fields of California and the other headed north to Oregon. Those who could read headed north, and those who could not went south.

Reflecting their commitment to literacy, Oregonians support eighty-nine daily or weekly newspapers spread throughout the state.[6] Despite these impressive numbers, Oregon really has one paper of record: the *Oregonian*. With the state's largest readership and statewide circulation, the *Oregonian* has been a force in Oregon politics since its founding in 1850.

SINGLE DAILY DOMINANCE: *PAX OREGONIAN*

The *Oregonian* was not always number one in readership or political clout.[7] Early in Oregon's history, it competed with its rival to the south, the *Statesman* (now *Statesman Journal*), in Salem. In the 1950s the *Oregonian*'s prominence was challenged by the *Oregon Journal*. The *Journal* served as a left-of-center, liberal, pro-Democratic paper with statewide circulation. Likewise, into the 1970s the *Oregonian*'s editorial page masthead stated its political bias clearly—"An Independent Republican Newspaper." In this era the canons of journalism did not require political neutrality but rather quite the opposite. The press could and often did take sides. Readers selected their paper based on a clear sense of ideological loyalty.

Like newspapers across the country that were being bought out, the *Oregonian* in 1950 became part of the Newhouse chain of papers. Then in 1959 a strike against both of Portland's daily newspapers changed everything. Initially, the strike led disaffected *Journal* employees to create a third statewide newspaper, the *Portland Reporter*. In 1961 the Newhouse chain bought the *Journal*, which was still being published, and merged the two papers. Then in 1965 the strike officially ended and the *Reporter* went bankrupt. The *Oregonian* became the sole statewide newspaper.

Today, the *Oregonian*'s power is widely evident. *Oregonian* articles are found in legislative files, and morning news programs on Portland-area radio and television stations crib from the *Oregonian*'s morning headlines and articles. The *Oregonian* serves as a primary means for state leaders to communicate with each other and provides them with a common base of information. The *Oregonian* is no longer solidly conservative. A more pro-environment editorial stance and opposition to many of the tax limitation measures of the 1990s reflect its new progressiveness. The *Oregonian* Web site, www.Oregonlive.com, provides an important source for information on state politics and has featured in-depth and critical coverage of the populist conservative activism of Oregon Taxpayers United and of the issues that concern progressives.

The *Oregonian* may play a central role in the state's media system, but its endorsements, like those of most newspapers, probably affect less-publicized elections, offices, and ballot measures far more than they do the voting outcomes in major campaigns. An example of this occurred in 2000, when the *Oregonian* endorsed George Bush, whom Oregon voters rejected, and twenty-one of its twenty-two picks for the state legislature won.[8] Yet the extent of the paper's influence even in these races was probably limited because many of these legislative candidates were incumbents. In 2002 the *Oregonian*'s endorsement of Ted Kulongoski may have slightly affected the extremely close governor's race, yet other factors were certainly more important. One way in which *Oregonian* endorsements help is through building name recognition and campaign support for lesser-known candidates in the pre-primary period.

More recently, millionaire Bob Pamplin launched the *Portland Tribune* in an effort to compete with the *Oregonian*. Pamplin also bought the suburban newspaper *News Times*, which covers Washington county. Pamplin's strategy is to cover local markets thoroughly, competing in the circulation wars with the *Oregonian* via local-only coverage rather than with the old-style way of competing via progressive or conservative editorial stances.

REGIONAL NEWSPAPERS

The Salem *Statesman Journal* is one of the more prominent daily newspapers in the state, especially during Oregon's biennial legislative sessions, when it assumes parity with the *Oregonian* as the paper of record. But outside of its unique status as the local paper of the Salem beltway crowd, the *Statesman Journal* is primarily a regional paper, as is Eugene's *Register-Guard* and Pendleton's *East Oregonian.*

Other local papers of note include the Albany *Herald Democrat* and the Corvallis *Gazette Times* in the mid–Willamette Valley, the *Daily Astorian* on the northern Oregon coast, the Medford *Mail Tribune* in southern Oregon, the *Baker City Herald* and the Ontario *Daily Argus Observer* in eastern Oregon, and the *Bend Bulletin* in central Oregon.

Locally owned newspapers once played a central role in the everyday life of Oregon communities. They often had to strike a difficult balance between journalistic objectivity and boosterism. But in the process such local papers reflected the communities they served and balanced the view offered by the *Oregonian* or the *Journal*. In the late 1940s, as Floyd McKay notes, Oregon

> had no large newspaper chain owners; the men who edited the papers also owned them, which gave them added standing in an age that was still dominated by Main Street businessmen. This generation of editors was strongly committed to the idea of personal involvement in the community. Any roster of community leaders would have included editors such as Charles A. Sprague in Salem, Bill Tugman in Eugene, Robert Ruhl and Eric Allen Jr. in Medford, Ed Aldrich and J. W. Forrester in Pendleton, Bob Sawyer and Bob Chandler in Bend, Merle Chessman in Astoria, and Claude Ingalls in Corvallis. How many editors' names today are known beyond the walls of their own newsrooms?[9]

In contrast, many of Oregon's local newspapers are now owned by outside chains. For example, the Salem *Statesman Journal* is a Gannet newspaper. In autumn 2002 the Ashland *Daily Tidings* and the Medford *Mail Tribune* went from one major newspaper chain to another when Lee Publishing sold them to the Dow Jones Company, publishers of the *Wall Street Journal*. Despite their distant ownership, local papers still provide the most extensive coverage of community affairs, dwarfing the reporting of local radio and television. The *Associated Press* covers state and regional issues, so smaller local papers can put their limited resources into reporting on local politics and issues. Community papers also serve as a primary means for local political leaders to track local events and concerns and to promote themselves.

PORTLAND'S ALTERNATIVE PAPERS

Willamette Week is Portland's main alternative newspaper. Founded in 1974 by Ron Buel, former aide to Portland mayor Neil Goldschmidt, it is printed weekly and has a history of solid investigative reporting. *Willamette Week* publishes a regular report card of metro-area legislators, which reaps considerable attention among political insiders. The Portland *Observer* and the *Skanner* serve Portland's African American community. In addition to the Portland-based papers, many smaller papers and newsletters are published to reflect all sorts of diverse perspectives on local and state issues. Publications such as the *Eugene Weekly* and the *Thymes* of Corvallis present issues and views that regular local newspapers cover minimally, if at all. Nearly every coffeehouse in Oregon has stacks of these usually free papers, providing readers some alternate versions of what is happening and what is possible in Oregon.

THE CHANGING CHARACTER OF NEWS REPORTING

Journalism has changed significantly over the last several decades. The regional press, influenced by national press coverage of such events as the 1973–74 Watergate scandal, focuses increasingly on investigative reporting of regionally significant stories. Ironically, the biggest story in recent years in the state—the allegations of sexual harassment against Senator Bob Packwood—was broken by the *Washington Post*. Moreover, the *Post*'s revelations came just weeks after the very close 1992 election in which Packwood defeated Les AuCoin.[10] A local bumper sticker was quickly created, using the *Oregonian*'s front-page font: "If It Matters to *Oregonians*, It's in the *Washington Post*."

Despite the tardy coverage of the Packwood story, the *Oregonian* provides most regional issues with close investigative coverage at some point. Recent investigative reporting has included stories on the Immigration and Naturalization Service office in Portland, on the Bonneville Power Administration, and on the urban-rural divide—or as the *Oregonian* put it—"the nine states of Oregon." The *Oregonian* provides the most systematic and widely distributed analysis of ballot measures, important information for voters considering issues pushed by progressives and populist conservatives.

The *Oregonian*'s unique role raises a very important issue: is one dominant paper a good recipe for informing the public? Tom Mason, author of a book on Oregon politics, argues that "when there is one paper, it becomes the sole source of public fact for both print and other media. The *Oregonian* is the practical public record. Competition between print and electronic [media] is competition for advertising and not competition between like products."[11]

Changing times led to some important firsts for the *Oregonian* in recent years. Bill Hilliard, who started working at the *Oregonian* as a copy boy, became its first African American editor, in the 1980s. He also was elected president of the National Association of Newspaper Editors and Publishers and moderated the 1980 presidential debate between Jimmy Carter and Ronald Reagan in Cleveland. Under Hilliard's leadership, the *Oregonian* became fully computerized.

THE RISE OF PUBLIC JOURNALISM

Sandra Rowe replaced Hilliard and was the first female editor of the *Oregonian*. Rowe has promoted "public journalism" as the modus operandi of the newspaper. Public journalism uses polling and other demographic information to assess reader interests and then responds to those interests. In a sense, the readership becomes the paper's constituency, to be served much as legislators serve their districts. Critics argue that public journalism reflects how the industry is overly concerned about profit lines, demographic niches, and the advice of market consultants.

In practice, Rowe reorganized staff into working teams focusing on various political beats—state government, education, health, and local government. She also hired a significant number of new writers and increased the ethnic and gender diversity of the paper's journalistic core. Public journalism has been successful in some areas, like health coverage, but it has not strongly enhanced the coverage of politics.

In the last decade some print journalists became household names among the readers of the *Oregonian* and the Salem *Statesman Journal*. Steve Duin, now a prominent *Oregonian* columnist, moved from covering the Portland Trailblazers to reporting on politics and the state legislature. He was joined by Jeff Mapes, now the senior political writer for the paper, whose beat includes state and election-year politics. Ron Blankenbaker at the *Statesman Journal* was revered by the Salem crowd for his ability to "[walk] the journalistic tightrope between being a well-informed insider and writing interesting pieces without burning his friends."[12] However, with public journalism the cast of journalists keeps changing; journalists seem to have term limits. With the exception of Jeff Mapes at the *Oregonian*, tag-team reporting has replaced the days of the good-old-boy system and of star reporters.

THE ROLE OF COMMERCIAL RADIO AND TELEVISION

In November 1962, KGW television in Portland broadcast a documentary on pollution in the Willamette River called *Pollution in Paradise*. The documentary's creator was Tom McCall, a failed congressional candidate and well-known radio and television personality in Portland. The documentary, airing in the same year that Rachel Carson's *Silent Spring* brought environmental concerns to a national audience, pushed the legislature to pass the strongest antipollution laws up to that time. The documentary also made McCall a statewide political force.[13] The upstart medium of television challenged the political influence of newspapers. Oregon politics would never be the same.

Radio and television stations in Oregon reflect national trends. The number of independently owned stations has plummeted since 1980. Loosened federal regulations promoted the rise of huge companies that now own dozens of different media outlets, and individual stations have primarily become profit centers for distant corporate owners. Nowhere has the change been more evident than in the broadcast media's political coverage.

Oregon's electronic broadcasting industry dates to the earliest days of radio. By the end of the 1920s most of the country and nearly all of Oregon could receive radio programs. Almost immediately, national networks sprang up. The Mutual Network, the Columbia Broadcasting System, and the National Broadcasting Corporation all struck deals with radio stations across the country to provide programming to local areas. With the networks came national news coverage. When Charles Lindbergh crossed the Atlantic Ocean in 1927 on his solo flight, most Americans heard about the news on the radio before they read about it in the next day's newspapers.

The number of commercial radio stations in Oregon went from twenty at the beginning of World War II to fifty by 1953.[14] These radio stations were most often owned by businesspeople or by the local newspapers. Several of them spawned some of the early television stations (KOIN in Portland, KMED in Medford). The spread of FM stations in the 1960s and 1970s increased the number to 110 by 1979, and many stations had doubled their time available for programming by having both AM and FM capability.

Commercial television grew from the first station in 1952 (KPTV in Portland, followed closely by KBES, now KOBI, in Medford), to five stations in 1953 and twelve by 1978. More expensive to run, television stations increased their viewing area through extensive systems of translators all across the state. Stations in southern Oregon helped develop some of the first widespread cable television systems in the country.

Even as the number of radio and television stations grew in the 1980s and 1990s, changes in federal rules about ownership decreased the number of station owners. By the 1990s national companies owned up to 75 percent of Oregon's television and radio stations. As local stations became primarily profit centers for large companies, broadcast news went from being a service specific to particular communities to a generic formula. The formula is the same nationwide. Crime stories and fires predominate. Weather is the single most watched part of television news. Stations that use helicopters, such as those in the Portland area, skew coverage as news directors seek to justify huge aircraft expenses by using them in every news show. Station resources going to political reporting and documentaries like *Pollution in Paradise* have declined greatly.

Commercial television underwent further change in the early 1990s, when cable television franchises began to dominate most Oregon media markets.

These franchises are required to broadcast local television stations and provide a certain portion of their channels for public access (C-SPAN is an example of this at the national level). However, with just two companies dominating the Oregon market (AT&T and Charter Communications), programming is becoming national, and regional concerns receive declining attention.

The effects of this change can be seen in Medford. From the 1960s to the 1980s Medford was home to a local cable company whose primary purpose was to ensure that the many small valleys of southern Oregon received television signals. Among other stations, the Medford cable system showed two San Francisco–area channels and several from Portland. People in Medford had a sense of the region's issues and how those issues were dealt with by the main commercial centers to the north and the south. With the arrival of national cable systems, Medford no longer gets any news coverage outside of the immediate southern Oregon region. Viewers can share new recipes discovered on the Food Channel with others across the country, but they no longer see what is happening in their neighboring urban centers.

THE LAST HURRAH?

In many regards the 1970s and 1980s were a golden era of politics and electronic journalism in Oregon, since the state's politics was replete with colorful, charismatic, and issue-oriented leaders on both sides of the political aisle, and the state's television coverage at times excelled. The Democrats had Vera Katz, the first women speaker of the state House and later mayor of Portland, and Barbara Roberts, a state legislator who became secretary of state and then governor. The GOP had two media-savvy U.S. senators, Bob Packwood and Mark O. Hatfield. Norma Paulus and Dave Frohnmeyer also provided the GOP with a strong media presence. Paulus served as state legislator, secretary of state, and superintendent of public instruction. Frohnmeyer advanced from the state legislature to become attorney general and is now the president of the University of Oregon.

Neal Goldschmidt also contributed to and benefited from television's strong local political coverage in the 1970s. Goldschmidt's appearances on a monthly public affairs program, hosted by Dick Klinger on KGW-TV, helped establish the Portland mayor's regional profile. Residents outside Portland sometimes called the show to ask the mayor questions, assuming he was their mayor. Undoubtedly this kind of experience led Goldschmidt, after a stint as secretary of transportation in the Carter administration, to run successfully for governor in 1986. In a twist of irony he was forced to drop plans for reelection after the media made his impending divorce very public. Tabloid journalism had come to Oregon. But it would take fourteen years for the Goldschmidt sex scandal story to break before Oregonians would read the story behind the story of why he didn't run for reelection or higher office.

The state's leading television journalist in the 1970s and early 1980s may have been KGW-TV's Floyd McKay. McKay knew all the players, followed the legislature carefully, and kept his viewers informed on important local and state issues. McKay was the last journalist to be allowed to do half-hour political shows and documentaries along the lines of McCall's *Pollution in Paradise*.

The nationalization of broadcasting has brought uniformity and a deemphasis on politics to local stations. Floyd McKay observes how, on a cross-country trip, he "tuned in to local news programs and could not find any regional differences; the same blonde twit, deep-voiced slightly older man, wisecracking sports guy and bouncy weatherman with his electronic wizardry greeted me all the way from Washington DC to Portland."[15]

More than the format has changed; the content of the news has been significantly downsized. In a study of local television news, Mark Fitzgerald found that government and politics received 15.3 percent of the coverage time in eight major cities, whereas crime received 29.3 percent and calamities and natural disasters 10 percent. Another study of fifty-eight local news programs found that most stations aired an average of only forty-five seconds of candidate discourse during the 2000 elections.[16] Coherent progressive or conservative views are subsumed by the need for good lively pictures on television. Subjects must fit into the thirty-second sound bite on television, the top-of-the-hour news summary on radio, or the glitzy front-page sidebar format as used in *USA Today*. We hear less of the candidate's voice. Instead, we are given the voice-over by a reporter with accompanying pictures. Floyd McKay puts it this way: "Television has abandoned any pretext of a community leadership role . . . and . . . has become a deregulated tower of babble."[17]

As a consequence, it is increasingly unlikely that reporters or politicians will galvanize citizens to support strong policy actions such as McCall's efforts to clean up the Willamette in the early 1970s. Progressives seeking to build support for activist government policies find it more difficult to sell the public on their concerns and ideas, and both progressives and conservative populists turn to paid advertising to promote their views.

TALK RADIO

Commercial radio plays a community leadership role very similar to that of television. Local radio is increasingly dominated by talk shows. It is possible to hear national talk-show hosts like Rush Limbaugh, G. Gordon Liddy, Ron Reagan, or more recently, liberal Al Franken. around the clock. They have been joined by regional talk-show jockeys at Portland's KXL and KPAM (initially dubbed "Radio Free Oregon"). Like talk-show radio at the national level, which is decidedly conservative, the Portland media market features KXL's conservative Lars Larson. Given Larson's prominence in so many aspects of Oregon politics, it is not surprising that antitax activist Bill Sizemore was also a prominent figure on talk radio until his recent demise, which was caused by successful lawsuits brought against his Oregon Taxpayers United organization by public employee unions.

Compared to the general public, talk-radio listeners are political activists. They are more conservative, more likely to vote, and more likely to engage in other public communications, such as public hearings. However, the talk-radio audience is also fairly small, encompassing at most about 10 percent of the electorate. Talk-radio programs differ greatly from the public-service-oriented coverage in commercial radio and television up to the 1970s. Talk radio seeks higher ratings (and higher profits for owners—most often national companies like Clear Channel radio) through controversy. Truth and analysis are often casualties of this approach. And when talk radio does not properly contribute to the bottom line, station management pulls the plug and inserts another nationally syndicated show highlighting music or psychology.

PUBLIC BROADCASTING IN OREGON

Public broadcasting provides a partial exception to the depressing story of declining attention to serious news on commercial television and radio. It is only a partial exception, however, because news coverage in public broadcasting largely means public radio. There is a national televised public news program, the *Lehrer Report*, broadcast by Oregon Public Broadcasting, but it rarely covers Northwest regional stories. Only the largest public television markets, such as KQED in San Francisco, can afford regular programs devoted to state and local news.[18] Radio is far less expensive and thus has been in a better position to develop serious news coverage.

Three public radio networks in Oregon feature regional and state news programs. Oregon Public Broadcasting (OPB) started in Corvallis in 1922 and is now based in Portland, though broadcast by several stations and numerous transmitters. KLCC/KLCO started in 1967 and remains centered in Eugene but with stations in central Oregon and along the coast. The third system, Jefferson Public Radio (KSOR), has covered southern Oregon since 1969 and is based in Ashland. Of the three networks, OPB has the largest audience by far.

The audience for news programs on public broadcasting stations has grown partially because of the news "gap" created by the declining commercial news coverage. In Oregon, this trend became evident by the late 1980s but was strongly accelerated by National Public Radio (NPR) and its virtual full-time coverage of the brief war in the Persian Gulf in 1991. Those consistently interested in serious news and public affairs programming are, of course, a decided minority of the population—probably not more than 15 percent of adults—but they are the most influential citizens. The National Public Radio audience, for example, has been found to be much better educated, more affluent, and older than the average citizen. For example, in the U.S. only about 7.5 percent of citizens have postgraduate degrees, but in the NPR audience, more than 32 percent do. Among households in 2000, median income nationally was $46,354, but in the NPR news audience, it was $75,110.[19]

Public broadcasting is strikingly popular in Oregon. Portland's dominant public radio station, KOPB, beat all commercial stations in 2000 in radio ratings during "drive time" (rush-hour) slots. Public radio is more popular in Portland, when adjusted for population, than in any other large city in the nation, except for Minneapolis and Washington DC. Furthermore, public broadcasting has a larger audience in Oregon—measured as a proportion of state population—than any other state. Moreover, that audience includes disproportionate numbers of influential people, including political and business leaders, so even the strong audience numbers understate the impact of public broadcasting on public policy.[20]

The "public" part of the funding for public broadcasting has declined greatly. Budget crises in 1979 and 1991 led to significant reductions of state support for and connections to public broadcasting.[21] Today OPB is recognized as a nonprofit organization, and its Federal Communications Commission (FCC) broadcasting license is now held by the "community" rather than by the state or the university, though it retains ties to the state. By the early 1990s less than 20 percent of the OPB budget came from the state, and the legislature eliminated all state funds in 2002. About half of the budget comes from listeners and viewers who make contributions, allowing them to become "members," though they have no formal powers over programming or management. The balance of the funding comes from corporate, foundation, and other large private contributions. The other two networks have faced similar financial problems, but each remains affiliated with higher education and survives on a mix of funding sources.

THE STRUCTURE AND CONTENT OF PUBLIC BROADCASTING

The news operations at OPB, KLCC, and KSOR are similar. Each has a news director and a few reporters. They normally assemble an afternoon news program Monday though Friday. Weekend offerings are usually limited to quick "billboard" news summaries inserted into NPR coverage. Typically, the local, state, and regional news program is broadcast in the afternoon, just before or after NPR's *All Things Considered*, the oldest NPR news program.

Oregon's public radio system distinguishes itself by its detailed stories on local, state, and regional politics, economics, and culture. The longer news features routinely run for three to four minutes, and often longer. This is quite a bit of time when compared to the fifteen to thirty seconds available to radio news reporters at commercial stations. In addition, public radio routinely offers news analysis, now missing from commercial stations. Perhaps most important, state ballot initiatives and the initiative process receive sustained attention on public radio, even though these very important topics are often too complex for effective coverage on commercial radio or television. Environmental and natural resource management controversies are also more prominent here than nationally.

This approach evidently works for the audience that listens to public radio. In a statewide survey in 1996, it was discovered that among state news sources, OPB had the highest rating for trust of its reporting of any major news source (though "local newspapers" were not far behind).[22]

There is some limited local, state, and regional news on public television in Oregon as well. Beginning in the mid-1990s a program called *Seven Days* tried the *Washington Week in Review* format, with reporters and editors simply sitting around a table, reviewing and analyzing the news. *Seven Days* has been successful enough for five years to attract a core audience among Salem insiders and the state political cognoscenti, but it rarely exceeds an audience of forty thousand. However, given the complexity of public policy issues and popular distaste for politics, a commercial-sized audience may not be realistic.

THE OLD AND THE NEW MEDIA TODAY

Local media is no longer the day-to-day independent player in Salem or the Portland metro area that it was in earlier times. Today, it merely chronicles the combatants and their stories. Ironically, the decline of an active partisan media has contributed to a climate conducive to legislative polarization and paralysis, punctuated by the successes of various populist conservative ballot measures. Up through the 1960s the partisan press, particularly the *Oregonian* and the *Oregon Journal*, played an important role in elevating more "establishment" Republicans and Democrats and fostered a candidate pool filled with people who focused on building consensus and educating the public on issues. The partisan press applied consistent pressure on the parties and candidates to address issues and their possible solutions seriously. Television initially fit this model when it provided programming that addressed public issues in a more sustained and in-depth manner. The political polarization in recent years on many state issues, such as the budget battles of 2002, arises partially because politicians face less pressure for a broad state or community perspective. Absent the moderating influence of the press of previous decades, Republicans and Democrats focus on narrower constituencies and rely more on advertising to communicate to the public. This situation enhances the ability of aggressive populist conservatives or progressives to define the public agenda through the initiative process.

The nationalization of the media in Oregon has homogenized news coverage and led to a media that emphasizes the politics of confrontation—warring ballot measures and diminished civility in the legislature. Conflict and personalities are "in," compromise and civility are "out." The former "sells," the latter does not. You've got to have that "sizzle" to get market share, that Nielson rating. Moreover, as political news and analysis coverage declines, politicians and issue advocates turn to special interest contributors for the funds needed to buy thirty-second capsules of advertising time. The importance of advertising and the role of money in determining public awareness and views of the issues are demonstrated by the fact that ballot-measure campaign committees spent over $30 million in the 2000 elections.[23]

Another notable question regards whether television has contributed to the general decline in the participation of citizens in all community activities, including politics. In his book *Bowling Alone*, Robert Putnam makes a powerful case that Americans are participating much less in community activities of all types, including bowling leagues. He argues that this decline of social activities reflects and contributes to a broad erosion in the connection and commitment of citizens to public affairs, noting the decline since the 1960s of participation in public meetings (down 35 percent) and party politics (down 40 percent).[24] Television and other media forms that emphasize individualized activities contribute to this process throughout the country. Putnam's argument hits home for at least some in Oregon. Peter Ames Collins reports in a 2002 *Oregonian* article about how Portland neighborhoods used to be communities in the fullest sense, communities where recreation, education, and city politics were community activities. Now, in once-lively neighborhoods such as Portland's Woodstock district, one sees only the flickering lights of televisions, and the citizens are more likely to view government as a service to be consumed rather than as something they own.[25]

Things are no longer different here. The market pressures that homogenize and reduce political coverage in commercial media are unlikely to reverse, but change is inevitable. Futurists claim that the Internet will become the dominant means of communicating the news, promising more open communications for all while also fostering strongly biased unaccountable presentations of alleged facts. Internet use for information is inversely related to the age of the individual. Older people still tend to rely on newspapers and broadcast journalism. Within the capitol building during legislative sessions, the newspapers remain the dominant source of information. Patterns of Internet use have interesting political implications. Given that individuals can readily filter their information sources to suit their ideological predispositions, the Internet promotes ideological communities that have no geographical dimension. How this will affect politics and government in the future remains to be seen.

Hope for a revival of the oldest media—the local community-based newspaper—remains. Floyd McKay argues that newspapers today in Oregon are better than ever. "The product is good—more informative, better written, and much better produced. Newspapers have been counted out every time a new medium appears, but they remain the most resilient of the mass media. The lead must be taken by editors who are willing to take a stand in, for, and with their local communities."[26]

McKay speculates that the newspapers might attempt "to define and discuss broader community and even state goals, linked via the Internet to smaller audiences focused on the news and issues of their communities and willing to engage in dialogue concerning these local needs."[27] In this regard, www.Oregonlive.com comes to mind. The *Oregonian* site provides a broader platform for developing active citizenship than do typical Internet sites because it combines relatively comprehensive news and opinion with a focus on state and local matters. Oregonlive.com seeks to promote community education and cooperation. For politics, this could mean bringing citizens, pundits, and politicians together in a context featuring information and interactive debate. With the rise of blogging, a grassroots revival in journalism might be on the horizon. Stay tuned.

60 mem House 2yr terms 69,000

30 mem Senate 4yr terms 120,000

CHAPTER EIGHT

The Legislature

Richard A. Clucas

The big news at the end of the 2001 legislative session was not what had happened, but what had not: the session ended with little conflict. The surprising cooperation was a far cry from the closing of the previous session.

The 1999 legislative session was seen by many as one of the most divisive in Oregon's history. The session was marked by a bitter political fight between Republican Party leaders, repeated conflict between the legislature and the governor, and highly visible battles over public school funding, abortion, gasoline taxes, and the state's $11 billion budget. Normally, the legislature adjourns by late June or the first few days of July, but conflict kept the legislature in session until a quarter past three in the afternoon on July 24, making it the third-longest session on record until then. In the months that followed, state newspapers reported that the session was characterized by "sniping and little else" and that it "broke new ground" in partisan bickering.[1]

Although the criticisms of the 1999 session were severe, this was not the first time the Legislative Assembly had been criticized for its performance. Almost every legislative session throughout the 1990s received harsh reviews.[2] The 2003 legislative session was no exception to this trend either, as conflict among the legislators over how to fix the state's budget deficit led to the longest session in the state's history. The 2001 session was thus surprising because it did not break down into the same pattern of conflict. Yet even that session was not free of criticism. Although the session was unusually collegial, it was criticized for accomplishing little. Plus, legislative action came to a standstill for a few days when Republican and Democratic legislators squared off over redistricting legislation.

The continuing problems in the Oregon legislature have made it the brunt of considerable criticism in the press and in the public. Yet it should be pointed out that the criticism of the legislature is not unique to Oregon. Since the 1960s the American public has grown increasingly cynical and distrustful of politics and politicians, with much of its wrath directed specifically at legislative politics.

Why does the legislature at times seem incapable of functioning? Is there something wrong with our legislative system? Many of the nation's leading scholars argue that the real problem is not state legislatures per se but a lack of public understanding of legislative politics. Certainly, the public often has valid reasons to criticize the legislature, but many of the problems that are associated with legislative politics simply reflect the nature of representative government.[3] In Oregon the problems confronting the legislature, to a large extent, reflect differences in public opinion and political attitudes across the state, especially the split between progressives and conservative populists. In recent legislatures, disagreements between these two sides have been at the root of much of the conflict. In the 2001 session some of the most outspoken conservative populists were no longer in office, which helped reduce the conflict, but the differences between the two sides still made it difficult to adopt major legislation.

The purpose of this chapter is to help explain the forces that shape legislative politics in Oregon and, at times, make it difficult for the legislature to act.

PROVIDING REPRESENTATION

The main theme we have tried to emphasize throughout this book is the importance of both progressivism and conservative populism in shaping Oregon politics. With the possible exception of the initiative process, there may be no place where the conflict between these two sides is more apparent than in the state legislature, for it is here that the diverse interests of the state ultimately come together to forge the state's laws. The reason that this split is so important here is that the legislature is at the heart of the state's system of *representative democracy*. In a representative democracy, or republic, citizens elect representatives to make laws for them. In Oregon voters elect individuals to represent them in the state House of Representatives and Senate.

The individuals who serve in the Oregon legislature are elected from *single-member districts*, which means that each one represents a separate geographical area of the state. As described in earlier chapters, regional differences play an important role in Oregon politics. For example, Portland, which is the most urban and demographically diverse city in Oregon, has among the most progressive voters in the state and tends to elect Democrats. Many of the other communities in the Willamette Valley also tend to be quite progressive, with the exception of some of the more suburban and rural areas. On the eastern side of Oregon, which is more rural and less demographically diverse, one finds stronger support for conservative populist ideals and Republican candidates. The southern parts of the state also tend to be more influenced by conservative populism.

In the first chapter we explained how these differences can be seen in voting behavior across the state. The differences in voter attitudes are important to legislative politics because they affect how legislators behave. Despite the widespread perception that politicians are not concerned about voters, most legislators do in fact take stands that reflect their district and constituents. Because constituencies differ, legislators come to Salem with different concerns and policy preferences. The importance of constituency can be seen by comparing the voting behavior of Portland representatives to that of the representatives from the eastern regions of the state.

Many interest groups create what is called a "scorecard" at the end of each legislative session, which shows the percentage of times that individual legislators supported the group's positions on key votes. These scorecards help reveal the legislators' positions in particular policy areas. For example, the Oregon League of Conservation Voters (OLCV) produced a scorecard after the 1999 legislative session that ranked the members according to the percentage of times they supported pro-environment legislation. The Oregon Education Association (OEA) created a similar scorecard that assessed legislators on education legislation, and the Christian Coalition created one focusing on social issues.

On all three scorecards, the voting records of the representatives from Portland were far different from those from the east. On average the legislators from Portland supported the OLCV almost 76 percent of the time, whereas the eastern representatives supported the league only 9 percent of the time. Similarly, the Portland representatives supported the OEA more than 81 percent of the time and the Christian Coalition less than 32 percent. Yet the eastern representatives supported the OEA 41 percent of the time and the Christian Coalition by almost 78 percent.[4]

These regional differences can be seen in table 8.1, which shows the average support scores for the representatives in each of the seven regions introduced in the first chapter. Because representatives' districts do not always follow county lines, the regions in table 8.1 are not exactly the same as those in table 1.1. Even so, the table makes clear that the regional differences

Table 8.1. Average Interest-Group-Support Scores, 1999

Region	Oregon League of Conservation Voters	Oregon Education Association	Christian Coalition
Portland	75.6	81.3	31.4
University counties	84.0	90.8	16.8
Portland suburbs	43.5	48.9	59.0
North Coast	71.7	84.7	24.7
Mid–Willamette Valley	16.1	31.4	83.9
Southern Oregon	22.9	37.7	73.0
Eastern Oregon	9.3	41.1	77.9

reflected in the voting behavior of Oregon residents is also reflected in the vote of state representatives.

Certainly, not all state legislators do a good job of representing their constituents, yet these numbers tell us that constituents do matter. Why are constituents important? The answer, legislative scholars argue, is related to the type of people elected to state legislatures.[5] In general, the individuals who are elected to represent a district are born in that district or at least have deep roots there. Over the years they develop close personal ties to community members and groups. Once in office the members continuously interact with constituents in a variety of different settings, from college classrooms to business luncheons to political rallies. Because of these ties, legislators routinely convey the concerns of their districts as they decide what action to take. Legislators also are motivated to think about their constituents because of their desire to be reelected. Yes, some legislators are less responsive to constituents than others, but most are supportive of the community that has sent them to Salem. One of the main reasons, then, that conflict occurs in the legislature is that there are these differences in districts across the state.

LEGISLATIVE FUNCTIONS

There are three main functions performed by legislators and legislatures: representation, lawmaking, and oversight.

Representation

The first function performed by legislators is to represent the people who live in Oregon. In the most basic sense this means that legislators are expected to represent the values and beliefs of their constituents as the legislature considers public policy questions. In modern American politics, however, the representational role of the legislature has expanded beyond this traditional role. Today, most legislators represent their constituents not only in the policy-making process but also in all government activities. In particular, legislators play an important role in helping constituents who have encountered problems with the state bureaucracy. A legislator's effort to represent constituents in this manner is referred to as *constituency service* or *casework.*[6]

Lawmaking

The legislature produces most of the state's laws, except for those adopted through the initiative process. The legislature considers bills on almost every type of issue imaginable, from anatomical gifts to military affairs to workers' compensation. In each biennial session during the 1990s, more than three thousand bills were introduced and around a thousand became law.

The most important legislation that is considered every session is the state budget. In actuality, the budget consists of several different bills, one for each state agency plus a reconciliation bill at the end of the session. The reconciliation bill is sometimes referred to as the "Christmas tree" bill because it includes money for individual legislators' pet projects. The budget is important because it establishes where the state will spend money each year; thus, it affects everyone in the state. Concern over state spending is so great that the budget often dominates the debate in each session and is one of the main causes for delaying the legislature's adjournment.[7]

Oversight

The legislature's effort to investigate how government agencies are administering state programs and spending state funds is referred to as *oversight*. The legislature can exercise oversight through a variety of methods. The simplest way is for legislators or their staffs to talk informally with bureaucrats on particular issues or concerns. At the other extreme, legislators can formally review agency rules and hold hearings on agency activities.

PART-TIME LEGISLATURE

Legislative politics is not just shaped by the differences in constituencies. Each state legislature has its own structures, rules, customs, and membership, all of which can influence the character of its politics. The Legislative Assembly is also affected by other factors besides the split between progressives and conservative populists.

One of the key forces in shaping politics in the legislature is its status as a part-time, amateur body. By amateur, I mean that the legislature does not have the same level of organizational support as Congress, it does not meet full time, and its members are less likely to be career politicians. The U.S. Congress comes to order in early January of each odd-numbered year, and it does not adjourn until two years later. The members of Congress are given large staffs, a liveable salary, and a variety of perquisites, from franking privileges to life and health insurance.

Oregon's Legislative Assembly convenes on the second Monday in January of every odd-numbered year and usually adjourns about six months later. Each legislator is allotted an allowance of $26,083 during the regular session for personal staff, services and supplies, and legislative newsletters. Members may hire as many staff members as they want with these funds, but only two are eligible for fringe benefits. These limitations mean that each legislator can hire no more than two full-time personal staff members each. Members are paid $15,396 a year, plus $85 a day in expenses while the legislature is in session.

Until the 1960s most state legislatures resembled Oregon's in the sense that they did not have the professional support and structure found in Congress. From the mid-1960s through the 1980s, however, a reform movement swept the nation, as state after state moved to modernize its legislature. California was among the leaders of this movement. It raised legislators' pay, removed constitutional restrictions on session lengths, and hired more staff. The increase in pay was meant to allow legislators to make a career of legislative service. The removal of the session limits and the hiring of more staff were meant to give state legislators the professional support they need to do their jobs.

Oregon was not immune to these trends, but overall the reform movement did not create the same level of professionalism in the Legislative Assembly as seen in California and many other states. The state's most comprehensive effort to modernize its legislature came in 1967, when the legislature created an advisory committee to study and recommend reforms. The result of the committee's work was compiled into a report entitled "Oregon's Legislative Future," which laid out a series of proposals for improving the legislature. Since the committee concluded its study in 1968, the state has adopted some, but not all, of the committee's proposals.

Perhaps the most significant step taken to modernize the legislature occurred in 1975, when the Legislative Assembly approved an expansion of
the capitol to supply more offices and meeting rooms for legislators and
support staff. The addition also provided space for an underground parking
garage. The 1968 Legislative Future report had recommended a 50,000-
square-foot addition; the Capitol Wings Addition, as the expansion was
called, added almost 190,000 square feet, more than doubling the capitol
facilities. A few other proposals from the report have also been enacted,
including giving the legislature the power to call itself into special session
and creating a compensation committee to help set legislators' salaries.
In 1975 the Legislative Assembly created the Legislative Revenue Office
to obtain better nonpartisan analyses of tax-related issues. In 1978 voters
passed a constitutional amendment requiring Senate confirmation of almost
all gubernatorial appointments, a power not given the Senate in the past. In
the mid-1980s, the legislature began to fund staff for legislators when the
legislature was not in session. Today, each legislator is allocated just under
two thousand dollars per month to pay for interim staff. Both state houses
have reduced the number of committees from a high of more than thirty in
the mid-1900s to around fifteen or sixteen today. The state has also adopted
an open-meeting law, which was one of the proposals of modernization
reformers nationwide.

In other areas many of the committee's proposals have not been adopted;
consequently, the legislature has retained an amateur air. Many of the
committee's organizational reforms have been ignored or rejected, including
increasing the size of the legislature, reducing the authority of the Emergency
Board, and limiting the total number of committees in each house to eleven.
Even though a compensation committee has been created, the legislature
retains control over its own compensation. Funding for staff support remains
limited. Where the reform committee recommended that the legislature add
a separate fiscal session in even-numbered years, the legislature continues
to meet solely in odd-numbered years, except when it is called into special
session. Finally, while legislative salaries have risen in current-dollar terms
over the past few decades, legislative pay has remained unchanged since the
early 1960s when adjusted for inflation. Because the pay is not sufficient to
make ends meet, most members retain an occupation outside the legislature.

In general, many Oregonians are supportive of the legislature's more
amateur status, believing that it makes legislators more responsive to constituents. Yet not everyone agrees. Many scholars see more professional
legislatures as being more effective and independent than amateur ones.[8]

ELECTION RULES

A state's election rules also play an important role in shaping legislative politics, both by spurring political battles and by shaping the character of those who serve.

The sixty members of the House are elected for two-year terms. The thirty members of the Senate are elected for four-year terms, with half the Senate up for reelection every two years. One difference between the Legislative Assembly and Congress is that state senators, like their House counterparts, are elected from individual districts of approximately equal size. The state legislative district boundaries are drawn so that each state Senate district is made up of two House districts.

The district boundaries are redrawn every ten years, after the federal census, in order to adjust for changes in each district's population. This redistricting routinely spurs a major political battle because it can affect an individual member's reelection chances and possibly which party controls the legislature. The Legislative Assembly has the initial responsibility to redraw the district lines. If it does not approve a redistricting plan by July 1 of the year after the federal census, then the secretary of state is given the task. The battle over redistricting is so contentious that the legislature has not actually completed the redistricting since 1911.[9]

This was true in 2001 as well, despite the otherwise cooperative tone of that session. In fact, the debate over redistricting produced what was by far the most prominent political fight during the 2001 session. Incensed by a proposal from the Republican majority to pass the new redistricting plan as a resolution rather than as a bill, House Democrats staged a five-day boycott of the legislature, arguing that use of a resolution for redistricting was unconstitutional. Republicans proposed using a resolution because it would not need to be approved by the Democratic governor as would a bill. When the Democrats walked out, the Republicans hired process servers to force the Democrats back to work, but none of the Democrats could be found. The Democrats returned when it became clear that the resolution would fail.[10]

Among the most important election rules affecting legislative politics in recent years has been the state's term limits law, which was of the strictest in the nation until the law was overturned by the Oregon Supreme Court in January 2002. Under the law individuals could serve for no more than twelve years in the legislature. Of those twelve years, no more than six could be served in the House and eight in the Senate. After the introduction of this law in 1992, there was an increase in the turnover of members and a decline in the experience of officeholders. It also allowed newcomers to move more rapidly into important leadership positions.[11]

MEMBERS

Who serves in a legislature can also affect its politics. In general, most members of the Legislative Assembly are white, middle-aged, and male. In 2001 there were one Latino and four African Americans in the Legislative Assembly at the start of the session, though one African American resigned to run for another office. The average representative was fifty-one years old, the average senator fifty-seven. There were twenty-two women in the House and eight in the Senate. About 40 percent of the members were born in Oregon. After Oregon, the second most common place of birth was California. The Republican Party has held a majority of seats in the House since 1991 and a majority in the Senate from 1995 to 2002. In the 2001 session the Republicans held sixteen of the thirty Senate seats and thirty-two of the sixty House seats. In 2003 the Republicans and Democrats both held fifteen Senate seats, and the Republican membership in the House rose to thirty-five.

As for occupation, business leads the way. In the 2001 session more than one-third of the House and nearly half of the Senate members either listed themselves as business owners or as being employed in some particular type of business. The second most common occupation was government work. Many legislators list their occupation as being a "legislator" or they list a previous political office. Along with these two occupations, there were several farmers, educators, health care workers, journalists, and a variety of professionals.

In general, the composition of the legislature has changed little over time, with a few exceptions. The most important change may be the number of women elected. In the 1960s only a handful of women served in the legislature. Today there are still fewer women than men, but the numbers are closer. Since the early 1990s around 25 percent or more of the members in each house have been women. This increase is important because there is evidence that women legislators behave in a different way than do male legislators and pursue different issues. Women legislators tend to be more supportive of legislation concerning families, children, and women's issues.[12]

There have also been some important changes in the occupation of members. In particular, the number of attorneys and farmers has declined, and the number of individuals who list government service as their career has grown. This last statistic is an interesting one. Despite the fact that the Oregon legislature is less professional than many, it has a growing number of legislators who identify their profession as politics. Certainly, a large number of them are professional politicians in the sense that prior to being elected they were already involved in legislative politics, serving as aides, journalists, or lobbyists. After leaving the legislature, many will seek other political offices or a career related to politics, such as lobbying.

LEGISLATIVE LEADERSHIP

The two most powerful leaders of the legislature are the speaker of the House and the president of the Senate. Both of these leaders are formally elected by the entire membership of their chamber at the beginning of each session. In recent years the majority party in each chamber has controlled who is elected to these positions. Before each session the members of the House majority party nominate a candidate for speaker, and members of the Senate majority nominate a candidate for president. These nominees are then elected in the formal vote. The election of these leaders has not always followed party lines, however. From 1961 to 1973, for example, a bipartisan coalition selected the Senate president.

The House speaker and the Senate president play a dual role. On one hand they serve as their chamber's formal leader, which means they perform a variety of duties to help the legislature function. Among other tasks, the speaker and the president distribute committee assignments, select committee chairs, refer bills to committee, preside over the legislature, and oversee administrative details. On the other hand both individuals serve as the leaders of their political parties. In this role they plan strategies, negotiate compromises, and work to further their party's goals.

The Republican and Democratic parties in both houses also elect someone to lead their caucuses. A "caucus" refers to all the members of one party within each chamber. The four caucus leaders are the House majority leader, House Democratic leader, Senate Republican leader, and Senate Democratic leader. The main job of the caucus leaders is to promote their party's political and policy goals. Although they are not the top leaders in their parties, the caucus leaders in the majority party often play a more hands-on role in planning strategy and championing party goals than the speaker and president. The caucus leaders, along with their staffs, also provide various services to their party members, including writing legislation, conducting research, helping with constituency service, and handling media relations.

The cochairs of the Joint Ways and Means Committee also make up a key part of the leadership. All committee chairs play an important role in the legislative process because they have considerable power over committee activities. The chairs of the Ways and Means Committee are particularly important, however, because this committee puts together the state budget for the legislature. As a joint committee, the committee is composed of members from the House and the Senate. The committee has two cochairs, one from each house. The chairs of the House and Senate revenue committees are also considered important because these committees oversee taxes and revenue-related issues. Finally, there are a number of lesser leadership positions within each party. These include deputy leaders, assistant leaders, and whips.

Overall, the leaders of the Oregon legislature are considered among the most powerful legislative leaders in the nation. One recent study ranked the Oregon House speaker as the fifth most powerful speaker in the nation.[13] But even though the leaders are powerful, there are limits to their ability to exercise that power. Most legislative scholars argue that legislative leaders are agents of their followers, which means that leaders must work to further their followers' goals. Because the party caucus controls leadership selections, the leaders must pay attention to what the party wants. As a result it is not the leaders per se who ultimately control power but the party caucuses. If a caucus grows unhappy with its leaders, it can replace them. This is just what happened at the start of the 1999 session when the Republican caucus threw out the sitting speaker, Lynn Lundquist, because he had been too supportive of Democratic legislation.

THE LEGISLATIVE PROCESS

The legislative process is often considered a "conservative" process in the sense that it encourages slow change. The reason it is considered conservative is that each step in the process provides an opportunity for opponents to defeat legislation. Conversely, for bill supporters each step requires bringing together a different coalition of legislators to support the legislation. As a consequence the process makes it difficult to pass legislation.

The difficulties in passing laws can be seen when observing the legislative process in Oregon. It is here, as the bills move through the process, that battles are fought among the different interests within the state—progressives versus conservative populists, east versus west, or one coalition versus another. Because there is conflict in the state, many bills are unable to survive the legislative process, or if they do they are compromises.

How a Bill Becomes a Law

The legislative process begins with an idea for a new law or a change in an existing one. Anyone can have an idea for a bill—a private citizen, an interest group, the governor, or a member of the legislature. In order for the idea to be considered by the legislature, it must first be written out as a bill and introduced into the legislature. The Office of the Legislative Counsel works for the Legislative Assembly to draft bills in proper legal form. After a bill is drafted it can then be formally introduced. Only legislators, legislative committees, and state agencies can introduce legislation. For an agency to introduce legislation, however, it must submit ("prefile") its proposal before the beginning of the session.

After a bill has been introduced in the House, the speaker refers it to a committee for consideration. In the Senate, the president refers bills to committee. Legislative committees play a central role in the legislative process. It is in committee that hearings are held and legislation tends to get the most intense scrutiny. The chairperson of each committee has considerable influence over the committee's actions, since he or she has the power to schedule bills for consideration. If a chairperson opposes a bill, it is more difficult, though not impossible, for the bill to become law. A large proportion of the bills introduced each session "die" in committee because the committee chairs have not put them on the agenda. If a chair is willing to consider a bill, he or she will schedule hearings and then a work session. Hearings provide an opportunity for private citizens, lobbyists, agency representatives, and others to testify on the bill before the committee. A work session is where committee members sit down to discuss and decide the content of bills. A majority of committee members must agree for a bill to be passed out of committee.

After a bill leaves committee, the full chamber may then consider it. If scheduled, a debate may take place and a vote taken. For most legislation, a majority vote of the entire membership is needed for a measure to be approved. Tax measures require support from two-thirds of the legislators. One of the reasons that committees are considered powerful in the Oregon legislature is that amendments are not allowed on the House floor. If legislators want changes to a bill after it has reached the floor, they must return it to committee.

To reach the governor, a bill must pass through all of these steps in both houses. In addition, the final wording of the bill as it leaves the House

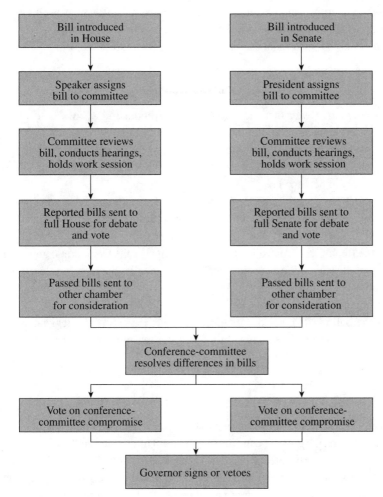

Figure 8.1. The Legislative Process

and Senate must be exactly the same. If the wording is not identical, then one or both houses must alter its language. When neither house is willing to compromise, the House speaker and Senate president may put together a conference committee composed of members from both houses to find a compromise. If this committee is able to work out a compromise, both chambers must then approve the committee's proposal.

Once a bill has passed both houses with identical wording, it then goes to the governor, who has three options: sign the bill into law, veto it, or do nothing and allow it to become law without his or her signature. A two-thirds vote of both houses is needed to override a gubernatorial veto.

Bill Referrals

An alternative way that the legislature can produce new laws is to place proposed legislation on the ballot for voter approval. Such action is called a legislative referral. From 1902 through the end of the 2001 session, the legislature placed 369 proposals on the ballots. Of these, 206 were approved by voters to become law.[14]

In the 1999 session the legislature placed twenty-one measures on the ballot, setting a record for the number of referrals made in any legislative session (see figure 8.2). The large use of referrals that year reflected an effort by the Republican-controlled legislature to bypass the Democratic governor in getting legislation enacted. Unlike regular bills, ballot referrals do not need the governor's approval. With the greater cooperation among members during the 2001 regular session, however, only seven measures were placed on the ballot.[15] (Figure 8.2 includes referrals passed by the legislature in subsequent special sessions.) Only four referrals appeared on the ballots in 2003 and 2004 combined.

LEGISLATIVE-GUBERNATORIAL RELATIONS

In recent sessions strong disagreement and conflict have marked the relationship between the governor and the legislature. The conflict can be seen in both the large number of referrals that the legislature put onto the ballot during the 1999 session and in the number of vetoes exercised by the governor in recent years (see figure 8.3). In large part the conflict between the two sides has reflected the impact of the state's divided political character. In 1995 both chambers of the Legislative Assembly had a Republican majority for the first time since 1955. As a result the conservative populist part of the state was able to exercise greater influence over the legislature's actions than it had in years. Also in 1995 Democrat John Kitzhaber began the first of his two terms as governor. With the Legislative Assembly more sensitive to conservative populist concerns and the governor more sensitive to progressive ones, the result was frequent conflict between the two. The conflict reached a peak in the 1999 session before subsiding somewhat in 2001. Yet it did not vanish. In 2002, with tax revenues down because of the recession, the

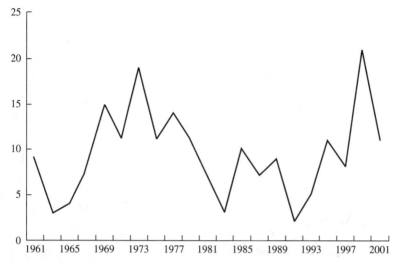

Figure 8.2. Legislative Referrals, 1961–2001

differences between the two sides reemerged as the Legislative Assembly and the governor tried to find ways to balance the budget in five separate special sessions. The prospects for continued conflict remain high, given the fact that the 2002 election placed another Democrat (Ted Kulongoski) in the governor's office, created an evenly divided Senate, and allowed the Republican Party to continue to control the House. Yet Kulongoski vetoed only seven measures in 2003, the lowest number of vetoes since 1971. The decline in vetoes likely reflected the split in party control of the Senate.

Over the years some of the most intense conflict between the legislature and the governor has been over the budget. Most often, when there is conflict between the two branches over budgeting or any major policy proposal, the top legislative leaders and the governor will negotiate a compromise. Part of the reason that there was less conflict in the Legislative Assembly during the 2001 regular session was that the legislative leaders and the governor made a conscientious effort to work together and find a middle ground on policy matters. On some occasions, however, the governor may try to negotiate with individual members of the legislature directly if he cannot work out an agreement with the legislative leaders. In 1999, for example, the governor met with a group of seventeen Republican and Democratic legislators in order to find some compromise on the budget. Similarly, the end of the

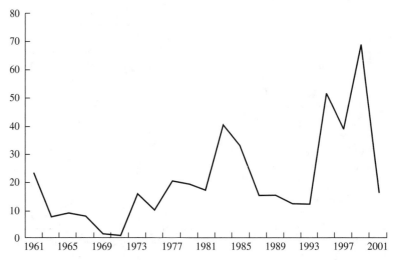

Figure 8.3. Gubernatorial Vetoes, 1961–2001

fifth special session in 2002 came after a handful of Republican legislators decided to oppose their party's leaders and began to talk directly with the governor about a compromise.

THE INTERIM

How does the legislature deal with issues or problems that arise when it is not in session? The legislature has two specific mechanisms that it can use to address problems that arise during the interim.

First, the state constitution allows the governor or a majority of members from both houses to call a special session of the legislature. From 1860 to 2001 the legislature was called for thirty special sessions, with an average length of nine days.[16] Because of the budget problems in 2002, the Legislative Assembly met in five special sessions, including the first one ever called by the legislature itself. In total, the legislature met for fifty-two special session days in 2002. Second, the Emergency Board, created in 1913, can address state funding problems when the legislature is not in session.[17] Today, the board consists of nineteen legislators, including the House speaker and the Senate president. The Emergency Board is given the power to allocate additional funds to state agencies when an emergency arises during the interim. In addition, the board can transfer funds within an agency's account and authorize an agency to spend money beyond the amount allocated in the agency's budget. Although the Emergency Board can help allay problems, the amount of money that it can spend is limited to what has been appropriated by the legislature.[18]

To be sure, the legislature does not entirely quit working during the interim. The Senate convenes approximately every three months to vote on executive appointments. In addition, legislators are assigned to interim committees that continue to examine policy proposals and to exercise oversight of the administration. Because the legislature is not in session, the interim committees often have more time than regular committees to analyze policy proposals in depth. As a result the committees often produce important bills to be considered in the next legislative session. In 1998, for example, the interim Senate Education Committee developed a bill allowing charter schools to exist in the public school system. The bill emerged as one of the major policy debates during the 1999 session and was eventually signed into law. Although there were other charter school bills under consideration during that session, the Education Committee's bill was considered by many to be the best because of the amount of work that the interim committee had put into it.[19]

THREATS TO REPRESENTATIVE GOVERNMENT?

Although I have emphasized that most legislators are concerned about their districts and the future of the state, the public has become increasingly disillusioned with state legislators and the legislative process. As a result Oregon has witnessed two important changes in its political system: the introduction of term limits and the increased use of the initiative process. Even though the Oregon Supreme Court struck down the term limits law, the potential remains that term limits will be reinstated if supporters are successful in placing a new law back on the ballot. The imposition of term limits and the increased use of initiatives are important to examine because many legislative scholars and political observers see both of these practices as potentially threatening to the state's system of representative democracy.

In much of the initial empirical research coming out on term limits, legislative scholars identified a number of problems that appear to be created by term limits. These include a greater concentration of power in the executive branch and among interest groups, a decline in expertise and knowledge among legislators, greater conflict between members, and less capable legislatures.[20]

There has been no scholarly study on how term limits have affected

Oregon's legislature, yet many of the newspaper analyses of term limits have come to similar conclusions. In an article that provided the most in-depth analysis of the state's term limits law to date, journalists for the *Statesman Journal* concluded that term limits were at least partially responsible for many of the recent problems in the legislature, including the conflict in the 1999 session that delayed adjournment. Among other consequences, the *Journal* argued that term limits reduced legislators' experience and knowledge, generated greater turmoil in the capitol, made it more difficult for major policy initiatives to be enacted, weakened the power of the legislature, and increased the power of the governor, interest groups, and lobbyists.[21] The problem, the *Journal* argued, is that by forcing continuous turnover, term limits reduced the legislators' understanding of the political process and of policy issues. With less understanding of the process and policy, legislators became more dependent on these other actors in taking action and less able to develop comprehensive public policies.

Similar concerns have also been voiced about the state's growing reliance on the initiative. One of the main criticisms of the process is that it makes the legislature work harder to address state problems because legislators must now spend a larger share of their time reacting to successful initiatives or threats of future ones. In addition, many initiative opponents criticize the process because it does not give voters any other options but to vote for or against a proposal, whereas the legislative process is designed to find compromises among the different interests in the state.[22]

Despite these concerns, it is important to keep in mind that not everyone sees either term limits or the initiative as being threats to representative democracy. The state's term limits law was enacted with almost 70 percent of the popular vote. Although there have been no recent surveys on the popularity of term limits in the state, it is quite likely that such limits retain considerable support. The reason that term limits are popular is because many supporters, including initiative advocates, feel that the state government has not been responsive to the public's concerns. Term limits are seen as a way to keep the legislature more closely tied to voters by regularly bringing in new members. The initiative is seen as a way to get legislation enacted in areas in which the legislature has been unwilling or unable to act, such as in reducing property taxes (Measures 5 and 47), protecting property rights (Measure 7), or allowing physician-assisted suicide (Measure 16). For supporters of term limits and initiatives, neither of these practices constitutes a threat to democracy. Rather, they are designed to make the political system more democratic.

Whether term limits and the initiative process actually harm or heighten democracy, they certainly cannot be held solely responsible for all that has made lawmaking more difficult in Salem. The conflict and gridlock in Salem reflect, in large extent, the vast political split in the state itself. As long as voters continue to be divided between progressivism and conservative populism, the legislature will face conflict, as it did throughout most of the 1990s, or have difficulty passing innovative legislation, as was the case during the 2001 session. As long as voters do not agree on what is best for the state, neither will legislators. Such is the nature of representative democracy.

CHAPTER NINE

Governor

Jerry F. Medler

State governments are not clones of the federal government, and nowhere is this clearer than in the executive branch. Perhaps the most important feature that distinguishes Oregon's executive branch from its federal counterpart is the limit on the governor's control of state government.

Some of the restraints facing the governor are similar to those confronting the president. Both the president and Oregon's governor, for example, operate under the separation of powers. But in the state, the governor confronts additional challenges. Whereas presidents choose the members of their cabinets, Oregon governors work with five "cabinet-level" officers who are independently elected. These officers share the executive power with the governor. Whereas the president oversees most of the federal bureaucracy, the governor oversees only a small portion of Oregon's. At the federal level direct democracy does not exist; in Oregon it often surpasses the governor in shaping the direction of the state.

Combined, all of these factors as well as others have set limits on the governor's ability to control the state government. As a result, Oregon's governor is, comparatively speaking, a relatively weak executive in the mosaic of U.S. governments.

This chapter addresses two major themes. The first is the limited power of Oregon's governor. The second is that the executive branch, like other parts of Oregon politics, has been affected by the conflict between the state's progressive side and conservative populism. The conflict is not about who is elected governor but on the pressures that come to bear on the governor's office. In general, moderate centrists have held the governorship in recent years. Nevertheless, Oregon governors have had to contend with the shifting political tensions that have been created by the split between the state's progressives and conservative populists. Before looking at the causes and consequences of these two themes, it is important first to explain the role of the governor and the other five executives.

THE GOVERNOR

The governor is the chief executive officer of Oregon's government. As such, the governor performs a variety of roles, from serving as the ceremonial leader of the state to handling some of the most important duties of the state government. There are five particularly important roles performed by Oregon governors.

Policymaker

When candidates seek the governor's office, they routinely lay out their vision of Oregon's future. Once in office there is the widespread expectation that governors will pursue their vision by championing their political goals through the legislative process. Because of this expectation, governors are compelled to participate in the legislative process. In fact, governors are sometimes referred to as a state's chief legislator because of how active they are in policymaking. To help attain their policy goals, governors are given greater staff support than any other officeholder in the state. Governor John Kitzhaber's main policy staff in 2002 consisted of more than twenty individuals, from his press secretary to specialists in specific policy areas.[1]

The most important legislation the governor places before the legislature is the state's budget. Oregon, like most states and the federal government, uses a highly structured budgeting process (see chapter 13). The dynamic of budgeting is an elaborate pas de deux between the executive and legislative branches of government. The Budget and Management Division puts together the proposed budget based on the governor's goals. The legislature responds to the governor's proposal, adding here and cutting there to reflect the members' spending preferences. Because the budget is so important, it demands a great deal of attention from the governor and legislators alike.

Administrator

The governor is the top administrative officer in the state, overseeing a large share of the state bureaucracy. One of the primary ways in which the governor influences the state's bureaucracy is through appointments.

Historically, agency jobs were used for patronage politics, a practice by which partisan politicians were able to appoint their supporters, family, and friends to the public payroll in return for electoral support. However, modern state governments have reformed this process by creating a professional civil service. Despite these reforms, the governor still controls the selection of the top management of many state bureaus, which provides the governor with some influence over the bureaucracy's actions and the way that laws are implemented. The governor's role in managing the bureaucracy is limited, however, because of the existence of the five other executives and the widespread use of boards and commissions to oversee many state agencies.

Appointer of Commissioners and Board Members

Oregon government was created in the nineteenth century in an agrarian culture where most people lived on farms or worked in agriculture. In this milieu state government was considered to be an occasional activity. The amateur politicians elected to the legislature were expected to attend to their duties in the capitol for only a few months every other year and then go home. In lieu of a strong, professional state government, Oregon took care of most government business through boards and commissions whose citizen-members were entrusted with policy-making authority. This citizen-based approach to government still exists today. These boards and commissions routinely handle many of the most important policy matters confronting the state. They also oversee numerous departments and agencies, including the selection of some top personnel.

Three boards are particularly noteworthy. The Public Utility Commission oversees telephone service in the state, as well as privately owned gas and electric companies. The Transportation Commission oversees the expenditures of the state's motor-fuel taxes. The Land Conservation and Development Commission directs Oregon's land-use planning program.

The governor nominates or appoints the citizens who serve on these boards. While governors have little direct influence in the business of these boards and commissions, their power to select board members gives them an important role in shaping the board's behavior and, in turn, the performance of Oregon government.

Chair of the State Land Board

The governor is one of three members of the State Land Board, along with the secretary of state and the state treasurer. The governor also chairs the board. The State Land Board was created when Oregon entered the nation, to oversee state-owned school land and to manage the Common School Fund. As part of the Oregon Admission Act, Congress set aside 6 percent of the state's land for the use of public schools. The board was created to oversee this land and any income generated from it. The income from the land is deposited into the Common School Fund and then distributed to public schools across the state.[2]

Today, the board oversees almost two million acres of state land and contributes more than $20 million per year to public schools.[3] In addition to managing state-school lands, the board oversees the Oregon territorial sea (including the seabed), the land under all of Oregon's navigable waterways, and the petroleum and mineral rights attached to all of these state lands. As chair and member of the board, the governor plays a critical role in the policy issues it addresses.

Appointer of Judges

Judgeships in Oregon are nonpartisan, elected positions. Constitutionally, judges are required to seek the approval of voters and to run for office every six years. On the surface this arrangement gives the impression that judges are politically independent from the governor and other branches of government. However, the actual practice is more complex.

If a judge dies, retires, resigns, or is recalled from office, the governor is empowered by the state constitution to name a replacement for the remainder of the judge's unfinished term. This provision for an interim appointment serves to make the selection of Oregon judges more like the federal appointment of judges. Essentially, this allows the governor to select fellow partisans or political compatriots for appointments to the bench. These appointed judges, like all judges, must face the voters periodically for reelection. However, if no one challenges the appointed judge, which is often the case, the judge is reelected. As a result the governor can play a significant role in shaping the political makeup of the state courts, including the state supreme court. In fact, gubernatorial appointments tend to be the rule, not the exception. Since 1950, for example, thirty-two people have taken a seat on the supreme court. Eight of these judges (25 percent) were initially elected to the bench, while twenty-four (75 percent) were appointed by the governor (see chapter 11).

SHARED EXECUTIVE POWERS

As with other states, Oregon has more than one executive. The governor is the chief executive, yet the state constitution subdivides the executive function of government into six different offices. Each of these executive positions has its own area of responsibility and power. Each executive is also independently elected. Along with the governorship, these offices are the secretary of state, treasurer, attorney general, commissioner of labor and industries, and superintendent of public instruction.

Secretary of State

The secretary of state is considered the "number two" position among the state's executives. Constitutionally, the secretary of state succeeds the governor in the event of death or disability. Informally, this position is seen as a political stepping-stone to the governor's office.

The secretary of state is in charge of elections, which often makes the position quite visible to the public. As secretary of state, Phil Keisling, for example, generated considerable attention in his efforts to promote Vote by Mail and other electoral reforms.[4] One of the most important election-related duties of the secretary of state is to oversee the redrawing of legislative redistricting plans when the legislature is unable to complete this task. Although this task technically falls to the legislature, the partisan stakes are so high that the legislature has not completed redistricting since 1911.[5] This was the case again in 2001 when Secretary of State Bill Bradbury drew the district lines.[6]

Perhaps more important than these electoral duties, the secretary of state has the power to conduct audits of state agencies. The secretary of state also acts as the state's chief records officer, overseeing all official state records and the state archives. In addition, this person serves as one of three members of the State Land Board.

State Treasurer

The state treasurer serves as the state's banker, receiving, overseeing, and managing state funds. The largest investment fund managed by the treasurer is the Public Employee Retirement System (PERS) accounts, which fund the retirement of most public employees (state and local) in Oregon. In addition, the treasurer manages the State Industrial Accident Fund (SAIF), which provides workers' compensation insurance for most Oregon employers. The treasurer is also a member of the State Land Board.

Much of the treasurer's work is routine and follows accepted accounting and banking procedures. For example, the treasurer is responsible for issuing and retiring government bonds issued by the state of Oregon. However, other functions can be more controversial. For example, setting premiums charged to employers for SAIF coverage or payments made to injured workers has generated considerable debate within the state.

Attorney General

The attorney general serves as Oregon's lawyer, providing legal services to all state agencies, including counsel in all court cases involving the state or its agencies. The attorney general issues written legal opinions on questions of state law. These opinions guide public policy unless overturned by the courts or by the passage of new legislation. One other important legal task given to the attorney general is the writing of ballot titles for proposed initiatives. The ballot title is a short description of the proposed initiative measure. In recent years this responsibility has become time-consuming and contentious. In addition the attorney general also oversees the state's Department of Justice. In this position, the attorney general is charged with administering a great variety of policies, including child-support payments, crime victims' compensation, and consumer protection.

Commissioner of Labor and Industries

The Bureau of Labor and Industries was created as part of the early-twentieth-century Progressive movement to protect workers and children in a newly industrializing economy. The commissioner was originally a partisan position but recently has been made nonpartisan. The commissioner's role has evolved to include diverse responsibilities. The office's original concern with the well-being of workers is still addressed through the Wage and Hour Division, but its mission has expanded to include more modern concerns, such as overseeing apprenticeship programs, protecting civil rights, and providing various business services.

Superintendent of Public Instruction

This position is relatively new (it was created by the legislature in 1951) but serves over a half million Oregon students (K–12). Statewide education policy is the shared responsibility of the legislature and the appointed State Board of Education. The Oregon Department of Education is responsible for implementing state education policies. The superintendent of public education is both the executive head of the Department of Education and the administrative officer of the board. In this dual role the superintendent provides policy recommendations to the board and oversees the operation of the department.

CONSTRAINTS ON POWER

One of the major research topics that has interested state politics scholars over the past four decades is gubernatorial power. Since the 1960s scholars have attempted to identify the factors that make some governors more powerful than others in shaping the direction of state politics. Much of the research has focused on what are called the governor's "institutional" powers. These powers refer to specific structural aspects of a governor's office that can either strengthen or weaken a governor's ability to attain his or her goals. The number of separately elected statewide officials in the state, the potential for a governor to be reelected, and the amount of control that a governor has over the budget are all examples of institutional factors thought to influence a governor's power.[7]

In general, Oregon governors have fairly weak institutional powers, making it difficult for them to achieve their policy goals. In fact, one nation-wide study identified only fourteen states in which the governor had less institutional power than in Oregon.[8] The governor's powers seem even less formidable when compared with those of the president. Although a number of different institutional factors affect the power of Oregon governors, five are particularly important: the separation of powers, the presence of direct democracy, a weak party system, divided government, and separate constituencies. These factors are not unique to Oregon, but their presence plays an important role in defining gubernatorial politics in the state today.

Separation of Powers

The architecture of Oregon government reflects the same basic structure as that of the federal government. Power is separated into three parts: the executive, the legislative, and the judicial branches. The purpose of this separation is to create a weak government that makes it difficult for any one group to exercise power. With this separation of powers, governors cannot force their demands on the other branches.

However, the Oregon Constitution goes further than the U.S. Constitution in separating powers. First, the state constitution, like many other state constitutions but unlike the nation's, includes a separation of powers clause. This clause explicitly prohibits one branch from exercising the functions of another branch. Second, the constitution subdivides the executive function of government into several parts. As a result of having plural executives, Oregon's governor does not even oversee the entire executive branch; rather, the governor shares control with these other elected offices. The governor's powers are further weakened by the use of boards and commissions to oversee many policy areas.

Direct Democracy

Oregon voters amended the state constitution in 1902 to provide for the initiative, referendum, and legislative referrals. The effect of these Progressive Era reforms has been to reduce the leadership capacity of elected officials, especially the governor. In most states one of the primary powers often associated with the governor's office is the ability to control a state's agenda, especially by choosing the timing of when particular policy proposals are introduced.[9] In Oregon the governor remains a highly visible political actor who is able to set the state political agenda in many areas. Yet the initiative process gives other actors a platform for placing proposals on the agenda as well. To the extent that governors must respond to the proposals of these actors, the power of the office is diminished.

Conservative populists have been particularly successful in helping to set the tone of political debate in Oregon in recent years by championing initiatives, though they have not been alone in using initiatives to try to set the agenda. The reason that many of the conservative populist proposals have been successful in shaping debate is that they frequently touch on issues that are highly salient to voters across the political spectrum. This is particularly true of some tax reform proposals, such as Measures 5 and 47. Because tax limitations are one of the central goals of conservative populists, these measures generate immediate support, helping them to move quickly onto the political agenda. At the same time many progressive opponents see these proposals as dire threats to government programs and services, equally motivating them to work against the initiatives. With such highly salient initiatives repeatedly on the ballot, along with a number of more progressive ones, the governor has difficulty controlling the agenda and leading the state.

The ability of the legislature to place measures directly on the ballot, or what is called a legislative referral, also reduces the governor's power. Under the state constitution, the legislature can place a proposed change in state law or a constitutional amendment on the ballot if a majority of members in both houses approves. The referred legislation, however, does not need the governor's approval. As a result the legislature can circumvent the governor by placing legislation directly before voters.

As with the initiative, the use of legislative referrals has also grown in recent years, reflecting in part the ideological split within the state. Although it would be inaccurate to classify Democratic governor Kitzhaber as a strong ideologue, he certainly falls within the progressive camp. The Legislative Assembly, on the other hand, had a Republican majority for Kitzhaber's entire tenure. In the late 1990s the split between the two branches grew particularly severe as the ideological differences between these two sides frequently led to very public clashes. This conflict peaked in the 1999 session, when Republican legislative leaders decided to use the referral power more often so that they could sidestep the governor on policy proposals they supported. In total the legislature placed a record twenty-one measures on the ballot, in part to avoid gubernatorial vetoes.[10] In the 2001 regular session, however, the Republican leaders decided to forego that strategy, reducing the number of referrals to seven, the fewest since 1993.

Weak Parties

Just two years after the introduction of direct democracy in the state, Oregon voters used their newfound power to pass legislation requiring the use of primary elections to select party nominees. Ever since the passage of this progressive reform, Oregon has selected candidates for public office through the mechanism of intraparty elections. As a consequence political parties in Oregon are weak. This is important to our understanding of the office of the governor because it means that governors often cannot rely on party politics to augment their relatively powerless formal position.

Although many Americans view political parties as being undemocratic, party organizations can play a vital role in a democratic system, serving to link leaders with citizens and providing a mechanism for encouraging political leaders to work together. Historically, incumbent governors in many states have taken on the unofficial role of state party leader. Governors benefit from this position because it encourages cooperation from other elected officials. In Oregon, however, the governor enjoys little political advantage as the titular head of the party because of the use of primary elections, which reduces the parties' control over nominations. Oregon, of course, is not unique in use of primary elections. Yet Oregon parties are also weakened by the fact they do not make preprimary endorsements, which is common in states with strong party systems.[11] Moreover, the organizational structure of Oregon parties is considered to be weaker than in most states.[12] With primary elections and weak party organizations, and without preprimary endorsements, the candidates must rely on their own personal efforts and their own personal campaign organizations to get elected. Because of this independence state legislators do not have close political ties to the party organization and the governor.

The character of general elections in the state also does little to forge bonds between the governor and legislators. Even after a candidate wins a primary election, the party plays only a secondary role in the general election campaign. With a winning organization in place, party nominees are loath to abandon that organization for one directed by the party. Consequently, the parties have only a limited role in the general elections. In the end governors gain only a little from serving as the head of the state political party.

Divided Government

Even though party ties provide little help to the governor, they are not entirely unimportant. In particular, when members of the same party control both the legislature and the governor's office, they do provide some advantages to the governor. Unified party control, in effect, removes the tensions of partisan conflict from the state government, which can help the governor to play a larger role in leading government. When party control is divided, however, the governor has more difficulty leading.

One of the reasons that Oregon governors have had problems leading in recent years is that the state has repeatedly faced divided government. From 1959 to 2003 the Oregon legislature was reconstituted by elections twenty-three times (see table 9.1). Unified government characterized only four legislative sessions during that period, and divided government occurred nineteen times. The problem has not just been a partisan divide; the ideological differences between the legislature and the governor, described above, have been quite deep.

Table 9.1. Partisan Control of Oregon Government

Year	House	Senate	Governor	Status
1959	Democrat	Democrat	Republican	Divided
1961	Democrat	Democrat	Republican	Divided
1963	Democrat	Democrat	Republican	Divided
1965	Republican	Democrat	Republican	Divided
1967	Republican	Democrat	Republican	Divided
1969	Republican	Democrat	Republican	Divided
1971	Republican	Democrat	Republican	Divided
1973	Democrat	Democrat	Republican	Divided
1975	Democrat	Democrat	Democrat	Unified
1977	Democrat	Democrat	Democrat	Unified
1979	Democrat	Democrat	Republican	Divided
1981	Democrat	Democrat	Republican	Divided
1983	Democrat	Democrat	Republican	Divided
1985	Democrat	Democrat	Republican	Divided
1987	Democrat	Democrat	Democrat	Unified
1989	Democrat	Democrat	Democrat	Unified
1991	Republican	Democrat	Democrat	Divided
1993	Republican	Democrat	Democrat	Divided
1995	Republican	Republican	Democrat	Divided
1997	Republican	Republican	Democrat	Divided
1999	Republican	Republican	Democrat	Divided
2001	Republican	Republican	Democrat	Divided
2003	Republican	Tied	Democrat	Divided

Different Constituencies

A final institutional factor that can constrain governors is that they have different constituencies from the members of the state legislature. Governors are elected statewide. Legislators are elected from individual districts from across the state. Because their constituencies differ, there is no assurance that the two branches will work together even if the same party controls both branches. While governors may champion particular policy proposals that they think are valuable or popular, legislators may see little support for these proposals in their districts. As a result the governor's proposals may meet opposition in the legislature.

Differences in constituency have played an important role in Oregon politics over at least the past two decades, helping to further constrain the governor's influence. The constraints placed on the governor by having a different constituency base from that of legislators have been particularly pronounced in the state because the constituency bases of the two branches differ along both partisan and ideological lines. In large part the governor's office as well as the offices of the other statewide executives have been dominated by Democrats since the late 1980s. Except for the office of commissioner of labor and industries, no Republicans have been elected to a statewide office since 1988. Thus, the constituency for the governor has tended to be more progressive. On the other hand the Republican Party, drawing from a more conservative populist constituency base, has controlled the state House of Representatives since the 1990 election and the Senate from 1995 to 2003. In 2003 the Senate was split evenly between the two major parties. In essence, then, it is not just the party divide that separates the two branches but a difference in constituencies.

INFORMAL RESOURCES FOR LEADERSHIP

Even though there are important constraints on the governor, the governor is able, on occasion, to play a significant role in shaping public policy in the state. What factors are important in helping a governor to lead? Certainly, a governor's personality, energy, and outlook can be important.[13] Yet governors also rely on a range of resources to further their positions.

Veto Legislation

The Oregon governor has the power to veto, or reject, legislation. With this power the governor can say "no" to legislation he or she dislikes. Although the legislature can override a veto with a two-thirds vote of both houses, it is very difficult to do so. Thus, in a real sense, the veto gives the governor the final say on legislation. Some scholars argue that the veto power also gives the governor the ability to force legislators to keep the governor's policy goals in mind as they write legislation.[14] In so doing, the veto not only gives the governor the power to say no but it also provides a resource to shape the legislation that does pass.

The use of the veto varies greatly with the strategic situation between the governor and the legislature. For example, Governor Kitzhaber was given the nickname "Doctor No" because he used his power to veto legislation so frequently in the late 1990s (see figure 8.3).[15] In large part this tendency to use the veto is precipitated by divided government. When the governor and the legislature are of different parties, legislators may feel free to produce legislation as they see fit without consulting the governor, or may even challenge the governor. Likewise, the governor may feel free to veto legislation. The upshot is legislative gridlock.

Kitzhaber's heavy use of the veto also reflected the strong ideological differences he had with the Republican-controlled legislature. In 1999 the number of vetoes reached a record high of sixty-nine. In part, the increase that year reflected an overt decision on the part of the Republican Party leadership in the Legislative Assembly to send bills to the governor, as one Republican leader phrased it, to make a "philosophical statement" even though they knew the governor opposed the bills. In the 2001 session, the Republican leaders told their members that they wanted to abandon that practice and instead look for ways to compromise with the governor.[16]

Initiative Leadership

The introduction of the initiative has, as described above, undermined the governor's ability to set the agenda. However, the initiative can also provide some benefits to governors. On several occasions governors have seized the initiative bull by the horns, so to speak, and taken their policy vision directly to the electorate in the form of an initiative measure. By sponsoring initiatives, the governor can seek legislation without having to battle with the legislature. In so doing, the initiative provides the governor with an alternative means to lead the state, one that may be particularly valuable when the legislature is unsympathetic to the governor's position.

Symbolic Resources

As the chief executive officer of the state, the governor is in the politically enviable position of being "newsworthy." That is, governors frequently appear before the public because their proposals, their actions, and even their public appearances are considered news. This inherent newsworthiness offers opportunity for governors to focus public attention on problems, issues, and policy proposals. As ceremonial head of state, the governor represents Oregon at different types of events in the state, across the nation, and around the world. Although many of these occasions are decidedly apolitical, the governor frequently uses these appearances to make a political point or to offer a policy proposal.

Partisan Leadership

Even though Oregon's party system is very weak, the governor can, on occasion, use his position as party leader to his advantage. Governors are in a particularly good position to draw on partisan ties to their advantage when their party controls both houses of the Legislative Assembly. However, governors can also provide a variety of benefits to fellow party members, which can help them build personal ties and ultimately achieve their political goals.

Perhaps the most obvious support the governor can provide is in election campaigns. As the most visible actor in state government and as the titular head of the party, the governor is ideally situated to make financial appeals on behalf of the party or individual candidates. Likewise, the governor's presence at a rally or political event for a candidate can help bestow media attention on that candidate. All of these activities can help build the governor's relationship with fellow party members, which can help them to attain policy goals later on.

GUBERNATORIAL POWER TODAY

Of all the modern governors in Oregon politics, the one who is almost always portrayed as the most successful is Tom McCall, who served in the governor's chair from 1967 to 1975. McCall successfully championed a variety of new programs and used his office to aggressively address an assortment of state problems. Among other victories, he pushed through legislation establishing the state's broad land-use planning rules, creating new pollution restrictions on water and air quality and providing for bottle recycling (the bottle bill). He pushed the adoption of the Beach Bill, which extended public ownership of oceanfront land, and the Bicycle Bill, which set aside state transportation money for bicycle and foot trails. He also pushed through a major reorganization of the executive branch. This was not to say that McCall won every battle. For example, one of his most prominent defeats was his effort to restructure the state's tax system, which was turned aside by voters in a 1973 special election. Nor does it say that there has been universal praise for these policies. Yet in the number of victories and the breadth of the policies, few of the more recent governors can compare.

Why was Tom McCall so successful? Why have subsequent governors been less so? It is difficult to answer this question because so many different factors can influence political power. When comparing only a handful of governors, it is easy to over- or underemphasize the relative importance of any given explanation. Plus, efforts to measure power, or influence, are wrought with hazard because power is an elusive concept. Yet there are a number of different factors that do separate McCall's tenure from his successors and that undoubtedly influenced his success. Some of these factors are institutional; others are more personal.

Looking at the personal explanations first, there are a number of different characteristics about McCall and his policy pursuits that may have made him particularly successful. Even though state politics scholars have devoted considerable attention to understanding institutional power, many recognize that various personal factors related to individual governors can also matter.[17] One of the primary personal qualities frequently offered to explain McCall's success was his background in both print and television journalism. In his biography of McCall, Brent Walth argues that McCall's media knowledge helped him shape news coverage and build support for his proposals in the public. McCall was seen as being particularly adept at staging media events and turning out memorable quotes. Perhaps the best illustration of McCall's ability to generate media interest was his 1971 admonition to nonresidents: "Come visit us . . . But for heaven's sake, don't come here to live."[18] There may be no words uttered by an Oregon governor that have been more repeated than those.

McCall also pursued a policy agenda that included a number of issues that, in general, enjoyed widespread public support. This was particularly true of his efforts to protect the environment. The years in which McCall served as governor overlapped a period of time in which environmental protection was frequently at the top of the political agenda throughout the nation. It was in the late 1960s and early 1970s that Congress created the Environmental Protection Agency and enacted such laws as the Endangered Species Act, the Water Quality Improvement Act, and the National Environmental Policy Act. Concern over the environment was also important in Oregon. In 1970, for example, a majority of respondents in a statewide poll identified pollution as the state's biggest problem.[19]

Not all of McCall's success, however, can be attributed to personal qualities. The political context in which McCall served was considerably different from the one today. McCall did not confront all the same institutional constraints faced by some of his successors. Perhaps the most important difference is that the split between progressives and conservative populists was not as severe as it would become later. McCall himself was a progressive Republican, which is a rarity among Oregon political leaders today. Yet in the 1960s and 1970s a number of progressive Republicans held prominent political office. McCall, like most of his successors, confronted divided government throughout his tenure, yet the divide between the two branches was not so severe then. For most of McCall's tenure, it was only the Senate that held a Democratic majority. Yet that majority did not control the Senate. Rather, the Senate was controlled, as it had been since the early 1960s, by a bipartisan coalition.

Although other factors were certainly important as well, McCall benefited from strong leadership skills, a popular agenda, and a political environment that was more open to these major policy proposals. More recent governors have not always had these same benefits. To most political observers in the state, the biggest difficulty Kitzhaber confronted as governor, a difficulty that limited his policy record, was that the state is far more politically divided both within the public and among elected officials. Elected statewide with the support of progressive voters in 1994, Kitzhaber faced a legislature in which a majority of members were elected from districts in which conservative populism is very strong. The governor and the legislature have been able to work together at times, as they did during the 2001 regular session, but the ideological gulf within the state and among elected officials is so wide today that it is difficult to put together a record that is as broad as McCall's.

THE PEOPLE WHO SERVE

Who serves as Oregon governor? Perhaps the most significant pattern in modern Oregon politics is the fact that most recent governors have generally been from the population centers of western Oregon, particularly the Willamette Valley and, more recently, the I-5 corridor. That is to say, the governor of Oregon has come from the region of the state that contains the vast majority of Oregon residents and is considered the most progressive. Despite this heritage it is difficult to categorize many of the recent governors as being ardent champions of progressive legislation.

In general, most recent Oregon governors have been moderates, whether elected as Republican or Democrat. While Oregon has been swept by the conflict between progressivism and conservative populism, the voters have been consistent in rejecting gubernatorial candidates who are not in the political middle. No recent governors could be classified as conservative populist. The last Republican governor, Vic Atiyeh, is considered to have been a moderate, pro-business leader. Of all recent governors, McCall was probably the most active reformer in the progressive tradition of Oregon

Table 9.2. Recent Oregon Governors

Governor	Years served	Hometown	Political experience
Mark Hatfield (Rep.)	1959–1967	Dallas	State legislator Secretary of state
Tom McCall (Rep.)	1967–1975	Portland	Secretary of state
Robert Straub (Dem.)	1975–1979	Eugene	State legislator State treasurer
Victor Atiyeh (Rep.)	1979–1987	Portland	State legislator
Neil Goldschmidt (Dem.)	1987–1991	Portland	Portland mayor U.S. Transportation secretary
Barbara Roberts (Dem.)	1991–1995	Portland	State legislator Secretary of state
John Kitzhaber (Dem.)	1995–2003	Roseburg	State legislator State Senate president
Ted Kulongoski (Dem.)	2003–present	Portland	State legislator Attorney general Supreme Court justice

policymaking. Yet he was a Republican. Though moderate, most of the other recent governors have tended to lean toward the progressive side.

Even though it is difficult to label other recent governors as being ardent champions of progressive ideals, their background from the Willamette Valley has certainly influenced their outlooks. Most modern Oregon governors have come to office with an urban political perspective, which has caused them to be particularly attentive to the needs and problems facing those Oregonians living in the relatively dense populations of Oregon cities and suburbs. Conversely, Oregon governors often do not have extensive direct experience with the political culture of the less densely settled parts of Oregon. (See table 9.2.) Consequently, governors are often less well-acquainted with the needs and concerns of loggers, fishermen, coastal farmers, and other groups from these areas. The one exception to this may be Kitzhaber, who is from the southern Oregon community of Roseburg.

In addition to having roots in the Willamette Valley, all recent governors have come to office with some previous political experience. Many, in particular, have served in the Legislative Assembly. While this experience often leaves the governor with a good understanding of how the legislative process works, it does not necessarily provide the governor with a clear picture of the executive branch and the political skills needed to function outside the halls of the capitol.

The ability of Oregon governors to control Oregon politics has been limited in the past, and the office does not seem likely to become more powerful, at least in the foreseeable future. Many of the structural characteristics that limit the governor's influence, including the separation of powers and the use of plural executives, are deeply entrenched in the state's political system and will not be altered. Moreover, some of the main political factors that have weakened the governor do not appear likely to change either. The Oregon party system shows no sign of resurgence. It seems unlikely that initiative sponsors will soon quit using initiatives to press for change.

But even more important, the constraints placed on the governor because of having a different constituency base from that of the Legislative Assembly are not likely to go away overnight. Future governors will continue to have to grapple with a population and a legislature that are split between progressives and conservative populists. It is possible that the state may not confront divided government in the near future and that someone will be elected governor who is especially adept at leading. Yet it is unlikely that the split between progressives and conservative populists will vanish anytime soon. Hence, Oregon governors are likely to continue to find considerable resistance to major new policy proposals, no matter their party or their ideology. Moreover, the governor's office is likely to continue to play a constrained leadership role.

CHAPTER TEN

Bureaucracy

Douglas F. Morgan

During the past decade Oregonians placed nearly two dozen petitions on the ballot to circumscribe the discretionary authority of their administrative agencies.[1] Most of these measures failed, but in November 2000 the voters passed Measure 7 by a 53 percent to 47 percent margin. Although overturned by the state supreme court in October 2002, this measure would have emasculated state and local agencies by requiring "fair market" compensation for any loss in property value resulting from state and local regulatory actions. In 2004 a revised version of the Measure 7 initiative was again on the ballot for voter approval. Ironically, while Oregonians continually seek to restrict the administrative discretion of their state agencies, they simultaneously have increased agency discretion to build and manage prisons, improve and expand the state transportation infrastructure, stimulate the economy, regulate the environment, and increase the minimum wage rate.

The contradictory attitude of Oregon citizens toward their state bureaucracy emanates from the deeply embedded conservative populist and progressive traditions that influence the state's political life. According to conservative populists, career administrators should play only an *instrumental* role by listening to what the people want, to be "on tap, not on top," and to exercise only the authority that is expressly given to them by the citizens. In practice, however, the bureaucracy plays an enormously active and *constitutive* role in producing the social, economic, and environmental conditions that have made Oregon unique. This constitutive role is a legacy of the progressive tradition, in which administrators play a leadership role in democratic governance through the application of their professional expertise, the accumulation and analysis of extensive information, and the exercise of wide discretion in formulating and implementing public policy.

This chapter examines how tensions from conservative populism and progressivism influence the organization and control of state administrative agencies. Initially, the chapter illustrates how these tensions influence the daily work that agencies perform on behalf of the citizens of the state. From there, it explains how these two different perspectives influence the character of the state's bureaucracy.

POPULIST AND PROGRESSIVE INFLUENCES

The state bureaucracy plays a very significant role in the daily lives of Oregonians. Figure 10.1 illustrates a bit more precisely what we mean when we speak of Oregon's bureaucracy. It includes approximately 40,000 employees, about 166 for every 10,000 residents, thirty-eighth in the country per capita.[2] The state bureaucracy is organized into six independent administrative structures overseen by six separately elected political officials: governor, superintendent of public instruction, treasurer, secretary of state, commissioner of labor, and attorney general. Together, these elected offices oversee more than two hundred separate agencies, commissions, and departments, most of which operate quite autonomously.

All Oregon state agencies face the common and very difficult task of reconciling the contradictory sets of expectations that grow out of Oregon's progressive and conservative populist traditions. The two following cases illustrate how these prominent political traditions help shape the bureaucracy.

THE DEPARTMENT OF ENVIRONMENTAL
QUALITY AND THE PROGRESSIVE TRADITION

The Department of Environmental Quality (DEQ) received a call from a Mr. Q complaining that the oil recycling business run by his neighbor Ms. P was polluting the environment.[3] Ms. P runs a small business that recycles used crank case oil collected from automobile repair shops. The DEQ staff frequently receive similar calls and typically respond by making a phone call to the business, a site visit, and a follow-up meeting with the neighbor. During these conversations the staff members use a variety of negotiating skills learned from professional training programs. Through these negotiations Ms. P agreed to change some of her storage practices to allay the neighbor's concerns. The DEQ staff assured Mr. Q and Ms. P that the operation was consistent with the law. However, Ms. P wanted

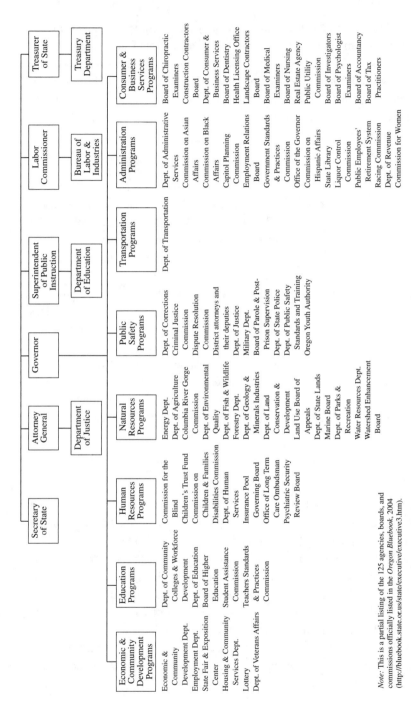

The following lists appear under each program heading in the organizational chart:

Economic & Community Development Programs
Economic & Community Development Dept.
Employment Dept.
State Fair & Exposition Center
Housing & Community Services Dept.
Lottery
Dept. of Veterans Affairs

Education Programs
Dept. of Community Colleges & Workforce Development
Dept. of Education
Board of Higher Education
Student Assistance Commission
Teachers Standards & Practices Commission

Human Resources Programs
Commission for the Blind
Children's Trust Fund Commission on Children & Families
Disabilities Commission
Dept. of Human Services
Insurance Pool Governing Board
Office of Long Term Care Ombudsman
Psychiatric Security Review Board

Natural Resources Programs
Energy Dept.
Dept. of Agriculture
Columbia River Gorge Commission
Dept. of Environmental Quality
Dept. of Fish & Wildlife
Forestry Dept.
Dept. of Geology & Minerals Industries
Dept. of Land Conservation & Development
Land Use Board of Appeals
Dept. of State Lands
Marine Board
Dept. of Parks & Recreation
Water Resources Dept.
Watershed Enhancement Board

Public Safety Programs
Dept. of Corrections
Criminal Justice Commission
Dispute Resolution Commission
District attorneys and their deputies
Dept. of Justice
Military Dept.
Board of Parole & Post-Prison Supervision
Dept. of State Police
Dept. of Public Safety Standards and Training
Oregon Youth Authority

Transportation Programs
Dept. of Transportation

Administration Programs
Dept. of Administrative Services
Commission on Asian Affairs
Commission on Black Affairs
Capitol Planning Commission
Employment Relations Board
Government Standards & Practices Commission
Office of the Governor
Commission on Hispanic Affairs
State Library
Liquor Control Commission
Public Employees' Retirement System
Racing Commission
Dept. of Revenue
Commission for Women

Consumer & Business Services Programs
Board of Chiropractic Examiners
Construction Contractors Board
Dept. of Consumer & Business Services
Board of Dentistry
Health Licensing Office
Landscape Contractors Board
Board of Medical Examiners
Board of Nursing
Real Estate Agency
Public Utility Commission
Board of Investigators
Board of Psychologist Examiners
Board of Accountancy
Board of Tax Practitioners

Top-level boxes: Secretary of State; Attorney General → Department of Justice; Governor; Superintendent of Public Instruction → Department of Education; Treasurer of State → Treasury Department; Labor Commissioner → Bureau of Labor & Industries.

Note: This is a partial listing of the 125 agencies, boards, and commissions officially listed in the *Oregon Bluebook, 2004* (http://bluebook.state.or.us/state/executive/executive3.htm).

Figure 10.1. Oregon Administrative Structure

more than informal assurances from the agency staff, so the agency head issued an official ruling that formally declared that the operation did not violate the law. In this case the law cited was Oregon Revised Statutes (ORS) 183.410.

After several years Ms. P modified her operation and Mr. Q complained again. After negotiations with Ms. P broke down, the agency determined that the oil recycling operation constituted a danger to public safety. The dispute, as called for by administrative procedures, went to a hearing, which resulted in a finding by the hearing officer that Ms. P's operation was in violation of state law (ORS 183.415).

The agency's decision to adopt the findings from the hearings was quite controversial because doing so would force the closure of many similar businesses in the state. However, many members of the public supported the ruling because it protected them and their businesses. Given the limited number of interest groups involved in the dispute, the agency decided to use the new "negotiated rule-making" authority that was created in 1997. The new process seeks to create consensus agreement of all the interested parties through formal participation in the rule-making activity (ORS 183.502). After a protracted process of discussions and compromise, facilitated by a neutral third party, the committee produced a proposed policy, which the agency decided to adopt as a final administrative rule. No one requested a formal hearing, so the agency simply put the rule into effect.

In this case the DEQ played a very active constitutive role in determining what public policy means in the daily lives of ordinary Oregonians. It relied on a combination of expertise in science, economics, and politics to create a workable solution that met the test of public acceptability. The DEQ and other administrative agencies are provided with a wide array of legal tools to accomplish their work, but these tools also severely constrain how the work is to be done both substantively and procedurally. This is true whether the agency handles child custody cases, social service eligibility, regulatory violations, land-use approval, pollution mitigation, habitat and wildlife protection, transportation planning, or licensing requests. In all of these instances administrative agencies seek to use the progressive tradition's reliance on bureaucratic expertise and discretionary authority to exercise a leadership role in solving state problems, but they must also operate within clearly defined boundaries of democratic accountability. The following case illustrates how these boundaries of democratic accountability may quickly change for administrators.

LAND-USE PLANNING AND THE POPULIST TRADITION

While Oregon's progressive tradition has led to an emphasis on bureaucratic expertise and discretionary authority, the bureaucracy is also affected by the state's populist tradition. Increasingly, administrators must adjust to the growing activism of conservative populists. The passage of Measure 7 in 2000 is an excellent example of how Oregon's populist tradition can affect the bureaucracy.

Measure 7 grew out of a conservative populist movement in the late 1980s to place limits on state and federal regulations affecting natural resource and land development. One critical target for those seeking to restrict the impact of Oregon's progressive environmental policies was the land-use planning system.

Oregon's land-use law, based on Senate bill 100, which Governor McCall pushed through the legislature in 1973, created the first comprehensive land-use planning law in the nation. Oregon progressives consider it a premier example of how government can strike a socially beneficial balance between social and individual interests.[4] Conservative populists view such regulations, whose costs are generally absorbed by property owners, as a direct attack on fundamental American liberties. The bureaucracy is caught in the middle, since it is obligated to implement the law in face of powerful political and legal attacks.

Fundamental elements of Oregon's planning system include 1) the State Land Conservation and Development Commission (LCDC), which develops and amends the basic goals and rules for state and local planning; 2) provisions for public participation in the rules process and for affected landowners to be notified and to have the opportunity to participate in decision making; 3) the creation of comprehensive city and county plans that include "urban growth boundaries," which can change only through a public process and beyond which growth is severely restricted; and 4) policies that encourage regional cooperation, transportation planning, resource land protection through tax incentives, and transportation planning. In response to complaints by a powerful coalition of development interests and rural resource users, the legislature established the Land Use Board of Appeals (LUBA) to handle appeals of LCDC decisions before they can go to the courts.[5]

In the simplest terms possible, the acres in Oregon have been categorized and can be used only in ways allowed for by their designation. Generally, planning programs are developed and managed by county or city agency officials who use their expertise to judge how and when to tailor LCDC guidelines to specific local conditions. The LCDC develops and adjusts the basic state rules for planning, and the LUBA handles appeals from those dissatisfied with local policies or decisions.

Landowners who feel the government illegitimately restricts their development rights find the open planning and appeals process more frustrating than fair if their personal goals conflict with the government's purposes. Accordingly, they have increasingly turned to the courts and the initiative system for relief.

The conservative populist movement to radically alter Oregon's planning process crystallized in a conflict between a hardware store owner and the City of Tigard. The battle began in 1987, when the owner of A-Boy Plumbing in Tigard asked the city for permission to expand her store. The city told the owner, Florence Dolan, that she could expand the store if she would set aside part of her property for drainage and a bike trail. Dolan offered to sell the land to the city for fourteen thousand dollars. When her offer was rejected, Dolan then fought the city through the State Land Use Board, the Oregon Court of Appeals, the Oregon Supreme Court, and eventually all the way to the United States Supreme Court. Ultimately, the U.S. Supreme Court ruled in the 1994 *Dolan v. Tigard* decision that the city had used an inappropriate standard in deciding to take a part of Dolan's property as a condition for allowing her improvements. This case remains a landmark in the federal judicial trend to expand the impact of the Fifth Amendment's requirement that landowners be provided "just" compensation when a government takes their land.

For Tigard, the loss was expensive. The city had to compensate Dolan for lost use of her land plus the much greater costs of her litigation as well as the city's own costs relating to the suit.[6] Dolan's victory vindicated those who felt that Tigard, and many other governments and their agencies, overreach their constitutional powers.

Oregonians in Action, which had provided Dolan with about $100,000 in legal aid, sought to build on this success to promote a broader public reevaluation of Oregon's regulations. When Oregonians in Action helped to qualify Measure 7 for the ballot in 2000, they used Dolan's story to build voter support. The story was appealing because it conveyed the conservative populist idea that the government bureaucracy was unconcerned about citizens and their tax money.

In the voters' guide in that election, the Dolans contributed the following statement in support of Measure 7: "We support Measure 7 because it will cut down on endless litigation like ours. If Measure 7 would have been in place in 1987, the City would have purchased our land for $14,000, instead of fighting us every step of the way and eventually wasting one and a half million of your hard earned dollars. Please vote yes on Measure 7."[7]

With this appeal and with many progressive leaders focused on fighting other initiatives on the ballot, Measure 7 passed.

Dolan's successful appeal to the U.S. Supreme Court resulted in the establishment of a new and stricter standard of review by administrators who are involved in taking private property for public purposes.[8] At the time of Dolan's request for a permit to expand her business in 1987, Tigard administrators had little doubt that they were properly exercising their authority under state land-use law.[9] In *Dolan v. Tigard* city administrators lost a significant land-use battle; if Measure 7 had become law, state and local agencies would have found their discretion to implement laws severely circumscribed by their limited budgets. It is likely the sentiments and policy issues of Measure 7 will strongly influence Oregon politics in the future; therefore, it deserves a bit more attention.

The key provisions of Measure 7 included that 1) property owners should be paid "just compensation equal to the reduction in fair market value to their property" that occurs as a result of any state or local regulation that restricts the use of their property; 2) "historical and commonly recognized nuisance laws" are not affected if they are narrowly construed; 3) the law does not apply when governments are minimally implementing required federal laws; and 4) the law does not apply to regulations regarding pornography, controlled substances and alcohol, or gaming.[10]

Although Measure 7 and most other property-rights reform proposals would not forbid regulations that affect property use, the expenses of compensation for extensive programs would prohibit far-reaching programs such as Oregon's land-use planning system. Property rights activists hold that this is as it should be, arguing it is wrong for individuals to bear the burden for broad community benefits. Their concerns go beyond regulations; they are also angry over the use of the power of eminent domain, where governments actually take land outright for "public uses." Their arguments are bolstered by cases where governments condemn property only to transfer it to other private interests, such as when housing or farm properties are condemned in order to allow for large-scale commercial developments.[11]

Unfortunately for property rights activists, Oregon initiatives are permitted to affect only one section of the constitution, and since the provision regarding properties involved in pornography related to the Fourth Amendment, to free speech, and to press rights, the court struck down the measure.

Measure 7 may have been overturned but the conservative populist sentiment and political interests behind it are a permanent part of Oregon's political system. This is reflected in a revised version of Measure 7 that passed in 2004 as Measure 37. The next few sections demonstrate how this populist influence consistently triumphs over Oregon's latent progressive concern that public administrators exercise their professional expertise independently in their work.

POLITICAL CONTROL OF THE OREGON BUREAUCRACY

Political oversight of the state bureaucracy reflects Oregon's long tradition of nonpartisanship and weak party control, and its populist desire for decentralized authority. Two long-time career administrators observed that they had never been asked their party affiliation in more than twenty years of public service, even when appointed by the governor to serve at the highest and most trusted levels of government.[12] A former director of the Department of Administrative Services, Jon Yunker, observed that most elected officials take a "Driving Miss Daisy" attitude toward the bureaucracy: they want the ride to go smoothly, they do not want any surprises, and they do not want rapid acceleration. In short, elected officials have reflected the attitude of the general citizenry, which does not want the bureaucracy to take excessive risks with its tax dollars and wants good, reliable service at an affordable price.[13]

Former governor Barbara Roberts believes these conditions helped to make Oregon's career public service among the best in the nation. Because they are kept out of partisan political battles and because legislators have respected the neutral advice they get, administrative agencies have played a powerful role in shaping the public policy initiatives that have made Oregon famous. Roberts sees that this could change. For example, she speculates that in the 1990s, term limits led to having legislators who increasingly relied on the expertise of paid lobbyists.[14]

The sheer number and independence of Oregon agencies makes it difficult for governors to control the bureaucracy. Figure 10.1 captures the breadth and depth of this complexity and independence. Each of the six separately elected state officials is in charge of an independent set of administrative structures and processes. The governor appoints only 32 of the 136 agency and commission directors.[15]

Governors and other elected executives gain some special power because they not only appoint department heads but also have controlling influence over the appointment of the "deputy of each division within a department of state government" and all "principal assistants and deputies"(ORS 240.205). But most of the 136 agencies are beyond the political reach of the governor's direct authority because they are governed by independent commissions whose chair and members are appointed for fixed and usually staggered terms, with the advice and consent of the Senate.

ORGANIZATIONAL STRUCTURE AND CONTROL

One of the unusual features of the Oregon state bureaucracy is the diversity of organizational structures, which reflects the contradictory influences of conservative populism and progressivism. Even in its original form, the Oregon Constitution featured populist aspects, as it sought to protect the interests of farmers and small businessmen from the emerging corporate power of railroads and banks, while also trying to keep governors and other potential centers of political power in check. The current system of bureaucratic control developed piecemeal over time as the legislature and voters considered how the state should respond to diverse and specific issues, often creating progressive programs with conservative populist management controls. The following examples of Oregon's three most prominent models for organizing administrative agencies illustrate the influence of both of these commitments.

Exclusive Control by the Governor

The Department of Administrative Services (DAS) is one of the few agencies created explicitly to work on behalf of the governor. Today's DAS was created in 1993, completing a long period in which diverse management agencies were consolidated and centralized bit by bit.[16] The DAS reflects Oregon's strong progressive commitment to the efficient and effective management of the public's business through reliance on professional expertise and technical competence.

The mission of the (DAS) is "to improve the efficient and effective use of state resources" through the provision of centrally provided services and systems, including purchasing, fleet, personnel, management information, and budgeting and finance (ORS 184.305). Despite its progressive mission, the DAS is vulnerable to populist control because the governor can very directly influence the agency's leadership.

The DAS is one of the very few state agencies that explicitly provides that the governor "may assume the office of director of the department whenever and for whatever time the Governor deems advisable" (ORS 184.315). While there are a handful of agencies, like the Department of Human Services (ORS 409.100) and the Department of Transportation, where the directors work at the "pleasure of the governor," these appointments still require the advice and consent of the Senate. This is not the case with the DAS.

Strong Commissions Having Weak Governor Control

Most state agencies in Oregon are not like the DAS but reflect Oregon's commitment to conservative populism, with its distrust of government and its emphasis on citizen control of and access to governance institutions. Most commissions operate with five to seven members, appointed by the governor, and serve two- to six-year usually staggered terms. These appointments provide the governor some influence but much less than when he or she directly selects the director.

For example, when appointing members to their four-year terms on the Oregon Transportation Commission, the governor must consider geographical distribution and receive Senate consent. Furthermore, no more than three members can belong to the same political party (ORS 184.612). The Oregon Transportation Commission has far-reaching policy authority because it is required by statute to "develop and maintain a state transportation policy" and has the "general power to coordinate and administer programs relating to highways, motor vehicles, public transit, transportation safety." (ORS 184.617–8). Accordingly, the director of the transportation commission has a very subordinate role to the commission. In fact, the statute charges the director with the responsibility of preparing and submitting implementation programs to the commission for approval.

Compared with the Department of Transportation, the Department of Veterans' Affairs (DVA) is under much greater administrative control by the governor. The department has a nine-member advisory committee, which has only the authority to make recommendations. However, there is an unusual provision in the law, one that requires the governor to have "the written approval of the Advisory Committee" (ORS 406.210) before making an appointment of a new director. This provision once prevented Governor Goldschmidt from filling a vacancy after pressuring the director to resign.

Not favoring a change, the advisory committee simply exercised its statutory veto over a new appointment.

Independent Commissions Having Little Governor Control

Most of the Oregon's administrative agencies are controlled by very independent commissions. The Racing Commission and the Liquor Control Commission demonstrate how the commission structure can frustrate centralized control by the governor or the legislature. The Oregon Racing Commission consists of five members appointed for four-year terms by the governor, with the advice and consent of the Senate. The governor may remove any commissioner "for inefficiency, neglect of duty, or misconduct in office" only after a public hearing and ten days' notice (ORS 462.230). Complex detailed steps in the removal process further limit gubernatorial efforts to control the commission membership for partisan or policy purposes.

The Oregon Liquor Control Commission is even more independent of the governor. The commission consists of five members appointed for four-year terms, with no more than three persons chosen from the same party. The governor designates one person to serve as chair. But the law provides that the commission "shall appoint an administrator who shall serve at its discretion. The administrator shall be subject to policy direction by the commissioners, and shall be the secretary of the commission and custodian of commission records" (ORS 471.705–710).

The overall pattern of Oregon's administrative structure reflects a commitment to the conservative populist tradition of decentralized control, with a secondary emphasis on progressive concerns for efficiency and effectiveness. This pattern was established early in Oregon's history with the creation of the first predecessors of the state's existing administrative agencies (Fish and Wildlife, 1878; Department of Transportation, 1913). The pattern continued as the state took on increasing regulatory and social welfare responsibilities after the turn of the century and into the New Deal (Labor and Industries, 1903; Department of Forestry, 1907; Public Utility Commission, 1915; Public Welfare Commission, 1934). The commission model was also favored in the 1960s and 1970s, when each significant political constituency sought to have its own commission to provide oversight of its interests. These more recent commissions include the Asian Affairs Commission, 1995; Black Affairs Commission, 1983; Commission on Women, 1964; numerous product promotions commissions, such as the cherry commission, hazelnut commission, and fescue seed commission; and the professional self-regulatory commissions, such as those for teachers, radiologists, and dentists. The numerous populist commissions create an administrative system in which the governor's ability to control agencies for either policy or managerial ends is limited.[17]

Besides relying on political and organizational controls to ensure the popular accountability of administrative agencies, the United States has become famous for developing an entirely new system of control: administrative law. The purpose of this separate body of law is to structure the exercise of administrative discretion through a set of laws governing how rules are made and, more generally, how administrators may use their power to influence public policy. This section explores some of the more important dimensions of Oregon's administrative law system and how the state's populist tradition has influenced its practice.

Administrative Rule Making and Adjudication

Administrators need to make policy choices, or discretionary judgments, to implement policies. One of the more difficult problems in modern government is how to bind administrators to the rule of law system when the basic laws created by the legislative branch cannot possibly anticipate all of the circumstances and conditions administrators face. Administrative rule making is the process for accomplishing this "gap-filling" role.

After World War II the federal government and all of the states began to adopt guidelines that administrators must follow when developing the detailed rules and procedures to be used in implementing broad legislation. In the DEQ and land-use planning cases at the beginning of this chapter, all the steps taken by administrators were carefully spelled out in a set of guidelines known as the Oregon Administrative Procedures Act (APA). This act was adopted in 1957 and has been significantly revised in subsequent legislative sessions. The provisions of Oregon's APA are set forth in ORS, chapter 183.[18] They outline the procedures for the making of agency rules, how and when the rules shall be published, how contested cases shall be conducted, and how hearings officers are to conduct proceedings. A new section on alternative dispute resolution was adopted in 1997. The act also includes provisions for judicial review of agency action. These administrative rule-making procedures have been described by one of the leading legal scholars as "one of the greatest inventions of modern government."[19]

At the heart of the administrative rule-making process is the principle of "notice and comment," which requires agencies to notify citizens when they consider developing or changing an agency policy, procedure, or practice that "substantially affects the interests of the public." The agency must include a statement of the need for the rule and how the rule meets the need. But the need does not have to be documented. The "need" contemplated by ORS 183.335(2)(b)(C) is the need "that the rule-proposing agency *perceives*."[20] This "burden of proof" standard is far less than what is required of federal agencies, which must meet the test of "substantial evidence based on the record taken as a whole."[21]

During the rule-making process citizens can comment on the proposed rule, and the agency is required to keep a record of all submitted materials. All proposed or adopted rules are required to be published in a monthly publication, called the *Oregon Bulletin*.[22] The administrative rule-making process serves three key objectives of our broader "checks and balances" system: 1) to obtain useful information that broadens and deepens an understanding of a problem and its possible solutions, 2) to legitimate the processes of governance by providing notice and opportunities for participation, and 3) to provide a check against the arbitrary and capricious exercise of governmental authority.

One of the unusual features of Oregon's administrative rule-making process is the definition of a rule. This is critically important because rules provide employees with guidelines on what policy means, how to set priorities, and how to interpret and apply their discretionary authority. For example, if the director of the state police issues a directive that makes countering drug trafficking a higher priority than the recovery of stolen property, is the director engaged in rule making? Or consider, for example, the simple question of whether a state Department of Environmental Quality (DEQ) administrator in Burns, Oregon, can allow a solid-waste operator to cover disposed debris with dirt only once a week in contrast to a DEQ administrator in the Portland metropolitan area who may require debris to be covered daily. The amount of debris, the density of the population, and the prevailing winds may create quite different health hazards at the two separate sites. Where is the line between administrative rule making and routine management oversight and control?

Oregon's Administrative Procedures Act APA defines "rule" very broadly to include "directive, standards, regulation or statements of general applicability that implements, interprets or prescribes law or policy or describes procedure or practice requirements of any agency." Although interagency or internal statements, regulations, or directives that do not "substantially affect the interests of the public" are excepted, this very inclusive definition means that Oregon agencies have very little discretion in deciding what is a rule and what is not a rule (ORS 183.310). The result is that agencies must follow rule-making procedures in all cases where practices and policies "substantially affect the interests of the public."[23] This contrasts sharply with the United States APA, which draws a clear distinction between substantive/procedural rules and interpretive rules (which are exempt from rule-making requirements).[24] As a consequence, in the state police and DEQ examples cited above, the directors of both state agencies would have to follow rule-making requirements that can be avoided by federal agency officials.

Oregon's far-reaching requirement to use the formal rule-making process rather than internal management guidelines and interpretive rules creates some unintended consequences.[25] Because Oregon administrators have little discretion to formally accommodate local conditions and special circumstances, agencies sometimes appear rigid and bureaucratic. Second, agencies have adopted a variety of techniques to avoid the extra expense and time delay (two to five months) of making rules. For example, some agencies distinguish between "employee guidelines" and "policies." The former are considered supervision and management issues, thus avoiding the need for rule making. Finally, many agency informal rules and procedures are never officially promulgated according to the procedures outlined in ORS, chapter 183. Some small agencies simply lack the staff necessary to follow all the rule-making procedures. For others, it is worth the risk of operating with unpromulgated rules in order to save money, preserve managerial discretion, and provide geographic flexibility. Agencies vary in their motivation to write rules. For example, the Department of Corrections has a well-organized constituency who will readily sue the department if there is the slightest departure from required rule-making protocols. The attorney general provides "Model Rules" to assist agencies in formulating rules and to promote uniformity in the nature and style of their rules.[26]

Despite their variation, state agencies are much more accountable for their practices, rules, and rule making than Oregon's cities, counties, local school boards, and many special district governments. Except in land-use planning, local governments very rarely promulgate their administrative rules, procedures, and practices through any formal process. In the rare cases where public rule making is used, locating the final rules may be difficult.

Oregon provides citizens with numerous points of access to information and the rule-making process, but citizens rarely use these access points.[27] Few individuals show up at hearings on proposed rules as is allowed by state law (ORS 183.335). Citizens rarely use their right to petition an agency to adopt, amend, or repeal any rule (ORS 183.390). Interested parties to a rule-making process frequently do not use their right to automatically stop the process for no less than twenty-one and no more than ninety days by simply making a request of the agency (ORS 183.335(4)). Citizens do not use their right to request the Legislative Counsel to review any existing or proposed rule to determine the rule's constitutionality and whether the agency is authorized to make such a rule (ORS 183.720). Citizens seldom invoke their right to request a public hearing on a rule-making process (ORS 183.335). Finally, citizens do not often turn to the judiciary to influence the rule-making process. The judicial options include getting their names on the attorney general's rule-making notification list, filing a direct action on a promulgated rule in the court of appeals, challenging a rule during a contested case hearing, and asking for a declaratory judgment against a rule.

In 1997 the legislature added an additional "populist" provision that requires agencies to notify the legislature of all administrative rule-making activities (ORS 183.335(14)(15)). The potentially invasive impact of this provision in micromanaging the affairs of an agency can be largely avoided by refraining from rule-making activities during the legislative session.

In addition to rule making, Oregon administrative agencies frequently perform the same function as courts in their adjudicative role in deciding individual cases. For example, whenever an agency revokes a license from a driver or any professional possessing a license to practice, or removes children from the custody of parents, or revokes a person's parole or probation, the agency is engaged in administrative adjudication. It is deciding the outcome of an individual case by applying and interpreting existing rules rather than by developing new rules. Oregon's Administrative Procedures Act (ORS 183.413–470) sets forth the guidelines that administrators are required to follow when engaged in these "contested case" or adjudicative activities. The decisions made by administrators under these guidelines create an administrative common law within an agency.

SOME PROGRESSIVE TRENDS

Oregon has introduced some important progressive changes in recent years. For example, Oregon's administrative agencies have been at the forefront of the nationwide trend for measuring the results and outcomes of administrative programs. Government accountability and efficiency are areas where conservative populists and progressives may converge because they both agree on the need to improve public service and reduce government costs. Disenchantment with traditional measurements of administrative processes, such as counting the number of clients served or the number of applications processed, led the Oregon legislature to take a bold step in 1989 and create the Oregon Progress Board.

The new agency was charged with keeping Oregonians focused on the future by developing and implementing a state strategic plan for achieving the following three goals: 1) quality jobs, 2) safe, caring, and engaged communities, and 3) a healthy, sustainable environment. These goals are organized into seven areas with ninety quality-of-life indicators that are measured and reported on annually.[28] This performance-based program is referred to as "Oregon Benchmarks." During the first years of its existence (1989–1997), the Oregon benchmarking process was primarily used as a policy tool to harness the multiple streams of city, county, and state agency spending and program activities to a set of commonly shared goals. In 1997 the legislature made the board a permanent part of state government and began to use the benchmarking process increasingly as a management tool to shape state agency performance. In 2001 the legislature transferred the board into the Department of Administrative Services, thus ensuring increasing penetration of the benchmarking process into the operational planning of all agency activities. Agencies must now undertake benchmark-based planning, budgeting, and development of their management systems. The first annual reporting of these performance measures was successfully delivered in January 2004.

There is some evidence that this shift in focus from policy inputs to social outcomes may improve program effectiveness. In a study done for the Milbank Memorial Fund, Howard M. Leichter and Jeffrey Tryens found that Oregon exceeded the nation in its improvement in some benchmarks (such as reductions in infant mortality) but fell farther behind the national average in others (change in number of abused children, for example). Still, the study praised how the benchmark system has promoted common understandings and trust between agencies and local governments regarding how to measure and improve social well-being.[29]

Benchmarking has also promoted alternate perspectives on how to solve social problems. For example, the system led state and local officials to consider how changing practices in both the private and public health systems can improve prenatal conditions rather than simply recommending a system based on state-administered regulations or spending. In this sense Oregon Benchmarks, with its broad approach to social-quality measuring, may allow for more emphasis on private approaches to solving social problems, something conservative populists value.

Agency productivity is also encouraged through a separate special Productivity Improvement Revolving Fund, administered by the Department of Administrative Services. This fund is used for "making loans, grants, and matching funds or cash awards available to state agencies or units for implementation of productivity improvement projects" (ORS 182.375). The program is relatively small, with a balance of $700,695 in September 2002. Many of the programs center on upgrading technology or information systems, such as an eighty-five-thousand-dollar grant to the Department of Agriculture for developing scalable intranet applications.[30] There are no distinct programs for punishing agencies for inefficiencies, though the tightening budget provides politicians and administrators with incentives for finding wasteful practices.

The state has also taken steps to tighten bureaucratic ethics and accountability by placing restrictions on conflicts of interests. These conflicts are broadly defined to include using one's official position or personal knowledge for private gain. Conflicts of interest are discouraged by prohibitions against certain departing administrators working for agencies as lobbyists or consultants within a specified period of time and against public employees accepting funds or gifts. Public officials must also disclose assets and business and personal relationships that may conflict with their official duties.[31]

Finally, Oregon has been innovative in its efforts to use formal, consensus-based approaches to create rules and negotiate disputes after rules have been made.[32] The key to the process is the use of an impartial third party to facilitate discussion among the interested parties and to find appropriate solutions. Once begun, the parties commit to abiding by the results of the process, although any party has the right to withdraw from participation while the process continues. The purposes of collaborative rule making are four-fold: 1) to reduce the time, money, and effort expended on developing and enforcing rules, 2) to reduce the time for policy implementation, 3) to create higher compliance, and 4) to develop more cooperative relationships between agencies and the parties affected by agency rules and policies.

Agencies that have used collaborative decision making and negotiated dispute resolution have found the process beneficial. A few agencies have been reluctant to use this new statutory authority, believing it creates pressures to accept a result that may not be in the larger public interest. Others believe that the existing rule-making process can accomplish the same results.[33]

ENDURING ISSUES AND CONFLICTS

The history of Oregon's administrative processes might be read as the simple story of democracy triumphing over bureaucracy. Beneath the surface, however, is a deep and abiding tension between three competing responsibilities the bureaucracy has in maintaining Oregon's democratic health: 1) being responsive to public wishes and preferences, 2) providing efficient and effective administration, and 3) supporting the political policy objectives of elected officials. The impact of these tensions is indicated in *Governing Magazine*'s assigning a grade of C+ to Oregon for its overall government performance, with nine states receiving lower grades. The report notes how Oregon's grades are strongly influenced by the impact of conservative populist efforts to restrict state and local revenues, as well as problems in its information technology system.[34]

The importance Oregonians place on having a bureaucracy that is directly responsive to the will of the citizens is demonstrated by the numerous independent commissions, the many access points citizens have to the bureaucracy, and the strong open meetings laws. But these populist-appearing processes can be misleading. For example, the attorney general interprets Oregon's open meetings law to require that government business be conducted openly, not that there be high levels of participation.[35] This interpretation recognizes the importance of efficient and effective public agencies, a hallmark of the state's progressive heritage. This concern for efficiency and effectiveness is echoed in Oregon's productivity and benchmarking legislation, in its ethics law, in its use of negotiated dispute resolution, and in its design of the Department of Administrative Services.

A review of the role of administrative agencies in Oregon state government reveals a deep disjunction between the "espoused theory" of democratic governance and a "theory in action." The espoused theory is quite hostile to the bureaucracy, but the "theory in action" places administrative agencies at the very center of implementing all of the good things that many Oregonians take the most pride in—the bottle bill, beach protection, medical insurance for the poor, clean air and water, community policing, watershed restoration, effective transportation, and dozens of other similar services that produce a high quality of life.

One of the yet unresolved issues is what role the bureaucracy will play in the future of Oregon politics. Increasing economic and demographic growth, declining revenue sources, term limits, the globalization of the economy, mandated federalism, and rising regulatory requirements are a recipe for increasing citizen frustration and demands for more responsive mechanisms of governance. Will the Oregon bureaucracy continue to succeed in using its administrative tools to strike an acceptable balance between its instrumental role in executing the popular will and its constitutive role in effectively conducting its duties? Most of the tools are in place to enable the bureaucracy to succeed, including the authority to use advisory committees, collaborative dispute resolution, and negotiated rule making. If these tools become widely used, the future looks bright for the central role the bureaucracy can play in Oregon's unusual system of democratic governance.

CHAPTER ELEVEN

Judiciary

James C. Foster

When the Lloyd Center, a large indoor shopping mall, was built in Portland, Oregon, in the 1960s, it represented a novel approach to commercial development. Covering fifty acres, with a perimeter of one-and-a-half miles, the Lloyd Center originally included some sixty commercial tenants and an ice-skating rink. On November 14, 1968, Donald M. Tanner and several others were in the mall distributing invitations to a meeting of the "Resistance Community" to protest the draft and the Vietnam War. Responding to a customer complaint, security guards employed by the Lloyd Corporation informed Tanner and his colleagues that they were trespassing on private property and would be arrested if they did not leave. Tanner and his colleagues left.

The antiwar activists then filed suit in the United States District Court for the District of Oregon, claiming their ejection from the Lloyd Center violated their right to distribute handbills in the mall, a right protected under the First Amendment to the United States Constitution. Tanner and his colleagues won their case, and when the Lloyd Corporation appealed, Tanner won again in the United States Ninth Circuit Court of Appeals. But Tanner lost in the United States Supreme Court. Writing for a five-to-four Court, Justice Lewis Powell wrote that under the First Amendment, property does not "lose its private character because the public is generally invited to use it for designated purposes."[1]

Almost twenty-one years after Donald Tanner was asked to leave the Lloyd Center premises, Lois Stranahan was arrested outside a Fred Meyer store in southeast Portland. Stranahan had been gathering signatures for initiatives concerning sales taxes and the rights of initiative petitioners. A Fred Meyer official asked her to leave. When Stranahan refused she was arrested by a Portland police officer.

Stranahan sued Fred Meyer in Oregon Circuit Court for false arrest. Her attorney argued, in effect, that the store's official had arrested her in violation of her rights under the Oregon Constitution. Fred Meyer replied by asking the judge to rule that Stranahan had no constitutional right to trespass on its private property. The circuit court agreed with Stranahan. When Fred Meyer appealed, the Oregon Court of Appeals also sided with Stranahan. For a divided court Judge William Riggs noted that "at the time of Stranahan's arrest, this court had recognized that petitioners have a right under Article I, section 8, of the Oregon Constitution, to gather signatures at the Lloyd Center."[2] The Oregon Supreme Court, however, reversed the appeal court's decision in 2000. In so doing, it did not base its decision on the U.S. Constitution but on a section of Oregon's constitution.[3]

JUDICIAL FEDERALISM

The third chapter of this book made the point that Oregon politics is affected not only by forces within the state but also by the federal government. The tale of these two Oregon court cases illustrates this fact. It is an account about judicial federalism. To understand the role of the courts in Oregon politics, it is valuable to begin by examining judicial federalism as well the state's constitution, because both provide the foundation upon which the state's judicial system is built. It is also important to look at judicial federalism because Oregon's judiciary has been at the forefront of the movement bringing it about.

Oregonians, like all Americans, hold dual citizenship. We are citizens of the United States and of our state. We live under two constitutions: the United States Constitution and the Oregon Constitution. We also are subject to the jurisdiction of a dual system of courts: the federal courts and the state courts. Judicial federalism refers to fact that there are two separate yet interrelated judicial systems.

The story of the two court cases shows the dual character of our political system. Tanner sued to vindicate rights he claimed under the First Amendment to the United States Constitution. Stranahan based her case on rights she claimed under Article I and Article IV of the Oregon Constitution. Tanner lost under the U.S. Constitution as interpreted by the U.S. Supreme Court. Stranahan's case was decided under the Oregon Constitution as interpreted by the Oregon Court of Appeals, and eventually the state supreme court.

How is it is possible for an Oregon court to differ with the U.S. Supreme Court with regard to exercising free speech, as the appellate court did, when the U.S. Constitution says that the Constitution and federal laws "shall be the supreme Law of the Land"? This situation is possible because the U.S. Supreme Court has interpreted the U.S. Constitution as permitting states to provide greater protection. The ability of Oregon to go beyond the U.S. Constitution was explained in a subsequent case, *Pruneyard Shopping Center v. Robins*. In that case the U.S. Supreme Court wrote that its reasoning in the Tanner decision "does not . . . limit the authority of the State to exercise its police power or its sovereign right to adopt in its own Constitution individual liberties more expansive than those conferred by the Federal Constitution."[4]

The two court cases demonstrate an important point. While we have emphasized the unusual character of Oregon politics throughout this book, Oregon politics is, in many respects, a variation on broader American patterns. With regard to rights protections, Oregon's constitution is both similar to the federal constitution and different. Tanner and Stranahan sought to exercise free speech rights—a guarantee all Americans cherish. Their particular exercise of free speech clashed with another cherished American right, private property. Nevertheless, unlike Tanner's tale, Stranahan's story was played out exclusively in Oregon courts, on Oregon constitutional terms.

OREGON'S ROLE IN JUDICIAL FEDERALISM

Why does the nation's political system allow this dual court system to exist? Why are some court decisions based on the U.S. Constitution and others based on state ones? There is nothing in the U.S. Constitution that explicitly establishes this dual system, and for many years state courts rarely turned to state constitutions when deciding cases involving individual rights. This was true even in cases in which the wording of state constitutional provisions were different from parallel provisions in the U.S. Constitution. Thus, in a case such as Stranahan's, the courts would not have turned to the state constitution in years past but would have looked no further than the First Amendment of the U.S. Constitution to reach a decision. Why were state constitutions ignored? It is difficult to say, though some legal scholars argue that the courts thought that either the wording differences between state and federal constitution were unimportant or that the two constitutions needed to be treated uniformly.[5]

Beginning in the 1970s, however, a number of legal scholars began to argue that state courts ought to rely on their state constitutions in protecting individual rights, rather than looking only toward the federal constitution.

Among the leaders of this movement was Hans Linde, a University of Oregon Law School professor, who was appointed to the Oregon Supreme Court in 1976. In a series of articles and court decisions, Linde wrote that state constitutions should not be ignored and, more importantly, that judges should look first at state constitutional protections before turning to the U.S. Constitution. In one of his most quoted statements, Linde wrote "a lawyer today representing someone who claims constitutional protection and who does not argue that the state constitution provides that protection is skating on the edge of malpractice."[6]

Linde's work helped spawn a national revolution of sorts, helping to revitalize state constitutions and encouraging judges to turn to their own state constitutions for deciding cases. To be sure, not all states have adopted this "new judicial federalism." In fact, some studies indicate that most states, except a few more liberal ones, have continued to rely primarily on U.S. Supreme Court decisions in rights cases.[7] Even so, Linde's efforts helped offer a new tool for state courts to use to protect individual rights while moving Oregon to the forefront of this new movement.[8] Linde was such an important figure among legal scholars that he was considered one of the nation's top state court judges of the twentieth century, before retiring in 1990.[9]

Finally, it is important to recognize that Linde's leadership in new judicial federalism was in many ways consistent with the state's progressive heritage. Judicial federalism was innovative, and it offered an alternative way for state courts to protect civil rights and liberties at a time when the U.S. Supreme Court was becoming less willing to use the federal constitution to protect those rights and liberties.

THE EVOLVING CONSTITUTION

What is it that has made Oregon's constitution different from the broader American pattern? To a large degree the differences in the state's constitution reflect the state's progressive heritage and, more recently, the importance of conservative populism within the polity. When the constitution was originally written, it was influenced by the political concerns of the Jacksonian Democrats, who controlled a majority at the constitutional convention. The content of the constitution began to see considerable change, however, with the rise of the Progressive movement and the introduction of the initiative process. Since the initiative was introduced, progressives and conservative populists, as well as other actors, have used the process to reshape the state's constitution. Initially, many of the constitutional reforms adopted through the initiative were tied to the Progressive movement. Since then political activists in the state have repeatedly used these resources to put their stamp on the constitution.

The Progressive movement, which began in the 1890s, was led by William U'Ren and Republican Jonathan Bourne Jr. In 1902 the reformers were able to get the state constitution amended for the first time since 1859, adding the initiative and referendum. A recall amendment was added in 1908. Combined, these reforms became known as the "Oregon System." In the decade immediately after these reforms were enacted, as the Progressive movement was breaking apart, an alliance between the Ku Klux Klan, the Federation of Patriotic Societies, and the American Protective Association dominated Oregon politics. In 1922 the Klan and the Federation of Patriotic Societies, along with the Scottish Rite Masons, sponsored an anti-Catholic initiative to compel all children to attend public schools. The law, which was adopted by voters in 1922, was eventually nullified by the U.S. Supreme Court as a violation of the due process clause of the Fourteenth Amendment.[10] Yet the proposal represented one of the first in a long line of efforts by the state's conservative side to use initiatives to champion its ideals.

Adoption of the Oregon System made Oregon's constitution, like those in many other states, highly mutable. In other words the constitution is subject to frequent change. The initiative can be used in eighteen states to amend their respective constitutions. The result is that state constitutions in these states have become long and detailed and perhaps less understandable. Over the past 212 years the U.S. Constitution has been amended only 27 times. As of 1998 the fifty state constitutions had been amended more than 6,000.[11] In this regard Oregon's constitution is typical; since 1857 it has been amended more than 220 times.

OREGON VARIATIONS ON AMERICAN THEMES

In most respects Oregon's constitution resembles the U.S. Constitution and other state constitutions despite all of these amendments. It establishes the *fundamental law* for the state, outlines the formal structure of the state's government, specifies various procedures governing the state, and declares rights.

Yet in other respects Oregon's constitution is different. These differences can be seen not only in its treatment of free speech but in other areas as well. The state's treatment of religious freedom is another good example. Heated debate over the appropriate relation between religion and government is as American as apple pie. In Oregon, however, religion is the explicit subject of no less than five provisions of the state's Bill of Rights, and implicitly of a sixth. These provisions guarantee "freedom of worship" and "freedom of religious opinion." They also prohibit religious qualifications for elected office, the use of state money for religious purposes, and the use of religious tests for witnesses and jurors. The number of provisions is remarkable considering Oregon today has the highest proportion of residents (17 percent) in the nation who identify themselves as "nonreligious."[12]

The Oregonians who drafted the state's original constitution valued protecting religious exercise and thereby sought to use the constitution to wall off the spiritual realm from the sphere of government. The six provisions reflected their concern to protect, as Roger Williams, the seventeenth-century American clergyman put it, the divine "Garden of the Church" from the corrupt "Wilderness of the World." In the state's more secular environment today, this emphasis on religiosity has clearly changed, as most Oregonians would now probably stress the need to separate government from religion. As a result the Oregon Constitution continues to reflect the values of state citizens, even though the wording in these sections has not changed.

In more recent years the state's constitution has grown more distinct because of the broad spectrum of changes brought by initiative. Many of these changes have come through the efforts of conservative populist and progressive leaders. These changes include amendments severely limiting the state's power to tax, allowing adoptees to have access to their birth certificates, mandating the use of Vote by Mail in all state elections, creating term limits, allowing physician-assisted suicides, and requiring the government to compensate landowners when government regulations reduce property value.

Overall, then, what one finds is that the state's constitution has some similarities to those of other states and the U.S. Constitution but also some uniqueness onto itself, which reflects its political heritage.

THE ORGANIZATION OF THE JUDICIAL BRANCH

Oregon's judicial branch has three major levels: the supreme court, the court of appeals, and circuit courts. In addition, there are a number of less prominent lower courts (see figure 11.1). Each of these courts plays a different role within the judicial system, which is determined by the jurisdiction it has been granted by the state. Jurisdiction refers to the power

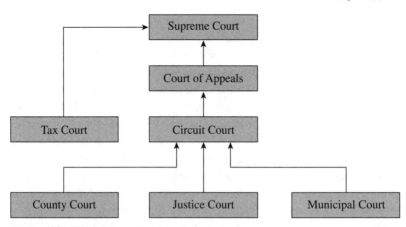

Figure 11.1. Oregon Court System

a court has to hear particular types of cases at particular times in the judicial process.

The jurists who occupy these various benches share similar qualifications. Each must be a citizen of the United States, a member of the Oregon Bar, and an Oregon resident for at least three years. Judges of the court of appeals also must be qualified to vote in the county where they live. With the exception of judges serving in Multnomah County, circuit court members also must reside in the judicial circuit where they preside. All Oregon jurists are elected on nonpartisan ballots for six-year terms.

Oregon Supreme Court

At the apex of the Oregon judiciary is the Oregon Supreme Court. The current court was created by an initiative adopted in November 1910. This Progressive Era measure significantly modified the original 1857 Judicial Department Article (VII) of the Oregon Constitution, making it more closely resemble the Judicial Article of the U.S. Constitution. An important exception is that the Oregon Constitution specifies that the justices on the supreme court and the judges on other courts "shall be elected by the legal voters of the state or of their respective districts." For federal courts, the president appoints jurists with the advice and consent of the Senate. The justices on the Oregon Supreme Court also elect one of their own to serve as chief justice.

The primary duty of the court is to serve as the state's court of last resort. As such, it mostly examines decisions handed down by the Oregon Court of Appeals. There are a few types of cases that can go directly to the supreme court without first going through the court of appeals. In particular, death penalty appeals go directly to the supreme court, as do rulings from the Oregon Tax Court. The supreme court also has *original jurisdiction* on some cases, which means that it has the power to hear those cases first. For example, the court hears challenges to the titles assigned to initiatives, as described in chapter 5. The court also has original jurisdiction on cases involving the redistricting of the state legislature.

The seven justices of the Oregon Supreme Court have broad discretion over their docket and can generally choose which cases they will review on appeal. The votes of three or more supreme court justices are required to allow a petition for review of a court of appeals decision. When the supreme court chooses not to consider a court of appeals decision, that lower court's resolution of the dispute becomes final. Overall, approximately four hundred to five hundred cases are filed with the supreme court every year.

The court also has some administrative duties. The chief justice oversees the Oregon Judicial Department, which means that he or she serves in the top management position for the entire state court system. The supreme court itself also determines who is admitted to the Oregon Bar, which allows it to control who can practice law in the state.

Oregon Court of Appeals

The Oregon Court of Appeals is just below the supreme court in the state's judicial hierarchy. The court of appeals is the busiest intermediate appellate court in the country, with more than four thousand mandated cases filed in 1999.[13] The court has jurisdiction over most civil and criminal appeals in the state. It also hears appeals of administrative agency actions. To manage its heavy caseload, the court is divided into three "departments" of three judges each, which is then assigned a group of cases.

The judges in each department have several options with regard to how they dispose of cases assigned to them. Most of the time the judges affirm the trial court outcome without writing a formal opinion. The department also can vote to reverse the trial court or to remand (return) the case to the trial court for further examination.

The Oregon Legislative Assembly created the court of appeals in 1969. Originally, it was a five-judge court. Membership was expanded to six judges in 1973 and to ten in 1977. The chief justice of the supreme court appoints a chief judge from among the ten members of the court of appeals.

Circuit Courts

Most court cases enter Oregon's judicial branch through the circuit courts. These are the state's trial courts of general jurisdiction, which means they have the authority to try most criminal and civil cases. Criminal cases are those in which an individual is charged by the government with violating the state's criminal law. These include charges of murder, kidnapping, or assault. In general, a civil case is a case between two or more private parties over an alleged violation of state civil laws. In some civil cases, however, the government can be one of the parties involved. Civil cases include contract disputes, divorce proceedings, and automobile injury claims. Cases involving tax law enter the court system through the Oregon Tax Court, however, rather than through the circuit courts.

All thirty-six counties in Oregon have their own circuit court. In total, there are 163 circuit judges statewide. In order to aid the administration of the courts, the state has divided the courts into twenty-six judicial districts. Most districts consist of one county, though in the less populated areas of the state, the districts are composed of more than one county. The chief justice of the Oregon Supreme Court appoints the presiding judge in each judicial district. This person then serves as the top court administrator in the district, overseeing the court's operation and budget.

Like the Oregon Court of Appeals, the circuit courts have very busy dockets. Data from the National Center for State Courts show that circuit court filings in 1999 totalled 19,131 per one hundred thousand Oregonians, with more than 630,000 overall. Because court organizational structure varies widely from state to state, comparing the workload of trial courts is difficult and problematic. Nevertheless, looking at the rate of filings in trial courts of general jurisdiction of Oregon's Pacific Coast neighbors, one finds that Oregon is closer to California than to Washington: filings in California superior courts totalled 26,000 per one hundred thousand residents (8,617,833 total); filings in Washington superior courts totalled 4,220 per one hundred thousand residents (242,928 total).[14]

Since the 1990s political debate has swirled around the need for new circuit judge positions, particularly in the Portland metropolitan area, and the Legislative Assembly's failure to create and fund them. The 1998–1999 Joint Committee on the Creation of New Judgeships of the Oregon Judicial

Department and the Oregon State Bar commented, "there has been very little increase in the number of judicial positions in recent years. Despite the pressures of governmental budgets, an increase in judicial capacity is necessary to serve the citizens of the state."[15]

County Courts, Justice Courts, and Municipal Courts

Outside the state-funded system of courts, locally funded county, justice, and municipal courts also exist in Oregon. Six counties have county court judges with limited jurisdiction to adjudicate juvenile and probate matters. Justice courts have existed in Oregon since prior to statehood in 1859, when they were common throughout the state. At present there are thirty justice courts in nineteen Oregon counties. In misdemeanor criminal prosecutions, justice courts share jurisdiction within their county with the circuit court. With some exceptions, justice courts also can try small claims and civil jurisdiction, and other petty violations occurring within the county where they are located.

Finally, most Oregon cities also have a municipal court, which tries cases under city ordinances. Two of the most common cases that these courts hear are minor traffic infractions and parking violations. Besides having jurisdiction on city matters, these courts can also hear criminal cases involving misdemeanor violations of state law that occur within the city's boundaries.

OTHER IMPORTANT ACTORS

There are three other actors besides the courts that play a central role in the state's judicial system. These are the state court administrator, the attorney general, and lawyers.

State Court Administrator

The state court administrator oversees the day-to-day operation of the state's courts. Among the most important responsibilities are managing the records of all cases on appeal to the court of appeals and supreme court, and publishing the various reports of written decisions handed down by the various courts. The court administrator is appointed by the chief justice.

Attorney General

Although organizationally located within the executive branch of Oregon government, the attorney general is the state's chief legal officer and head of the Oregon Department of Justice. Among other duties, the attorney general oversees the legal affairs of all state agencies, prepares written opinions about questions of law, and represents Oregon in all civil and criminal cases. The attorney general is elected every four years. State law places a two-term limit on the time an individual can serve in this office.

Oregon Lawyers

As of 2001 there were roughly 11,500 attorneys actively practicing in Oregon, ranking it approximately in the middle of the fifty states, both in terms of the number of lawyers and the ratio of lawyers to overall population. Oregon State Bar Association data indicate that Native Americans make up a scant 0.5 percent of lawyers in active practice, blacks 0.7 percent, Hispanics just over 1 percent, and Asians just shy of 2 percent. Slightly less than one-third of Oregon lawyers in active practice are women. There are three law schools in the state that are accredited by the American Bar Association: Northwestern School of Law at Lewis and Clark College in Portland (founded in 1915); the University of Oregon School of Law in Eugene (1884); and Willamette University College of Law in Salem (1883).[16]

The Oregon State Bar plays a key role in the oversight of the legal profession. Among its most important duties is to license lawyers and to discipline them for misconduct. The bar also provides a variety of professional programs to aid lawyers and a variety of educational programs to make the public more familiar with the state's legal system. The bar, which was created in 1935, is a professional association of lawyers. A lawyer must be a member of the bar to practice law in the state.

THE POLITICS OF SELECTING JUDGES

Judges make choices. To be sure, they make their choices within a context of legal, institutional, and interpersonal constraints.[17] But judges exercise discretion, nevertheless. They are relatively independent. Oregon jurists, like their colleagues in other judiciaries, exercise their relative independent discretion in a society that, formally at least, is committed to the idea of popular sovereignty.

Despite a cultural inclination to perceive law as separate from politics, Americans implicitly understand that, as one scholar put it, "Even in a government of laws, men make decisions."[18] Understanding this, Americans have debated various means of selecting judges in order to hold them accountable while still insulating judges from partisanship.

Nationally, there are five modes of judicial selection: partisan election, nonpartisan election, "merit" selection, gubernatorial appointment, and appointment by the legislature. During the early twentieth century, Progressive leaders nationwide advocated the use of nonpartisan elections to choose judges. In more recent years the merit system is more typically associated with progressive reformers, who seek to insulate judges from partisan politics. Despite labels such as "nonpartisan" and "merit," all the various selection procedures are political.

A mixture of de jure and de facto selection processes exists in Oregon. Since 1910 Article VII of the Oregon Constitution has specified that "[t]he judges of the supreme and other courts shall be elected by the legal voters of the state or of their respective districts for a term of six years." This constitutional mandate is supplemented by a statute (ORS 254.005) defining judicial elections as nonpartisan.

Combined, these two laws say that Oregon judges are elected in nonpartisan elections. In other words the formal mechanism for selecting judges reflects the state's progressive heritage. Yet two other constitutional provisions allow for an alternative method of selection. Article V of the constitution specifies that when a judicial vacancy occurs, "the governor shall fill such vacancy by appointment." Article III exempts governors' judicial appointments from requiring Senate confirmation.

Although, formally, Oregon jurists are selected through nonpartisan election, in practice the governor plays the key recruitment role. Characteristically, when a vacancy occurs on the bench, the governor draws from the ranks of sitting judges to fill it. For example, if a vacancy occurs on the Oregon Supreme Court, a member of the court of appeals typically is appointed; if a vacancy occurs on the Oregon Court of Appeals, a circuit court judge usually is appointed. When a vacancy occurs on a circuit court, the Oregon State Bar Association conducts a poll among attorneys practicing in the circuit where the vacancy exists to find out who they think should be selected. The findings from this "preference poll" are provided to the governor, who makes an appointment. This process is different from the selection of federal judges because the Legislative Assembly plays no role in confirming appointments.

Individuals who are appointed to fill vacant Oregon judgeships serve out the remaining term of office. Then they are eligible to stand for election at a retention election as an incumbent. Over the past twenty years, approximately 85 percent of Oregon judicial positions—roughly 150 judicial vacancies—have been filled by gubernatorial appointment. All but two of these appointed judges have been retained. Most of them (132 out of 150) ran in uncontested retention elections. In the May 2000 primary only 7 of the 73 Oregon judicial seats up for election had more than one candidate.

MONEY IN JUDICIAL ELECTIONS

Nationally, concern is growing about the role of money in judicial elections, or what is called "buying the bench."[19] This situation is troubling for two reasons. First, societal expectations and professional ethics require judges to exercise their discretion in impartial—that is, nonpartisan and detached—ways. Second, when donors to judicial campaigns are the very individuals and groups who regularly appear before the same judges whose campaigns they underwrite, the potential for a conflict of interest (or the appearance of one) is significant.

Particularly egregious examples of cash flowing into campaign coffers of candidates in judicial elections from special interests, law firms, and corporations come from a host of states from around the nation: Alabama, Louisiana, Ohio, Nevada, Pennsylvania, Texas, and West Virginia. The "cash-nexus" effect is pervasive: in California, for example, a recent study "found that the cost of the average superior court race in the Los Angeles area more than doubled every year, increasing twenty-fold from 1976 to 1994."[20]

Thus far, Oregon's selection process has been relatively insulated from the "injudicious" effects of money.[21] However, the process has been affected. The $407,000 raised for the primary race for a seat on the Oregon Supreme Court in May 2000 was the second most expensive judicial electoral contest in state history. The most expensive was the 1998 primary race for an open Oregon Supreme Court seat. Five candidates raised approximately $427,000 combined. Expenditures in another supreme court race in 2002 was expected to reach over $350,000. These recent races have been considered the exception, however, and not the rule, though the appearance of three high-spending races in such a short period does suggest that the state may be heading toward more costly elections. Because there have been so few expensive campaigns in the state in the past, there have been few charges that the state court is being influenced by campaign contributions.

THE POLITICS OF THE COURTS

On June 25, 1998, the Oregon Supreme Court voted unanimously to strike down Measure 40, the "victim's rights" amendment that was added to the state constitution in 1996. The *Armatta* decision, as it was called, had a profound effect on the court's treatment of constitutional initiatives, as was spelled out in chapter 5.[22] Yet it also marked the beginning of a series of court decisions that has angered many conservative populist leaders, and led to charges that the state judiciary has a marked liberal bias. Among other actions since then, the court has overturned legislative term limits, limited the ability of initiative sponsors to gather signatures on private property, and released a death-row inmate who had been convicted of raping and killing a two-year-old girl.

The court's decisions in these cases spurred a push by some conservative populists to seek changes in the election of judges. An initial effort in 1998 received a great deal of media attention but was eventually abandoned. However, conservative reformers were able to place two initiatives on the 2002 ballot, both of which sought to change the election process. One called for choosing justices from districts, the other for allowing voters to choose "none of the above" when they are dissatisfied with the other candidates. Although both initiatives were defeated, the results were close, especially for the district-elections measure, which lost with 49 percent of the vote. The court cases have also led to some of the most competitive judicial elections in recent history, including those cited above. In addition, the 2002 supreme court race mentioned above was considered the first in two decades in which interest groups became actively involved in trying to throw out an incumbent justice.[23] Conservative populist leaders also point out that five of the state's seven supreme court justices are registered Democrats and that the Democratic Party's dominance of the governor's office since the mid-1980s means that the party has had the ability to shape the membership of the court system.[24]

Others disagree with the charges of liberal bias. Progressive leaders point in particular at the supreme court's decision to overturn the prolabor Measure 62 as evidence that the court does not have a bias. Measure 62, which was adopted by voters in 1998, established a clause in the constitution protecting the rights of labor unions to collect funds through payroll deductions. The court threw out the measure based on the same legal reasoning used in the *Armatta* decision as well as the term limits case.[25] Others point out that the court has been reaching a unanimous decision in almost all of its cases in recent years, even though there is the partisan split on the bench.[26] The unanimity suggests that the decisions do not reflect strong ideological or partisan bias.

Many of the state's top legal scholars argue that the court, rather than pushing a partisan or progressive agenda, has been making a more concerted effort in recent years to be more consistent in how it interprets the constitution. The author of one recent study of the Oregon Supreme Court argues that the court has begun more regularly to apply an "originalist" approach to interpreting the constitution. By originalist, he means that the justices try to consider the framers' intentions when they wrote the constitution. To do this the justices closely examine the text and study the history of the particular enactments that are important in a case. They also examine appropriate case law. The author argues that the court began to declare explicitly its intent to use an originalist approach in the 1992 case *Priest v. Pearce* and has been more consistent in applying it since the Stranahan decision in 2000.[27] Other legal scholars have also dismissed charges of partisanship, arguing instead that the court tends to be pragmatic or that it is hard to pigeonhole.[28]

In one sense, however, the court has clearly pursued a course that has traditionally been associated with more liberal jurisprudence. In supporting judicial federalism and the right of state courts to look at state constitutions when reaching a decision, the court has supported an approach that is often considered more liberal than alternative approaches because it allows for greater protection of civil rights and liberties. In another way, the court has pursued a course that is more closely tied to conservative jurisprudence. By adopting an originalist approach, the court has been following a line of reasoning that has more frequently been associated with conservative legal scholars.

CRIMINAL JUSTICE

Oregon's criminal justice system has gone through considerable change over the past few decades. Two decades ago the system was considered in particularly poor condition. Prisons were overcrowded, and with that overcrowding the state was compelled to release most prisoners before the end of their sentences. In addition, there was a great deal of inconsistency in sentencing. In the late 1980s the state's Criminal Justice Council issued sentencing guidelines to standardize sentencing and address the problems of overcrowding. The state also embarked on an expansion of its prison system, adding more than twenty-three hundred beds. The reforms were highly praised for making sentencing more uniform and improving a system that was considered broken.[29]

Many Oregonians, however, remained dissatisfied with the system. Many conservative populist leaders, in particular, argued that state penalties were too weak and criminals released too early. In the 1990s the state saw new changes in its criminal justice system, this time ones brought through the initiative process. In 1994 voters passed Measure 11, creating mandatory and longer sentences for a variety of violent and property crimes. Two years later the voters passed Measure 40, the victim's rights bill, which was subsequently overturned by the supreme court.

Reaction to Measure 11 has been mixed. Supporters of the measure argue that it has brought down the crime rate and produced a fairer system. Critics of the measure, including Oregon judges and public defenders, argue that the law undercuts judicial independence. The problem, these critics maintain, is that by restricting judges' ability to tailor sentences to convicted offenders, it shifts discretion to prosecutors, who then have the power to decide whether to prosecute and how to charge. The result compromises an essential aspect of the judicial role.

The crime rate in Oregon has indeed dropped over the past several years. In fact, a recent study by the Oregon Office of Economic Analysis found that the crime rate reached a twenty-five-year low in 1999.[30] Yet the crime rate has declined nationwide since 1992, and it is difficult to determine to what extent, if any, the rate decrease in Oregon was related to Measure 11. The law is very popular, however, among voters. In 2000 opponents to Measure 11 placed an initiative on the ballot to overturn the measure. The proposal received less than 30 percent of the vote and was handily defeated in every county, including Multnomah and Lane. One effect of Measure 11 has been an increase in the prison population in Oregon. As of January 1, 2002, the state's prison population was 11,034. By July 2003 the population was expected to grow by 7.8 percent and to reach 11,892. According to estimates by the state Office of Economic Analysis, 41 percent of this growth is related to Measure 11.

Despite the decline in crime, the overall crime rate in Oregon tends to be higher than in other states in the nation. A study by the state Office of Economic Analysis reported that Oregon had the tenth highest total index crime rate in the nation in 1999. The index crime rate includes reports of both violent crimes, such as murder, rape, and robbery, and property crimes. The cause of the high crime rate is due primarily to a high number of property crimes. Overall, the state is ranked eighth in the nation in property crimes, with larceny-theft and burglary the most common. In violent crimes, however, Oregon ranked 28th in the nation. Not surprisingly, the crime rates are higher in the metropolitan area. In violent crimes the metropolitan area is two to three times higher than the rest of the state.

FOUR CONTEMPORARY CONTROVERSIES

In 1831, a French aristocrat, Alexis de Tocqueville, arrived in Newport, Rhode Island. He and his companion spent over nine months traveling widely in the United States, a nation then just over fifty years old. Upon his return to France, Tocqueville wrote his classic *Democracy in America*. Among his most famous insights is his observation that "[s]carcely any political question arises in the United States that is not resolved, sooner or later, into a judicial question."[31] For Oregon, one might add that there is scarcely any political question confronting the Oregon judiciary that is not also a controversy elsewhere. There are four nationwide political controversies, in particular, that are confronting Oregon's judiciary as well.

First, as discussed above, the increasing influence of special interest money in judicial elections has sparked a national debate. In Oregon the de facto importance of gubernatorial appointments, and the prevalence of uncontested retention elections in selecting jurists have retarded somewhat the incursion of extravagantly funded campaigns. Nevertheless, the recent appearance of more expensive races suggests that the state's judicial selection process may not be immune to the national trend.

Second, Oregon has embraced the movement toward mandatory sentencing policies—requiring longer terms of incarceration, for a broader number of crimes, applied to a wider age range of offenders. In 1994 Oregon voters adopted a mandatory sentencing initiative, Measure 11. Although the law is praised by supporters and is popular among voters, it is harshly criticized by many within the judicial system.

Third, like voters in other states with the initiative and referendum, Oregonians are debating whether "too much direct democracy" is a good thing.[32] The number of initiatives and referendums placed before Oregon voters has mushroomed, and as it has, Oregon's constitution has expanded. For supporters of the initiative, the basic principles at stake are free speech and democracy. For critics, the growing use of constitutional initiatives in this era of high campaign spending and special interest politics is tantamount to declaring open season on constitutional principles. Moreover, the rising number of initiatives has inundated the courts with new cases, including time-consuming battles over initiative titles (see chapter 5).

Fourth, in Oregon, as elsewhere throughout the United States, when judges nullify laws passed by legislators, on constitutional grounds, or when they reverse criminal convictions because of due process violations, controversy ensues. Critics of American courts are quick to label such actions "political," and call them unacceptable usurpations that undermine representative government or jeopardize public safety. Oregon judges are subject to similar criticisms. In addition, because Oregon judges can rule on the constitutionality of ballot measures adopted under the state's initiative and referendum procedures, they are subject to the added criticism that they stifle the "will of the people" expressed through "direct democracy." As a result of these criticisms, there has been a demand for changes in judicial elections.

Given the prominence of all four of these controversies, not only in Oregon but in other parts of the nation, it is clear that Oregon's judiciary is not unique. Yet Oregon's judiciary is different, in many respects, from those in other places. To a large extent, the controversies confronting the state judiciary are shaded by the state's political character, especially its reliance on the initiative and the split between progressives and conservative populists. In sum, what one finds is that Oregon's judiciary is indeed a variation on broader American patterns.

CHAPTER TWELVE

Local Government

Alana S. Jeydel

Americans often pay little attention to the affairs of local governments, yet these governments greatly affect our lives. Among their many responsibilities, local governments record our births and deaths, they decide how our children will be educated, they build roads, they provide fire and police protection, they oversee zoning, they collect taxes, they decide how to spend the money they raise, and they set rules on such mundane matters as whether we can bring dogs to the neighborhood park and what level of noise is permissible in the community. Because local governments affect so many aspects of our lives, it is essential to examine them.

In Oregon the Progressive movement had a significant impact in shaping the character of local governments, as it helped make these governments more independent from the state and it led to the introduction of new governmental structures. Today, local governments still operate under many rules championed by the Progressives. Yet the state's conservative populism has also affected local governments in recent years, especially in their ability to raise revenue.

TYPES OF LOCAL GOVERNMENTS

There are several types of local governments in Oregon, from those of cities to those of counties to such obscure entities as ambulance districts and television translator districts. Despite this diversity we can categorize local governments into two main groups: *general-purpose governments* and *special governments*. General-purpose governments are local governments that provide many different functions and have authority over a broad array of public policy matters. The two most common types of general-purpose governments are those of cities and counties. Although the regional government for the Portland metropolitan area, or what is called Metro, is also a general-purpose government, it performs fewer functions than city governments.

Special governments perform only one function or a limited number of functions. School districts are the most prominent type of special government, but there are many others, including ambulance, cemetery, fire, port, and television translator districts. These types of governments are also referred to as single-purpose governments.

Cities

There are 240 cities in Oregon. When Oregon was founded, the state government exercised considerable control over cities as well as other local governments. On some matters, such as the building of roadways, cities were able to make decisions without the state's interference. But in many areas, the state refused to grant the cities the authority to act. The state did this by including restrictions in a city's charter limiting the city's authority to only specified tasks.[1] City charters lay out the city's legal authority.

The problem confronting cities was that they did not have any legal basis to challenge the state. There is no mention of cities or local governments in the U.S. Constitution, so they do not enjoy the same type of sovereignty as states. In the late 1860s there was a series of judicial decisions handed down by Iowa judge John F. Dillon that spelled out the relationship between local governments and the state. The judge's decisions, which became known as *Dillon's rule*, made it clear that cities were subservient to the states and that they could, in general, exercise only the powers expressly given to them by the state government.[2]

The Progressive movement changed the position of cities within state politics. Unhappy with the legislature for rewriting city charters to benefit individual businesses, Progressives called for granting cities *home rule*, which would allow cities to act as they saw fit on a much broader array of policy matters. It would also allow cities to write their own charters and limit the state's ability to alter these charters.[3]

With the passage of Measure 6 in 1906, Oregon cities were given constitutional home rule as well as the use of the initiative and referendum. The introduction of home rule meant that cities had greater authority to act and that local residents had greater influence over city affairs. Over time, however, the power of cities to exercise home rule has been reduced, particularly through court rulings. The most important of these rulings came in the case of *City of La Grande and City of Astoria v. Public Employees Retirement Board* in 1971, which involved the state's power to force cities to offer certain employee benefits. The Oregon Supreme Court made it clear that the state has considerable power to preempt local ordinances and rules.[4]

Historically, Oregon has been unusual in the extent to which it has granted home rule to cities as well as to counties. In 1993 the U.S. Advisory Commission on Intergovernmental Relations identified the state as leading the nation in the amount of authority it grants to local governments.[5] Today, however, it is likely that the state's record on home rule would not be rated as highly because of court rulings.

Today, cities perform a variety of tasks, including providing many of the most basic governmental services. These include police and fire protection, water and wastewater management, street maintenance, land-use planning, social services, business licensing, and recreational activities.

Throughout the United States, there exist three forms of city government: *mayor-council, city commission,* and *council-manager.* In many states the size of the city tends to determine its choice of government form; this also appears to be the case in Oregon.

While the forms of city government have significant differences, they share a few key common characteristics (see table 12.1). All cities have a council or commission that serves a legislative function in creating and passing policy and provides some oversight of the city administration. Almost all have some type of executive, either a mayor, a manager, or a city recorder. All have administrators to carry out the administrative function of government (writing regulations and implementing the policies passed by the legislative branch). Although this separation of powers is similar to that used in the federal and state governments, it is usually not as rigid. There is more sharing of powers within local government.

Mayor-Council Form

Textbooks frequently identify two types of mayor-council governments. In a *weak-mayor system* the city council controls city politics, and the mayor's power is very limited. In these cities the mayor is charged primarily with presiding over the city council and serving as the city's top ceremonial leader, though he or she may also have some administrative powers.

Under a *strong-mayor system*, the mayor plays a larger role in the city, leading it in a manner that is similar to how the governor leads the state.

Table 12.1. Forms of City Governments

	Mayor or Manager	Council or commission	Administrative Departments	Empoyed in
Weak mayor-council	Acts as ceremonial leader; chairs council; has few administrative powers	Sets city policy; directly runs administration	Answer to council; administer programs	Most small cities (populations under 2,500)
Strong mayor-council	Recommends legislation; chairs council; heads bureaucracy; has strong appointment powers; has veto power	Sets city policy; can override veto	Answer to mayor; administer programs	Beaverton
Commission	Chairs commission; distributes commissioner assignments; prepares budget	Sets city policy; oversees administration	Have commissioners serving as department heads; administer programs	Portland
Council-manager	Hired by council; implements city policies; runs administration; hires/fires personnel; develops budget; provides support to council members	Sets city policy; oversees administration	Answer to manager; administer programs	Most larger cities (populations over 2,500)

In general, the mayor runs the city's administration, including hiring and firing personnel (with the council's approval), preparing the city budget, signing all official documents, and sometimes even having veto power. The city council can exercise some oversight over the administration, but it tends to play a more removed role, leaving the day-to-day operation to the mayor. Like state governors, the mayor is also expected to propose legislation.

In Oregon one finds both of these forms of government as well as governments that are somewhere between these two types. Most of the smaller cities in Oregon (with populations under twenty-five hundred) are considered to use the weak-mayor system, though there are considerable differences in the amount of power that mayors are given in these cities. In some cities the mayor plays a small role; in others, the mayor may hire and fire personnel, propose legislation, or have veto power. Beaverton is the only city in Oregon that is considered to operate under the strong-mayor system.

Commission Forms

In this system of government, the city commission is vested with all the powers of government. The commission is similar to a city council, except that the members of the commission also serve as the heads of individual city departments. One member also serves as mayor. In essence, the commissioners serve two roles: when assembled, they act as a small legislature or city council; as individuals, they each act as part of the bureaucracy by overseeing individual city departments.

The commission form of government was among the major reforms advocated by Progressives in the early part of the twentieth century. Progressives believed that the commission form would lead to more efficient and effective government.[6] Today, Portland is the only city in the state, and one of the largest cities in the nation, with the commission form of government.

Portland's charter divides the administration of the city into five departments and numerous bureaus. The mayor's most important power is to decide which commissioner will oversee each department and bureau. The mayor also chairs all council meetings and prepares the city budget each year. Although the mayor may appear to have a lot of power, this is not the case. The mayor's vote on matters before the council counts the same as the vote of each of the commissioners. Thus, the mayor is considered to have no more power than any other commissioner.

Council-Manager Form

This system of government has an elected council and a professional manager or administrator. The council is responsible for setting city policy, exercising broad oversight of the administration, and hiring the manager. The manager is responsible for running the city on a daily basis.

Along with commission system, many Progressive reformers advocated the use of the council-manager system. To many Progressives, city governments needed professional leadership, not partisan politics. The council-manager form was championed as a way to bring more expertise into government. Today, this system of government is very common in Oregon. Currently, most Oregon cities with populations over twenty-five hundred have the council-manager form of government.

COUNTIES

There are thirty-six counties in Oregon. Counties were created to provide services from and for the state, including administering elections, tracking vital statistics, and collecting taxes. Cities were created to provide services to the people, such as police protection, schools, and roads. This difference is not as valid today because counties have taken on a wider range of duties. The primary reason that the counties have become more active is that they, like cities, have been granted the power of home rule. Since the Progressive movement, reformers have sought to extend home rule to counties, but it was not until 1958 that state voters adopted a constitutional amendment allowing counties to adopt home rule charters. Nine have since done so. In 1973 the state expanded the power of all counties to allow them to have greater home rule. In addition, the change in the state constitution in 1958 extended the use of the initiative and referendum to counties.

As a result of these reforms and other changes in state law, counties now perform a variety of different duties, including road maintenance, law enforcement, health care, public housing, election administration, and tax assessment.

As with cities, the structure of county government is fairly similar across the state. Each has a board that serves a legislative function and provides some oversight of the county administration. Each has an executive. Most also have several independently elected officers, including county assessor, clerk, sheriff, surveyor, and treasurer. There are three forms of government used in home rule counties: the county administrative plan, the county manager plan, and the elected executive plan (see table 12.2).

Table 12.2. Forms of County Governments

	Executive	Board or council	Administrative Departments	Empoyed in
County administrative officer	Is appointed by board; implements board policies; may run administration; hires/fires personnel; supervises budget	Size set by charter; sets county policy; shares administrative responsibilities with administrator	May answer directly to administrator, though not in all counties; administer programs	Home rule counties (Benton, Jackson, Josephine, Lane, Umatilla, and Washington)
County manager	Is appointed by board; implements board policies; runs administration; hires/fires personnel; supervises budget	Size set by charter; sets county policy; oversees administration	Answer to manager; administer programs	Home rule counties (Clatsop and Hood River)
Elected executive	Is independently elected; chairs board; implements board policies; runs administration; hires/fires personnel; develops budget	Size set by charter; sets county policy; oversees administration	Answer to elected executive, excepting independently elected offices; administer programs	Home rule counties (Multnomah)
County court system	Chief executive is the county judge; chairs court; runs administration; may perform some judicial functions	Is the court, consisting of county judge and two other elected commissioners; sets county policy; oversees administration	Answer to county court, excepting independently elected offices; administer programs	General law counties (Crook, Gilliam, Grant, Harney, Malheur, Morrow, Sherman, Wasco, and Wheeler)
Board of commissioners	Position is rotated among board members; some are elected; chairs board; may run administration	Consists of 3 to 5 elected commissioners; sets county policy; oversees administration	Answer to board, excepting independently elected offices; administer programs	General law counties (all others)

County Administrative Plan

This system of government has an elected governing board (the county commission) that fulfils the legislative function. The board then appoints an administrative officer to fulfil the executive function. The amount of power and responsibility given to this administrator differs across counties. In general, there are two types of county administrative plans. Some commissions appoint a "county administrator" who is given considerable power over the county's administration. This person directs the county's general governmental functions, such as staffing and finance, and develops issues for the board to consider. The county administrator also has authority over county departments. Other county commissions appoint an "administrative officer." This person also oversees the general government function and develops issues but does not have authority over county departments. The administrative officer is less independent than a county administrator and, in many ways, acts primarily as a staff position to the board.

County Manager Plan

The county manager system is very similar to the county administrative plan, with one major difference. In the county manager plan the county commission tends to be part-time, focusing almost exclusively on policy considerations with less attention devoted to oversight. In these counties the manager plays the leading role in running the county's administration. Under the county administrative plan, on the other hand, the county commission tends to be more active in supervising the county's administration.

Elected Executive Plan

This system is similar to the strong-mayor form of city government. There is an elected chief executive and an elected governing body. The chief executive, or chair, oversees the administration of the county, presides over board meetings, prepares the county budget, and signs all official board acts. The board, on the other hand, sets the county's policies.

Counties that have not adopted home rule charters are called "general law" counties. These counties use one of two types of governmental structures. In the "county court" system, two commissioners and a county judge run the county. The county judge functions as the chief executive and may exercise some judicial functions. In general, these judicial functions are limited to probate and juvenile court. In some county court systems, however, the chief executive is called the county judge but no longer has any judicial functions. This is true, for instance, in Wasco County. The county court system is found only in nine counties in the eastern part of Oregon. The remaining general law counties use an elected board of commissioners. The board serves as the local legislature and often plays a major role in directing the bureaucracy.

As with cities, there are some exceptions to these generalities. For example, Washington County, which has home rule, has an elected executive, yet it also has a county administrator. Josephine and Umatilla counties, which also have home rule, do not have administrators. In addition, some general law counties have government structures that resemble those of home rule counties. For example, Deschutes, Jefferson, Linn, Polk, Union, and Yamhill have administrative officers.

REGIONAL GOVERNMENTS

To many government reformers today, the only way that many local problems will be solved is to create regional governments. The reason that regional government is considered valuable is that many problems do not recognize traditional political boundaries. The problems associated with crime, pollution, transportation, economic development, and urban growth do not automatically stop at a city's edge but often affect an entire region. Regional government is said to allow for regional solutions.

Following in its progressive tradition of restructuring government so that it is better able to address problems, Oregon has created one of the most powerful regional governments in the nation. Metro was created in 1979 to address some of the major problems confronting the twenty-four cities and three counties in the Portland metropolitan area. Today, Metro is the only elected regional government in the nation and the only one to be organized under a home rule charter.

Metro was initially formed through the merger of the Columbia Region Association of Governments and the Metropolitan Service District. When these two merged, the state legislature transferred their responsibilities to Metro and then granted Metro several additional powers. According to its 1992 charter, Metro has primary responsibility for "regional land-use and transportation planning, and is further empowered to address any other issue of 'metropolitan concern.'"[7] Metro also oversees the Oregon Convention Center, the Portland Center for the Performing Arts, PGE Park, the Multnomah County parks system, the Oregon Zoo, and the Portland Expo Center.[8]

Even though Metro is the only regional government in Oregon with home rule, there are several voluntary associations of governments in the state that also act as a form of regional government. Associations of governments have been in existence for decades, but in the 1970s they began to play a more vital role. At that time, Governor Tom McCall divided the state into fourteen administrative regions. The existing associations of governments were then encouraged to adopt the same physical boundaries as the administrative regions.[9] These associations are now called councils of governments (COGS).

Today, the state Blue Book lists nine councils of government in Oregon. One of the main roles of these councils is to help foster cooperation between the local governments in their regions. The legislature has granted some limited powers to COGS. One main area in which COGS have power is in providing services to the elderly. For example, the Oregon Cascades West COG provides in-home case managers to senior citizens to arrange providers for household tasks. It also provides hot meals to seniors in twelve dining centers located throughout Linn, Benton, and Lincoln counties.

SCHOOL DISTRICTS

School districts are the most visible special government in the state. There are 198 school districts in Oregon serving 567,660 students in 2000.[10] An elected board governs every school district. The primary functions of the school board are to develop educational programs, set curriculum guidelines, produce the district's budget, oversee personnel matters, and maintain facilities.

Of all the types of local governments in Oregon, the school district has been among those that have been most affected by the growing activism of conservative populists. In particular, school politics were drastically altered by the passage of two ballot measures in the 1990s that were designed to reduce government spending and cut taxes. In 1990 Oregon voters adopted Measure 5, rolling back property tax rates. Seven years later, state voters passed Measure 50, which set a limit on future property tax growth for individual properties.[11] The combined effect of these two measures has been to significantly reduce the property tax as a source of revenue for local governments and to turn the problem of school funding into a major political battle in the state capitol. In order to help the schools survive, the state has had to play a larger role in providing funds to local districts. In 1990 approximately 27 percent of school funds came from the state. Today, the amount is 70 percent.[12]

The school districts have been affected not only by these conservative populist trends but also by some progressive ones. In the past there was little uniformity in the programs and offerings across the state because each district had considerable power to set the curriculum. The state board of education, which oversees the schools, did set some guidelines on the number of hours that needed to be devoted to particular subjects, but there were great differences between the districts in how they responded to these guidelines. In 1991, however, the legislature enacted the Education Act for the Twenty-first Century, which established state performance standards for all public schools. Although local districts continue to have considerable freedom in developing specific programs, they now must be continuously attentive to these statewide expectations.

SPECIAL DISTRICTS

Along with schools, there are more than 950 other special governments in Oregon. Each performs a single function, or a limited number of functions, in a particular region of the state. Translator districts, for example, provide television-broadcasting support in more remote areas of the state where adequate television programming is not available. One of the most common types of special government are the port districts, which manage the bays, rivers, and harbors. Among the twenty-two port districts in the state is the Port of Portland, which not only oversees marine activities in Clackamas, Multnomah, and Washington counties but also manages the Portland International Airport.

In total, there are twenty-eight different types of special-service districts in the state. These include ambulance, cemetery, fire, hospital, park and recreation, sanitary, transportation, water conservation, and water control districts.

SOURCES OF REVENUE

During the 1998–1999 fiscal year, local governments across Oregon, including schools, generated more than $10.5 billion in general revenue. There were four main sources used to raise this revenue: property taxes, state payments to local governments, federal aid, and user fees. As discussed above, the effort by conservative populists to roll back taxes has had a profound effect on local government revenue and, in turn, local politics.

Historically, property taxes have been the largest source of revenue for most local governments in Oregon. In 1991–1992, when Measure 5 was just beginning to be phased in, property taxes still accounted for almost 40 percent of all local government general revenue. In 1998–1999, however, they accounted for only 24 percent of revenue.[13] The decline in the property tax has meant that local governments have had to scale back programs and look for alternative sources of funding.

During that same period of time, payments from the state to local governments more than doubled, helping to offset some of the lost revenue from the drop in property taxes. In 1991 the state provided $1.7 billion in payments to local governments, or almost 27 percent of local budgets. In 1998 it provided almost $3.9 billion, or 37 percent of these budgets. However, much of this state increase went to schools and not to other types of local government. In addition to these payments, local governments also receive funds from the state in revenue-sharing from taxes on cigarettes, liquor, fuel, and public utilities.[14] Payments from the federal government (federal aid) also increased during this period, rising from $390 million to $737 million. Of the four sources of revenue, however, federal aid has remained the smallest.

Local governments have also increased the amount of money raised from user fees to help compensate for the decline in revenue, but the growth in fees has not been large. User fees are the monies charged by various agencies of local government to citizens for the rendering of various services, such as for building permits, business licenses, and recreational activities. In 1991–1992, user fees accounted for 23 percent of local budgets; by 1998–1999, they accounted for 26 percent.[15]

INTERGOVERNMENTAL

Even though cities have more autonomy than they did prior to the Progressive Era, there are still limits to what they can do. The limitations placed on local governments, however, do not just come from the state but from other governments as well. Along with the state, the federal government can also restrict the activities of local governments. In addition, local governments often have to find ways to work with each other in order to attain their goals.

Federal-Local Relations

As discussed in the first chapter, the federal government can influence states in a variety of ways. The federal government can pass laws that preempt or supersede state laws. It can mandate that states take certain actions. It can place conditions on federal aid to force states to behave in certain ways. The federal government also owns more than 50 percent of the land in Oregon, which gives it direct control of a large chunk of the state. All of these federal constraints on the state government also affect local governments.

The federal government's involvement in local areas is not always controversial, such as when it provides funding for a local highway or for emergency aid to private citizens. But in some cases, federal programs can lead to a strained relationship with local governments. The federal government's use of what are called "unfunded mandates" has caused particular problems for local governments. A federal mandate refers to a federal program that requires states or local governments to perform a specific service or activity. An "unfunded" mandate is one that the federal government does not pay for. The Americans with Disabilities Act (ADA) provides a good example. Under the ADA all units of government that receive federal funding are required to make public buildings, facilities, and services available to individuals with disabilities. Given that local governments receive some federal support, they are required to meet the ADA rules. Yet the federal government did not provide financial support to help local governments do so.

In recent years the federal government's involvement in issues dealing with environmental protection and property rights has also caused controversy in some parts of Oregon. For example, in the last few months of his administration, President Bill Clinton created the Cascade-Siskiyou National Monument in southern Oregon. Even though the monument was highly praised by environmentalists, many local residents opposed the president's actions. In July 2001 the Jackson County Commission asked U.S. Interior Secretary, Gale Norton, to decrease the size of the Cascade-Siskiyou National Monument from 52,947 acres to 16,580 acres. The commission argued that this reduction was necessary to protect the property rights of individuals who own land in the monument.[16] While this scale back has been put on hold, at least temporarily, the controversy in the community remains. Furthermore, many smaller communities, especially those that depend on natural resources for their livelihood, have been critical of federal timber regulations and the Endangered Species Act, viewing them as threats to their economic survival.

While the federal government may be able to affect local government activities, the relationship between the two levels of government is not just a top-down one. Local governments often lobby the federal government to help their position, and members of Congress try to protect local interests.

Relations among Local Governments

Local governments often need to work together in order to solve joint problems, prevent duplication of efforts, and promote efficiency. When there are joint problems, local governments will often work together informally to find solutions. On occasion, however, local governments will turn to more formal mechanisms to bring about better cooperation. One of those methods is through a council of governments, described above. One of the major responsibilities of COGs is to provide coordination and cooperation between the local governments in their region. Even though membership is voluntary in COGs, they provide a valuable means to help local governments work together. In addition, there are several statewide groups that help build cooperation between local governments. These include the Association of Oregon Counties, the League of Oregon Cities, the Special Districts Association of Oregon, and the Oregon Regional Councils Association.

Another method local governments use to work together is to sign an intergovernmental agreement. Through an intergovernmental agreement, local governments can, in effect, hire other local governments to handle some of their functions. Intergovernmental agreements are beneficial because they can make governmental services more effective and efficient by reducing the duplication of efforts.[17] Among the areas in which local governments enter into these agreements are police and fire protection, ambulance service, road maintenance, animal control, water and sewer utilities, public health, parks and recreation, and planning.

The Progressive movement had a profound effect on local governments in Oregon. Even after almost one hundred years, the influence of progressivism is still very visible. Local governments have greater autonomy because of home rule. Most of the larger cities in Oregon have either the council-manager form of government or the commission system, both of which were championed by Progressives. The initiative and referendum also are found among cities and counties. The state's progressive heritage can also be seen in a number of newer innovations, including the creation of Metro and the passage of education reform.

Yet the real story in local government today may not be this progressive heritage, but the role played by conservative populism. With the passage of Measures 5 and 50, local governments have found themselves struggling to provide services with smaller budgets. In the past few years, many local governments have had to cut programs and find alternative sources of funding to balance their budgets. In the next few years, the financial problems brought by these reforms may worsen. During the 1990s the state government was able to channel money to some local governments, especially schools, to help compensate for the decline in revenue. The state was able to help out, in large part, because the strong economic growth in the 1990s expanded the state's budget. As the economy slows, as it was beginning to do in 2001, the state will be less able to help schools.

On top of the financial problems created by Measures 5 and 50, local governments face one other challenge brought about by the state's conservative populism. In the 2000 election voters passed Measure 7, an initiative that requires all governments in the state to compensate property owners when government policies reduce property value. Even though the state supreme court has since overturned the measure, the support for protecting property rights in the state is quite strong, and it is likely that voters will be given another chance to pass a revised version of that measure.

Looking back through this record of reform and change, it is clear that the state's progressive heritage and its support for conservative populism have played a central role in shaping local government, just as it has in other aspects of state politics.

CHAPTER THIRTEEN

Fiscal Policy

Mark Henkels

Oregon's public budget patterns reflect a balance of the tradition of a progressive activist government and the more recent conservative populist antitax policies. Oregon's historic reliance on a graduated income tax (those who earn more pay a higher rate) reflects its progressive tradition. Yet the state, in many regards, has turned away from this heritage. This change can be seen in the tax code. Because of inflation, most taxpayers today are actually in the highest income tax bracket of 9 percent.[1] Even so, Oregon's reputation as "tax hell" is no longer appropriate, as conservative populist policies have dropped its total state and local tax burden as a percentage of personal income from number twelve in the nation in 1990 to forty-one in 2001, according to the conservative Tax Foundation's ranking system.[2]

Passage of measures to cut property taxes in 1990 (Measure 5), 1996 (Measure 47), and 1997 (Measure 50) epitomize how conservative populists powerfully influence Oregon governments through "tax revolt" ballot measures. In recent decades all significant efforts to reform Oregon's tax system involved public votes. Even when the legislature passed revenue measures independently, such as the 1999 legislated increase in the gasoline tax from twenty-four cents per gallon to twenty-nine cents, opponents placed the bills on the ballot by petition referenda. Accordingly, the popularity of fiscal conservatism (antitax, smaller government) in Oregon has driven budget changes in the past twenty years.

This chapter features four main elements. First, there is an overview of the design and nature of state and local budgets. The second section of the chapter looks at state and local revenue options. Taxes may be as inevitable as death, but the options for raising revenue have very different strengths and weaknesses. A third part of this chapter looks at some of the truly distinctive aspects of Oregon's public finance system. Finally, we consider local government budgets by looking at Salem's budget and some aspects of public school district funding.

OVERVIEW OF STATE AND LOCAL BUDGETS

Three fundamental aspects of state and local fiscal policy are noteworthy: 1) state and local governments are inextricably connected and so are their budget systems, 2) comparisons between budgets can be misleading, and 3) state and local governments have multiple budgets.

State and Local Government Budgets Are Connected

State and local budgets are connected in two principal ways. First, states subsidize many local government activities. For example, the state provides 70 percent of local school funds in Oregon. As a consequence, changes in state budgets strongly affect local programs, and vice versa.

A second critical connection between state and local budgets is that local governments are basically subject to state law. This is a result of what is called "Dillon's rule," discussed in the next chapter. Local governments cannot tax or spend anything unless state law allows it. Oregon's property tax cuts of the 1990s demonstrate this. These ballot measures limit local property taxes even if the local community strongly favors more taxes and services.

Comparisons Can Be Misleading

While comparisons can educate, they can be misleading if not done with care. Two areas of state and local fiscal policy can be particularly confusing. First, tax comparisons between states should consider *all* sources of revenue, including local revenues. State and local revenue systems vary greatly in their reliance on the "big three" of taxes: sales, income, and property taxes. In addition, local governments frequently tax or charge for specific services according to state laws. Analysis based on comparing a single revenue source can misrepresent the government's overall tax impact and its revenue history.

Second, though generally budget change happens incrementally, which means through small changes, sometimes a major budget change can happen quickly. The most rapid changes occur when major "tax revolts" and very strong economic recessions or booms occur. Information from the early 1990s misrepresents Oregon's property tax system today. The 2001–2002 state legislature was forced to have five special sessions in order to compensate for a 15.3 percent ($1.75 billion) shortfall from revenue projections used to create the original 2001–2003 budget.[3]

States Have Multiple Budgets

When people refer to the "state budget," they usually mean something called the "general funds/lottery" budget. In fact, there are several "state budgets," each with its own revenue sources and characteristics. Local governments also usually have multiple budgets.

PARTS OF THE BUDGET

The four different state operating budgets in Oregon are the total funds budget, the general funds/lottery budget, the other funds budget, and the federal funds budget. Each agency or department in the state has its own mixture of reliance on these budgets. Where the money comes from has important consequences for the agency. For example, an agency that depends more on money from the federal funds budget is more likely to be controlled by federal mandates and other requirements. Agencies funded largely from the general funds/lottery budget compete with many other programs in the legislature, and their funding is influenced by legislative politics. Shifting program funding from one revenue stream to another can have important distributional consequences. For example, property tax cuts during the 1990s caused the state to send more state money to local school districts. This, in turn, meant that general funding for higher education was cut, resulting in a 70 percent increase in tuition.

Oregon has a two-year budget, which is different from many other states and from the federal government, which use a one-year budget. The state budget begins on July 1 of each odd-numbered year and runs through June 30 two years later. Unless otherwise labeled, the spending figures here come from the 2003–2005 legislatively approved budget. These numbers incorporate the budget impact of voters rejecting Measure 30 in February 2004, when antitax groups successfully overturned a temporary tax surcharge through the referendum process. The defeat of Measure 30 led to cuts of $544.6 million from the original budget approved by the legislature in 2003.[4] State revenue pattern figures are generally taken from the Governor's Budget for 2003–2005, which is the original budget proposal presented by the

Table 13.1. Components of the Oregon All Funds State Budget, 2003–2005
(in billions of dollars)

General funds/lottery	10.95	(29.4%)
Other funds	18.15	(48.7%)
Federal funds	8.02	(21.9%)
Total funds budget	37.202	(100.0%)

Source: Based on *Update: Budget Highlights, 2003–2005 Legislatively Approved Budget* (Salem: Oregon Legislative Fiscal Office, 2004), 1.

governor in 2003. Despite recent fluctuations, the fundamentally incremental nature of state budgets means that the underlying patterns noted here are likely to continue.

The All Funds State Budget

The all funds state budget (sometimes referred to as the "total funds budget") contains the totals of three other budgets (see table 13.1). The all funds budget shows how much money passes through the state government. The size is deceptive, however, because the legislature cannot easily control significant elements of the total. The all funds budget is useful only in comparisons where the facts contained within it are known.

The General Fund

The general funds budget is the political keystone of the state's financial system. Arguments and comments about "the state budget" usually concern the general funds or the general funds/lottery budget because the legislature and the governor have the greatest control over these parts of the budget. Although technically separate, the lottery funds are usually included with the general funds for practical purposes. Generally, the legislature can spend general funds/lottery money as it wishes, except it must cover any specific mandates required by existing laws.

Few state programs are funded as their supporters would like. The creation (or authorization) of programs is a separate issue from their funding (or appropriation). In Oregon appropriations are formally adopted and tracked, but there is no formal system, as there is for the federal government, for estimating how much authorized programs should receive. Advocates who successfully promote the creation of programs are sometimes disappointed when the legislature fails to fund them as they wished. Without changing

Table 13.2.   Priorities in General Funds and Lottery Revenues, 2003–2005
(in billions of dollars)

K–12 education	4.905	44.7%
Human services (Medicaid, welfare, work programs, etc.)	2.298	21.0%
Other education (higher education, community colleges, special education)	1.531	14.0%
Public safety (corrections, law enforcement)	1.225	11.2%
All other programs	0.996	9.1%
Total	11.97	100.0%

Source: Update: Budget Highlights, 2003–2005 Legislatively Approved Budget (Salem: Oregon Legislative Fiscal Office, 2004), 3.

the basic authorizing laws, the legislature in 2002 cut various social service programs and eliminated direct general funding for the Oregon Progress Board entirely.[5]

As table 13.2 shows, education gets the lion's share of the general fund. The impact of the property tax limits of 1990 and 1997 on the state general funds budget is dramatically illustrated by the fact that general funds/lottery spending on K–12 schools increased by more than 250 percent from the 1989–1991 budget to the 1997–1999 budget. General funds spending on higher education barely grew at all during the same period, although total spending on higher education went up significantly because of tuition increases.[6] These figures also make one important political fact clear: cutting the state budget significantly without cutting K–12 education would be extremely difficult.

Oregon's general funds/lottery budget is funded primarily by the personal income tax, as can be seen in table 13.3. Oregon's income tax is one of the highest in the country. General funds/lottery budget numbers in table 13.3 also reveal that lottery funds do not come even close to the amount needed to fund education. When personal incomes decline, the legislature must cut spending or raise taxes to balance the budget. The results are dramatically evident in the budget struggles that started in 2001. As the economy slowed and income taxes fell short of projections, the legislature made direct cuts, spent and borrowed from various reserve funds, and increased various charges and fees. Voters strongly rejected temporary income tax increases to counter revenue shortfalls by voters in January 2003 and February 2004. The public antitax attitude and the powerful presence of nationally supported antitax activists make it extremely unlikely that legislature will support significant tax increases for years.[7] Programs relying on state general funds

Table 13.3. Principal Sources of Oregon General Funds and Lottery Monies
(in millions of dollars)

Personal income tax	9,915	87%
Corporate income tax	376	3%
Miscellaneous taxes and fees, other sources	589	5%
Lottery funds	550	5%
Total	11,430	100%

Source: Ted Kulongoski, *Governor's Budget: State of Oregon, 2003–2005* (Salem: Department of Administrative Services, 2003).

face budget uncertainty until Oregon regains a stable positive economic growth pattern.

Lottery funds were initially dedicated to "economic development," but public ballot measures of the 1990s broadened how they could be spent. Lottery funds are now significantly controlled by mandates such as one passed by voters in 1998 that requires 15 percent of lottery funds be spent on parks and natural resources. Unfortunately for the parks and natural resource programs, these guarantees do not prevent the governor and legislature from reducing the other general funds going to those programs. Thus, the gains from the lottery mandate were somewhat offset by cuts in the general funds.

Other Funds Budget

The other funds budget encompasses monies not included in the other categories. Other funds are typically generated by dedicated taxes and fees, rotating funds, and other less flexible revenue sources. Some areas of other funds are paid for by "user pay" revenues such as tuition or licenses. Advocates of such fee systems note that it is equitable under the "benefit principle" because consumers bear the costs of their consumption, though in practice, fees may not accurately reflect the costs or benefits of the service.[8] Dedicated taxes, or "earmarked taxes," are those that can be spent only on particular programs. For example, fuel taxes and motor-vehicle fees in Oregon can be spent only on transportation programs. The state Transportation Department receives well over 90 percent of its money from such other funds.

Some of the money found in other funds comes from rotating funds, where investments earn some of the current income. The veterans' housing program, for example, generates money for new loans from revenues earned on the repayment of old loans. The largest single fund in the other funds budget is the Public Employee Retirement System (PERS). PERS has a large investment fund that is supplemented by new general funds. Funds with large investment components are strongly affected by fluctuations in financial markets. Investment income and other earnings made up $6.68 billion (82 percent) of the total of $8.14 billion raised in PERS in 2000. At the end of 2002, the PERS system was projected to have a $17.1 billion shortfall over the next twenty-five years because its benefits structure is based on very optimistic predictions about the stock market.[9] The magnitude of the problem can change rapidly, though, because changes in the stock market alter investment revenues rapidly.

In general, other funds budget items are difficult to change for legal and political reasons. Many of these reasons are embodied in the Oregon Constitution, and some are defended by well-organized interest groups, such as those for public employees or veterans. The history of PERS demonstrates the political complexity of some "other funds." In 1979 Oregon had high unemployment but also strong inflation. This "stagflation" meant that government revenues were not growing, but pressures to increase compensation for public workers were mounting. To please workers while controlling expenditures, state and local governments in PERS agreed to pick up the 6 percent of employee pay that went toward retirement funds. Employees received no actual raise but saw 6 percent more take-home pay. The state and local governments had to pay 6 percent more into the retirement funds but avoided the extra employer payroll taxes, such as social security and disability payments, that accompany a normal raise.

A major shift in PERS almost occurred in 1994, when Oregon Taxpayers United successfully promoted Measure 8, which sought to force employees to pay the 6 percent charges again. The measure won by less than a thousand votes, but lawyers for public employee unions convinced the state supreme court to overturn Measure 8 because it violated the state's constitutional protection of contractual agreements. The battle continued, however.

Minor benefit reductions for newer employees were passed in the mid-1990s, but a genuine turning point occurred in 2003. That year, despite strong union support in his election, Governor Kulongoski promoted major changes in PERS. Kulongoski was concerned about how PERS was requiring increasing amounts of state and local general funds to make up for the dramatic stock market declines after 2000. On May 9, 2003, the governor signed bills that would save state and local governments seven hundred million dollars between 2003–2005 by 1) updating the life expectancy tables used to determine benefits (thereby reducing benefits payments), 2) stopping cost-of-living increases for PERS retirees, 3) eliminating the 6 percent employer contribution, and 4) limiting the 8 percent guaranteed annual return that some employees receive. These dramatic reforms still face significant legal challenges. Public employee unions immediately turned to the state courts, asserting that the reforms violated contractual agreements guaranteed by the state constitution. The case reached the state supreme court on July 30, 2004.[10]

Federal Funds Budget

The state government serves as a funnel for federal grants. Federal grant monies going to the states are nearly always dedicated to specific programs, although states may have some flexibility in how to use the money within those policy areas. Medical assistance programs provide an example of the flow of these funds into the state. In the 1999–2001 actual budget, medical assistance programs received 57 percent of their $3.46 billion in funds from the federal government, the same percentage in Governor Kulongoski's 2003–2005 proposed health service budget.[11]

Federal funds have associated problems because Congress inevitably intervenes in programs receiving federal funds. Some federal interventions are quite specific, such as forbidding spending federal money on assisted suicide. Some conditions are broad, such as requiring states to have work requirements and time limits in welfare programs. Federal grants often have matching requirements that distort state and local budget priorities. For example, the federal government may make money available for mass transit systems but require local and state governments to provide an equal amount of new money for the project.

Capital Budgets and Bonds

Capital budgets are created to account for spending on major projects that will be paid for over many years. Major new buildings are a typical element in a capital budget. For example, instead of paying for the construction of a new dormitory out of a single year's budget, the state charges the public university for the costs over the life of the building; the costs are essentially shifted to the operating budget over time. Oregon's capital budget is not included in table 13.1 because capital budget projects are actually paid for by the other types of budgets.

Capital budgets are often funded through bonds. Bonds are loans that finance the construction of a facility or the provision of a service and are paid off over period of time. The government raises funds by issuing bonds to investors. The bonds are then repaid out of a government's general revenue stream ("general revenue bonds") or by money generated by the new facility ("revenue bonds"). An example of a revenue bond would be an improvement in a water system that is paid for by future water charges. The public's willingness or unwillingness to approve bond measures often reveals whether a community favors conservative populism or progressivism. No communities pass all bonds, but some, such as Corvallis, are much more likely to do so than are more conservative areas.

STATE AND LOCAL REVENUE OPTIONS

Political battles over taxes have two dimensions. The first dimension concerns how much money the government needs or should have. This time-less fight places fiscal conservatives advocating a very limited government against the progressive view that government services should enhance social opportunity and equity. The proper size of government deserves thought, but here we will consider the other side of the tax debate: the best way to raise government revenues.

Traditionally, state and local governments have depended on three major revenue sources: property taxes, sales taxes, and income taxes. Some analysts describe state and local budgets as being a "three-legged stool" because of the dominance of these three revenue sources. States with only two legs are considered off balance because they rely mainly on two revenue sources. Such states tend to have much higher tax rates in their two revenue sources. In addition, revenues in these states are strongly affected when either of their main tax sources change. Oregon's lack of sales tax gives it only two legs, making a higher income tax necessary. Until Measure 5 the state also had high property taxes. Across the Columbia River, Washington residents have no income tax but they pay high sales taxes.

Probably the most controversial aspect of taxes, beside their sheer costs, is their fairness. There are a variety of different ideas regarding what constitutes a "fair tax." In Oregon many of the battles over taxes reflect different opinions as to what is fair. One way to evaluate the fairness of a tax is to use the "ability to pay" principle of equity. This approach assumes that those who earn more can afford to pay a higher percentage of their income in taxes. The ability to pay principle holds that *progressive* taxes, those that require wealthier people to pay a higher tax rate, are desirable. Accordingly, taxes that take a greater percentage of the earnings of low-income earners than high-income people are *regressive* and undesirable.[12]

Another approach to equity emphasizes the "benefit principle," which postulates that those who benefit from a service should pay for it. The benefit principle is notable also for its link to the market system, because the funding of services by beneficiaries would connect price to use. Some argue that "flat," or "proportional," taxes, which take the same percentage from all taxpayers, are most fair.

Property Taxes

In Oregon counties administer and collect property tax revenues and distribute them to various local governments, including school districts. Basically, the property tax requires three steps: 1) assessment—determining the value of the property for tax purposes, 2) application of the tax rate to that property, and 3) collection. For example, the owner of a house assessed at $100,000 in an area with a total property tax of 1.5 percent would have a tax of $1,500 that year. Often, properties receive special assessments, the payments of which promote nonrevenue goals. To promote agriculture and better timber practices in Oregon, for example, farmland and timberland is specially assessed at lower values.

The voters' refusal to adopt major property tax cuts in the 1980s, despite rapidly increasing property values, testifies to the historical strength of Oregon's progressivism. Finally, over twenty years after Californians fundamentally altered their system through Proposition 13 in 1978, Oregonians passed a major property tax reduction in the form of Measure 5 in 1990. Measure 5 had three central elements: 1) after a short phase-in period, property tax rates were limited to a total of 1.5 percent of the assessed value, with school districts receiving half of a percent (0.5 percent) at most; 2) the state government must compensate local school districts for their lost revenues; and 3) counties must update property-value assessments every three years. Before Measure 5 property tax rates varied greatly in the state; more urbanized areas, like Washington County, near Portland, had overall tax rates of 2.5 percent to 3 percent, most of it going to the school districts.[13]

Many residential property owners were disappointed in the effects of Measure 5 on their tax bills. Initially, the phase-in delayed some savings. Far more important, Measure 5's requirement that assessments be more current meant that many people in areas with outdated assessments and fast-rising property values (most notably in the Portland metro area) received lower tax rates but on much higher property values. The homeowner whose property was assessed at $100,000 in 1990 might find that it was reassessed at $250,000 by 1994. Even with a 50 percent rate cut, this person would owe more in taxes. Homeowners in the Portland suburbs, the staunchest supporters of Measure 5, benefited the least since their assessments were often out of date in 1990 and their values were rising the fastest. Once the new rates were established, homeowner taxes would continue to rise as fast as their property values. Business and industrial interests benefited the most because their property values generally grew at a much slower rate and their assessments were usually more current.[14]

Even with rising assessments for many metropolitan homeowners, the tax savings of business and industrial properties and in areas of stagnant property values meant Measure 5 reduced local revenues greatly. Before 1990 the property tax rates for Oregon school districts nearly always topped the half-a-percentage-point limit, with many district rates being three to five times as high. Property tax revenues for other local governments were generally not affected because they rarely exceeded the one-percent limit prior to the measure's passage. Hopes that the state would prevent schools from harm were generally in vain. While the state school fund grew from $611.3 million in 1990–1991 to $1,750 million in 1995–1996, school property tax revenues declined by $631.6 million; also, enrollments grew and inflation continued. As dramatic as the shifts in state support seem, the net change was a 4 percent decline in per pupil spending between 1990 and 1996. The impact on other state-funded programs varied because some could "backfill" with increased charges (such as tuition). Overall, thirty-one of seventy-one state agencies had less actual money to spend in 1993–1995 than in 1991–1995, and many other programs had increases that did not keep pace with inflation and caseload increases.[15]

Dissatisfied with Measure 5's outcome, Oregon voters approved Measure 47 in 1996, which Bill Sizemore's Oregon Taxpayers United sponsored. Measure 47 was confusing, so the legislature submitted a revised version to state voters in the form of Measure 50, which voters approved in 1997. Measure 50 had three key elements. First, assessed values would be calculated for 1997–1998 on the basis of the 1995–1996 real market less 10 percent, ensuring all property owners a savings of at least 10 percent. Second, increases in assessed values were limited to 3 percent per year. Together, these first two elements separated property tax assessments from the market value of the property. Henceforth, assessed values were to be calculated from the discounted 1995–1996 base with no more than a 3 percent increase. Given that property values frequently increase more than 10 percent annually in high-growth areas, such as Bend or the Portland suburbs, tax assessments will increasingly fall behind market values there. Properties may be reassessed to market value only when they are subdivided, rezoned, lose exemptions, or have major new construction.[16]

Two other elements of Measure 50 deserve special note. First, local governments were given the option of passing option levies up to the amount that would have been raised under Measure 5. Essentially, a local government could create a levy that raises the amount of revenue lost due to the property tax assessment lag from Measure 50, effectively raising the tax rate over 1.5 percent These local option levies cannot be permanent and may not exceed five years for operating levies and ten years for capital levies. Second, unless they are placed on general election ballots in November of even years, local property tax increases and bond measures require a "double majority": a majority of eligible voters must turn out, and a majority must approve the levy.

Measures 5 and 50 have powerfully altered state and local fiscal policy. Funding for public primary and secondary schools shifted from being 30 percent from state general funds to 70 percent between 1990 and 1997. Approximately $2 billion per year of the state's general fund was spent on K–12 education in the 2001–2002 budget cycle.[17]

Property taxes are unpopular. One reason is that they come as a single lump-sum bill. Each October, Oregon property owners receive the notice from the county that they owe a big chunk of money, generally over a thousand dollars and sometimes much more. Although counties generally allow payments in partial sums, the property tax bills have significant shock value, especially right before the autumn elections. Also, so many people contest property assessments that counties have well-established processes for handling appeals. Finally, property taxes can be particularly difficult on people on fixed incomes. A house bought for $50,000 in Beaverton in 1965 could easily be worth $250,000 today. This can create a problem for long-tem owners with fixed or declining incomes, even with the limits in Measures 5 and 50.

The fairness of property taxes is unclear. Though rich people generally live in more expensive houses, they also tend to pay a lower percentage of their income on housing than lower income families. In addition, the wealthy tend to own business or other properties that are taxed. Often people think that renters do not pay property taxes, overlooking how landlords figure in taxes when calculating their rent charges. Some experts argue that local taxes and services are an important part of how local governments compete to attract and keep businesses and residents. This approach, sometimes called the Tiebout model, views locally based fiscal systems like property taxes as desirable, since the quality of life in communities is connected to their taxing and spending decisions. This model is similar to the benefit principle, which says fairness occurs when taxpayers directly benefit from the government services they fund.[18]

Property taxes have one real strong point: they are more stable and predictable than other revenue sources. Because assessments change relatively slowly, property taxes are more predictable year to year than sales or income taxes, though they certainly change over time.

Sales Taxes

Oregon has no general sales tax. Efforts to reform Oregon's tax system often include implementing a sales tax despite their consistent rejection by voters. Sales taxes have several notable characteristics. First, they are usually shared between a state and its local governments. Often the local governments have the power to choose, within limits, how much tax they will add to the higher state rate. Second, sales taxes are relatively simple for the government to administer because retailers actually do the collecting. The state typically has to oversee only the process for accuracy and honesty.

Sales taxes are generally regressive but can be made less so by excluding basic necessities of food, clothing, and medicines. Still, the less affluent generally spend a higher percentage of their incomes paying this tax when it is present. To be more progressive, a sales tax could include personal services, such as legal or financial counseling, which the wealthy and the elderly use more. But expanding sales taxes in this way is politically dangerous. Florida repealed its tax on services after only six months of operation in face of powerful political opposition, led by advertisers and supported by Democrats and the elderly.[19] Sales taxes are usually more stable than income taxes but not nearly as predictable as property taxes. Economists often support the sales tax concept because such "consumption taxes" encourage more saving and investment.

Income Tax

Oregon state government runs primarily on personal income taxes. This has a few implications for the state budget. When times are good, tax revenues soar. Economic growth of the 1990s allowed the state to compensate significantly for the property tax cuts from Measures 5 and 50. However, when times go bad income tax revenues drop almost immediately. This created the budget crisis of 2002–2003, which fits the patterns of dramatic rises and falls established when Oregon lived in the boom-and-bust cycle of the timber industry.

Oregon's system is often highly ranked for equity, since its income tax system has higher rates for higher incomes. Richard Winters rates Oregon the fourth most progressive state tax system.[20] These ratings are a bit misleading, however, since taxpayers reach the highest category in Oregon's tax schedule at a relatively low income: $6,100 of taxable income for singles and $12,200 for married couples filing joint returns in the year 2000.[21] Overall, Oregon's tax schedule provides for three tax rates: 5, 7, and 9 percent. Oregon provides an earned income credit, which allows low-wage workers to keep more of their earnings, but the impact is small. Earned income credit is a progressive concept, but in Oregon only 148,000 claims were processed, and these taxpayers received an average of only forty-six dollars each.[22]

Oregon actually has two income taxes. The personal income tax, which all wage earners pay, accounts for about 80 percent of general funds/lottery revenues, and the corporate income tax contributes about a tenth as much. Income taxes are easy for the state to administer because employers or the taxpayers themselves collect the money. While nobody likes taxes, income taxes are accepted by most Oregonians as a fact of life.

Other Revenue Sources

The state also receives revenue from three significant but lesser other sources: excise taxes, gambling, and user fees. These sources play an increasingly important role in state and local budgets.

Since the 1980s most states have used at least some form of gambling as a source for revenue. Oregon's "lottery" is actually dominated by video poker, which brings in over three-fourths of the revenue. The desirability of state-supported gambling and of a gambling-supported state, is a matter of significant public disagreement. While gambling revenues are regressive in that lower income people gamble disproportionately more, the public seems to consider it fair because gambling is a personal choice.

Two points about gambling revenues deserve special emphasis: 1) gambling does not raise money on the scale that general income, sales, and income taxes do, and 2) gambling revenues are addictive. Once adopted, states tend to depend increasingly on gambling revenues because of their popularity.

Excise taxes are taxes placed on specific goods. Often they are dedicated to specific programs, such as how fuel taxes are spent on highways. Except for luxury taxes, applied in some states, excise taxes are regressive because they are commonly placed on things that both rich and poor alike use: fuel, liquor, and tobacco. Excise taxes can be relatively popular. "Sin taxes" on alcohol and tobacco raise the price of things our society condemns publicly. Other excise taxes, such as the fuel tax, are not so well received. In spring 2000 voters rejected an effort by the Oregon legislature to increase the gasoline tax by five cents per gallon.

User fees are charges directly levied for the use of public services. They include camping fees, tuition, bus tokens, and fishing licenses. User fees, like gambling revenues, are viewed by many as being more equitable because only those using the public resource pay for it. They can be regressive, however, because higher income earners tend to use public services proportionately less. One problem with high user fees is that sometimes they discourage optimal use of public services. For example, low mass-transit fees encourage people to take mass transit and can free up highway and parking space for others and help preserve the business center's tax base. Similarly, raising tuition may make students pay for their education, but it also reduces access for the less wealthy and reduces the overall quality of the workforce.

Both excise taxes and fees are considered desirable when analyzed according to the benefit principle. Fishing licenses, tuition, and other use-related fees, and dedicated taxes such as the fuel tax fund are paid for by the direct beneficiaries of the services. The benefit principle justifies taxes on cigarettes and alcohol because drinkers and smokers tend to use public services more.

OTHER KEY BUDGET FEATURES

In addition to the basic structure of budgets described above, some special aspects of the budget process that strongly influence the overall nature of

Oregon's revenue and spending system deserve attention. Of the innumerable possible specific aspects that could be selected, these four features were chosen because of the significance of their impact or because of the fact that they operate uniquely in Oregon.

Tax Expenditures

First, like most states Oregon has an extensive system of exceptions to its basic tax rates. These are known by many names, such as "tax loopholes," "tax breaks," or by their technical name: *tax expenditures*. A tax expenditure is money that the government would get under the basic tax law but that it does not receive because of exceptions made to the basic tax laws. Tax expenditures reward people for certain activities and can be seen as a subsidy for those activities. They include discounts on property taxes for farmers, mortgage deductions for homeowners, and the depreciation of business buildings. In his proposed 2003–2005 budget, Governor Kulongoski estimated that deductions, exemptions, discounts, and credits will cost Oregon's state and local governments about $27 billion in revenues. Property tax exemptions are projected to exceed $19 billion, nearly three times the amount of money to be collected.[23]

The Kicker

Oregon has one budget law that is unique: the "2 percent kicker." Simply put, the kicker is the legal requirement stipulating that if income tax revenues exceed projections for the biennium by more than 2 percent, then all the revenue above the projection must be sent back to the taxpayers. Personal income taxes and corporate income taxes are considered separately in determining and distributing kicker funds. Table 13.4 lists the size of revenue surpluses for both of these taxes since the 1991–93 fiscal year. The table also shows the percentage of the tax revenue returned through the kicker, and how business and personal tax kickers may vary. In 1995–1997 businesses received a greater percentage of their taxes back than individual taxpayers. In 1997–1999 and 1999–2001 the opposite occurred; business revenues were too low to trigger the kicker but individuals benefited.

The legislature voted to keep the personal income tax kicker in 1989–1991 and the corporate kicker in 1991–1993 in order to meet the demands for more state money for schools. Keeping the kicker will require a public vote in the future, however, since voters placed this requirement in the state constitution in the November 2000 elections.

Table 13.4. Tax Revenue Surplus and Kicker Payments

Biennium	Personal tax revenue surplus (in millions of dollars)	Percentage of personal tax revenues returned as kicker	Corporate tax revenue surplus (in millions of dollars)	Percentage of corporate tax revenues returned as kicker
1991–1993	60	(no kicker)	18	(kicker kept by state)
1993–1995	163	(6.3)	167	(50.1)
1995–1997	431	(14.4)	203	(42.2)
1997–1999	167	(4.6)	69 (deficit)	no kicker
1999–2001	254	(6.0)	44 (deficit)	no kicker

Source: Oregon Legislative Revenue Office, Oregon's 2% Surplus Kicker: 2001 Update, Salem, September 2001.

This recent history of the kicker illustrates the difficulty budgetmakers have predicting revenues over the life of each two-year budget. Some analysts believe excess revenues should be invested in a "rainy day fund" from which they can be drawn when times turn bad. Others think that the money should simply be spent because it reflects economic growth that is probably accompanied by an increased demand or need for state services. Conservative populists believe that government gets too much already and that keeping the kicker only builds in demands for future budget growth.

The Impact of Initiatives

Progressive policies collide head-on with conservative populist activism when the public votes on measures that affect government taxing and spending. Initiatives affect state and local budgets in three ways.

First, both conservative and progressive policy advocates promote mandates as a way to push government funds toward their favored programs. Often mandates are explicit, such as when voters passed Measure 66 in 1998 requiring the state to direct 15 percent of lottery funds to natural resource and park programs. At other times the mandates are not written in budget terms but have great budget impacts. When voters passed Measure 11 in 1994 adopting the "three strikes and you're out" mandatory sentencing law, they not only changed the sentencing code but also forced state legislators to spend hundreds of millions of dollars more on state prison programs than previous projected.

Second, initiatives can be used to change tax rates directly. Conservative populists did so in 1990 with Measure 5. Measure 23 in the 2002 election would have created a comprehensive health care system financed by new income taxes.

Third, initiatives can be used to make future tax changes difficult. Examples include Measure 47/50's "double majority" provision and 1996's Measure 25, which requires a three-fifths majority in the state legislature to pass any tax increases.

Oregon's State-Spending Limit

In 1979 the state legislature passed a law forbidding the state general funds budget to grow faster than the growth of personal income in the previous two years. Generally, if times are good, this limit has no impact because the legislature does not seek to go above the limit anyway. The limit creates problems when an economic dip makes the spending limit lower than some people think is necessary for good policy. In the three biennia from 1987 to 1993, the legislature suspended the limit to avoid drastic program cuts. Overall, this law ratchets down the proportion of general fund spending relative to the general Oregon economy.[24]

LOCAL GOVERNMENT BUDGETS

Local budgets differ from the state and federal budgets significantly. The first distinctive aspect of local government budgets is that they are completely subject to state law. Although the state does not continuously meddle in local budgeting, it strongly shapes these budgets through laws that affects revenue, such as Measure 5, or policies that regulate how local governments perform particular services.

Local governments also have highly variable revenue structures, though they rely predominantly on state funds and property taxes. Many special districts, particularly sewer and water districts and public power cooperatives, are funded entirely from charges to their consumers. Cities have perhaps the most complicated revenue streams. Salem receives money from fees and charges, grants, property taxes, licenses and fines, and various bonds.

Oregon school districts have the simplest revenue patterns because they basically rely on property taxes and state funds, with another 10 percent or less coming from the federal government.

Like the state, cities have multiple budgets. The most visible and flexible local government funds are in the general funds category. Property taxes account for the largest component of Salem's general fund revenues, supplying about 44 percent of the $72 million available in the 2001–2002 budget. The second major source is franchise fees, which provided more than 13 percent. Franchise fees are charges for use of public rights of way. For power and electricity, for example, the utilities pay about 5 percent of their local revenues to maintain their lines in city streets, alleys, and sidewalk spaces. The rest of the revenue comes from a diverse blend of fees, grants, fines, and transfers from other programs. General funds spending is dominated by police (almost 30 percent) and fire service (21 percent), followed by a diverse array of lesser community services and operating funds.

Cities and counties also have a wide range of specialized funds that may be funded entirely by a specific tax or fee, such as those for Salem's water and sewer fund. These programs each have specific revenue sources and legal limitations. Of Salem's all funds resources of $220.9 million for 2001–2002, the general funds' $72 million is about 32.6 percent, or nearly one-third, of the total. The water and sewer fund is next, at $55.7 million, or about 25 percent.[25]

Public school funding in Oregon paid for over 540,000 students, 35,000 teachers and aides, and 1,250 school sites in 2003. Because the state general fund provides about 70 percent of the money, how the state allocates money between the districts is important. Fundamentally, the state's "equalization" formula is based on the premise that spending per student should be equal throughout the state. The state supplements local property tax funding to make per student spending equal in each district. State allocations are then adjusted to reflect variable local circumstances, specifically the district's number of students, student costs, teacher experience, transportation needs, and construction costs. Districts receive more money if they have greater student needs, like a large number of disabled, non-English-speaking, or low-income students.[26]

Overall, school funding across the state has become more equitable since Measure 5 passed in 1990. Previously, local property taxes determined funding levels. Wealthy areas could fund good schools much more easily than poorer districts. Today, the state ensures that all districts provide a minimum amount of funding to their schools. Previously well-funded districts like

Portland and Corvallis have suffered because the new state formula does not match their historical levels of spending, but districts with lower property values or where citizens were not supportive of property taxes benefited.[27]

Frustrated by the funding cuts to the Portland area schools, some Multnomah County residents have taken the potentially revolutionary step of adopting a local income tax whose revenue goes primarily to public schools. Advocates of this policy say that the increased dependence on state funds has hurt Portland schools disproportionately and unacceptably. Portland's adoption of a local income tax reduced the progressive Metro area voters' concern for statewide school funding. Thus, the new tax in Portland reduced pressure for statewide school funding reform and probably helped doom the state legislature's income tax supplement when it went before the voters in February 2004. Ultimately, the Portland area's new approach to supporting schools may lead to greater school funding inequities in Oregon. The new tax's supporters say that equality based on bringing standards in Portland so far down was not desirable anyway. Public school advocates in other cities, such as Corvallis, are considering similar ideas as well.

BUDGET PRESSURES AND TRENDS

State legislatures are always under fire as they make their budgets. Local budget sessions can be just as contentious. The lines typically are drawn between the conservative populists, who argue that the government does too much or that cutting government waste could make up for any tax cuts, and progressives, who advocate for a more active and well-funded government.

Two major factors beyond the control of the combatants influence what they fight over. First, the state of the economy determines budget possibilities. Inflation, growth, and unemployment rates determine both the revenue levels and the demands for publicly financed services. The need for the state legislature to come up with about $1.75 billion in cuts or revenue increases in 2002 dramatically illustrated this fact, as did the magnitude of the kicker payments of the late 1990s. Second, Oregon's budget priorities may be affected by federal policies. Changes in Medicaid, to note the most important example, can powerfully influence the state and local budgets because half of the funding for the Oregon Health Plan comes from Washington. Cutbacks on the federal side create pressures for the state to increase its spending or cut back on health care for the poor.

Whether Oregon will continue as a relatively low-tax state depends ultimately on the voters. Conservative populist groups such as Oregon Taxpayers United defined the fiscal agenda in the 1990s through ballot measures. Yet Oregon voters seem unwilling to fully embrace conservative populism. None of the Oregon Taxpayers United three major tax limitation measures in the November 2000 election passed. Progressives could not be too pleased, however; the same voters embedded the 2 percent kicker in the state constitution and increased the deduction allowed for federal taxes on state's tax returns. And in January 2003 and February 2004 voters overwhelmingly rejected tax increases designed to fill the temporary budget shortfalls, leading to cuts in state services and education.

As of 2004 Oregonians statewide have clearly chosen budget cuts over tax increases when the choice arises. This pattern has led to the emergence of local efforts to provide revenue for protecting service levels and improving local education systems. For example, Multnomah County passed Measure 26/48 in May 2003 that will institute a local income tax of 1.25 percent to provide additional local funding for eight school districts and for law enforcement and social services. Other localities may be moving this direction as well (like Benton County), but the appeal of such measures in areas dominated by populist conservatives is suspect. The movement of progressive local jurisdictions toward local funding options demonstrates the current inability of the more progressive statewide leaders and groups to sell their vision of how government can best serve Oregonians.

CHAPTER FOURTEEN

Environmental Policy

Brent S. Steel and Denise Lach

Logging, agriculture, grazing, mining, and fishing have all been important to Oregon's economic and social fabric, as symbolized by their presence on the official state seal. However, increasing public interest—especially in urban areas—in protecting wildlife habitat, fish species, wilderness, recreational access, and other nonextractive uses coupled with questions about traditional resource management practices have become the subject of increasing controversy and litigation, particularly with regard to public forests, rangelands, and rivers. At the heart of this debate are differing values and interests concerning the natural environment and the proper relationship of humans to their ecological surroundings. These views in turn are connected to different conceptions about environmental policy and the management of Oregon's natural resources.

There are those who believe we should *conserve* natural resources in ways that protect the resources for human purposes. The bounty of Oregon's environment has always been used, first by Native Americans and later by white settlers. The moderate climate in western Oregon promotes growth of all types of biological life, from wild berries to four-hundred-foot Douglas fir trees, from fish-filled rivers to fields of elk and deer herds. The more arid climate on the east side of the Cascade Mountains provides less natural bounty but has been domesticated through irrigation technology, which has supported viable agriculture and forestry for many decades. Oregon farmers and ranchers, for example, often view themselves as stewards of the environment, arguing that unless they take care of the land they own, it will not provide them with a living. They point to habitat conservation areas and easements, wild birds that feast on their crops and plowed fields, and sustainable yields of timber. Individuals who live in or rely on the rural landscape often express the view that we must "continue to rely heavily on natural resource industries which have recently faced serious downturns."[1] The conservation worldview is typically expressed by those who have developed and supported environmental policies that protect the natural world for human use, including Oregon's groundbreaking bottle and beach bills, discussed below.

Others argue, however, that we should *preserve* natural resources even if human needs are not met. The preservation viewpoint is a relative newcomer to Oregon, emerging during the early part of the twentieth century and finding strong proponents beginning in the 1960s. Human impacts, preservationists argue, have devastated the environment, and society needs to act to protect pristine areas and to restore degraded areas. The need to preserve is often expressed by many urban Oregonians, who are less likely to be involved in resource industries and employed, instead, in the rapidly growing service and high-tech sectors.[2] Progressives in Oregon have built both policy and movements that reflect the preservation ethic, including the recent Sustainability Act (2002) and land-use planning rules that limit the sprawl of urban areas into farmlands and forestlands.

The goal of this chapter is to provide a brief introduction to these differing value orientations toward the environment, and toward environmental policy in Oregon. We begin with a brief history of environmental policy in Oregon and then discuss the development of competing environmental management paradigms evident in Oregon. The concluding sections of the chapter discuss the policy environment and the actors involved in the natural resource and environmental policy process in Oregon.

HISTORY AND CONTEXT OF ENVIRONMENTAL POLICY IN OREGON

The environmental policy of Oregon reflects the state's transformation from a resource-extraction economy beginning in the mid-1800s to a postindustrial society in the latter part of the twentieth century, when high-tech, global companies such as Intel, Hewlett Packard, and Nike came to economic prominence. Concern for the protection of natural resources was not an important policy priority during most of Oregon's history. The environment was seen as something to conquer in order to improve the quality of human life, and there was little concern about sustainable harvesting of resources. According to W. Douglas Costain and James Lester, this period can be characterized "as a period of resource exploitation by a rising industry, during which time natural resources were subordinated to political objectives of industrial development, homestead settlement, and the promotion of free enterprise."[3] The *Oregon State of the Environment Report 2000* describes this period: "Early in Oregon's history, people saw the abundance of natural resources as something ready to be harvested, vast riches to be cut, plowed, or caught. Yet the intensity of harvest outpaced the land's natural ability to replenish, and as early as the 1920s, wheat lands in the Columbia Plateau were losing topsoil, grasslands in eastern Oregon were grazed bare, and the once looming salmon industry was in decline."[4]

During the early twentieth century, there was growth in the number of individuals and groups interested in natural resource conservation both in Oregon and across the country. With proponents such as W. J. McGee and Gifford Pinchot, environmental policy in Oregon and the United States began to reflect a resource conservation philosophy. A multidimensional conservation policy has evolved over time but is grounded on several ethical and political principles concerning natural resources: wise human use and development of resources, preservation of natural resources for future generations, and democratic allocation of those resources for the greater public good.[5]

The conservation ideology reflects a "human centered orientation toward the non-human world," putting humans, their needs, and satisfactions as the primary focus in all relationships with the natural world.[6] Moreover, it assumes that the nonhuman part of the environment is "material to be used by humans as they see fit."[7] The natural world is treated as a *resource* that humans can use for their own purposes rather than as the setting that all humans and nonhumans require for life. At the heart of the conservation ethic is the idea of stewardship—that humans have a responsibility to maintain the environment in a way that allows its use by future generations. Thus, providing for continuing human use becomes the primary aim of natural resource management, whether for commodity benefits (such as timber and forage) or for aesthetic, spiritual, or physical benefits (such as outdoor recreation).

This conservation ethic was implemented during President Theodore Roosevelt's administration (1901–1909), under Gifford Pinchot's guidance. During this time the national forest system expanded from 41 to 159 reserves, and government sought more efficient use of forest resources for the good of the country. Oregon senator Charles McNary (1917–1944), a republican, was instrumental in promoting expansion of the U.S. Forest Service through cosponsorship of the Clark-McNary Act (1924) and the McSweeny-McNary Act (1928). A conservation management philosophy continues to be advocated by many officials and employees in federal resource agencies such as the U.S. Forest Service and the Bureau of Land Management BLM.

Conservationists promoted the huge Columbia River system, with eighteen dams harnessing the great power of the river to produce electricity at over 150 hydropower projects. This inexpensive energy source drove economic growth in the northwest throughout the second half of the twentieth century and helped to build Oregon's cities and economy. Hydroelectric power is still a dominant source of energy for the region, and the water stored in reservoirs behind the dams plays a significant role in Oregon's agriculture—especially in eastern and central Oregon, where the climate and landscape is hot and dry during the growing season.

Some of the more significant innovations adopted during this period include the creation of the Oregon Beach Bill in 1967, guaranteeing public access to beaches; the Department of Environmental Equality in 1969; the 1971 Oregon Bottle Bill, requiring deposits on beverage containers; and the 1971 State Forest Practices Act, which regulates private forestry practices and harvests.

By the second half of the twentieth century, however, it was apparent to many citizens that the conservationist approach was not working well in many parts of Oregon. As described in the *Oregon State of the Environment Report 2000*: "By the 1960s, it was clear that parts of Oregon's environment were not healthy. . . . Oregon's political leaders responded with a series of landmark initiatives to clean up Oregon's waterways and limit urban sprawl. Led by Governor Tom McCall [R], Oregon became a leader in protecting water quality, green way preservation, land-use planning, protection of agricultural land, and recycling. Also, in cleaning up the Willamette River, the State demonstrates that environmental quality need not be sacrificed for economic growth."[8]

During this same period a new approach to environmental policy was emerging in Oregon. Drawing on the ideas of thinkers like John Muir and Aldo Leopold, the preservation ideology shifted away from concentrating on human use of the environment and turned to a more "biocentered" or "ecocentered" philosophy.[9] From this perspective the natural world (of which humans are one of many components) holds value in itself, regardless of any use we might have for it. The world is perceived as a complex web of biotic and abiotic elements, each with its own contribution to making the whole system function. The role for natural resource management from this perspective becomes one of balancing human use with protection of the larger ecosystem.

Innovative environmental policies growing out of the preservation world-view include the 170-mile Willamette River Greenway; statewide land-use planning, including an urban growth boundary to limit sprawl across natural landscapes; the Northwest Power Planning Council; and the Oregon Salmon Plan. The Northwest Power Plan Act (1980), for example, brought together representatives from the four Columbia River states (Oregon, Washington, Idaho, and Montana) to collaboratively oversee the multiple uses of the river, in particular to balance human use (hydropower, irrigation, and transportation) with wildlife habitat. When several salmonid species were listed as threatened or endangered under the Endangered Species Act of 1973 ESA, the Oregon Salmon Plan was implemented to create place-based and voluntary councils responsible for managing stream recovery in local watersheds. In 2002 the Oregon legislature signed the Sustainability Act, directing state agencies to consider environmental and community costs in their practices and policies. The bill was developed by a group of Republican and Democratic legislators, the Associated Oregon Industries (a private sector lobbying group), and Defenders of Wildlife (a nonprofit environmental group). Oregon is viewed by many as a model of visionary environmental and natural resource policy; this is a legacy of both conservationist and preservationist ideals and policies. Table 14.1 lists major events in the environmental history of Oregon.

Throughout the late twentieth century and early twenty-first century, however, new efforts at environmental preservation have sometimes clashed with traditional conservation values, resulting in public controversy and frequent litigation. Many social scientists who study environmental policy describe this conflict in terms of "changing paradigms." Since Thomas Kuhn's book *The Structure of Scientific Revolutions* was published, social scientists have used the term "paradigm" to describe how people think about and interpret the world around them.[10] A dominant social paradigm (DSP) is a worldview that is pervasive in a society and often reflected in values concerning proper public policy. Belief in the DSP is, by definition, so accepted that most people take its assumptions as self-evident. When a significant number of people start to question the accuracy and relevance of the DSP, the paradigm shifts. Some social scientists argue that we are now in the process of replacing the DSP with a new environmental paradigm (NEP). These two competing paradigms, with their starkly different stands on environmental policy and natural resource management, have been described by social scientists such as Riley Dunlap and Kent Van Liere.[11] The DSP worldview reflects anthropocentric beliefs and conservation ethics, mainly

Table 14.1. A Brief Environmental Policy History of Oregon

1864	First salmon cannery opens in Astoria.
1887	An *Oregonian* investigation concludes that the Columbia River is being fished out.
1891	Congress grants the president power to establish forest reserves in the region.
1900s	Columbia white-tailed deer, mountain goats, and coastal sea otters virtually disappear because of hunting and habitat loss.
1902	Crater Lake National Park is created.
1913	Beaches are declared a public highway, preventing private development.
1925	State park system is created.
1930	Oregon Fish Commission survey estimates that half the state's salmon habitat has disappeared.
1933	First Tillamook forest fire burns 311,000 acres of timber.
1939	Second Tillamook forest fire burns 220,000 acres of timber.
1951	Oregon imposes the first statewide laws to control air pollution.
1967	Governor Tom McCall signs Oregon Beach Bill, guaranteeing public access to state beaches.
1971	Governor Tom McCall signs the Bottle Deposit Bill, the nation's first law requiring refundable deposits on soda and beer bottles.
1972	The Forest Practices Act passes, regulating harvest practices on 11.7 million acres of nonfederal state forestlands.
1973	State lawmakers pass a law creating statewide comprehensive land-use planning.
1975	Portland limits downtown parking because the city had violated the federal air-quality standard for carbon monoxide fifty times.
1980	Power Planning Act creates NW Power Planning Council to develop remedy for fish and wildlife problems associated with operation of federal hydroelectric dams.
1983	State legislature requires garbage services to offer curbside recycling.
1986	Nineteen animals and nine plant species are listed as endangered or threatened, including the northern spotted owl, the coho salmon, the western pond turtle, and the western painted turtle.
1997	The Oregon Plan for Salmon and Watersheds is established. The plan sets out how federal, state, and local government agencies, watershed councils, and scientists are to restore diminishing salmon and steelhead runs.
1998	The Oregon Salmon Plan (implemented by executive order) commences management of salmon streams using local and voluntary watershed councils; timber harvests hit the lowest level in seventy years, lumber- and wood-products jobs decline to 50,316 and high-tech jobs increase to 70,302.
1999	Nine salmon and steelhead runs are listed under the Endangered Species Act.
2000	Portland Harbor is listed as a Superfund site; voters pass Measure 7 (overturned in 2002 by Oregon Supreme Court); Sustainability Act passed by Oregon Legislature.

(*See sources next page*)

that natural resource management policy and practices should be directed toward goods and services that benefit humans.

The NEP, in contrast, has a biocentric view toward natural resources and emphasizes the protection and preservation of ecosystems. It can be summarized in the words of Aldo Leopold: "A thing is right when it tends to preserve the integrity, stability, and beauty of the biotic community. It is wrong when it tends otherwise."[12] The NEP suggests that continued population growth, urbanization, and consumption of natural resources will have serious socioeconomic, political, and ecological consequences up to and including the long-term survival of the human species. Table 14.2 presents the major assumptions and orientations of the two rival paradigms.

Differences between these paradigms may underlie the conflict over environmental policy in Oregon. The debates may also reflect differences between urban and rural perspectives due to differing economic interests, as well as progressive and conservative perspectives concerning proper government policy. For example, efforts to preserve old-growth forests have been described as the imposition of urban values at the expense of resource-based livelihoods and cultures. The survey data presented in table 14.3 provide some insight into how urban and rural Oregonians view natural resources and the environment. A representative random sample of Oregonians conducted in 1999 showed that urban residents were more likely to endorse the NEP and progressive policies, and their rural counterparts tended to be much more conservative (see table 14.3). For example, 81 percent of urban residents agreed with the statement "greater efforts should be given to protect wildlife on public lands" compared to 32 percent of rural residents.

Another factor contributing to environmental policy conflicts in Oregon is the large role of federal landowners. Approximately 57 percent of Oregon's 61 million acres is owned and managed by the federal government. This includes thirteen national forests with 15.6 million acres managed by the U.S. Department of Agriculture's Forest Service and 15.7 million acres managed by the U. S. Department of the Interior's Bureau of Land Management. Practices on federal lands are directed by policies originating

Sources: The *Oregonian*, *The Oregon Story, 1850–2000* (Portland: Graphic Arts Center Publishing, 2000); Oregon Public Broadcasting, "The Oregon Trail Timeline," http://www.pbs.org/opb/oregontrail/teacher/timeline; William G. Robins, *Landscapes of Promise: The Oregon Story, 1800–1940* (Seattle: University of Washington Press, 1997).

Table 14.2.   Elements of Conflicting Environmental Policy Paradigms

Dominant Social Paradigm (DSP) Anthropocentric	New Environmental Paradigm (NEP) Biocentric
Nature to produce goods and services primarily for human use.	Nature for its own sake.
Emphasis on commodity production over environmental protection.	Emphasis on environmental protection over commodity production.
Primary concern for present generation.	Primary concern for future generations.
Science and technology will solve problems of resource scarcity.	Science and technology create as many problems as they solve.
Economic and population growth need not be restricted.	Economic and population growth must be limited.
Emphasis on competition and markets.	Emphasis on economic, political, and social cooperation.
Old politics, determination by experts.	New politics, consultative and participative.
Centralized and hierarchical decision making.	Decentralized and participatory decion making.

Source: Adapted from Gregory Brown and Charles Harris, "The USDA Forest Service: Toward the New Resource Management Paradigm?" Society and Natural Resources 5 (1992): 231–45.

in national policy debates, which may not reflect the environmental values of Oregonians. For example, years of political activism and litigation resulted in the 1990 Northwest Forest Plan, which shifted U.S. Forest Service goals away from timber production in the Pacific Northwest to habitat protection for the northern spotted owl and the marbled murrelet, both listed under the ESA.

In combination with economic forces and technological changes in the timber industry, the reduction in logging on federal lands in Oregon required by the listings devastated many rural timber communities. This led to an adverse reaction from those dependent on the resource as well as from many political conservatives. Both groups claimed that "spotted owls and marbled murrelets were not worth jobs and payrolls."[13] The affected communities rebelled against the government when they "discovered that the national forests and lands administered by the Bureau of Land Management . . . belonged to all the people of the United States, not the locals, and that interest groups thousands of miles away had a valid voice in crafting land use policy and use of public resources."[14] As discussed in chapter 3, this ultimately contributed to eight rural Oregon counties voting on "county

Table 14.3. Urban and Rural Public Values Concerning the Environment

	Urban Oregon (percent agree)	Rural Oregon (percent agree)
The economic vitality of local communities should be given the highest priority when making environmental decisions.	47	72
Livestock grazing should be banned on public rangelands.	36	14
Clear-cutting should be banned on public forestlands.	62	29
Endangered species laws should be set aside to preserve jobs.	19	57
More wilderness areas should be established on public lands.	67	30
Greater efforts should be given to protect wildlife on public lands.	81	32
Greater efforts should be given to protect fish on public lands and waterways.	72	61

Source: "Survey of Public Lands Issues in the Pacific Northwest," Program in Public Affairs, Washington State University–Vancouver, 1999.

supremacy" and "wise-use" ordinances in the 1990s. One such ordinance that was considered in Grant County (1995) stated, "Shall the people of Grant County refuse to recognize Federal management of certain public lands?" This ordinance was passed by 72 percent of the voters.[15]

Another conflict among federal policy, local communities, and different worldviews is taking place in Oregon's Klamath Basin. As discussed in chapter 3, farmers, Native Americans, commercial and recreational fishers, and environmentalists are engaged in an enormous policy dispute over water use and rights in the basin. Klamath Lake is home to two endangered sucker species (lost river and shortnose), and its tributaries contain endangered salmon species. Protection of endangered fish habitat requires that Klamath Lake be kept at a minimum level of 3,130 feet (above sea level). As a result of a drought during 2000–2001, lake levels dropped, and the BLM determined that water allocation must be restricted to protect fish habitat; project water was cut off to about twelve hundred farmers in the spring of 2001 after many had already planted their crops. Farmers, business people, and others in the Klamath Basin area organized to protest the decision; pictures of a standoff at the head gates to the dam made the front page of newspapers around the country. This issue is yet to be resolved, but many Oregonians still question environmental protection choices that displace historical human uses.

One place where there has been much cooperation between federal, state, and local governments, interest groups, and local communities is on the project laid out in *The Oregon Plan for Salmon and Watersheds*, established by the legislature in 1997. As with many other Oregon environmental policies, it is an innovative attempt to create public and private partnerships to restore watersheds and increase salmon runs in Oregon. This approach for fish and watershed restoration is considered innovative for the reasons provided by the governor's Natural Resources Office: "In contrast to endangered species recovery and environmental protection plans that rely primarily on regulatory approaches, the Oregon Plan represents a new way of restoring the natural system—the 'Oregon Approach.' The approach meshes scientific actions with local watershed-based support. It relies on teamwork between governments and constantly monitors results. Enforcement of current laws is combined with voluntary and cooperative actions. This plan will require an unprecedented level of cooperation and coordination."[16]

The Oregon Plan was approved in April 1997 by the federal agency responsible for managing salmon and steelhead under the Endangered Species Act—the National Marine Fisheries Service. This was the first time that a state gained federal approval of a locally designed and implemented restoration effort. It is one of the first statewide attempts at an ecosystem management where local citizens are directly involved with federal and state agencies and scientists that have a role in fish management. As such, it has generated much regional, national, and international interest among scholars, managers, and policymakers interested in new and innovative policies to resolve difficult environmental policy issues.

PUBLIC AND INTEREST GROUP INVOLVEMENT
IN THE ENVIRONMENTAL POLICY PROCESS

Recent studies of public participation in politics in the United States and Oregon suggest that a new style of participation has emerged over the course of the last several decades. Postwar economic growth, prosperity, and political stability have created an increasingly knowledgeable public that places new demands on government. Contemporary grassroots citizen organizations and social movements are more likely to engage in such "elite challenging" political activities as demonstrations and boycotts than previous generations of activists.

Contemporary political conflicts arising over complex issues such as environmental management have generated a multitude of interest groups, many of which draw citizens into the political process via single-issue concerns. Environmental organizations proliferated in Oregon as concern for the environment increased during the 1970s, mobilizing citizens, challenging traditional natural resource management practices, and presenting new proposals for public debate.

The formation of environmental groups has been key in helping many citizens deal with the complexities of environmental issues. The environmental movement has been characterized by many social scientists as an "eruption from below," with demands for increased citizen input in the policy process. Environmental groups have pushed for increased democratization as a fundamental component of environmental and natural resource policy. The activities of environmental interest groups illustrate the populist aspect of progressivism discussed in chapter 1. However, at times, certain progressive elites with support from environmental groups—such as former governor Tom McCall—also have played an important role in Oregon's environmental policy.

Political scientist Ronald Inglehart argues that there are two distinct forms of political participation.[17] The "elite-directed," or traditional, mode of political action is represented by sociopolitical institutions (such as political parties, bureaucrats, and industry) that are hierarchical in nature and that organize citizens into action through "top-down" mobilizations. The "elite challenging," or populist, mode of political action, generally more issue-specific, operates outside traditional political channels and often utilizes unconventional, sometimes disruptive, tactics to influence public policy.

The environmental movement is a form of elite-challenging and progressive populist activism in which certain segments of the public—typically in Oregon's urban areas—oppose the existing political agenda and seek to impose constraints on polluters, policymakers, and the like. For example, Alexander Mather characterizes forest management in the United States as driven by public opinion in conflict with government and those who would exploit the timber resource.[18]

According to political scientist David Truman, groups that perceive threats to existing values and who are put on the defensive tend to increase their group cohesiveness, which results in greater political activity.[19] In response to the populist behavior of the environmental movement, resource-extraction groups are motivated to network and establish a common front against more stringent environmental protection policies. Instead of competing against one another, as the market-based economy model would predict, industries work in concert to take advantage of all political opportunities to oppose the environmental movement.

A 1993 study of Oregon interest groups involved in environmental policy issues reveals the diversity of such groups and of their resources.[20] This study found several hundred interest groups attempting to influence the environmental policy process concerning the management of public forests and rangelands. The types of groups formally involved in the Oregon natural resource and environmental policy process included the following:

Environmental Protection/Conservation: Individual membership groups interested in the preservation or conservation of public lands. Examples include 1000 Friends of Oregon, Sierra Club, Portland Audubon Society, Oregon League of Conservation Voters, and the Oregon Natural Resources Council.

Passive Recreation: Membership groups representing, for example, hiking, cross-country skiing, mountain climbing, and wildlife-watching interests. Examples include the Mazamas and Chemeketans (mountain climbing groups), and the Oregon Nordic Club.

Intensive Recreation: Membership groups representing, for example, fishing, hunting, snowmobile, or powerboating interests. Examples include the Pacific Northwest 4-Wheel Drive Association, Northwest Steelheaders Association, and the Oregon State Snowmobile Association.

Industry-Related Groups: Professional and membership groups representing natural resource extraction interests on federal lands. Examples of these groups include mining groups, logging groups, and wood products unions. Examples include the Society of American Foresters, the Society for Range Management, and the Western Forestry and Conservation Association.

Industry: Nonmembership commercial organizations interested in natural resource extraction from public lands. Industries in this category include sawmills, logging companies, millworks, mining companies, timber-trucking companies, and helicopter logging concerns, such as the Southern Oregon Timber Industries Association, the Western Mining Council, and the Oregon Forest Industries Council.

Social scientists have identified various strategies that interest groups use to influence public policy. Central among these strategies are lobbying elected officials and bureaucrats, grassroots organizing to mobilize public opinion, building coalitions with other like-minded groups, and making eco-

Table 14.4. Interest Group and Industry Strategies to Influence Environmental
Policy (mean score)

Strategy	Group Type				
	Environmental	Passive Recreation	Intense Recreation	Industry-related	Industry
Testifying before a legislative committee	3.1	2.7	2.6	2.2	3.5
Making appeals to government agency personnel	4.9	2.4	2.2	2.5	3.2
Building coalitions with other groups	2.3	2.6	2.1	2.0	2.0
Instigating a letter-writing campaign	1.4	2.7	2.2	3.8	4.1
Releasing information through the mass media	2.6	3.7	3.8	3.2	3.8
Organizing a political protest	2.1	6.0	5.0	3.0	5.1
Filing court suits	3.4	3.0	5.6	4.0	5.4
	N=126	N=28	N=142	N=32	N=133

Index: 1=most effective method used, 2=second most effective, etc.
Source: Brent Steel, Peter List, and Bruce Shindler, *Directory of Oregon Forest Interest Groups* (Corvallis: Extension Forestry Program, Oregon State University, 1993).

nomic contributions to the political process. The Environmental Federation of Oregon, for example, is a consortium of thirty-two nonprofit groups working together to raise money and lobby both locally and nationally. The strategy used by an organization may be influenced by various factors, including the types and amounts of resources available, the perceived effectiveness of the strategy, and the governmental structure in place. Large memberships may give interest groups an advantage in letter writing, public demonstrations, and volunteers to carry out activities. Organizations with few members but large budgets may focus on influencing the election of key decision makers or on lobbying such decision makers after the election. The latter has been the preferred strategy used by industry, and as a result, industry has benefited significantly from government programs or subsidies.

Table 14.4 provides some insight into the strategies used by interest groups and industry to influence environmental policy in Oregon. The data displayed in the table are from the 1993 study of interest groups involved in Oregon environmental policy. The strategies listed in the table range from traditional forms of influence, such as testifying before legislative committees, to populist forms such as organizing political protests and letter-writing campaigns. All organizations were asked to rank-order the effectiveness of each method. Mean scores indicate that environmental groups rely much more on elite-challenging tactics such as letter writing, political organizing, and releasing information through the media than do industry or industry-supported groups. Only in building coalitions are the strategies of environmental and industry groups similar. Industry groups, using their traditional access to the power structure, find testifying and appealing to government agencies most effective.

STATE OF THE ENVIRONMENT

What has been the impact of Oregon's various innovative and often contro- versial environmental policies? The Resource Renewal Institute, a nonprofit, nongovernmental organization supporting innovative environmental man- agement strategies, recently named Oregon as the most sustainable state in the nation. Oregon was noted for its strong sustainability plan, the Oregon *State of the Environment* report, land-use planning, pollution prevention legislation, support of renewable energy, a climate action plan, an emission inventory, open-space protection, recycling priorities, and innovative public transportation.[21] The *Oregon State of the Environment Report 2000*, pro- duced for the Oregon Progress Board by a panel of scientists from Oregon's universities, reported, "Overall, the science panel found that Oregon has made great strides in resolving critical problems of the past. Oregon's land use laws have limited the loss of forest and farmland. Coastal zone man- agement has helped to reverse the loss of estuarine habitats. Forest practices rules have contributed to protection of forest streams. Recent changes in federal forest management emphasize protection of biodiversity on federal forests and rangelands. Yet, the panel also found that Oregonians now face a new set of environmental challenges that existing policies and programs may not be sufficient to address."[22]

In general, the report and recognition from the Resource Renewal In- stitute paint a positive picture of Oregon's environmental policies at the beginning of the twenty-first century. At the same time, there remain areas for improvement. For example, 67 percent of the major water facilities in

Oregon have expired Clean Water Act permits—the fourth worst record in the United States.[23] The Willamette River, which runs within twenty miles of the homes of 70 percent of all Oregonians is in trouble. Fish are contaminated and unfit for consumption; sewage overflows limit swimming, boating, and fishing; the Portland Harbor qualifies as a Superfund site; and 99 percent of the river's historic spring Chinook runs are gone. Environmental problems reported in Oregon's *State of the Environment Report* include inadequate water supplies, poor water quality, loss of wetlands, degraded riparian areas, depleted fish stocks, diminished biodiversity, and waste and toxic releases across the state.[24] The Resource Renewal Institute also mentions poor air quality in urban areas, lack of "right to know" legislation, and low voting rates as problems that need to be addressed by Oregon's environmental policies.[25]

The *2000 Benchmark Performance Report* by the Oregon Progress Board provides a grade for sixteen benchmarks in environmental policy (see table 14.5). For those benchmarks where data are available, Oregon's environmental policies have led to "above average" results in seven areas (that is, benchmarks 75, 77, 78, 79, 80, 81, and 84), and there are "below average" results in six other areas (benchmarks 76, 83, 85, 87, 88, and 90). Above-average results are evident for air quality, wetlands preservation, stream quality, instream water rights, preservation of agricultural lands and forestlands, and hazardous waste site cleanup. Areas with poor results include carbon dioxide emissions, solid waste, wild salmon and steelhead restoration, the health of native fish, wildlife, and plants, and the amount of state park acreage.

As discussed throughout this chapter, there are multiple visions for how we should care for Oregon's environment. In addition, there are many actors with often-conflicting missions for managing Oregon's natural resources. The population of Oregon continues to grow, and it is increasingly concentrated in urban areas. New industries with global connections are shifting economic and political power to urban areas, away from rural communities, which have economies based on resource extraction. These differences and changes have resulted in a record of both great policy innovations and stunning setbacks as Oregonians struggle to find ways to balance the values reflected in the DSP and the NEP, and in the ideas advocated by the state's progressive and conservative elements.

On the near horizon, Oregon will be challenged to develop effective water quality and allocation policies that reflect increasing demand for municipal and industrial uses even in the face of emerging shortages for irrigation,

Table 14.5. Oregon Environmental Benchmarks: The 2000 Benchmark
Performance Report

Benchmark	Description	Grade
75	Air quality: Percent of Oregonians living where the air meets government ambient air quality standards	A
76	Carbon dioxide emissions: Carbon dioxide emissions as a percentage of 1990 emissions	F
77	Wetlands preservation: Percentage of wetlands in 1990 still preserved as wetlands	A
78	Stream water quality: Monitored streams doing better and worse in terms of temperature and chemical/ biological pollutants	A for some streams, B– for others
79	Instream water rights: Percentage of key rivers meeting instream water rights for 12 months	A
80	Agricultural lands: Percent of agricultural land in 1970 still preserved for agriculture	A
81	Forest land: Percent of forest land in 1970 still preserved for agriculture	B
82	Timber harvest: Actual harvest levels as a percentage of sustainable harvest levels	NA
83	Solid waste: Pounds of municipal waste landfilled or incinerated per capita	F
84	Hazardous waste site cleanup: Percent of identified Oregon hazardous waste sites cleaned up or being cleaned up	A
85	Wild salmon and steelhead restoration: Percent of wild salmon and steelhead populations in key sub-basins that are at target levels	F
86	Marine species at risk: Percentage of assessed marine species at risk	NA
87	Native fish and wildlife: Percent of native fish and wildlife species that are healthy	D–
88	Native plant species: Percent of native plant species that are healthy	F
89	Nuisance invasive species: Number of nuisance invasive species established in Oregon	NA
90	State park acreage: Acres of state-owned parks per 1,000 Oregonians	F

Source: Oregon Progress Board, The 2000 Benchmark Performance Report, Salem.

power, and fish recovery. New state and federal laws require Oregon to set total maximal daily contaminant loads (TMDL) for streams; the regulations are likely to curtail existing practices and drive changes in agriculture and urban development. Oregon's traditionally inexpensive hydropower energy sources are being limited to meet species recovery requirements and energy requirements by other western states. "Brownfields"—contaminated sites that need to be restored for productive use—are becoming major issues for both rural and urban communities.

None of these issues is unique to Oregon; every state is facing some variation of these resource management concerns. What may be unique to Oregon is reputation for creating innovative environmental policies. The bottle bill, comprehensive land-use planning, and voluntary watershed management policies all were developed in response to seemingly intractable resource problems (waste and pollution, sprawl, and endangered species). Even now, the Department of Forestry is examining ways that state forests can be certified as "sustainable" to encourage ecosystem management practices. The DEQ is building partnerships with industry and individuals to create TMDLS through collaborative methods. Many state agencies are also collaborating with federal agencies and nongovernmental groups to create sustainable resource-based communities, such as those in the Blue Mountains of eastern Oregon, and to implement the Oregon Plan for Salmon and Watersheds.

The *Oregon State of the Environment Report* gives policymakers and the public a baseline understanding of the current conditions of our natural resources. Oregonians have experience and success in designing innovative policies for complex natural resource management issues. With leadership and public support, there is every likelihood that Oregonians will create environmental policies that are responsive to the emerging challenges.

CHAPTER FIFTEEN

Health Policy

William Lunch

Oregon's health care policy is widely viewed as a reflection of the state's innovative progressivism, and John Kitzhaber's successful effort to promote what became known as the Oregon Health Plan reflects what might be called a political culture of innovation. That is not the whole story, however. The struggle to build a comprehensive health care system on the foundation of the Oregon Health Plan has been significantly limited by resistance from businesses and by inadequate revenue caused by the tax reductions sponsored by populist conservatives.

This chapter describes health care policy in Oregon in three sections. First, there is an overview of health care policy in the United States and of the Oregon Health Plan. Second, John Kitzhaber's sponsorship, promotion, and defense of the health plan is described. Finally, the implications of the Oregon experience with the Oregon Health Plan for national health care policy are briefly addressed.

NATIONAL HEALTH CARE PATTERNS AND THE OREGON HEALTH PLAN

Health care in the United States is paid for mainly by three major entities: employers, Medicare, and Medicaid. A small number of people receive care by purchasing services on their own. First, most citizens who receive health care insurance receive it through their employers. Private employers provide health insurance to about 44.6 percent of Americans. Government workers and their families (including military personnel and their families), representing about 14.5 percent, are also usually covered, bringing the total percentage insured by employers to about 59 percent. Employer-based insurance may be fully or partially paid for by employers. Recipients may

Table 15.1. Health Care Insurance in the United States, 1998

Insurance provider	Number of recipients (in millions)	Percentage of citizens*
Private employers	120	44.6
Government employers	39	14.5
Medicaid	41	15.2
Medicare	39	14.5
Individual purchase	16	5.9
Uninsured	43	16.1

* Percentages add up to more than 100 because some citizens receive coverage from more than one source.
Source: National Coalition on Health Care, "Health Care Facts," November 1998, http://www.info.nchc.org.

purchase insurance on the open market or through some form of group plan, such as those provided by some unions. About 6 percent of Americans purchase health insurance themselves.

Second, Medicare pays for health care for about one American in seven. Medicare is an entirely federal program that provides health insurance to almost all elderly (over age sixty-five) and disabled citizens—about 14.5 percent of the population. Medicare does not cover some important medical costs, such as prescription drugs, though recent federal legislation provides for future coverage of some prescription costs.

Third, 15.2 percent of Americans qualify for Medicaid, a health insurance system for the poor funded jointly by the federal government and the states. States are responsible for administering Medicaid programs but must operate according to federal guidelines unless the federal government allows an explicit exemption (a "waiver"). Medicaid has become a major segment of state budgets—it grew from 10 percent of state spending in 1987 to almost double that by the midnineties. Recently, Medicaid costs have increased rapidly—by 13 percent in fiscal 2002 after rising 9 percent the previous year.[1] The largest single cause for increased costs was higher pharmaceutical prices, but enrollments also increased after states relaxed eligibility requirements in the nineties and after the 2000–2001 recession struck. In addition, as Michael Reagan points out, long-term-care costs, primarily for elderly patients, have grown rapidly in recent years. Long-term-care patients make up only about 25 percent of all Medicaid beneficiaries but take more than 60 percent of the national Medicaid budget.[2] Oregon's medical assistance programs increased in cost by 13 percent between the 1999–2001 and 2001–2003 budgets, reaching a total of $2.97 billion with over $450 million coming from the state general fund.[3]

Finally, approximately forty-four million Americans were uninsured in 1998, about 16 percent of the population. Some of them pay for medical care themselves, but most of the uninsured cannot afford to pay. Their medical care is essentially paid for by overcharging those who have insurance. Thus, those with insurance indirectly pay the bills for a poor, uninsured person who walks into an emergency room.

States play a major role in providing health care because they administer and help finance Medicaid. State Medicaid policies influence how many residents qualify for Medicaid and thus influence the number lacking health care insurance. Plans to extend coverage to the uninsured often incorporate changes in Medicaid. In Oregon the expanded Medicaid program is known as the Oregon Health Plan (OHP).

The OHP has been regarded as innovative from the time when it was conceived and proposed by the then state senator (later governor) John Kitzhaber in the late 1980s. The Oregon plan is built on the foundation established by the national government in 1965, when the Medicaid program began almost as an afterthought to the Medicare bill. Its original sponsors thought it would be a small program, but Medicaid rapidly became one of the most important and expensive national health care programs. Because the states play a central role in shaping and administering Medicaid, there are state-by-state differences, even though the federal government provides most of the funding. Those differences have increased during the past fifteen years.

Traditional Medicaid plans offer families with incomes at or below the poverty level (among people under sixty-five, mainly single mothers and their children) health care coverage, generally through traditional fee-for-service arrangements. In recent years a number of states have shifted Medicaid patients into Health Maintenance Organizations (HMOs), which control costs by limiting coverage. However, under the traditional approach, most Medicaid programs provide health insurance that covers any illness or injury, assuming physicians and hospitals willing to take Medicaid patients at low reimbursement rates can be found.

At its height the OHP extended health care coverage to more than a hundred thousand of the working poor who would otherwise not have been covered in the traditional Medicaid plan—those who were employed in jobs that did not provide health insurance and who did not earn enough to afford private health insurance—by explicitly limiting the number and type of treatments, or "medical procedures," available. Following the severe recession of 2001–2003, however, the number of working poor covered by the OHP has been reduced to about twenty-five thousand.

The OHP stretches public health dollars by spreading them across more poor patients. Consequently, not all medical treatments are available to those under the plan. The Health Services Commission establishes a "prioritized list of services" that ranks all medical procedures, from setting a broken leg to diagnosing and treating pneumonia or various forms of cancer, according to their effectiveness, cost, and impact on the quality of life. The OHP covers more people by funding only the medical procedures listed above a certain point on the list. Thus, more people may get vaccinations and prenatal care, but no one in the program receives experimental cancer care or organ transplants. Using this approach the OHP provided health coverage in the mid-1990s to more than 130,000 working and nonworking Oregonians who would not have been covered under the old Medicaid system.[4]

The original OHP also included provisions requiring employers either to provide health insurance or to contribute to a fund so employees could be covered by the state. These provisions were called "pay-or-play" provisions, but by whatever name, they were an employer mandate. Kitzhaber's intent was to establish universal health insurance coverage in Oregon using the OHP for leverage. This approach had national implications but faced continual challenges from both liberals and conservatives.

THE EVOLUTION OF THE OREGON HEALTH PLAN

Kitzhaber is a "new" Democrat who resembles Bill Clinton in that he has ideological flexibility and substantial political skills. But few Oregonians would compare the gregarious, backslapping Clinton with the often reserved and sometimes laconic Kitzhaber, a physician who was, for more than twenty years, a politician. From 1994 to 2002 he also served as governor of Oregon. In the argot of political science, Kitzhaber is a "political entrepreneur." The Oregon Health Plan was his idea. He assembled the group support to enact it and has been its most consistent champion, advancing it and defending it against attacks that came first from the left but now come mainly from the right.

Kitzhaber is unusual in politics because he was trained as a physician and practiced medicine (as an emergency room doctor) almost until his election as governor. In his medical practice he noticed many patients appeared in the emergency room only because they had delayed treatment for what began as ordinary, easily treated illnesses or injuries. He saw children with respiratory infections that had turned into pneumonia and minor injuries that had become seriously infected. As a consequence, such patients became more seriously ill, or their injures were aggravated further than if they had sought medical treatment sooner. Kitzhaber later recalled that many patients "had delayed seeking treatment for minor problems because of their concern over how to pay for the care. In each case, the minor problems had evolved into much more serious ones."[5]

In addition to causing human suffering, such cases had other disadvantages. The national government and the state of Oregon, through Medicaid, often paid substantially more for medical care in such cases than would have been needed had these patients gone to a clinic or sought routine care earlier. Kitzhaber also noticed that many easily preventable illnesses and medical conditions, because they were not prevented earlier, were frequently being treated at hospitals.

Kitzhaber entered the legislature in the late 1970s concerned primarily about environmental issues. After two years in the state House, he was elected to the state Senate, where he tried to focus again on environmental issues. But experiences in the emergency room persuaded him that changes were needed in state health care policies. In the 1987 legislative session, Kitzhaber (by that point the Senate president) supported changes in funding priorities for state Medicaid dollars to expand preventive treatments, such as prenatal care, even though that meant dropping Medicaid funding for some transplant operations.[6] But later that year the decision to stop funding transplants, which had not initially received much attention, became very controversial due to the Coby Howard case.

A seven-year-old boy from a poor family, Coby Howard had leukemia. Under the new rules, the state would not pay for a $100,000 bone marrow transplant that might have helped him. The boy died before his family could raise the money through private contributions.[7] During the intense controversy that followed, there was an attempt to repeal the new rules. Kitzhaber made the case for them; he argued that personalized cases such as this "are not policy decisions. They are reactive choices we make that are driven by emotionally charged situations."[8] Kitzhaber had strong credibility among his legislative colleagues, both because he was a physician and because of his leadership position. The repeal attempt was defeated.

In 1989 Kitzhaber persuaded the state legislature to adopt what would become the first draft of the Oregon Health Plan. It proposed to expand the number of Oregonians who could qualify for public health care through

Medicaid, but would do so by rationing the medical procedures available under the plan. At the heart of the plan was a prioritized list of some 700 "medical procedures." An original list was released in May 1990 based on a computerized formula that weighed the cost of treatment versus the "quality of well-being" that resulted.[9] The list was subjected to withering criticism for ranking treatments that were not perceived as vital far ahead of others that were. The formulaic approach simply did not adequately address the subjective feelings of citizens, patients, or health care professionals. After a firestorm of criticism, the original priority list was withdrawn. After an exhaustive series of public hearings and internal deliberations, the Health Services Commission, which included physicians, nurses, other health care professionals, and representatives of the public, released a significantly revised list, which included 709 "medical procedures," in May 1991.[10]

The plan proposed to use federal funds from Medicaid, adding to them the state funds previously committed to health care for the poor, plus an additional appropriation added to the state budget to show good faith. As the budgetary concession suggests, most of the early criticism of the plan came from the left. Many Oregon progressives initially denounced the OHP for "rationing" health care at the point when the state sought a federal waiver of Medicaid rules to start the plan. Liberals, such as Democratic representative Henry Waxman from Los Angeles, worried that once the prioritization of health care services was accepted, the list of covered services would shrink with tight budgets or that substandard care for the poor would become the norm.[11]

Additionally, as health care rose as a critical issue on the national public agenda in the late 1980s and early 1990s, liberals feared that the piecemeal and possibly inadequate coverage of state plans like the OHP might undercut support for a nationwide universal insurance program. They sought a much more sweeping and comprehensive health care reform, such as a Canadian-style single-payer system.

Kitzhaber argued that the United States already rations medical care but does so silently, excluding large segments of the working poor and the near poor because they cannot afford health insurance. He emphasized his own extensive liberal political record, reminding critics that as a medical student he had opposed the war in Vietnam and as a doctor he had joined the left-leaning Physicians for Social Responsibility. He also added, "I have impeccable liberal credentials in the social area . . . the difference is [that my critics] don't have to deal with fiscal limits."[12]

Democrats controlled the legislature when the plan was adopted, but

Kitzhaber, a centrist, sought the support of Republicans and business, and generally received it. He also was supported by the Oregon Medical Association (OMA), whose surveys indicated strong public support for the plan, and other organized health care interest groups.[13]

The plan needed a federal waiver but did not receive it for years. In fact, the first Bush administration tried to squeeze some political advantage out of a formal rejection of the Oregon plan.[14] Kitzhaber had the support of the Oregon congressional delegation, notably Senators Mark Hatfield (the then ranking Republican on the Senate Appropriations Committee), Bob Packwood (the then ranking Republican on the Senate Finance Committee), and the then representative Ron Wyden, a liberal Democrat from Portland. Packwood and Wyden served on key committees in their respective chambers. Packwood was evidently attracted to the plan's cool, rational priorities, but even his active support did not persuade the first Bush administration, which did not want to give Kitzhaber, a Democrat, such a major political victory.[15] Oregon finally received the waiver in 1993 from the Clinton administration, after Kitzhaber helped Clinton win Oregon in the 1992 election.

DEFENDING THE NEW PLAN

Almost as soon as the OHP went into effect, most criticism of it shifted to the right, as conservatives began to recognize the costs and implications of government expansion of health care in the plan. Conservative populists responsible for antitax measures, which have significantly reduced state and local revenues in Oregon, have been less visible in opposition to the OHP than traditional business-connected conservatives—the "enterprisers" in Andrew Kohut's "lifestyle" categorization of factions in American politics.[16] Part of the reason for the relative acquiescence by the conservative populists may be that because of their relatively low incomes, disproportionate numbers of rural Oregonians are among the patients covered by the plan. Instead, business conservatives in the suburbs have been most prominent as critics. But their criticism has not been persuasive for most voters, as the 1994 and 1996 elections revealed.

In 1994 the Democrats nominated Kitzhaber for governor. Kitzhaber had retired from the state Senate two years earlier, telling friends he was done with politics. His return apparently owed a great deal to his sense that he needed to protect the health plan. His Republican opponent in 1994, former congressman Denny Smith, tried to make a campaign issue out of his opposition to the health plan, calling it "a wide open entitlement."[17]

Smith ran television ads showing trains full of impoverished Californians migrating to Oregon seeking health coverage. If Smith could discredit the OHP, Kitzhaber's most visible policy accomplishment, he could discredit Kitzhaber.

Smith also tried to focus attention on the "pay-or-play" employer mandate provision due to start in 1996, hoping to capitalize on late-developing recognition by business leaders that the plan included aspects that would be costly to them.[18] But Smith was a weak candidate and his opposition to the health plan was, if anything, counterproductive. In the most Republican year in half a century, Smith lost by a substantial margin, even as the GOP took control of the state Senate for the first time in forty years.

The OHP had become something of a point of pride for many Oregonians. Public opinion polling showed it to be quite popular, if poorly understood. Kitzhaber designed it to appeal to most health care interest groups, such as physicians and hospitals, and many moderate Republicans. He had persuaded relatively conservative groups and politically influential individuals, including most Republican state legislators, that the threshold decision had been made: government is going to provide health care for many citizens. Having persuaded potential adversaries that they could not reverse that decision, he focused their attention on the second question: how should public health care be financed and delivered?

The answer to that question makes the plan appear quite *institutionally* conservative. The plan does not disrupt the third-party payment structure that dominates health care financing, nor does it require changes in the relationship between patients, physicians, and hospitals. The (OMA), the insurance industry, and most medical providers have focused on these points. When the plan was initially approved, there seemed to be a real chance that the United States might adopt a Canadian-style single-payer health care system. That prospect, while it contributed to opposition to the plan by the left, badly frightened established health care interest groups, making them more accommodating than they would probably have been otherwise.[19] But once the size of the Republican sweep in the 1994 elections became clear, prospects for expanded national public health care vanished. Nonetheless, Kitzhaber had been elected governor and his health plan was an issue in the campaign, so he could claim a mandate for it.

In 1995, with Republicans fully in control of the legislature for the first time in forty years, the OHP was a source of conflict. The number of "working poor" Oregonians who applied for the plan had exceeded expectations. Costs rose rapidly. Measure 5 forced an increase in state spending to keep elementary and secondary schools open, so Kitzhaber had to negotiate cuts in the OHP with the legislature.

At the time the highest priority for business was repeal of the employer mandate. The 1993 legislature had required congressional approval of the employer mandate, without which it would have been abandoned. Given that the new GOP-dominated Congress would not approve the mandate, opponents killed the requirement without action in Salem.[20] Kitzhaber reluctantly gave up the mandate in return for a somewhat higher OHP budget than the Republicans wanted. The larger budget was required because efforts to "shift the line" (reduce services among those on the list) were rejected by the national Health Care Financing Administration (HCFA). Since federal funds are essential to the plan, HCFA's opposition to shrinking the list ended the debate.

In the 1996 elections health care politics became a major focus. Three measures concerning health care appeared on the November ballot. First, a coalition of health groups, supported by Kitzhaber, qualified an initiative (Measure 44) to increase tobacco taxes by the equivalent of thirty cents a pack, for OHP expansion. Second, a group of chiropractors, naturopaths, acupuncturists, and "alternative health providers" circulated an initiative (Measure 39) to require insurers to cover their services. By early spring, the sponsors had collected only a small fraction of the necessary signatures. At that point Mark Nelson, the campaign consultant for the tobacco industry, persuaded his clients to contribute $750,000 to the alternative health group to pay "bounties" to petition circulators. He reasoned that if mainstream health care providers had to defend against the chiropractors, they would be much less able to devote time or money to the campaign for the tobacco tax. It worked; the bounties essentially purchased enough signatures to qualify Measure 39.[21] A wealthy fee-for-service physician personally financed petitioners to qualify a third health care initiative (Measure 35), this one to ban the capitation payment system and one that rapidly became known as the "decapitation" initiative.

Capitation payment compensates health care providers per person enrolled. Capitation payments are central to HMO programs and are advocated to help control costs by encouraging prevention and lower cost services, but many patient advocates contend that capitation indirectly discourages patients from seeking the best care.

But in the fall, Measure 44, supported by a coalition of health groups and progressives, was the main focus. The tobacco industry spent over five million dollars trying to defeat it, or almost five dollars per voter in Oregon.[22]

It was not enough. With Kitzhaber's support, Measure 44 passed with 56 percent of the vote. That success was widely interpreted in political circles as potent evidence of the health plan's political strength. Although quite different in substance, Measures 35 and 39 were tied together in extensive negative television advertising, which emphasized support for Measure 39 by the unpopular tobacco industry. Kitzhaber led the successful opposition to both initiatives.

Yet another property tax limitation (Measure 47) passed in 1996, so discussion in Salem quickly turned to shifting about one billion dollars (about 11 percent) of the state budget to public school funding. The new tobacco tax from Measure 44 was expected to raise about $160 million, not nearly enough to compensate for the property tax cut. Despite this fiscal situation, Kitzhaber announced plans to expand OHP coverage to women and children with incomes up to 180 percent of above the poverty line (up from 133 percent) and to include needy college students. He also proposed to create a state subsidy for private insurance for the working poor who made just enough to disqualify them from the OHP.[23]

CHANGES IN POLITICAL SUPPORT

At the time, some 380,000 Oregonians were covered by the OHP. Kitzhaber proposed to increase that number by a little more than 40,000. He argued that failure to expand the OHP would have violated the will of the voters, expressed in approval of Measure 44. Republicans, still in control of the legislature, resisted, but the state economy was strong and the governor's proposals, with some minor tweaking, largely passed. But many Republicans grumbled that they thought they had voted for a plan that would remove services from the bottom of the priority list if funds were tight. Instead, they were regularly asked for more money.

The initial additional cost to the general funds budget was less than seventy million dollars, but by the 1995–1997 budget the OHP added an additional two hundred million dollars to state health costs, and by the 1999–2001 biennium the OHP cost roughly seven hundred million dollars more than a standard Medicaid program would have. By 1999 OHP costs had risen very quickly—more than 25 percent in two years—so Kitzhaber felt obliged to propose cuts, recommending a waiting period for new applicants, a reduction in the list of covered procedures ("moving the line"), and an increase in copay requirements. Republicans proposed more extensive cuts to the health plan but failed to enact them.[24]

During the 1999 legislative session, Republican legislators began to say in public what they had been saying in private—that Kitzhaber had hoodwinked them when the OHP was originally adopted. They did not have the votes to impose extensive cuts, but by the end of the session, support and opposition to the OHP had clearly reversed. By 1999 progressives were publicly supportive; indeed, some health group leaders on the left were rather sheepish about their early opposition. By contrast, many Republicans now recognized that the most important result of the OHP had been to extend public health care to more of the poor and the near-poor, not quite their core constituency. Privately, many Republicans were furious, and late in the session they voted to eliminate legal authority for the health plan. They knew full well the governor would veto the bill, but its passage demonstrated that they were more willing than before to "go public" with their opposition.

After GOP legislators voted to cancel authorization for the OHP in 1999, it appeared that if a Republican won the presidency in 2000, the health plan would be in jeopardy because the federal waiver was due to expire in 2001. This prospect was ominous to OHP supporters because the process through which federal waivers are granted or denied is so Byzantine and obscure that killing the plan could be accomplished largely out of public view. Kitzhaber again showed his political acumen and flexibility. Once George W. Bush was declared the winner of the presidential election, Kitzhaber went to Washington and negotiated changes in the OHP that, in a sense, underscored its original design. Kitzhaber was helped in this by Bush's selection of Governor Tommy Thompson of Wisconsin as Secretary of Health and Human Services (HHS).

During the Clinton administration, the HCFA had largely rejected state proposals to "move the line" among the covered medical procedures. Health care professionals at HCFA reflected fears that the OHP would, line-by-line, slice away health coverage for the poor. The leadership of HHS kept its distance from the controversy. By contrast, Thompson, a governor noted for his focus on changing social welfare programs, knew Kitzhaber from the time when they were governors together and admired Kitzhaber's innovative approach. After closed-door discussions with Thompson, Kitzhaber presented a proposal to the 2001 legislature to split OHP patients into two groups starting in 2002: those who were largely healthy and probably not at risk for major problems versus those, such as the disabled or pregnant women, who could be expected to need extensive medical attention. The former group was to be covered by a reduced plan called "OHP Standard" (which advocates for the poor dubbed "OHP Minus"), and the second group would be covered by "OHP Plus," which would include all of the services that had been available under the plan in 2000. About a hundred thousand patients with "OHP Standard" became eligible for benefits equal to a little less than 80 percent of the former plan. With the money saved, the state was, for a time, able to expand coverage to include an estimated forty-two thousand additional beneficiaries (or about 12 percent), before recession-induced budget cuts struck.[25] This revision to the OHP benefits package seemed to mollify many of the Republican legislators who were so unhappy in 1999. As a result, the changes were adopted with much less political debate than the OHP produced in 1995, 1997, or 1999.

Despite its national reputation as liberal, Oregon is hardly liberal in fiscal matters. By the end of the 1990s Oregon's rank in per capita state taxes dropped to forty-fourth among the states.[26] Those deep tax cuts require that much state revenue (mainly from income taxes) must be spent on local schools, which suffered the greatest reduction in funding when property taxes were cut. Highly dependent on state general revenue, the OHP never developed as envisioned because of this grim competition for state money. As a result, Oregon's highly publicized and progressive health plan has not had the sweeping impact first envisioned.

In the 2002 elections, health care was again debated when an initiative—Measure 23—proposed to provide a state universal health care system, as had been proposed in California in 1994. Measure 23 would have increased state income and corporate taxes significantly to pay for a far-reaching and costly health care system. But the sponsors from the far left margin of Oregon politics failed to get support, even from their natural allies among labor unions, and the initiative was widely defeated, receiving only 21 percent of the vote. So for those without other health insurance, the OHP remained critical.

As this chronology should suggest, the saga of the Oregon Health Plan is hardly over. Kitzhaber's term as governor ended early in 2003, and though his successor—Ted Kulongoski—is a Democrat who supports the OHP, he is unlikely to devote the same level of personal or political commitment to the plan as Kitzhaber did.

Upon election, Kulongoski confronted a severe recession that greatly reduced state revenue, because Oregon is so heavily dependent on income tax revenue, a highly volatile source. The budget adopted by the 2001 legislature was rendered almost immediately obsolete because the national recession that began that year struck the Northwest in general and Oregon in particular harder than any other region. Between summer 2001 and fall 2002, there were five special sessions of the legislature to balance the budget—and legislators cut the budget repeatedly. They could have also adopted tax increases, but those were not considered until the very end, and a modest tax increase referred to voters by the fifth and last special session was rejected with 54 percent of the vote against it in January 2003.

With Kitzhaber gone and the legislature under the control of many Republicans who recalled earlier defeats at his hands, the OHP took a disproportionate fraction of the budget reductions in 2001–2002. Then in the 2003 legislature, budgets were reduced still more. In an effort to balance the state budget, at the end of the 2003 session legislators passed a temporary income tax increase only to have antitax activists place it on the ballot through the referendum process. The voters rejected the tax increase, Measure 30, soundly in February 2004. At that point it appeared that virtually all of the working poor who had been covered by the OHP would lose their coverage. That is, it appeared that between 2001 and 2004, the OHP had been almost completely dismantled. But in the closing days of the 2003 session, hospitals in Oregon agreed essentially to tax themselves in order to sustain at least a small fraction of those who had been covered by the OHP. They were concerned that without any remnant of the OHP, they would confront bearing the full cost of uninsured patients who appeared at the emergency room. If, however, the hospitals absorbed a small tax, the state would be eligible for federal matching funds, so hospital administrators could calculate that they would not bear all the cost for uninsured patients. As a result, a fraction of those once covered by the OHP, amounting to roughly twenty-five thousand patients, will still be covered by the plan—at least until the next legislative session.

NATIONAL IMPLICATIONS

The Oregon experience attempting to extend health care to almost everyone contains at least four lessons for other states and the nation. First, the venerable tradition of strong progressives to go for broke and to be broken was very much in evidence when the OHP had been adopted but had not yet received the federal waiver. But as the program began to serve clients, most progressives were converted.

Second, the unsentimental hardheadedness of the conservatives (at least regarding the poor) was temporarily abandoned when Kitzhaber proposed a program that seemed to hold out the promise of forcing the poor or at least their champions to make hard choices between services and cost. However, once the OHP began to be implemented, it dawned on conservatives that they might have been had. As a result, it is unlikely that the Oregon plan will be seen as offering much to conservatives if it is proposed at a national level. Still, if they are ever confronted with the prospect of a Canadian-style, single-payer government plan, which would end the third-party payer approach, the conservatives might once again see merit in Kitzhaber's approach.

Both liberals and conservatives have slowly realized that above all else, the OHP provides health care for a substantial number of the near poor. There is a parallel here to the enactment of Medicare (and Medicaid) as the partial culmination of a decades-long struggle to establish universal health care.[27] Changes of this magnitude do not happen easily in American politics, and when they do happen, they almost always take time.

Third, persistence matters. Kitzhaber worked for years at developing, crafting, and editing his plan, modifying it, compromising with opponents, publicizing it, gathering support, and making dozens of other efforts on its behalf before it began to be implemented. No legislative father ever worked harder to be present at the creation, except, perhaps, those who labored for decades to be present when the Civil Rights Act and Medicare were signed.

Fourth, political skill matters. Kitzhaber was not only persistent but also a bright and agile politician in the best sense of the word. It may be that only political scientists now admire political skill, but it is indispensable to the accomplishment of large goals in the complex, inconsistent, frustrating political system we have. In at least this dimension, Kitzhaber had far better focus than did Bill Clinton when the latter proposed his national health care plan in 1993–94. Of course, Kitzhaber had the advantage of being able to work as a state legislator, physician, and freelance policy wonk for many years before he became governor. Once he became governor, he was in a position to make the success of the health plan a priority for the state and, to an extent, the nation.

Whether the Oregon Health Plan comes to be viewed as an important step in the development of a comprehensive American health care system or just a distraction remains to be seen, but the story of its political evolution contains many lessons for those concerned about both health care policy and Oregon politics.

CHAPTER SIXTEEN

Social Issues

Melody Rose

As Patrick Buchanan, frequent Republican presidential contender, is fond of saying, "Economics is not the science that sends men to the barricades." Buchanan's declaration is less an observation about the dreariness of economic policy than a reflection on the contemporary interest in social issues. Gun control, affirmative action, end-of-life issues, and school prayer are more likely to move citizens to action than questions of fiscal or monetary policy.

This is no less true in Oregon. Social policy is riveting. In the November 2000 election, for instance, Oregon voters were faced with an initiative that would have prohibited public school teachers from positively referencing homosexuality in their classrooms. Measure 9 narrowly failed by a vote of 702,572 to 788,691. This vote demonstrates the complexity of the state's views on social issues and the state's tendency to resolve social policy battles not through legislation but through the initiative.

SOCIAL POLICY: A DEFINITION

Social issues are the most divisive political questions of our time. Political scientists distinguish social policy issues from other issue types for two reasons: their subject matter and the type of politics they inspire. Theodore J. Lowi classified policy types thirty years ago based on the type of coercion they use and the likelihood that the coercion will be felt. The more coercive the policy, the more contentious the politics will be around that policy.[1] Although Lowi did not integrate social policy into his original framework, more recently, others have done so.

Raymond Tatalovich and Byron Daynes argue that social policies are different from other forms of issue debates because they place restrictions on very personal behaviors.[2] Unlike policies that restrict business practices or redistribute money from one group of citizens to another, social policies regulate personal conduct. Laws that govern marriage and parenting decisions, for instance, have a very direct impact on citizens' choices and behavior.

Political divisions over social issues parallel the progressive and conservative populist split in Oregon. Progressives support government intervention in areas of economic equity and long-term social planning but believe government should not dictate personal lifestyles. Conservative populists generally take the opposite position, believing that market principles should guide economic policies and that the government should promote appropriately moral lifestyles.

The politics of social policies in Oregon and elsewhere tend to be polarized because citizens participating in social policy debates rarely see room for compromise on these deeply personal issues, which they often view as affecting their fundamental values. Social policy debates often include graphic visual images that are conducive to the print and television media. Social issues are therefore often amplified in the media because of their salience to the public. They are often resolved, in the end, through judicial review.

SOCIAL POLICY IN THE FEDERAL SYSTEM

Historically, social issues have been the sole responsibility of the states. The U.S. Constitution created a very narrow scope of influence for the federal government, designating only national security and interstate commerce issues to the federal government. All remaining issues, often referred to as "police powers," were reserved to the states. The founders believed that leaving social policies to the states would allow for better citizen participation in the debates, would allow for flexible policy outcomes based on the culture and demographics of each state, and would keep these divisive issues out of the national limelight. Although the twentieth century saw the growth of the federal government in the realm of social policy, states have begun to reclaim their conventional role in resolving social policy issues.

No state takes the right to establish social policy more seriously than Oregon. As the introduction to this book points out, Oregon is known for its strong culture of policy innovation and democratic participation. Oregon is also noted to have distinctly progressive views, protecting individualism and limiting government efforts to regulate social policy. While this reputation

Table 16.1.   Social Policy Initiatives, 1990–2004

Election (in November of)	Measure number	Ballot title	Outcome
1990	8	Amends Oregon Constitution to Prohibit Abortion, with Three Exceptions	Failed
1990	9	Requires Use of Safety Belts	Passed
1990	10	Doctor Must Give Parent Notice Before Minor's Abortion	Failed
1992	9	Government Cannot Facilitate, Must Discourage, Homosexuality, Other "Behaviors"	Failed
1994	13	Amends Constitution: Governments Cannot Approve, Create Classifications Based on, Homosexuality	Failed
1994	16	Allows Terminally Ill Adults to Obtain Prescription for Lethal Drugs	Passed
1994	19	Amends Constitution: No Free Speech Protection for Obscenity, Child Pornography	Failed
1996	31	Amends Constitution: Obscenity May Receive No Greater Protection than under Federal Constitution	Failed
1997	51	Repeals Law Allowing Terminally Ill Adults to Obtain Lethal Prescription	Failed
2000	5	Expands Circumstances Requiring Background Checks Before Transfer of Firearm	Passed
2000	9	Prohibits Public School Instruction Encouraging, Promoting, Sanctioning Homosexual, Bisexual Behaviors	Failed
2004	36	Changes Constitution to Acknowledge Only Marriage between One Man and One Woman	

Source: Bill Bradbury, *Oregon Blue Book, 2003–2004.*

may or may not be verifiable in other policy areas, it is very clear in the realm of social policy. A number of social policy debates have gripped Oregon in recent years: gun control, abortion, gay rights, assisted suicide, and medical marijuana issues. As table 16.1 reveals, many of Oregon's contemporary social policy debates are fought through the initiative process.[3] Still, nearly all of these recent debates have resulted in progressive policy outcomes, with Oregonians consistently preferring minimal government intervention in areas of personal decision making.

Of these myriad social policy debates, however, one stands out as consistently gripping this state: abortion. Although the state has thus far maintained a progressive policy despite a nationwide trend toward state regulatory restrictions on abortion, key changes in the state's political institutions guarantee that the debate in future years will intensify and may ultimately lead to some new policies.

While we see evidence of a growing conservative populist sentiment around social policy in present-day Oregon, that tendency is geographically specific. Progressive views on abortion are most widely held in the densely populated Willamette Valley, which runs north-south down the center of the state, though conservative populist ideas are evident from Yamhill County through Polk, Marion, and Linn counties. On either side of the Willamette Valley, social policy progressives are flanked by rural voters, whose views on abortion and other social policy issues are decidedly more conservative.

ABORTION POLICY IN OREGON

America experienced a nationwide trend in the 1990s toward restricting abortion access by both the federal and state governments. What has sparked this trend is a complex story involving the rise of a conservative populist social movement aimed at protecting traditional family values, as well as a general backlash against the progressive changes for women in 1970s. However, while most states passed restrictions on abortion during the last ten years, Oregon remained steadfastly progressive. In fact, it is no exaggeration to say that in the abortion policy debates, Oregon is clearly a progressive leader resisting a sea change in state social policy. Although table 16.1 reveals the opportunity that voters have had on several recent occasions to refine the state's lenient position through initiatives brought directly to the voters, they have consistently refused to do so. In certain key policy decisions, such as generous funding of abortion for indigent women, Oregon has taken the debate a step further, using government to protect a woman's access to abortion.

Oregon's uniquely progressive position is illustrated in table 16.2. Each state is allotted one point for each restriction it places on abortion (a waiting period, signed consent requirement, and so on); a point is subtracted for each state protection of abortion (full state funding, clinic access laws, affirmative constitutional protection of abortion, and so on). The combination of these numbers is the a state's abortion restriction score. Table 16.2 indicates the wide variance in state abortion policies in the year 2000: scores range from –2 (Oregon) to a high of 10 (Missouri). Oregon's score of –2 indicates the state's strong protection of abortion access.

Looking at the state's scores in a graphic format emphasizes Oregon's

Table 16.2. State Abortion Restriction Scores, 2000

State	Restriction	Protection Score	Total Restriction
Oregon	0	−2	−2
Vermont	0	−1	−1
Hawaii	1	−1	0
New Jersey	1	−1	0
Washington	2	−2	0
West Virginia	1	−1	0
Alaska	2	−1	1
California	3	−2	1
Connecticut	3	−2	1
Montana	2	−1	1
New Mexico	1	0	1
New York	2	−1	1
Arizona	2	0	2
Illinois	3	−1	2
Maryland	3	−1	2
Minnesota	4	−2	2
Colorado	3	0	3
Florida	3	0	3
Idaho	4	−1	3
Maine	4	−1	3
Massachusetts	5	−2	3
Nevada	4	−1	3
New Hampshire	4	−1	3
North Carolina	4	−1	3
Texas	3	0	3
Arkansas	4	0	4
Georgia	4	0	4
Iowa	4	0	4
Oklahoma	4	0	4
Wyoming	4	0	4
Delaware	5	0	5
Kansas	6	−1	5
Mississippi	5	0	5
Tennessee	5	0	5
Wisconsin	6	−1	5
Alabama	6	0	6
Indiana	6	0	6
Kentucky	6	0	6
Nebraska	6	0	6
Ohio	6	0	6
Rhode Island	6	0	6

South Carolina	6	0	6
South Dakota	6	0	6
Utah	6	0	6
Virginia	6	0	6
Louisiana	7	0	7
Michigan	7	0	7
North Dakota	7	0	7
Pennsylvania	8	0	8
Missouri	10	0	10

unique position. Figure 16.1 orders the states by their level of abortion restriction. The "most restrictive" states are those with abortion restriction scores of seven to ten; "restrictive" states have a score between four and six. The states with scores of one to three are marked "lenient" states, and the six states with scores from zero to negative two are "most lenient." This visual reflection of the Oregon position stands in stark contrast with most of the nation.

Still, the map misrepresents the social politics in Oregon to some degree. While the state has indeed prevented restrictions in the area of abortion, in very recent years it has done so only narrowly. Furthermore, recent institutional and political changes in the state could spell more dramatic and varied social policy outcomes in the years ahead.

INSTITUTIONAL AND POLITICAL CLIMATE CHANGES IN OREGON

Oregon has maintained access to abortion because of liberal voters in its urban core. The movement favoring more restrictive abortion access has historically been thwarted in the state legislature, where the short legislative session, dominated by urban liberals, gave short shrift to its policy claims. As table 16.1 indicates, during the 1990s the movement took its efforts to the initiative arena, where it could gain enough support to place its policy proposals on the ballot, though typically not enough to win passage.

In 1986 the Oregon Citizens Alliance (OCA) authored a ballot initiative, Measure 8, to ban abortion. In that same year, Oregon Right to Life (ORTL) offered another initiative, Measure 6, to end state funding for abortions. Both measures failed, but the OCA offered two additional ballot initiatives in 1990, one of which nearly passed.[4] Since 1990 the state's various pro-life organizations have tried numerous times to place additional abortion restrictions on the ballot but have failed to gather the requisite number of signatures. The recent inability of the conservative pro-life organizations to

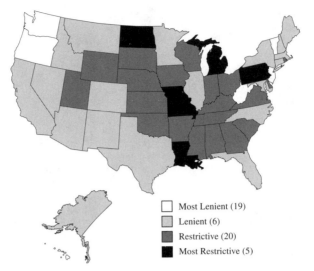

Figure 16.1. Abortion Laws in the United States, 2000

bring antiabortion initiatives to the voters may in part explain their renewed interest in legislative politics.

Three changes during the 1990s spell a different future for Oregon's social policies. First, the legislature changed party control during the 1990s, moving to Republican hands and creating a more receptive environment for the conservative social viewpoint. Second, the profamily movement has gained momentum in recent years, possibly making it more effective in its legislative demands. The three main Protestant prolife groups in Oregon, the OCA, the Oregon Christian Coalition (CC), and Oregon Right to Life, have grown both in size and in influence. Finally, and most important, the introduction of term limits in Oregon fundamentally changed both the legislative makeup and environment in Salem, opening new opportunities for the state's moralist movement to pursue change through legislative channels.

STATE LEGISLATIVE TERM LIMITS ENLIVEN THE MOVEMENT

By far the most direct political opportunity for the state's prolife advocates since the movement began was the state's legislative term limits. Until overturned by the state supreme court in 2002, Oregon's law prevented individuals from serving more than twelve years in the legislature. The law first came into full effect at the end of the 1997 legislative session, forcing the retirement of twenty-four state legislators. Twenty-two additional legislators were removed from office in the 2000 election.[5] Among the twenty-two retirees in 2000 were eight committed prochoice members.[6] Turnover of this magnitude in Oregon is unprecedented in the past quarter century. The large number of open seats in the 1998 election naturally created a firestorm of activity in the state for control of the 1999 session. The state's prolife movement organizations, long stymied by the inattentiveness of the legislature, heralded the 1998 election as an "opportunity to take the moderates out." Likewise, the state's prochoice leaders identified the 1998 state legislative races as a direct threat to the state's historically liberal policies.

In 1998 and 2000 prolife activists focused a greater effort on the legislative elections through enhanced candidate assistance, get-out-the-vote efforts, and voter education than ever before. Even OCA leader Lon Mabon, long hostile to legislative politics, articulated his frustration with the "silk-stocking Republicans" in Salem who do not actively pursue the prolife agenda and threw his assistance to a number of prolife candidates.[7] The OCA's effort to change the composition of the legislature was strengthened by the presence of ORTL in 1998. ORTL focused its efforts exclusively on the open-seat races in 1998, working to fill seats previously held by moderate Republicans with social conservatives, and the fledgling CC offered minimal election support.

By all accounts, prolife groups saw the 1998 election as their opportunity to elect socially conservative Republicans. This effort succeeded. The 1999 Republican caucus was identified by legislative members and interest group leaders on both sides of the abortion issue as the most favorable to prolife groups since the 1970s. M&R Strategic Services, the lobbyist for Planned Parenthood Affiliates of Oregon, labeled a majority of each house as reliably prolife. M&R counted sixteen consistently prolife state senators (out of thirty) and thirty-one consistently prolife House members (out of sixty) in the 1999 session. Of the forty-seven prolife legislators in 1999, fourteen were freshmen. Neither M&R nor Oregon NARAL produced analogous figures for previous legislative sessions because both groups viewed the likelihood of policy change in earlier sessions as too remote to warrant concern.

Unfortunately, ORTL did not provide a scorecard of the 1999 legislators to compare to Planned Parenthood's. The Christian Coalition did, however, and its assessment of the legislature's makeup confirms Planned Parenthood's numbers. While the CC's issues are broader than the single issue of abortion, it has compiled the best prolife scorecard available for the 1999 legislative session. According to the CC, thirty-four of the sixty House members supported the CC's agenda at least 50 percent of the time. In the state Senate, eighteen of the thirty members had CC support scores in excess of 50 percent.[8] Based on these numbers, the 1999 legislative session appeared headed for major abortion policy revisions.

The term limits law motivated prolife groups to shift their efforts to securing prolife seats in the legislature, but it presented a number of more subtle opportunities as well. Term limits affected the style and tenor of the session not just because the membership had changed but also because the institutional environment of policy development had created more favorable conditions for the prolife organizations. Term limits allowed younger, more conservative legislators to move up the leadership ladder swiftly. Given that there was overall less seniority in the institution, younger members (in this case, the more prolife members) were able to move into gatekeeping positions that allowed them to shepherd legislation through the process sooner in their careers. Oregon House speaker Lynn Snodgrass, a social conservative, publicly articulated on many occasions her commitment to passing prolife policy and to the advancement of her younger, more conservative colleagues. In a heated battle made possible through the election of new conservative legislators, Snodgrass replaced moderate Republican speaker Lynn Lundquist with the support of socially conservative freshmen after years of socially moderate Republican leadership.[9] Her stewardship of abortion legislation and her decisions in assigning committee chairmanships both encouraged sympathetic members to draft antiabortion bills and facilitated consideration of those bills. Snodgrass appointed many freshmen to desirable posts in order to accelerate their legislative experience. This fact acts as an incentive for freshman legislators to make names for themselves and to express boldness early in their tenure; as one participant observed, "term limits gets people moving faster." Detractors worried publicly that Snodgrass's ascendance to the speaker's chair would allow her to "turn the job into a pulpit for her religious conservatism."[10] In fact, Snodgrass announced that passage of antiabortion and antigay rights legislation would be her primary goals after passage of a charter schools bill.[11]

Term limits also encouraged consideration of abortion-related bills by creating among the new members a sense of policy urgency. The new conservatives were "vying for visibility," and they identified social policy bills as a sure way to attract press attention and gain name recognition swiftly.[12] Many legislators reported they felt rushed to effect public policy due to the limited tenure of their service. The term limits law created a sense of urgency for all of them: "Term limits create more heat than light," Representative Mannix poignantly commented.[13]

Finally, term limits diminished the deference that a freshman legislative class might otherwise pay to senior members, and encouraged individualism in the policy process. The new legislators did not share the sense of party loyalty or coalition building held by their more senior colleagues. According to one activist, "There is no currency in taking care of the team because the team turns over."[14] Lacking a sense of deference to their more moderate senior colleagues, freshmen legislators were liberated to pursue their own agendas. The record number of abortion bills introduced in 1999 may be partially the result of sponsors being insufficiently acquainted with one another to collaborate their efforts or of their lack of knowledge regarding past efforts at similar legislation.

In sum, the prolife movement in Oregon enjoyed unprecedented opportunities in the 1999 legislative session as a result of the high number of seats occupied by movement supporters; "they [freshmen legislators] may not have had the gavel, but they were effective."[15] As a result, prochoice forces prepared for the inevitable onslaught of abortion restriction measures that would be proposed during the session.

CONSERVATIVE CULTURE EMERGES: THE 1999 LEGISLATIVE SESSION

Due to enhanced political opportunities created through state term limits, the prolife movement was poised for unprecedented legislative influence in the 1999 session. In fact, representatives of the state's two largest prochoice organizations, NARAL and Planned Parenthood, reported that they felt their position was gravely threatened in that year.[16] And although there was a larger number of prolife bills drafted and considered in 1999 since *Roe v. Wade*, not a single prolife measure succeeded. Evidently, electing prolife legislators is not in itself enough to effect historic policy change.

Three bills surfaced early in the 1999 session as the most politically salient and likely to pass: restrictions on state abortion funding (HB 5029), minors' access to abortion (HB 2633), and late-term abortion (SB 1330). Restrictions in these arenas are prevalent throughout the fifty states, and public support is wide for these abortion hurdles. Of these three issues, the first two moved swiftly through the legislative process and were prevented from becoming law only by Democratic governor Kitzhaber's veto pen; the third bill, the so-called partial-birth measure, was surprisingly stymied at the speaker's request, much to the disappointment of the prolife community.[17] Snodgrass's stated reason for preventing floor consideration of sb 1330 was the governor's near-certain veto and pressure from moderate Republicans.[18] Conservative Republicans in the House speculated that Snodgrass may have felt her speakership would be threatened by a coalition of Democrats and moderate Republicans if she had allowed sb 1330 to move in the House.[19]

THE FUTURE OF SOCIAL POLICY IN OREGON

Despite the improved legislative climate for the prolife cause, the prolife movement was unable to change the state's progressive policy. Even though Kitzhaber has left office, the opportunity for prolife advances in the near future do not appear great. Replacing Kitzhaber is Democrat Ted Kulongoski, who was endorsed by NARAL. The election also led to an even distribution of seats in the Senate between Republicans and Democrats, making the task for prolife advocates more difficult. Moreover, given Oregon's historic commitment to abortion access, conservative Republican politicians may not be compelled to act without a powerful lobby behind them. What remains a substantial barrier to the prolife movement in Oregon is continued conflict among the prolife organizations themselves.

The unwillingness of the relevant prolife groups to coordinate their efforts and take advantage of their increasing opportunities in the state is striking. The three main Protestant groups have historically declined to work together on most issues; this preference for independent action was present even during the 1998 election and the 1999 legislative session. Even when opportunity for change was great, the organizations deliberately avoided coordination, citing philosophical and stylistic differences. In addition, the lobby is missing a key possible ally—the Catholic Conference. Salem legislators report the distinct lack of a Catholic presence on the abortion issue. In part, this fact is explained by the state's relatively small Catholic community.[20] In addition, the Catholic Conference often finds itself at odds with the prolife organizations on other issues such as welfare reform, child care, and poverty policy, making it difficult for Catholics to form a solid lobbying alliance with prolife Protestant groups.[21]

The three other prolife organizations (oca, cc, and ortl) each operate independently and are sometimes at odds with each other on substantive and strategic issues. ortl's Gayle Atteberry, for instance, argues that the oca's ballot initiatives delegitimize the movement as a whole because they are often too radical or even unconstitutional. Atteberry argues that to waste the time and resources of her organization for something unlikely to pass by voters and the courts is detrimental to the goal of future volunteer efforts.[22] Lon Mabon, for his part, claims his primary goal is to educate—not to legislate—so compromise succumbs to principle.

The OCA's extremism accounts in part for the rift between the local prolife groups, but other factors contribute to the disjointed nature of the movement as well. The state's Christian Coalition is a shoestring organization that has struggled to remain viable. Other states have thriving Christian Coalition branches; nationwide, the organization boasts over 1.8 million members and is one of the nation's largest Christian conservative organizations. Ironically, the state group's recent membership drive prevented the organization's participation in the 1999 legislative session, and so it remained peripheral to ORTL and the OCA.[23] The Christian Coalition's survival may well be the key to improved odds for the movement in coming years. The Christian Coalition is legendary for its recent ability to run successful local candidates and influence Republican Party policy goals. Given its philosophical approach, the Christian Coalition has the potential for coordination with ORTL.

What further weakens the state's Christian Coalition is the breadth of its issue concerns. The national organization's recent strategy has been to widen its issue concerns beyond the core Christian issues of the family in order to attract a larger membership; the national organization now expresses positions and produces voter education literature on matters relating to foreign policy, education, and taxes, amid a host of other issues.[24] Representative Mannix openly chastised the Christian Coalition for spreading itself across too many issues. "The gas tax? Really, that offends me."[25] Several legislators conveyed their disdain for the Christian Coalition's reach into areas well beyond traditional religious concerns. Not only does the organization's interest in wider policy arenas alienate it from the narrowly focused prolife groups and spread its meager resources thin as a result, this strategy apparently alienates the organization from some probable legislative allies as well.

The organizational strength of the prochoice lobby will also prevent change in the state's abortion law. Oregon's historic commitment to abortion rights is obvious in the consistent demise of the OCA's antiabortion ballot measures; it is also clear in the organizational power of NARAL. As one prolife legislator recently reported, during the 1999 legislative session, the prochoice organizations summoned a tremendous lobbying effort to protect the state's policies. "They were everywhere . . . the pro-life organizations are simply out-organized."[26] Oregon's prochoice organizations enjoy the advantage of defending the status quo. In 1999, when NARAL recognized a larger-than-usual threat to abortion rights, it was able to call upon a large and active membership to provide lobbying pressure beyond what the prolife organizations could summon.

Oregon has a recent history of social policy teeming with progressivism. This inclination is most evident in the case of abortion. However, Republican success in winning control of the state legislature, growing conservative social movement organizations, and the possible passage of a revised term limits law could catapult conservative ideals to new levels of power within the policy-making apparatus. In the 1999 legislative session, all that stood between the prolife organizations and policy change was a progressive governor and the organizations' own lack of coordination. Should these conditions change, the state's policies on abortion and other social policies, may shift dramatically.

The implementation of legislative term limits in Oregon encouraged the state's prolife activists to shift their focus from a strategy based largely on the pursuit of policy change through initiatives to a strategy of greater involvement in legislative politics. This shift produced more prolife legislators and more abortion bills than ever before. The activists themselves believe term limits greatly enhanced their political opportunity in the legislature by increasing the number of open-seat races in the state and by changing the policy-making environment itself.

However, changing the state's policies is still a formidable and politically risky task. One implicit feature of the term limitation law was that legislators were mindful of their limited time in office. While many I interviewed argued that term limits emboldened freshmen legislators to pursue divisive issues with courage, there was another, unstated consideration at play: the careers of these legislators were going to end sooner rather than later. Without the security of unlimited tenure and with an eye toward higher office, many of the members may have opted for policy moderation, despite their passionate rhetoric or their social movement allegiances. This point may help explain why Speaker Snodgrass, who became ineligible for reelection at the end of the 1999 session, abandoned her prolife position and the partial-birth-abortion-ban bill; she was the Republican candidate for secretary of state in the 2000 election.[27]

Prolife organizations naturally remain focused on increasing their support in Salem, considering how close they came to victory on several measures in 1992. The prolife movement has only recently shifted its efforts from the initiative process to the legislature, and in a very short time changed the nature of the abortion debate there in 1999. And 1999 was just the beginning.

Senator Eileen Qutub was quick to point out, "You have to remember there was no discussion of abortion [in the legislature] until 1995—we can't change policy overnight."[28] Policy success of a social movement through term limits was not immediate in Oregon, but this chapter has only accounted for the first legislative session since the law was implemented.

At the time of this writing, August 2004, it seems that two different trends are worthy of consideration in the realm of Oregon's social policy. First the the possibility that the profamily organizations detailed above may be joined in future battles by newer organizations such as the Defense of Marriage Coalition, whose mission is to prevent same-sex marriage. This development is of course in response to the decisions by Lane and Multnomah counties in 2004 to issue marriage licenses to some-sex couples. The efforts of the conservative populists in response to this county-level effort has been to produce a ballot measure for the November 2, 2004, election. Measure 36 passed by 57 percent and altered the Oregon Constitution to allow legal protection for only marriages between one man and one woman. The 1990s debate over abortion may well be eclipsed by the more recent battles over same-sex marriage.

In addition to this significant shift in social policy emphasis in Oregon, it is important to note that this chapter has indicated the dominance of the progressives over statewide social policy. However, another recent trend shows conservative populists, long thwarted in the arena of statewide measures and policymaking, have taken their efforts most recently to local venues. In both the issues of abortion and gay rights, the conservative populists have been active in rural areas in pressing for local ballot measures and restrictions. Patrick Buchanan's declaration that social issues send men to the barricades is still persuasive; however, the particular social issues and location in which they are debated will continue to shift. As this next chapter in Oregon's social policy battles unfolds, the rest of the nation will watch and wait.

CHAPTER SEVENTEEN

Education Policy

Brent S. Steel and William Lunch

Education in Oregon, especially its funding, has become one of the most controversial policy areas in recent years. On one hand, there is a general consensus among most Oregonians that providing K–12 public education is perhaps the most important function of government. Annual surveys conducted by researchers at Oregon State University between 1992 and 2000 indicate that more than 74 percent of the general public had "some" to a "great deal" of confidence in the local public school district, and public education was always among the "top three important issues" facing the state in any given year.[1] In addition, most moderate, conservative, and progressive legislators generally have been supportive of Oregon's K–12 public education system. However, at the same time, there have been frequent and numerous conflicts over school revenues (such as property taxes), funding levels, and specific education policies. A contemporary example of this conflict was the 2002 legislature's attempt to balance the state budget while providing adequate funding for the K–12 system. After an unprecedented five special sessions, the legislature decided on a package of borrowing money and referring a three-year income tax rate increase to voters for their approval in January 2003. The income tax referral failed by a vote of 46 percent in favor to 54 percent in opposition. As a result, state school support has been reduced, leading to many school districts cutting music and athletic programs, as well as the number of school days. This dire situation has received national attention from the comic strip *Doonesbury*, the *New York Times* and *Washington Post*, and several national news programs. Governor Ted Kulongoski has commented, "To do the job right . . . schools would need $6.7 billion for 2003–05, even if they and the Legislature take all reasonable cost-cutting measures."[2] The overwhelming majority of legislators want to provide adequate funding for schools yet are very polarized about whether to achieve this goal though new tax revenues, program cuts, or short-term borrowing.

Perhaps the greatest conflict over education policy has been between conservative populists, such as Bill Sizemore and his now defunct Oregon Taxpayers United OTU group, and education organizations such as the Oregon Education Association and the Oregon chapter of the American Federation of Teachers. As discussed previously in the book, Sizemore has been a constant critic of government taxes and spending, and of public schools. He has sponsored many initiatives not only to limit taxes and spending but also to weaken the role public employee and teacher unions play in the policy process. For example, in the 2000 general election, Sizemore's organization had two initiatives on the ballot that could have seriously hampered such organizations' efforts to influence education policy. Measure 92 would have amended the Oregon Constitution to prohibit public and private employee payroll deductions (such union dues) for "political purposes" without first receiving employee authorization for such expenditures. The measure, which failed by a 45 percent "yes" to 55 percent "no" margin, would have restricted the ability of teacher unions and other education organizations to contribute to candidates, support or oppose ballot measures, or collect signatures to place a measure on the ballot. Measure 98 would have added a new section to Oregon's constitution prohibiting anyone from using public resources— such as public buildings and spaces, equipment and supplies, or employee time—to collect or help collect political funds or contributions. This measure failed by a close vote of 47 percent "yes" and 53 percent "no."

After the election the conflict continued between Sizemore and the two education groups. The two groups successfully sued (OTU) over the two failed initiatives. A *Statesman Journal* article described the situation as follows: "The unions are seeking damages of $2.7 million, or three times what they spent in 2000 fighting Sizemore-backed measures which they claim should have been disqualified because of forged signatures. Racketeering laws allow them to seek triple damages. . . . A former Sizemore aide, Kelly Highley, has already pleaded guilty to signature forgery linked to those campaigns, and was sentenced to jail time and a $5,000 fine."[3]

On September 27, 2003, (OTU) was found guilty of racketeering activities including forgery, fraud, and conspiracy concerning Measures 92 and 98. The jury also ruled that the presence of these two measures on the November 2000 ballot forced the Oregon Education Association and the American Federation of Teachers to spend money to fight the measures, and both organizations were awarded a $2.5 million settlement. Subsequently, in April 2003 Multnomah County circuit judge Jerome LaBarre issued an injunction to remove OTU's tax-exempt status and barred Sizemore from organizing any similar organizations in the future.

Conservative populists such as Bill Sizemore are not only critical of the public school system but they have also targeted teacher unions and professional associations because they are considered to be some of the most powerful, influential, and progressive groups in the state. Research by Clive Thomas classified the K–12 lobbies (especially the Oregon Education Association, the Oregon Council of School Administrators, and the Oregon School Boards Association) and the higher education lobbies as some of the "most effective" interest groups operating in the state.[4] Therefore, any measures that curtail the groups' ability to raise funds for political purposes are considered highly desirable by certain conservative critics of the public school system.

This chapter will briefly discuss some of the main components of education policy in Oregon, including the various state and local agencies involved, school funding, student testing, the Certificate of Initial Mastery (CIM) and Certificate of Advanced Mastery (CAM), teacher education requirements, charter schools and vouchers, and higher education. The chapter concludes by considering how effective Oregon education policy has been.

HISTORY AND POLITICS OF EDUCATION POLICY

As with the environmental policy history of Oregon, the history of education policy also reflects Oregon's transformation from a rural natural resource and agricultural economy in the mid-1800s to a postindustrial society in the late twentieth and early twenty-first centuries (see table 17.1). The Oregon Territorial Legislature established the public school system in 1849, but few children had the opportunity to participate in the system. Not until 1922 was education made compulsory for all Oregon children. By 1885 there were 1,371 school districts in the state, with 49,176 students enrolled. In 2000 there were fewer school districts because of district mergers, but the number of students had increased to 574,635.

Throughout the history of Oregon's public education system, there have been many reforms and new policies. For example, teacher qualifications have increased over the years from a high school diploma and twelve weeks of additional training in 1919, to a four-year college degree in 1955,

Table 17.1.   Brief History of Oregon Education Policy

1833	First school in Oregon is established in Marion County.
1842	First college established (the Oregon Institute, now Willamette University).
1843	First public school established in Oregon City.
1849	Public school system created by Oregon's Territorial Legislature; Oregon Constitution assigns primary responsibility for public education to the legislature.
1869	First public high school established.
1873	First superintendent of schools appointed.
1885	School districts number 1,371, with 49,176 students.
1900	School districts number 2,094, with 97,745 students.
1919	Teacher requirements established (high school education plus twelve weeks of additional professional training).
1922	Compulsory education for children becomes law.
1925	School districts number 2,372, with 180,398 students.
1925	Average school year is 174 days.
1933	State government contributes approximately 2 percent of school funding.
1945	Constitution amended to allow voter participation in school board elections.
1946	State Basic School Fund established.
1951	State Board of Education established.
1953	School districts allowed to establish and collect local taxes.
1955	Four-year college degree required for teacher certification.
1973	Collective bargaining and other labor rights granted for Oregon teachers.
1973	First teacher strike in Oregon (Hillsboro).
1990	Passage of Measure 5 by Oregon voters, limiting property tax revenue for schools and local governments.
1991	Legislation requiring all districts to offer K–12 education passes.
1991	Legislature passes the Education Act for the Twenty-first Century.
1995	Major revision of Education Act by the legislature; establishes new academic standards for students and schools.
1997	Legislature eliminates tenure for K–12 teachers and places them on two-year contracts.
1997	Average state government share of local school budgets is 80 percent.
1999	Legislative council on the Quality Education Model (QEM, formed by House speaker Lynn Lundquist) issues report. The resulting QEM seeks to improve Oregon's K–12 system by linking funding to school performance.
2000	School districts number 198, with 574,635 students.

Sources: Adapted from *Oregon Blue Book*, http://bluebook.state.or.us/education/edu cationintro.htm, and "OEA and Education History," Oregon Education Association, http://www.oregoned.org.

to a master's degree in the 1990s. Today, standards are established by the Teacher Standards and Practices Commission, which is charged with ensuring "that every student in Oregon is taught by caring, competent and ethical educators."[5]

Since the passage of Measure 5 in 1990, there have been many changes and much conflict concerning education policy in Oregon. A current example of this conflict began in 1991, the first year during which k–12 school funding began to shift from predominantly local sources to state sources. Simultaneously, in its 1991 session, the legislature adopted ambitious goals for educational accomplishment and directed school districts to make curricular and structural changes that had the effect of centralizing and, to an extent, homogenizing education in the state.

The law that passed, almost unanimously, in 1991 is known formally as the Education Act for the Twenty-first Century, but among policy wonks it is usually called the "Katz bill," after Vera Katz, now the mayor of Portland, but at the time a state legislator who had just been deposed as speaker of the House. Katz is a Democrat, and Republicans had taken over the House in the 1990 elections at the same time Measure 5 passed. Katz was and is considered by many in state politics to be a gifted politician. Being in the minority for the first time liberated Katz from the leadership responsibilities she had when she was the speaker, allowing her to focus on education, one of her primary policy concerns. She brought in national education policy experts— in a context that featured deep concern over weak educational performance by American students, highlighted by the Reagan-era national commission on education—to persuade legislators that major changes needed to be made in state and local education policy in Oregon.

The Katz bill was an ambitious blueprint for state centralization of k– 12 education policy and curriculum. The innovations included substantial increases in the length of the school year and school day, more access to and a higher proficiency in using computers, regular testing, and familiarity with, if not proficiency in, a foreign language. In addition, the Katz bill envisioned substantial increases in teacher training and education, with the goal of notably higher standards of achievement for teachers. There was also an implication in the bill that teachers would be better paid and might be either hired by the state or assured that local district hiring policies would be subject to state standards.

In addition, the bill required high school students—in about the tenth grade—to take a qualifying exam to earn a Certificate of Initial Mastery (cim), in preparation for the Certificate of Advanced Mastery (cam) for those interested in continuing their education at colleges or universities. The CIM basically requires interested high school students to meet high standards in a variety of content areas (science, math, English, and language arts), and the CAM requires interested students to meet career-related standards in such areas as problem solving, teamwork, communication, and career development. Also envisioned were occupational internships, linking schools to local businesses and institutions and students to jobs; these were expected to be particularly important for students not planning to go to college. This model reflected a rather European approach to secondary education, fairly explicitly recognizing that many secondary students would be better served by a vocational rather than an academic track, but it also abandoned the pretense of equal academic treatment among high school students.

By 1995 it had become clear to new Republican legislative majorities (the GOP took control of the state Senate in the 1994 elections) that implementation of the Katz legislation would be very expensive, and most of its provisions were slowly abandoned. The goal of language proficiency, for example, would have required school districts to hire many new language teachers. Given the context of ongoing budget reductions for the largest (urban) school districts through the 1990s, the retreat was probably inevitable, but the aggressive centralization of curriculum reflected in the Katz bill was possible because the state was in the process of taking responsibility for the bulk of education finance just as local property taxes—and local control— were reduced.

Former House speaker Lynn Lundquist, a former teacher and a Republican, formed a legislative council to develop a Quality Education Model (QEM) in 1997. The QEM was an attempt to link school funding to school performance. In 1999, Governor John Kitzhaber and Superintendent of Public Instruction Stan Bunn appointed the Quality Education Commission to continue to work on this idea. The commission, composed of education, business and government leaders, subsequently released the Quality Education Model in 1999. In general, the QEM attempts to create a public school system whereby 90 percent of all students achieve statewide academic standards as defined by the Certificate of Initial Mastery. It suggests appropriate class sizes, courses, numbers of teachers and advisors, and funding levels. In response to the QEM, some conservative populist groups, such as the Cascade Policy Institute, issued studies and reports critical of the model. One such report by Richard Vedder argues that many of the assumptions underlying the QEM are flawed, including that of the relationship between class size and funding level, and students' performance.[6]

EDUCATION POLICY AND OREGON'S CULTURE WARS

The 1990s in Oregon education policy were dominated by contradictory developments that parallel the themes in much of this book—on one side, ambitious innovation, represented by the Katz bill, but on the other, decreased resources for public education as a consequence of declining property taxes. On the fiscal side, as has been discussed, the legislature and the governor have proven unable to fully compensate for reductions in local support given the growing constraints on state revenue and spending.[7] These contradictions were and are rooted more in cultural differences among regions and constituencies in the state than in economic differences—though cultural and economic change overlap considerably, and economic decline, particularly in rural areas, was certainly a factor in shrinking support for public education.

Another manifestation of education policy as a cultural-political football has been the ongoing battle over schools and school curriculum by cultural dissenters on the right (described here broadly as conservative populists), particularly supporters of the religious right. The Oregon Citizens Alliance made nationally visible efforts to restrict legal abortion and the legal rights of homosexuals from 1988 to 1994, but those efforts were by no means the only manifestation of strong dissent from some fundamentalist religious groups in the state.[8] Another important battleground has been the public schools. The dissenters on the right have objected to the content of much that is now taught in public schools, from evolution in biology to the contemporary emphasis on contributions made by minority groups to American history and on the writing of women in literature.[9] In response, some religious conservatives have withdrawn their children from public school and now teach them at home.

VOUCHERS, HOME SCHOOLING, AND CHARTER SCHOOLS

The effort by religious conservatives to remove their children from the public schools (while retaining public funding for private and parochial schools) began in earnest in Oregon with Measure 11 from 1990, an initiative that would have established a system of vouchers to allow parents who send their children to private or religious schools to receive public funds. The voucher school initiative was favored by conservative populists and by religious conservatives who hoped to use publicly funded vouchers to send their children to religious schools they could control.

James Madison would have noticed that the opponents of public schools were divided into two identifiable conservative "factions" (to use his term)—libertarians quite explicitly opposed to the existence of public schools, and religious conservatives who would have been happy to send their children to public school, but only if those schools would return to an earlier era in which the school curriculum featured religious instruction and where the roles of the sexes were sharply distinguished.

So while their goals were not entirely consistent, libertarians and religious conservatives had views that overlapped enough to allow them to agree on a broadly worded voucher initiative. But the sponsors of the initiative had evidently misread public opinion. Although there certainly was criticism of the public schools from mainstream sources, most voters were not prepared to make such a radical change in the school system. Measure 11 was overwhelmingly defeated, 68 percent to 32 percent.

In 1991, at the following legislative session, there was a concerted lobbying effort among home-schooling parents against educational regulations. The state Department of Education, interpreting the state education code, had allowed parents wide latitude if they wished to remove their children from public schools, but did require that the children be regularly tested to ensure that they were meeting minimum academic standards. The home-school lobby objected to the regulations, arguing that homeschoolers should be free of government oversight.[10] A bill was introduced in the House in the 1991 session to reduce government regulation of home schooling. With a new Republican majority in the state House, home-schooling advocates hoped that their bill would receive favorable treatment, and it did, at least in the House. The bill, however, met resistance in the Senate, which was narrowly under Democratic control, and from the Democratic governor, Barbara Roberts, who was a long-time advocate of the public schools. As a result, the House bill died in the 1991 session. The home-school advocates were fairly open in saying that the great majority of them—more than 90 percent—were religious conservatives seeking the elimination or evisceration of state education standards because they objected to the content of the contemporary curriculum, not just that it was taught in public schools.[11]

The next step for those opposed to public schools was to propose the establishment of a large number of charter schools as alternatives. Beginning in 1995, once Republicans had gained majorities in both the House and the Senate, many of the same forces that had been active in the battles over vouchers in 1990 and the deregulation of home schooling in 1991 shifted their focus to charter schools. The reform advocates called for changing state law to allow the creation of charter schools, which would have been almost entirely independent of any official oversight or accountability but would have had access to public funding on the same per-student basis as the public schools. The argument made was that the state should finance the education desired by parents, not by school boards or educators. The same strong opposition toward public schools—and schoolteachers—was clearly on display in legislative hearings on charter schools in 1995. The Republican victory across the political spectrum in the 1994 elections encouraged more direct attacks on education in general and schoolteachers in particular in the 1995 legislative session than had been heard previously.

Despite the high hopes of the charter school advocates, the governor threatened to veto a charter school bill if it did not include extensive accountability for public dollars. The leading Republican legislative sponsors of charter schools could not resolve differences within their own caucus. The result was a stalemate, and no charter school bill was enacted in 1995. Many of the same dynamics were present in the 1997 legislative session, but the rather unexpected comeback by some Democrats (including President Clinton nationally and some legislative Democrats in the state) caused the charter school advocates to begin to compromise on some points. Again in 1997 the Republican legislators who were most deeply involved in the charter school debate could not agree among themselves; hence, no bill was enacted.

In 1999, following Governor Kitzhaber's overwhelming reelection and additional modest Democratic legislative gains, the charter school advocates accepted compromises they had rejected earlier. Most of these compromises revolved around the rules governing how the charter schools could be established—principally, giving the school districts a limited veto (which could be overridden by a state board) when charter schools were proposed in that jurisdiction. Charter school advocates were not very happy with the compromise, but they had high hopes that scores of such schools would shortly be established and show the weaknesses of the public schools. Public school supporters feared such an outcome but recognized that the 1999 bill included many protections not in the earlier proposals.

Some three years later, there were twenty-three charter schools in the state, but neither the high hopes of the advocates nor the fears of the opponents have been realized. Public schools in Oregon remain largely as they were before the charter school bill was enacted, and the cultural dissenters on the right who were their most important supporters remain frustrated.

EDUCATION AGENCIES, BODIES, AND STATUTES

The Oregon Constitution requires the legislature to establish a "uniform and general system of common schools" and thus provides a superintendent of public instruction to oversee and administer the system. In 1951 the state Board of Education was established to set policies for the administration and operation of public elementary and secondary schools. The superintendent of public instruction and Board of Education are required to 1) "implement statewide standards for public schools," 2) "adopt rules for the general governance of public kindergartens and public elementary and secondary schools and public community colleges," and 3) "distribute basic school support funds to districts which meet all legal requirements and which maintain and operate a standard school."[12]

Additional agencies and organizations involved in Oregon's education policy include 1) the governor's Office of Education and Workforce Policy—responsible for coordinating the actions of state government, 2) the Department of Education and the Board of Education—responsible for coordinating prekindergarten through high school education programs, 3) the Office of Community College Services and the Board of Education—responsible for coordinating Oregon's seventeen community colleges, 4) the Oregon University System and the Board of Higher Education—responsible for coordinating the state's seven universities, 5) the Oregon State Scholarship Commission—responsible for university financial assistance programs, and 6) the Teacher Standards and Practices Commission—responsible for teacher preparation programs and licenses for teachers and administrators.

SCHOOL FUNDING

By the year 2000, approximately fifty-seven cents (57 percent) of each tax dollar collected by state government was spent to support the public education system, including 570,000-plus students in the public K–12 system, 400,000-plus students in Oregon's seventeen community colleges and workforce training programs, and the seven public universities and their various statewide educational and outreach programs. Thus, the portion of the state's general fund allocated to education is enormous when compared to that of other state programs such as human services (22 percent), public safety including law enforcement and prisons (12 percent), and all remaining government services (9 percent).

Determining the total state government share of the K–12 education budget

Table 17.2.   Spending per Pupil in Public Elementary-Secondary School Systems
in Selected Western States, 1999–2000 (in dollars)

State	Total spending	Total instruction	Total support services
Arizona	5,033	2,919	1,846
California	6,298	3,936	2,122
Colorado	6,165	3,586	2,364
Idaho	5,218	3,255	1,733
Montana	6,214	3,892	2,082
Nevada	5,736	3,423	2,137
Oregon	*7,027*	*4,161*	*2,631*
Washington	6,394	3,805	2,303
Regional average	6,011	3,622	2,152
National average	6,836	4,214	2,334

Source: U.S. Census Bureau, *Annual Survey of Local Government Finances*, 2000.

can be very complicated. The audited school district data for 2000–2001 showed the state share of all revenue resources (including federal and local government sources, trust funds, enterprise revenues, bond revenue, and beginning budget balances) for K–12 schools to be 37 percent. However, if one removes the beginning budget balance, the state's share increases to 47.3 percent, and if one removes long-term debt (bond revenue), it increases to 55.8 percent. If one focuses just on the revenue counted in the school equalization formula (which includes only state and local sources), the state's proportion increases to 70 percent of expenditures.

K–12 public school funding was primarily supported by local property taxes before the passage of Measure 5 in 1990. As discussed previously in this book, Measure 5 phased in a property tax limit over a five-year period, eventually reducing property taxes by 45 percent and limiting these taxes to 1.5 percent of market value. It also required state government to replace most of the lost property tax revenues for public schools over this five-year phase-in period. The end result of Measure 5 has been a decrease in local funding and authority in K–12 education and an increase in state funding and authority. Another consequence of this increased centralization has been more equity in funding for once poorer education districts—especially in rural areas—and a decrease in funding for once wealthier districts such as Corvallis and Lake Oswego.[13] The growth of K–12 spending in the state budget has made it the focus of statewide politics. In fact, many elected

Table 17.3. National Rankings of Selected Western States for Per-pupil spending
in Public Elementary-Secondary Schools, 1999–2000

State	For total spending	For total instruction	For general administration
Arizona	49	50	42
California	29	27	50
Colorado	32	36	41
Idaho	48	45	33
Montana	30	28	19
Nevada	40	42	40
Oregon	*19*	*22*	*35*
Washington	28	31	39

Source: U.S. Census Bureau, *Annual Survey of Local Government Finances*, 2002.

officials and political observers now believe that k–12 education funding is
one of the most contentious issues facing state government.

For the 2000–2001 academic year, statewide spending on public education
was approximately $5.1 billion. The largest component of this spending was
direct instructional activities (that is, salaries and benefits), which accounted
for $2.4 billion, or 47 percent of the total. The second largest component was
instructional and support services such as student counseling, psychological
and health services, and staff development.[14] This accounted for 33 percent
of total spending. The remaining 20 percent was spent on construction,
community services, and other services provided by school districts.

Although there was significant turmoil over school funding in 2002–2003,
with over ninety districts shortening the school year because of drastic budget
shortfalls, funding for k–12 public education in Oregon has historically
fared well when compared with many other western states, according to
U.S. census data.[15] Tables 17.2 and 17.3 provide some comparative data
concerning k–12 public school funding. According to U.S. census data for
1999–2000, k–12 funding in Oregon, at $7,027 per pupil, exceeded the
$6,011 average for other western states and the $6,836 national average
(see table 17.2). Expenditures for instruction (salary and wages) exceed
the regional average, yet are slightly below the national average. In terms
of national ranking in k–12 spending, Oregon ranks nineteenth in total
spending, twenty-second in instructional spending, and thirty-fifth in general
administration spending (see table 17.3).

Table 17.4.   Higher Education Share of General Funds Appropriations

Biennium	Total general funds (in dollars)	Higher education appropriation (in dollars)	Percent of general funds
1987–1989	3,733,830,147	456,745,185	12.2
1989–1991	4,585,476,617	536,744,094	11.7
1991–1993	5,596,713,833	587,844,839	10.5
1993–1995	6,399,967,929	560,666,918	8.8
1995–1997	7,373,000,000	512,958,573	7.0
1997–1999	9,349,900,000	584,401,883	6.3
1999–2001	10,752,385,000	755,074,000	7.0

Source: Oregon University System Budget Office, 2002.

The relative high priority given to K–12 funding has not been matched with community colleges and public higher education institutions. Since the passage of Measure 5, the proportion of the state general funds budget spent on public higher education has decreased from 11.7 percent in 1989–1991 to 7 percent in 1999–2001 (see table 17.4). This is in part due to the state's increasing responsibility to fund K–12 education since the passage of Measure 5.

Compared to other western states, Oregon now spends less per capita on public higher education, even when controlling for state income levels. The data displayed in table 17.5 for the 1997–1998 biennium show that Oregon spends $90.75 per capita compared to a regional average of $128.81 and a national average of $122.01. Oregon now ranks forty-fourth nationally for per capita higher education appropriations. This ranking may well decrease further in the future given the very difficult budget situation that existed in 2002–2003.

As a consequence of declining state support for higher education (and increasing costs), tuition and fees have been increased to keep pace. Despite strong recent efforts by legislators and the governor to slow or cap the growth of tuition and fees, they have increased nonetheless. For example, using Consumer Price Index adjusted dollars for tuition at the University of Oregon, tuition and fees for resident undergraduate students was $3,648 in 1997–1998 compared to $1,450 the year Measure 5 was passed.[16] This is a 152 percent increase in tuition and fees. The largest annual increase for tuition was the year immediately following the implementation of Measure 5.

Similarly, Oregon's community colleges have experienced dramatic increases in tuition due to tightened state and local budgets. The average annual

Table 17.5.   Appropriations for Public Four-Year Institutions in Selected Western
              States, 1997–1998

State	Appropriations per capita (in dollars)	National rank	Appropriations per $1,000 income (in dollars)	National rank
Arizona	161.43	13	6.65	17
California	125.49	27	4.58	32
Colorado	114.93	34	4.07	36
Idaho	174.77	10	8.08	6
Montana	132.56	23	6.53	18
Nevada	119.86	31	4.03	38
Oregon	*90.75*	*44*	*3.56*	*43*
Washington	110.66	38	3.95	40
Regional average	128.81		5.18	
National average	122.01		4.66	

Source: Oregon University System Budget Office, 2002.

tuition for Oregon's seventeen community colleges was $1,750 in 2000–
2001, up from $801 the year Measure 5 was passed—approximately a 118
percent increase.[17] Of course, not all of these increases reflect the impact
of Measure 5, but they do reflect the impact of state government taking an
increasingly important role in K–12 finance and having tighter budgets for
other services, programs, and higher education.

What has been the result of Oregon's various reforms and policy initiatives
in education? The 2001 Benchmark Performance Report by the Oregon
Progress Board provided a grade for twelve benchmarks in education policy
(see table 17.6). For those benchmarks where data are available, Oregon's education policy has led to "above average" results in some areas (benchmarks
18, 19, 20, 21, and 28), and in other areas there are "below average" results
(benchmarks 22, 24, and 25). Average results were obtained for benchmarks
23 and 26 (high school and college completion, respectively).

The benchmarks where above-average progress has been attained included the following: benchmark 18, percent of Oregon children entering
school ready to learn; benchmark 19, percent of third graders who achieve
established skill levels in reading and math; benchmark 20, percent of
eighth graders achieving established reading and math skills; benchmark
21, percent of high school students who have completed a structured work

experience, a measure tied to the Certificate of Advanced Mastery previously discussed in the chapter; and benchmark 28, percent of households using a computer to create documents/graphics or analyze data, or connect to the Internet.

Benchmarks where there was poor performance and need for improvement included benchmark 22, percent of public high school students who drop out; benchmark 24, percent of Oregon adults completing some college; and benchmark 25, percent of Oregonians who have completed an associate degree in professional education.

Another indicator of Oregon's success in education is scores from the Scholastic Aptitude Test (SAT), which is typically taken by college-bound high school seniors. Since 1990 Oregon's scores have always been higher than the national average and typically among the highest in the United States. Average math and verbal scores increased from 509 and 515 respectively in 1990 to 527 each in 2000.[18] These SAT scores, mandatory test scores of third, fifth, eighth, and tenth graders, and the benchmark data presented above, indicate that Oregon's education policy has contributed to much success.

As with many other chapters presented in this book, there are two Oregons in evidence here. While many children and young adults are increasingly successful in academics, there are others who do not fare so well. When examining those youth who drop out of high school and those who do not pursue a college degree, we find that rural and poverty-stricken Oregonians are at greatest risk, especially those who live in areas where economies based on natural resources (such as timber and fishing) have suffered.[19]

In December 2000 the Quality Education Commission (composed of eleven appointed members from industry, education, and government) issued a report to Governor Kitzhaber characterizing the status of Oregon's K–12 education system. Its summary of findings is perhaps an excellent summary of all the discussion and data presented here and a good way to conclude this chapter:

> Oregonians can be proud that with current school funding at the top of the second quartile (14th) we produce students who excel—Oregon Department of Education assessment data show we are getting payback from our focus on rigorous state standards and from our investment for all kids to meet or exceed those standards. Nonetheless, the commission points to areas for progress and the need for all schools to improve in reducing the disproportionately lower performance of students of color and those from low income homes. Are

Table 17.6. Oregon Education Benchmarks: The 2001 Benchmark Performance Report

Benchmark	Description	Grade
18	Ready to learn: Percent of Oregon children entering school ready to learn. Oregon kindergarten teachers indicate improvement for new students in all areas but motor development	A
19	Third grade skill levels: Percent of third graders who achieve established skill levels in reading and math	A for both reading and math
20	Eighth grade reading and math: Percent of eighth graders achieving established reading and math skills	B+
21	High school work experience: Percent of high school students who have completed a structured work experience	B
22	High school dropout rate: Percent of public high school students who drop out of grades 9 through 12 in any given year	D–
23	High school completion: Percent of Oregon adults (age twenty-five and older) who have completed high school or equivalent	C+
24	Some college completion: Percent of Oregon adults who have completed some college	D
25	Associate degree: Percent of Oregonians who have completed an associate degree in professional-technical education	D
26	College completion: Percent of Oregon adults age twenty-five and older who have completed a baccalaureate degree	C–
27	Adult literacy: Percent of all adult Oregonians with intermediate literary skills	NA
28	Computer/Internet usage: Percent of Oregon households that use a computer to (a) create documents/graphics or analyze data, or (b) connect to the Internet	B for creating and analyzing (a) and A for connecting (b)
29	Labor force skills training: Percent of Oregonians in the labor force who received at least twenty hours of skills training in the past year	NA

Source: Oregon Progress Board, *The 2001 Benchmark Performance Report,* Salem.

we doing well? Yes, the Commission believes Oregon schools are doing an exceptional job with the resources provided. Can we do better? The Commission is convinced we must do so if we are to become measurably the best system of schools in the country and the world.[20]

Of course, the main question now is: will Oregon's schools maintain an adequate level of funding and thus maintain this high level of accomplishment? At the time this chapter is being written, many school districts are laying off teachers, cutting school days, and cutting programs because of the state's budget shortfall. However, some local governments are taking matters into their own hands by promoting local tax increases to fund schools and other services. For example, Multnomah County passed Measure 26–48 on May 22, 2003, which will raise approximately $128 million a year through a 1.25 percent county income tax. However for most of the state, the current financial outlook is somewhat dismal and many parents are contemplating opting out of the public school system for private schools.

CHAPTER EIGHTEEN

Oregon in Perspective

Mark Henkels and Richard A. Clucas

A snapshot of Oregon today reveals a state at an apparent turning point. With the Oregon economy continuing to stagnate and with state revenue declining, the Legislative Assembly needed a record five special sessions in 2002 to find a way to balance the general funds budget. Over the course of the year, the legislature was forced to address a revenue shortfall totalling more than $1.3 billion in the $12 billion budget. The legislature responded in a piecemeal manner by increasing cigarette taxes, borrowing money from state trust funds, and cutting programs. Finally, in September 2002 the legislature sought to close the final budget gap with a three-year income tax increase. Recognizing the political risks of this decision, legislators referred the tax increase to voters in a January 2003 special election, rather than adopting the increase outright.[1]

The battle over the budget and the debate over a tax increase quickly moved beyond Salem politics and began to affect the ongoing gubernatorial race. The two major party candidates took opposing stands on the tax measure, and polls suggested that their positions could influence the outcome of the race.[2] Even though Democrat Ted Kulongoski won the race against Republican Kevin Mannix, he did so with only a forty-thousand-vote margin, suggesting that Mannix's antitax platform resonated with much of the public. The defeat of Measure 28 two months later affirmed that point. Without the tax increase, the Legislative Assembly was forced to devote the beginning of the new session in 2003 to finding an alternative way to balance the 2001–2003 budget. This time it relied on a range of cuts, fee increases, and funds transfers.

With the 2001–2003 budget behind it, the legislature then turned to the new crisis: the budget for the next biennium. Initially preparing an $11 billion budget, the legislature soon found itself again facing an unexpected shortfall. In May the state economist reported that revenue projections for the biennium were down more than $640 million from the January 2003 estimates. Later that day the governor began talk of raising beer and wine taxes and eliminating tax breaks to address the new shortfall. The battle over the budget kept the Legislative Assembly in session for a record 227 days as the legislators fought over a solution. Eventually, the legislature was able to adjourn when a group of moderate Republicans joined with the Democrats to approve a $1.2 billion tax increase. Yet the victory was short lived. Opponents of the tax increase were able to gather enough signatures to place a referendum on the ballot in February 2004. The voters overturned the tax increase, forcing the state to make cuts in social services, schools, and police protection.[3]

The state's continuing battle over the budget in 2002 and 2003 is important to think about because it tests Oregon's image. Oregon is often viewed as a progressive state, but clearly there is more to its politics than progressivism. The reality is that Oregon today is strongly divided, split between progressives and conservative populists, with both sides retaining critical sources of popular support and political influence, and with a future that is uncertain.

This chapter provides an overview of how this conflict has helped reshape Oregon government and politics, and considers what the future may hold. This task requires a discussion of the initiative process because it, perhaps more than any other aspect of the state's political system, has been the main stage where the conflict between progressives and conservative populists has played out.

THE OREGON SYSTEM REDUX

In the early 1900s Oregonians turned so frequently to the initiative and referenda to shape state law that these twin components of direct democracy were often called "the Oregon System." Initiatives have become such an important part of state politics in recent years that it may be fair to once again label the initiative process the "Oregon System" in the sense that initiatives are a defining element of modern Oregon politics. The total number of laws the initiative system produces is not the key point; the legislature produces much more legislation. Only 40 of the 106 initiatives that reached the ballot during the 1980s and 1990s actually became law. Initiatives are important because they can directly create major change in state policies and shape political debate. Over the past fifteen years, initiatives produced some of the state's most significant public policies, including property tax limits, term limits, physician-assisted suicide, tough sentencing rules, and a requirement that property owners be compensated when government policy reduces property values. Moreover, regardless of the final outcome, many initiatives dominated political debate in the state, as supporters and opponents fought very public battles to further or protect their political interests.

Why have initiatives reemerged as as being so important? Activists using the system, including Bill Sizemore, argue that it reflects growing public disillusionment with government. In chapter 5, however, Richard Ellis explains how the rise is linked to the growing use of signature-gathering firms by initiative sponsors. As a result, progressives and conservative populists now frequently turn to the process to try to transform their political ideals into law. The initiative has come to play a leading role in the conflict between the two sides.

The reemergence of the initiative as a key component of the state's political system has both immediate and long-term consequences. The legalization of medical marijuana and assisted suicide demonstrate how initiatives have had an immediate and visible impact on society. In both of these cases, Oregon residents were given new options in health care treatment overnight, options that had previously been denied to them.

The immediate impact of initiatives, however, may not be nearly as important as the structural changes they can bring over the long haul. The most significant example of the long-term effects of initiatives is in the state's revenue system. The property tax limitations of Measure 5 in 1990 and Measure 50 in 1997 significantly altered the sources of school funding and the state's role in education. Whereas local property taxes once supplied approximately 70 percent of school funds, today the state provides approximately 70 percent. Although hidden by the strong economic growth of the 1990s and by changes in other revenue sources, the effects of these measures intensified the competition for general funds among K–12 education and other programs, such as higher education and the Oregon Health Plan. After the economy slowed in 2001, the consequences of Measures 5 and 50 became unavoidable. State programs were squeezed especially hard because the state, along with its other responsibilities, now had to pick up a larger tab for K–12 education. Moreover, the revenue shortfalls were more immediate and larger, especially for the schools, because income taxes are less stable than property taxes. The fact that Oregon depends on income taxes for about 90 percent of its general revenue makes this situation particularly difficult.

Initiatives have also been important for giving political activists a power-ful springboard to influence public policy. No one has been more involved in the initiative process recently than Bill Sizemore. Sizemore has played a major role in shaping Oregon's political agenda over the past decade, even when championing some losing initiatives. For example, Measure 50, the property tax reform passed in 1997, was not an initiative. Instead, the legislature referred Measure 50 to the ballot in response to the even more severe cuts found in Measure 47, a Sizemore-sponsored initiative passed in 1996. Through his work on initiatives, Sizemore was also given a vehicle for entering the state's gubernatorial race in 1998. Thus, initiatives allow their sponsors to bring issues onto the state's political agenda and to pursue their own personal political ambitions.

Is the growing use of the initiative process good? Is it bad? The answer depends on whom you ask. In the past few years, many political observers, from state leaders to political scientists, have criticized initiatives, arguing that the initiative gives too much power to initiative sponsors and allows bad legislation to be enacted. These opponents believe that lawmaking should generally be left for the legislative process, where compromises can be worked out. Yet many conservative populist and progressive activists argue that the initiative is a much-needed mechanism for addressing policy issues on which the legislature cannot or will not act.

Whether initiatives are good or bad, what is important to understand is the critical role they play in the conflict between progressives and conservative populists, and how their increased use by both sides has, in turn, helped reshape other aspects of Oregon government and politics.

EVOLVING GOVERNMENT INSTITUTIONS

Beyond the initiative process, the conflict between progressives and conser-vative politics has altered Oregon politics in other ways. Perhaps the single most important institutional change in recent years was the election of a majority of Republicans to both houses in the 1994 election. The election marked the first time in forty years that Republicans had complete control over the Legislative Assembly. The election of a new Democratic governor (John Kitzhaber) that same year meant that the leaders of the two branches had quite different political values and goals. Legislative leaders were much more attentive to the concerns of conservative populists in the state, but the governor supported progressive policies. With divided government and different constituency bases separating the branches, state leaders have since been in frequent conflict and have had a difficult time finding solutions. The state is divided and so is the government.

The executive branch has also changed, especially because of the increased use of initiatives. The explosion of initiatives has helped reduce the governor's ability to set the state's political agenda. As governor in the late 1960s and early 1970s, Tom McCall produced his greatest accomplishments not through the ballot box but through traditional legislative processes. In recent years, on the other hand, Governor John Kitzhaber often found himself hedged in not only by the opposition's control over the statehouse but also by the constraining pressures of ballot measures. The governor remains the central voice in state politics, but the initiative provides other political actors direct entry to the state's political agenda. This has altered gubernatorial political strategies. Kitzhaber spent considerable political energy and capital fighting other people's initiatives, or championing his own, rather than working for change through the legislature.

The bureaucracy has not been immune to the conflict in the state or to change. Throughout the 1990s state agencies had to cope with the financial constraints placed on them by the passage of Measure 5 and Measure 50. During the same time conservative populist leaders sponsored three different initiatives to reduce administrative rules by allowing opponents to force the legislature to hear appeals on state rules.[4] Although these particular proposals failed, antiregulatory and antibureaucratic sentiment remains powerful. In chapter 10, Douglas Morgan argues that an effective administrative structure requires talented people who are willing and able to apply their expertise and experience to the task of implementation. Agencies that operate under constant close scrutiny, in fear of sanctions for minor errors, under pressure from special interests and from tightening budgets will not be able or willing to make the decisions needed to implement public policy effectively.

Oregon is considered to have had a long legacy of effective and creative administration, which is consistent with its progressive heritage. Conservative populists have an alternative vision of what makes good government, and because of that they are actively challenging Oregon's legacy. Conservative populists seek a smaller, less active government, one in which the bureaucracy plays a less intrusive role in private matters. What progressives may see as effective government, conservative populists are likely to view as overregulation or wasteful spending. Whereas progressives may prefer a problem-solving government, conservative populists frequently see government as the problem, and they oppose government activities that interfere with private economic activities or that increase taxes.

Finally, the split between progressives and conservative populists and the increased use of initiatives by these two sides have also impacted the state court system. As the ultimate judge of whether ballot measures are constitutionally legitimate, the court has been squarely in the middle of initiative-based battles. To some degree the courts have served as a bastion of defense for progressive interests, as they have overturned ballot measures limiting public employee benefits (Measure 8), tightening criminal punishments (Measure 26), and creating term limits (Measure 3). Yet the courts have also overturned at least one important progressive initiative that was designed to protect the power of labor unions (Measure 62).

In sum, it is clear that the conflict between progressives and conservative populists has changed Oregon politics. Much of this conflict has been fought through the initiative process, in the legislature, or between the legislature and the executive branch, yet the conflict can be seen at all levels of government in Oregon and in a wide swath of policy areas. Moreover, as this conflict has played out, it has transformed the role and position of government in the state, weakening the governor, threatening the bureaucracy, and making the courts more entangled in a web of political battles. Earlier chapters discussed the significance of this conflict in other aspects of Oregon politics, from debates over assisted suicide to battles over zoning.

Finally, it is worth thinking about what these trends mean for Oregon's political reputation. Looking back, it is clear that while the progressive side of the state remains potent, the more conservative side has been increasingly successful in shaping the public agenda and the direction of Oregon government and politics over the past decade or two. More than anything else, the efforts of conservative populists to limit the size and activity of government through the initiative process have been the most consequential. With the passage of property tax limits, the introduction of term limits, and the efforts to champion property rights, conservative populist leaders have enjoyed considerable success in shaping much of the political debate in Oregon, if not actual policy.

WHERE DOES THE OREGON TRAIL LEAD?

Where is Oregon politics headed? In answering this question, it is important to return to a discussion on the state's economy and demographics. One of the interesting and significant aspects of Oregon is that its political landscape parallels its physical geography. Geography matters in Oregon politics. This book has emphasized the importance of the state's progressive heritage and the emergence of conservative populism in shaping the state's politics. In many ways, the book could have focused instead on the state's political geography. Looking at the conflict between progressives and conservative populists, there is clearly a strong geographical element to this debate. The split divides the state between urban and rural areas, between east and west, and between much of the Willamette Valley and everywhere else in Oregon.

It is particularly important to understand this geographical dimension in order to get some sense of what the future holds for Oregon. Various parts of the state have experienced different kinds of change. The Portland metropolitan area has experienced a large increase in residents since the 1980s and a growing number of minorities. The area has become identified with high technology. The region around Bend, parts of southern Oregon, and the coast are also growing, but the growth in these smaller towns and rural areas reflects an influx of retirees from California and elsewhere. Some of the more rural areas of the state are also witnessing a rise in minority population, especially from Latinos settling in parts of rural Willamette Valley, in Umatilla, and in more eastern areas of the state. Other parts of the state are not growing as fast, and may even be declining as they suffer from the downturn in natural resources as an economic base.

Natural resources, such as timber, salmon, and wheat, no longer dominate the state's economy as they once did. High-tech and other industries are more important. The beneficiaries of these economic trends have been the urban areas; the losers have been the more rural areas. The state is facing new conflicts as it tries to confront population growth, more diverse communities, and changing economic realities.

While the defeat of tax increases in recent elections and the passage of such conservative populist proposals as the antiregulatory Measure 7 suggest that the state's progressive heritage may be on decline, these demographic, economic, and social trends suggest that progressivism should not be written off. As the Willamette Valley continues to grow and diversify, the urban parts of the state will undoubtedly remain a strong voice for progressive ideas.

Yet the most important political change may not come from the urban core but from the suburbs of Portland, since they are expected to experience among the largest rate of growth in the state.[5] In the past, outcomes of many of the big political battles between progressives and conservative populists have been decided in the suburbs, where the residents have not been as consistently aligned to either of these two camps. As their population grows, the suburbs may become even more critical to deciding the fate of public policy in Oregon, and in the process may make the state's politics seem less schizophrenic.

Of course even today, the rural/urban split is not as absolute as it sometimes appears. The success of the Republicans in controlling the Oregon statehouse in the 1990s in part reflects the fact that the fringes of the urban areas and the city of Salem are not as committed to progressivism as are other areas in urban Oregon. There is also a reservoir of rural Oregonians who have deep concerns about maintaining their resource-based economies but do not have a deep ideological bias against Oregon's traditional pragmatic approach to other public issues. It is well worth noting that despite his success in championing conservative populist ballot measures, Sizemore was able to attain only 30 percent of the vote in the 1998 governor's race. Despite stronger support in eastern and southern Oregon, he won only one county— Malheur.

One possible development may be that the state moves away from the centralizing patterns of Measure 5 and 50. Multnomah County's passage of an income tax in May 2003 to support its schools and social services may inaugurate a period of increasing local variation in taxes and services. A new model may emerge, one where communities compete by offering various combinations of taxes and services, if the legislature allows it.

In 2003 Oregon found itself in the same position it had been in several times over the previous year and a half—trying to find a way to fix the state's worsening fiscal position without any consensus on how to proceed. The real difficulty confronting Oregon, however, was not fiscal, but ideological. Underneath the debate over budgeting was a conflict that has come to structure much of Oregon politics in recent years. Oregon has long been recognized for its progressive tradition, yet it should be clear by now that it also has a strong conservative populist side to it as well. Over the past decade or so, these two sides have continuously sought to make their vision of society a reality, and in so doing they have fought each other and often dominated political debate. The battle over the budget represented a continuation of that larger conflict.

What will happen over the long haul is hard to know. Certainly there is the possibility that this split could decline in importance. The conflict could be weakened by factors such as demographic changes, shifts in the state's economy, or specific changes in the initiative process or government institutions. But for now none of those scenarios seem likely. While the budget crisis of 2003 appeared to have placed Oregon at a turning point, it is unlikely that the state will turn very far from where it is today—fighting over two perspectives on government and politics. The 2004 election was too recent to incorporate in this book, but the results clearly reaffirm the importance of the schism in the state, as both sides fought aggressively throughout the summer and fall over the presidential candidates, control of the state legislature, and several contentious ballot measures. In the end, neither side came out a clear victor. Democratic Party candidate John Kerry won the presidential vote, and the Democrats gained seats in both houses of the state legislature, but the conservative populists were able to pass a constitutional amendment banning same-sex marriages (Measure 36) and a statutory initiative (Measure 37) requiring state and local governments to pay landowners when land-use restrictions reduce property values, reviving the promise of the court-overturned Measure 7. The results gave no hint whatsoever that change is on the horizon. The reason that significant change seems unlikely is that the conflict between these two perspectives has grown deeply imbedded in the state's political culture. If there is one aspect of Oregon politics that best defines the state today, it would be this divide.

Notes

I. A STATE DIVIDED

1. Tony Howard Evans, "Oregon Progressive Reform, 1902–1914" (PhD diss., University of California, Berkeley, 1966); Warren Marion Blankenship, "Progressives and the Progressive Party in Oregon, 1906–1916" (PhD diss., University of Oregon, 1966).

2. Examples of Oregon's progressive tradition can be found in Gordon B. Dodds, *Oregon: A Bicentennial History* (New York: W. W. Norton, 1977) and Floyd J. McKay, *An Editor for Oregon: Charles Sprague and the Politics of Change* (Corvallis: Oregon State Press, 1998).

3. Dodds, *Oregon*, 156–60.

4. Kenneth M. Dolbeare and Klinda J. Medcalf, *American Ideologies Today* (New York: McGraw Hill, 1993); Michael P. Frederici, *The Challenges of Populism: The Rise of Right-Wing Democratism in Postwar America* (New York: Praeger, 1991); Kenneth Hoover, *Ideology and Public Life* (Belmont CA: Wadsworth Press, 1994). "Progressivism" is not a standardized term in political philosophy or political science. The definition used here fits easily into the range of descriptions found in the broad analysis of the term provided by James J. Connoly in "GAPE Bibliography: Progressivism," January 31, 1997, http://www2.h-net.msu.edu/ shgape/.

5. For more information on the Progress Board, the benchmark program, and the award, go to the Oregon Progress Board website: http://www.econ.state.or.us/opb.

6. *Governing's State and Local Sourcebook 2001* (Washington DC: Congressional Quarterly Press, 2001), 28.

7. Ernest Callenbach, *Ecotopia* (Berkeley: Banyan Tree Books, 1975); Brent Walth, *Fire at Eden's Gate* (Portland: Oregon Historical Society, 1994).

8. Alan Durning, *This Place on Earth* (Seattle: Sasquatch Books, 1996).

9. Dave Hogan, "Measure 7 Goes to State High Court Today," *Oregonian*, September 10, 2001, E1.

10. Brent Hunsberger, "Effects of Measure 7 Remain Up for Debate," *Oregonian*, November 20, 2000, A1; Dave Hogan, "Measure Seven Not Retroactive, Meyers Says," *Oregonian*, February 14, 2001, A1.

11. Charles Beggs, "Property Rights Initiative Thrown Out," *Corvallis Gazette-Times*, October 5, 2002, A1.

12. Thomas Bedenheimer, "The Oregon Health Plan—Lessons for the Nation, Part 1," *New England Journal of Medicine* 337 (August 28, 1997): 651–55; Thomas Bedenheimer, "The Oregon Health Plan—Lessons for the Nation, Part 2," *New England Journal of Medicine* 333 (August 28, 1997): 720–23.

13. Oregon Legislative Revenue Office, *Research Report 1–01*, Salem, January 8, 2001; Paul Warner, Oregon legislative revenue officer, telephone interview with Mark Henkels, September 23, 2002. The nature of these measures is explained more fully in chapter 13.

14. Charles E. Beggs, "Low-Income People Brace for Yet More Cuts in Oregon Health Plan," Associated Press State and Local Wire, June 27, 2004.

15. Gail Kinsey Hill, "Urban Areas Dominate Job Growth," *Oregonian*, February 26, 1999, B1.

16. McKay, *Editor*, 71.

17. Council of State Governments, *Book of the States 2001–2002* (Lexington KY: Council of State Governments, 2001).

18. Dodds, *Oregon*, 99–102.

19. Bill Bradbury, *Oregon Blue Book, 2001–2002* (Salem: Secretary of State, 2001).

20. Alan Tarr, *Constitutional Politics in the States* (Westport CT: Greenwood Press, 1996), 33; Council of State Governments, *Book of the States 2001–2002*, 3.

21. Tom Bates, "Oregon XXX-Rated," *Oregonian*, May 7, 1995, D1; Deborah Holton, "Sex-Store Plan Spurs Try for Zoning Rights," *Oregonian*, March 15, 1999, E1; Charles E. Beggs, "Campaign Donation Rules Cause Partisan Fuss," Associated Press State and Local Wire, January 8, 2001. The relevant court cases are *State v. Henry*, 302 Ore. 510, 514, 732 P.2d 9 (1987); *State v. Stoneman*, 323 Ore. 536, 920 P.2d 535 (1996); *State v. Robertson*, 293 Ore. 402, 649 P.2d 569 (1982); *Vannatta v. Keisling*, 324 Ore. 514, 931 P.2d 770 (1997).

22. When the amendment contains a supermajority-voting requirement, however, it must be ratified by a supermajority of voters. This is true whether the proposal has been placed on the ballot by the legislature or through the initiative process. The constitution also differentiates between amending and revising the constitution. If the legislature wishes to revise the constitution, it requires a two-thirds vote of each house to place on the ballot.

23. *Armatta v. Kitzhaber*, 327 Ore. 250 (1998).

24. Some recent examples include Mason Drukman, *Wayne Morse: A Political Biography* (Portland: Oregon Historical Society, 1997); Richard Neuberger, *They Never Go Back to Pocatello: The Selected Essays of Richard Neuberger* (Portland: Oregon Historical Society, 1988); and McKay, *Editor.*

2. PLACE, PEOPLE

1. Daniel Elazar, "The American Cultural Matrix," in *The Ecology of American Political Culture: Readings*, ed. Daniel Elazar and Joseph Zikmund II (New York: Thomas Y. Crowell, 1975), 20–21.

2. George Wilkes, *The History of Oregon, Geographical and Political* (New York: William H. Colyer, 1845), 54–56.

3. For a more detailed account of the formation of Oregon, see Elizabeth Orr, William N. Orr, and Ewart M. Baldwin, *Geology of Oregon*, 4th ed. (Dubuque, IA: Kendall/Hunt, 1992).

4. Keith S. Hadley, "Vegetation," in *The Pacific Northwest: Geographical Perspectives*, ed. James G. Ashbaugh (Dubuque IA: Kendall/Hunt, 1994), 99–116.

5. John Eliot Allen, *The Magnificient Gateway* (Forest Grove OR: Timber Press, 1984), 61; James W. Scott, "Historical Geography," in Ashbaugh, ed., *Pacific Northwest*, 3.

6. Gordon B. Dodds, *The American Northwest: A History of Oregon and Washington* (Arlington Heights IL: Forum Press, 1986), 26.

7. Dodds, *American Northwest*, 44–46.

8. Dodds, *American Northwest*, 40–41.

9. Frederick Holman, *Dr. John McLoughlin: The Father of Oregon* (Cleveland OH: Arthur Clark, 1907), 61–64; Robert J. Loewenberg, *Equality on the Oregon Frontier* (Seattle: University of Washington Press, 1976), 62–66.

10. Hubert Howe Bancroft, *History of Oregon*, vol. 29, *The Works of Hubert Howe Bancroft* (San Francisco: History, 1888), 305.

11. Loewenberg, *Equality*, 140–48.

12. Loewenberg, *Equality*, 156, 161, 166.

13. Walter C. Woodward, *Political Parties in Oregon: 1843–1868* (Portland: J. K. Gill, 1913), chapters 10–14.

14. Dodds, *Oregon*, 157–161; George Turnbull, *Governors of Oregon* (Portland: Binfords and Mort, 1959), 37–39.

15. Dodds, *Oregon*, 156–58; Thomas McClintock, "Seth Lewelling, William S. U'Ren, and the Birth of the Oregon Progressive Movement," *Oregon Historical Quarterly* 68 (1968): 197–220.

16. Dodds, *Oregon*, 166.

17. Leonard Schlup, "Republican Insurgent: Jonathan Bourne and the Politics of Progressivism, 1908–1912," *Oregon Historical Quarterly* 76 (1986): 229–44.

18. Dodds, *Oregon*, 197; David A. Horowitz, "Social Morality and Personal Revitalization: Oregon's Ku Klux Klan in the 1920s," *Oregon Historical Quarterly* 79 (1989): 365–84; Turnbull, *Governors*, 79–81.

19. Erasmo Gamboa, "The Bracero Program," in *Nosotros: The Hispanic People of Oregon*, ed. Erasmo Gamboa and Carolyn M. Buan (Portland: Oregon Council for the Humanities, 1995), 41.

20. Erasmo Gamboa, "A Personal Search for Oregon's Hispanic History," in *Nosotros*, ed. Gamboa and Buan, 11–20.

21. Brent Walth, *Fire at Eden's Gate: Tom McCall and the Oregon Story* (Portland: Oregon Historical Society, 1998), 440–441.

22. Measure 7 was found unconstitutional by the Oregon Supreme Court in 2002. See *League of Oregon Cities v. State of Oregon*, Oregon SC S48450, October 4, 2002. In 2004 property rights activists succeeded in passing a "son of Measure 7" initiative on the November ballot, Measure 37.

3. OREGON IN THE NATION AND THE WORLD

1. Barry Siegel, "As Oregon Becomes the Only Place on Earth with a Law Allowing Physician-Assisted Suicide, a Retired School Teacher Struggles with Terminal Cancer," *Los Angeles Times*, November 14, 1999, 1; "Key Figure in Assisted Suicide Movement Dies," *Oregonian*, May 29, 2000, C14.

2. Morton Grodzins, "The Federalist System," in *Goals for Americans: The President's Commission on National Goals* (Englewood Cliffs NJ: Prentice-Hall, 1960), 265.

3. Dodds, *Oregon*.

4. Mark Rom, "Health and Welfare in the American States: Politics and Policy," in *Politics in the American States: A Comparative Analysis*, 6th ed., ed. Virginia Gray and Herbert Jacob (Washington DC: Congressional Quarterly Press, 1996); Sanford F. Schram and Carol S. Weissert, "The State of U.S. Federalism: 1998–1999," *Publius* 29 (1999): 1–34.

5. Tom Detzel, "Kitzhaber Offers Plan for the Environment," *Oregonian*, May 3, 2001, A1.

6. William J. Mathis, "No Child Left Behind: Costs and Benefits," *Phi Delta Kappan*, May 2003, 679–86.

7. Oregon HAVA Plan Steering Committee, *Oregon Elections Plan: Implementation*

of the Help America Vote Act of 2002 (HAVA) (Salem: Secretary of State, 2002).

8. National Conference of State Legislatures, "Current Levels of Selected Unfunded Mandates and Underfunded National Expectations Imposed on State and Local Governmments," http://www.ncsl.org/standcomm/scbudg/budgmandateso3.htm.

9. John P. Salle, Office of Public Safety and Security, Oregon State Police, telephone interview with Richard Clucas, May 15, 2003.

10. U.S. Census Bureau, *Consolidated Federal Funds Report for Fiscal Year: 2001* (Washington DC: U.S. Government Printing Office, 2001).

11. Bill Graves, "Federal Largess Benefits OHSU," *Oregonian*, August 5, 1990, D1; "Hatfield's Lean Pork," *Oregonian*, April 6, 1996, D8.

12. David B. Walker, *The Rebirth of Federalism: Slouching Toward Washington* (Chatham NJ: Chatham House, 1995).

13. Oregon Department of Human Services, *Oregon's Death with Dignity Act Annual Report 2001* (Salem: Oregon Department of Human Services, 2001).

14. Jim Kadera, "Timber Towns Feel Losses," *Oregonian*, August 26, 1990, B1.

15. Michael Milstein, "Farmers Defy U.S., Escalate Fight," *Oregonian*, July 14, 2001, A1; Hal Bernton, "Worlds Collide in Klamath Basin," *Oregonian*, November 16, 1997, A1.

16. Rob Eure, "Land Grab," *Oregonian*, July 24, 1995, A1.

17. Jonathan Brinckman, "New Rules Set Up for Salmon," *Oregonian*, June 21, 2000, A1.

18. William Kevin Voit and Gary Nitting, *Interstate Compacts & Agencies* (Lexington KY: Council of State Governments, 1999).

19. Jim Lynch, "Gorge Landmark Still Empty Despite Ruling a Year after a State Court Decision in Their Favor," *Oregonian*, September 3, 2002, A1.

20. Oregon Economic and Community Development Commission, *1999–2001 Biennial Report: Status of Oregon's Economy* (Salem: ECDC, 2001).

21. U.S. Census Bureau, *Total U.S. Exports (Origin of Movement) via Oregon, Top 25 Commodities Based on 2001 Dollar Value* (Washington DC: U.S. Census Bureau, 2001).

4. PARTIES AND ELECTIONS

1. Paul Allen Beck and Marjorie Randon Hershey, *Party Politics in America*, 9th ed. (New York: Longman, 2001).

2. Elections Division, Secretary of State, http://www.sos.state.or.us/elections/elec hp.htm.

3. Robert E. Burton, *Democrats of Oregon: The Pattern of Minority Politics, 1950–1956* (Eugene: University of Oregon Books, 1970).

4. Burton, *Democrats*.

5. The office of superintendent of public instruction became nonpartisan in 1961.

6. Burton, *Democrats*; Dodds, *Oregon*.

7. Burton, *Democrats*.

8. Burton, *Democrats*; Dodds, *Oregon*.

9. Jeff Baker, "PDX Life Readings & Writings a Passion for Politics: Nader and His Party," *Oregonian*, January 25, 2002, 5.

10. Burton, *Democrats*.

11. Elections Division, Secretary of State, http://www.sos.state.or.us/elections/elec hp.htm.

12. Beck and Hershey, *Party Politics*.

13. Elections Division, Secretary of State, http://www.sos.state.or.us/elections/elec hp.htm.

14. Elections Division, Secretary of State, http://www.sos.state.or.us/elections/elec hp.htm.

15. Margaret Rosenfield, *All-Mail-Ballot Elections* (Washington DC: National Clearinghouse on Election Administration, 1995); Secretary of State, *Vote by Mail* (Salem: Secretary of State, 2000).

16. Jeff Mapes, "Oregon's Vote-by-Mail System Draws New, High-Level Criticism," *Oregonian*, August 9, 2001, A1.

17. Beck and Hershey, *Party Politics*.

18. David Hogan and Steve Suo, "Campaign Spending Heads Into Record Territory," *Oregonian*, October 23, 2000, A1.

19. Charles E. Beggs, "Spending Light for Governor's Race," Associated Press Newswire, October 6, 1998; David Hogan, "Governor's Race Looking to be Costly," September 11, 2001, B7.

20. Lisa Grace Lednicer, "Initiative Ruling by Court Leaves Terms Undefined," *Oregonian*, January 16, 2002, A1.

21. Elections Division, Secretary of State, http://www.sos.state.or.us/elections/elec hp.htm.

5. DIRECT DEMOCRACY

1. The term "referendum" is also used to refer to measures placed on the ballot by the legislature. Throughout this book, however, we have used the term "legislative referral" to refer to legislative measures.

2. *Libertarian Party of Oregon v. Paulus*, Civ. No. 82–521FR, slip op. At 4 (September 3, 1982).

3. *Meyer v. Grant*, 486 U.S. 414 (1988).

4. "One Donor Is Big Bucks Behind 3 of 11 Initiatives," July 24, 2002, press release available at http://oregonfollowthemoney.org/July2402.html.

5. Testimony on SJR3 before the Oregon Senate Committee on Rules and Elections, February 9, 1999.

6. Peter G. Gosselin, "Tax Cuts Seen as Spoiler—in Boom Times," *Los Angeles Times*, August 26, 2000; Jeff Mapes and Harry Esteve, "Healthy Economy Cools Oregon Tax-Cutting Fever," *Oregonian*, September 24, 2000; Brent Steel and Robert Sahr, *Oregon Governmental Issues Survey—2000* (Corvallis: Program for Governmental Research and Education, Oregon State University, July 2000).

7. Elizabeth Garrett and Elizabeth R. Gerber, "Money in the Initiative and Referendum Process: Evidence of Its Effects and Prospects for Reform," in *The Battle over Citizen Lawmaking*, ed. M. Dane Waters (Durham NC: Carolina Academic Press, 2001), 73–96.

8. Shaun Bowler and Todd Donovan, *Demanding Choices: Opinion, Voting, and Direct Democracy* (Ann Arbor: University of Michigan Press, 1998).

9. Kenneth P. Miller, "Judging Ballot Initiatives: A Unique Role for Courts" (paper presented at the annual meeting of the Western Political Science Association, San Jose CA, March 2000); Kenneth P. Miller, "The Role of the Courts in the Initiative Process: A Search for Standards" (paper presented at the annual meeting of the American Political Science Association, Atlanta GA, September 1999).

10. *Armatta v. Kitzhaber*, 327 Ore. 250 (1998).

11. The data presented in this section were provided by Jennifer Hannan, of the Appellate Court Records Section of the Oregon Judicial Department, and Keith Garza, staff attorney for the Oregon Supreme Court.

12. Keith Garza, interview with author, August 3, 2000.

13. Alana Jeydel and Brent S. Steel, "Public Attitudes Toward the Initiative Process: An Oregon Case Study" (paper presented at the annual meeting of the Western Political Science Association, Las Vegas NV, March 2001). Also see the City Club of Portland, "The Initiative and Referendum in Oregon," February 1996, appendix C, 61–68.

14. *Citizens Against Rent Control v. City of Berkeley*, 454 U.S. 290 (1981); *Meyer v. Grant*, 486 U.S. 414 (1988). Also see *Victoria Buckley v. American Constitutional Law Foundation*, 525 U.S. 182 (1999).

15. *Stranahan v. Fred Meyer*, 331 Ore. 38 (2000).

6. INTEREST GROUPS

1. James Madison, "Federalist Paper Number 10," in *The Annals of America* (Chicago: Encyclopedia Britannica, 1976), 216–20.

2. Oregon Legislative Revenue Office, *Research Report 1–01*, Salem, January 8, 2001; Paul Warner, legislative revenue officer, telephone interview with Mark Henkels, September 23, 2002.

3. Thomas Dye distinguishes interest groups and political parties: "An interest group seeks to influence specific policies of government—not to achieve control over government as a whole. A political party concentrates on winning public office in elections and is somewhat less concerned with policy questions." Thomas Dye, *Politics in States and Communities*, 10th ed. (New York: McGraw Hill, 2000), 106.

4. Alan Rosenthal, *The Third House* (Washington DC: Congressional Quarterly Press, 1993).

5. Ronald Hrebner and Clive Thomas, "Interest Groups and the States," in *Politics in the American States: A Comparative Analysis*, 7th ed., ed. Virginia Gray, Russell Hanson, and Herbert Jacob (Washington DC: Congressional Quarterly Press, 1999), 136–38.

6. *Capitol Club Membership Directory* (Salem: Capitol Club, 1991–1992 and 2001–2002). The Capitol Club is an organization of professional advocates (lobbyists) that provides a meeting place, message center, pay phones, and lockers for its several hundred members in the state capitol building. It also has a code of ethics, which members are required to follow. Most full-time lobbyists are members of the organization. Thomas Dye asserts that in most states, "hundreds of lobbyists never register under the pretext that they are not really lobbyists, but, instead, businesses, public relations firms, lawyers, researchers, or educational people" (Dye, *Politics*, 110). Oregon's clean politics reduces these distortions. The Center for Public Integrity documents that Oregon has 628 registered special interests and 600 lobbyists operating at the statehouse (Center for Public Integrity, "The Fourth Branch," April 23, 2002, http://www.publicintegrity.org).

7. Center for Public Integrity, "The Fourth Branch."

8. Hrebner and Thomas, "Interest Groups," 134–35.

9. Dye, *Politics*, 111.

10. *Capitol Club Membership Directory, 2001–2002*.

11. *Capitol Club Membership Directory, 2001–2002*; Secretary of State, *Oregon Blue Book, 1997–1998* (Salem: Secretary of State, 1997), 72.

12. Steve Suo, "Lobbyist Loopholes Make It Difficult to Break the Law," *Oregonian*, February 13, 2000, D2.

13. Information in this section is a compilation of opinions about lobbying and the legislative process based on "off the record" interviews with lobbyists in spring 2001 by Russ Dondero.

14. Anonymous legislator, interview with Russ Dondero, spring 2001.

15. Gary Moncrief and Joel A. Thompson, "Lobbyists' Views on Term Limits," *Spectrum* 74 (Fall 2001): 13–15.

16. Former legislator Tom Mason takes a different view and argues that Oregon has a "political environment dominated not by free speech, but by the ability to spend money." Tom Mason, *Governing Oregon: An Inside Look at Politics in One American State* (Dubuque IA: Kendall Hunt, 1994), 129.

17. National Institute of Money in State Politics, "Oregon 2000 Election Cycle," http://www.followthemoney.org. The numbers are based on official filings with the secretary of state.

18. Elections Division, Secretary of State, *Summary Report of Campaign Contributions and Expenditures, General Election, November 7, 2000*, Salem, 2002.

19. The details of "rulemaking" are covered in chapter 10 of this book.

20. Tomoko Hosaka, "Fish Agency Stuck in Quagmire of Conflicting Demands: The Department of Fish and Wildlife Is Criticized by Both Environmentalists and Wildlife Users," *Oregonian*, January 23, 2001, B1.

21. The state legislature and the Land Conservation and Development Commission has considered the impacts of SLAPPs in 2001. See "A SLAPP in the Face," *Oregonian*, May 15, 2001, C6.

22. Dave Hogan, "Sizemore Group Takes a Double Hit," *Oregonian*, September 28, 2002, A1.

23. Findings in this section are based on the observations of William Lunch, political analyst for Oregon Public Broadcasting.

24. Hrebner and Thomas, "Interest Groups," 134–35.

25. Harry Esteve, "Local antitax bid not so local," *Oregonian*, October 19, 2003.

26. "Oregonians Make a Painful Choice," *Oregonian*, January 29, 2003, B10. The defeat of Measure 30 in February 2004 would underscore public antipathy to new taxes.

27. Suo, "Lobbyists Loopholes," D2.

28. Anonymous lobbyist, interview with Russ Dondero, spring 2001.

7. MEDIA

1. Jeff LaLande, "The 'Jackson County Rebellion': Social Turmoil and Political Insurgence in Southern Oregon during the Great Depression," *Oregon Historical Quarterly* 95 (Winter 1994–1995): 450–55.

2. McCall's relationship with the mass media and his rise to national prominence

is described in Brent Walth, *Fire at Eden's Gate* (Portland: Oregon Historical Society, 1994).

3. See the work of Larry Sabato, *Feeding Frenzies* (New York: The Free Press, 1993); Steven Ansolabere and Shanto Iyengar, *The Media Game* (Englewood Cliffs NJ: Prentice Hall, 1992); Doris Graber, Denis McQuail, and Pippa Norris, *The Politics of News, the News of Politics* (Washington DC: Congressional Quarterly Press, 1998).

4. Floyd McKay, "News Media Loses Connection to Community, Voice of Citizens," *Pacific University Alumni Magazine*, Spring/Summer 1999, 28–35.

5. Oregon Legislative Revenue Office, *Oregon Legislative Revenue Report 1–01* Salem, December 2000, A11–A12.

6. Bradbury, *Oregon Blue Book, 2001–2002*, 202–08.

7. Founded in 1850, the *Oregonian* ironically opposed statehood "on the grounds that Democrats would control the government." Tom Mason, *Governing Oregon: An Inside Look at Politics in One American State* (Dubuque IA: Kendall Hunt, 1994), 164.

8. "The Oregonian's Endorsements," *Oregonian*, October 22, 2000, G5.

9. McKay, "News Media." An excellent analysis of the political and social contributions of one of these editor-owners can be found in Floyd McKay, *An Editor for Oregon: Charles A. Sprague and the Politics of Change* (Portland: Oregon Historical Society, 1998).

10. *Oregonian* reporters knew of the allegations against Packwood and were working on their own story. They also knew of the *Post*'s investigation as well. The *Oregonian* editorial staff endorsed Senator Packwood for reelection. A firewall existed between reporters and editors, which prevented knowledge of the impending scandal from reaching the editorial staff at the *Oregonian*. For a comprehensive story of Packwood's career and downfall, see Mark Kirchmeier, *Packwood: The Public and Private Life from Acclaim to Outrage* (New York: HarperCollinsWest, 1995).

11. Mason, *Governing*, 167.

12. Mason, *Governing*, 165.

13. The *Salem Statesmen Journal* published special editions that highlight McCall's impact on the Willamette, and how the clean-up campaign helped McCall's rise to national fame (August 25, September 1, and September 8, 1996).

14. McKay, "News Media."

15. McKay, "News Media."

16. Mark Fitzgerald, "Local TV News Lacks Substance," *Editor and Publisher*, May 24, 1997, 8–9; Tim Jones, "Inside Media," *Chicago Tribune*, February 8,

2001. Summaries of both articles are in Janda Berry Goldman, *The Challenge of Democracy*, 7th ed. (New York: Houghton Mifflin, 2002), 169–70.

17. McKay, "News Media."

18. Critics often focus on the effects of the private funding that now provides most support for public broadcasting. See James Ledbetter, *Made Possible By . . . : The Death of Public Broadcasting in the United States* (New York: Verso, 1997). For a more academic view, see Ralph Engelman, *Public Radio and Television in America: A Political History* (Thousand Oaks CA: Sage, 1996).

19. Data on audience composition and size were provided by Morgan Holm, news director of Oregon Public Broadcasting (OPB), and Virginia Breen, OPB director of radio. Data cited here are taken from an NPR survey conducted in fall 2000 and distributed to member stations.

20. William Lunch, one of the authors of this chapter, has served as the political analyst for Oregon Public Broadcasting for more than twelve years.

21. For more on Measure 5, see Bill Lunch, "Budgeting By Initiative: An Oxymoron," *Willamette Law Review* 34 (Summer/Fall 1998): 663–73.

22. "Media Use and Trust in Oregon," *Linkages*, Summer 1997, 4. OPB's rating as a "source you trust" was 3.75 on a five-point scale, the highest found in the survey. "Local newspapers" scored 3.57, the second highest.

23. Elections Division, Secretary of State, *Summary Report of Campaign Contributions and Expenditures General Election, November 7, 2000*, Salem, 2002).

24. Robert Putnam, *Bowling Alone: The Collapse of American Community* (New York: Simon and Schuster, 2000).

25. Peter Collins, "Together Yet Alone: Viewers Connect through Tube," *Oregonian*, September 22, 2002.

26. McKay, "News Media."

27. McKay, "News Media."

8. THE LEGISLATURE

1. Steve Law, "Political Bickering Produced a Messy, Productive Session," *Salem Statesman Journal*, July 26, 1999; Steve Law, "Lawmaking Talent Lost through Revolving Door, *Salem Statesman Journal*, February 13, 2000, 6A; James Mayer and Lisa Grace Lednicer, "Budget Cuts, Quiet Work May Define 71st Legislature," *Oregonian*, January 7, 2001, A1.

2. Jeff Mapes, "Legislature Conducts Management Session," *Oregonian*, July 6, 1997, A1; Jeff Mapes, "Animal House Session Ending in Division, Turmoil," *Oregonian*, June 10, 1995, D1; "Lawmakers Buoyed by End to Legislative Gridlock," *Oregonian*, May 5, 1993, D1.

3. Alan Rosenthal, *The Decline of Representative Democracy: Process, Participa-*

tion, and Power in State Legislatures (Washington DC: Congressional Quarterly Press, 1998).

4. The scorecards for all three groups are available online at http://www.olcv.org, http://www.oregoned.org, and http://www.coalition.org.

5. Rosenthal, *Decline.*

6. Rosenthal, *Decline.*

7. Steve Suo, "Lawmakers Slug It Out to Final Bell," *Oregonian,* July 25, 1999, A1.

8. Citizens Conference on State Legislatures, *The Sometime Governments* (New York: Bantam, 1971); Rosenthal, *Decline.*

9. Clay Myers, "Carving Up State Equitably Historically Tough," *Oregonian,* April 7, 1991, C11.

10. Lisa Grace Lednicer and David Hogan, "After Five-Day Walkout, House Gets Back to Work," *Oregonian,* July 1, 2001, A1.

11. Law, "Lawmaking Talent."

12. Sue Thomas, *How Women Legislate* (New York: Oxford University Press, 1994).

13. Richard A. Clucas, "Principal-Agent Theory and the Power of State House Speakers," *Legislative Studies Quarterly* 26 (May 2001): 319–38.

14. Bradbury, *Oregon Blue Book, 2001–2002.*

15. Tara McLain, "Next Ballot to Be Slimmer," *Salem Statesman Journal,* July 11, 2001.

16. The dates and lengths of all past special sessions are listed in Bradbury, *Oregon Blue Book, 2001–2002.*

17. Douglas Heider and David Dietz, *Legislative Perspectives: A 150-Year History of the Oregon Legislatures from 1843 to 1993* (Portland: Oregon Historical Society Press, 1995).

18. Bradbury, *Oregon Blue Book, 2001–2002.*

19. "Get the Fine Print Right," *Oregonian,* January 15, 1999, D10.

20. See John M. Carey, Richard G. Niemi, and Lynda W. Powell, *Term Limits in State Legislatures* (Ann Arbor: University of Michigan Press, 2000).

21. "Termed Out," *Salem Statesman Journal,* Special Report Series, February 13–28, 2000.

22. Mapes, "Legislature Conducts"; James Mayer, "Now, Not Even Taxes Are Certain," *Oregonian,* July 23, 2000, A1; Lisa Grace Lednicer, "Oregon's Ballot Reflects a New Era in Politics," *Oregonian,* October 1, 2000, A1.

9. GOVERNOR

1. Governor's policy staff Web page (http://www.Oregon.gov).

2. State Land Board, Division of State Lands, http://statelands.dsl.state.or.us:80/aboutslb.htm.

3. State Land Board, Division of State Lands, http://statelands.dsl.state.or.us:80/aboutslb.htm.

4. Phil Keisling, "What If We Had an Election and Nobody Came?" *Washington Monthly*, March 1996, 40–42.

5. Clay Meyers, "Carving Up State Equitably Historically Tough; Legislature Usually Found Unequal to Task of Reapportionment," *Oregonian*, April 7, 1991, CII.

6. Lisa Grace Lednicer, "Bradbury's Redistricting Plan Upheld by Justices," *Oregonian*, October 19, 2001, AI.

7. Thad Beyle, "The Governors," in *Politics in the American States: A Comparative Analysis*, 7th ed., ed. Virginia Gray, Russell L. Hanson, and Herbert Jacob (Washington DC: Congressional Quarterly Press, 1999).

8. Beyle, "Governors."

9. Alan Rosenthal, *Governors and Legislatures: Contending Powers* (Washington DC: Congressional Quarterly Press, 1990).

10. Steve Mayes, "A Record for Referrals Will Crowd Ballots; the Legislature Sets a New Mark by Sending 21 Measures to the Ballot," *Oregonian*, July 26, 1999, AI.

11. Malcolm E. Jewell and Sarah M. Morehouse, *Political Parties and Elections in American States* (Washington DC: Congressional Quarterly Press, 2001).

12. James L. Gibson, Cornelius P. Cotter, John F. Bibby, and Robert J. Huckshorn, "Whither the Local Parties: A Cross-Sectional and Longitudinal Analysis of the Strength of Party Organizations," *American Journal of Political Science* 29 (1985): 139–60.

13. Rosenthal, *Governors*.

14. Rosenthal, *Governors*.

15. David Steves, "Oregon Governor Set to Veto Fewer Bills this Year," *The Register Guard*, August 13, 2001.

16. Steve Mayes, "Kitzhaber Says He May Veto 32 More Bills," *Oregonian*, August 18, 1999, AI; Lisa Grace Lednicer, "Deal Completes Budget, Session Analysis," *Oregonian*, July 8, 2001, AI.

17. Beyle, "Governors."

18. Brent Walth, *Fire at Eden's Gate: Tom McCall and the Oregon Story* (Portland: Oregon Historical Society Press, 1998).

19. Walth, *Fire*.

10. BUREAUCRACY

1. Jordan Durbin, "The Impact of the Initiative and Referendum Process on Oregon

Administrative Discretion" (paper prepared for PhD independent study, Hatfield School of Government, Portland State University, spring 2001).

2. "State Government Employees," *Governing's State and Local Sourcebook 2002* (Washington DC: Congressional Quarterly Press, 2002), 47. Oregon ranks sixteenth in the number of local government employees per 10,000 population.

3. This example is drawn directly from a case provided by the state attorney general's office to demonstrate agency processes. See Oregon Department of Justice, *Attorney Generals' Administrative Law Manual and Uniform and Model Rule of Procedure under the Administrative Procedures Act*, Salem, March 27, 2000, 3–6.

4. An excellent example of how progressives view the McCall legacy can be found in "Paradise Lost: Searching for Tom McCall's Oregon," a series published in the *Salem Statesman Journal*, on August 25, September 1, and September 8, 1996.

5. Oregon Department of Land Conservation and Development, *Goals/Rule/Laws*, Salem, October 2002. Available at http://www.lcd.state.or.us/goalsrul.html.

6. Michael Ottey, "Tigard Digs into Coffers in Dolan Settlement," *Oregonian*, November 20, 1997, C2.

7. The full text of Measure 7 and voter pamphlet positions can be found at Elections Division, Secretary of State, *Official 2000 General Election On-Line Voters' Guide*, http://www.sos.state.or.us/elections/nov72000/guide/cover.htm.

8. *Dolan v. Tigard*, 114 S. Ct. 2309 (1994).

9. Patrick Reilly, former Tigard city manager, interview with author, October 1994.

10. Elections Division, *Official 2000 General Election On-Line Voters' Guide*. For a brief but fairly comprehensive review of the diverse views and the legal context of Measure 7, see Dave Hogan, "Measure Seven Goes to State High Court Today," *Oregonian*, September 10, 2001, E1. The Oregon Supreme Court's decision (*League of Oregon Cities v. State of Oregon*) can be found at http://www.ojd.state.or.us/.

11. Criticisms of recent local use of eminent domain can be found in Christian Bourge, "Abuse of Eminent Domain Debated," *United Press International*, May 22, 2002. A legalistic approach supporting a progressive view of property rights is presented in Charles M. Haar and Michael Allan Wolf, "Euclid Lives: The Survival of Progressive Jurisprudence," *Harvard Law Review* 115 (June 2002): 2158.

12. Fred Miller, interview with author, May 18, 2001; Jon Yunker, interview with author, June 28, 2001.

13. Yunker interview.

14. Barbara Roberts, former Oregon governor, interview with author, July 10, 2001. Roberts's concerns have emerged in other states, including Maine. David Broder

(among others) sees term limits as having broad effects on the legislature's ability to govern. Jim Brunelle, "The Reign in Maine," *State Legislatures,* September 1997, 28–29; David S. Broder, *Democracy Derailed: Initiative Campaigns and The Power of Money* (New York: Harcourt Press, 2000), 223–25.

15. Terry Bechdel, "Oregon State Boards and Commissions," (paper prepared for PhD independent study, Hatfield School of Government, Portland State University, spring 2001).

16. Bradbury, *Oregon Blue Book, 2001–2002.*

17. Miller interview. Miller is former director of the Executive Department under governors Goldschmidt and Roberts.

18. ORS, chapter 183, http://www.leg.state.or.us/ors/home.html.

19. Kenneth Culp Davis, *Discretionary Justice: A Preliminary Inquiry* (Baton Rouge: Louisiana State University Press, 1967), 65.

20. *Fremont Lumber Co. v. Energy Facility Siting Council,* 325 Ore. 256, 262, 936 P.2d 968 (1997).

21. Phil Cooper, *Public Law and Public Administration,* 3d ed. (Itasca IL: F. E. Peacock, 2000), 250.

22. Oregon Secretary of State, *Oregon Bulletin,* http://arcweb.sos.state.or.us/ rules/ bulletin_default.html

23. Amy Verant, interview with author, May 3, 2001.

24. 5 U.S.C. 553(b)A, 553(d)(2).

25. Interview with panel of six administrative rules coordinators for Oregon state agencies, June 28, 2001.

26. Oregon Department of Justice, *Attorney Generals' Administrative Law Manual,* appendix 1.

27. Interview with administrative rules coordinators.

28. Oregon Progress Board, http://www.econ.state.or.us/opb/.

29. Howard M. Leichter and Jeffrey Tryens, *Achieving Better Health Outcomes: The Oregon Benchmark Experience* (New York: Milbank Memorial Fund, 2002).

30. John Kitzhaber, *Governor's Budget: State of Oregon 2001–2003,* Salem, 2001, 1–2.

31. ORS, chapter 244, http://www.leg.state.or.us/ors/home.html.

32. ORS 183.502, http://www.leg.state.or.us/ors/home.html.

33. Interview with administrative rules coordinators.

34. Katherine Barrett and Richard Greene, "Grading the States: The Government Performance Project, 2001," *Governing Magazine,* February 2001. Available at http://governing.com.

35. Verant interview.

11. JUDICIARY

1. *Lloyd Corp. v. Tanner*, 407 U.S. 569.

2. *Stranahan v. Fred Meyer, Inc.*, 153 Ore. App 442, 958 P.2d 854 (1998).

3. *Stranahan v. Fred Meyer, Inc.*, 331 Ore. 38, 11 P.3d 228 (2000). In 1993 the Oregon Supreme Court ruled that initiative petitioners did have a right to gather signatures on private property. Jack Landau argues that the court's reversal in 2000 reflected a change in the court's philosophy, as it began to apply a jurisprudence of original intent more consistently. The 1993 case was *Lloyd Corporation v. Whiffen*, 315 Ore. 500, 849 P.2d (1993). Jack L. Landau, "The Unfinished Revolution: Interpreting the Oregon Constitution," *Oregon State Bar Bulletin*, November 2001, 9–20.

4. *Pruneyard Shopping Center v. Robins*, 447 U.S. 74 (1980).

5. Jason L. Landau, "Hurrah for Revolution: A Critical Assessment of State Constitutional Interpretation," *Oregon Law Review* 79 (2002): 793–890; Jack L. Landau, "Unfinished Revolution"; Don S. Willner, "A Second Look at Constitutional Interpretation," *Oregon Law Review* 67 (1988): 93–104.

6. Phyllis Skloot Bamberger, "Boosting Your Case with Your State Constitution," ABA *Journal*, March 1986.

7. Henry R. Glick, "Courts: Politics and the Judicial Process," in *Politics in the American States: A Comparative Analysis*, 7th ed., ed. Virginia Gray, Russell L. Hanson, and Herbert Jacob (Washington DC: Congressional Quarterly Press, 1999), 261.

8. Jason L. Landau, "Hurrah for Revolution."

9. Robert F. Nagel, *Intellect and Craft: The Contributions of Justice Hans Linde to American Constitutionalism* (Boulder CO: Westview, 1995).

10. *Pierce v. Society of Sisters*, 268 U.S. 510 (1925).

11. Council of State Governments, *Book of the States 1998–1999* (Lexington KY: Council of State Governments, 1999).

12. "Religion in Oregon," http://www.adherents.com/loc/loc_oregon.html.

13. National Center for State Courts, "Reported Total Caseload for All State Appellate Courts, 1999," http://www.ncsc.dni.us/divisions/research/csp/Tables%201–4.pdf.

14. National Center for State Courts, "Reported Grand Total State Trial Court Caseload, 1999," http://www.ncsc.dni.us/divisions/research/csp/tabl5–8.pdf.

15. Gleaves Committee, Oregon Judicial Department/Oregon State Bar, *Report of the 1997–98 Joint Committee on the Creation of New Judgeships*, Salem, 1998, comment #4, 25.

16. Data provided by Karen Garst, executive director, Oregon State Bar.

17. See Lee Epstein and Jack Knight, *The Choices Justices Make* (Washington DC: Congressional Quarterly Press, 1998).

18. Maurice Rosenberg, "The Qualities of Justice—Are They Strained?" in *Choosing Justice: The Recruitment of State and Federal Judges*, ed. Charles H. Sheldon and Linda S. Maule (Pullman: Washington State University Press, 1997); James C. Foster, "Rethinking Politics and Judicial Selection During Contentious Times," *Albany Law Review* 67 (2004): 821; James C. Foster, "The Interplay of Legitimacy, Elections, and Crocodiles in the Bathtub: Making Sense of Politicization of Oregon's Courts, *Willamette Law Review* 39 (2003), 1313.

19. Sheila Kaplan and Zoë Davidson, "The Buying of the Bench," *The Nation*, January 26, 1998, 11–18.

20. Kaplan and Davidson, "Buying of the Bench," 11.

21. Brennan Center for Justice at New York University Law School, "Reducing Injudiciousness in Judicial Elections," http://www.brennancenter.org/resources/re sources_act_injudic.html.

22. *Armatta v. Kitzhaber*, 327 Ore. 250, 959 P.2d 49 (1998).

23. Ashbel S. Green, "Appellate Judge Race Toughest in Years," *Oregonian*, April 8, 2002, B1.

24. James Sinks, "State Supreme Court to Be Tested in Coming Weeks," *The Bulletin*, September 23, 2001.

25. *Armatta v. Kitzhaber*, 327 Ore. 250, 959 P.2d 49 (1998).

26. Sinks, "State Supreme Court."

27. Jason L. Landau, "Hurrah for Revolution"; Jack L. Landau, "Unfinished Revolution"; *Priest v. Pearce*, 314 Ore. 411, 840 P.2d 65 (1992).

28. Sinks, "State Supreme Court."

29. Maureen O'Hagan, "The Crime that Changed Punishment," *Willamette Week*, September 23, 1998.

30. Oregon Office of Economic Analysis, *An Analysis of Reported Index Crimes in Oregon, 1975–1999*, Salem, 2002.

31. Alexis de Tocqueville, *Democracy in America*, ed. Phillips Bradley (New York: Vintage, 1945,), 290.

32. Jim Foster, "Oregon's Initiative Process: Does It Enhance Democracy or Demean Us?" *CLA Alum*, 11 (November 1994): 4–5; David S. Broder, *Democracy Derailed: Initiative Campaigns and the Power of Money* (New York: Harcourt Press, 2000), 223–25; Richard J. Ellis, *Democratic Delusions: The Initiative Process in America* (Lawrence: University Press of Kansas, 2002).

12. LOCAL GOVERNMENT

1. Bureau of Municipal Research and Service, *Background Information on Local Government in Oregon* (Eugene: University of Oregon, 1967).

2. Bureau of Municipal Research, "Background Information," 1–2.

3. Tony Howard Evans, "Oregon Progressive Reform, 1902–1914" (PhD diss., University of California, Berkeley, 1966).

4. *City of La Grande and City of Astoria v. Public Employees Retirement Board,* 281 Ore. 137 (1978).

5. U.S. Advisory Commission on Intergovernmental Relations, *State and Local Roles in the Federal System* (Washington DC: ACIR, 1982).

6. Bradley Robert Rice, *Progressive Cities: The Commission Government Movement in America, 1901–1920* (Austin: University of Texas Press, 1977).

7. Phil Keisling, *Oregon Blue Book, 1999–2000* (Salem: Secretary of State, 1999), 274.

8. Keisling, *Oregon Blue Book, 1999–2000.*

9. "Oregon Cascades West Council of Governments, A Brief History," http://www.cwcog.cog.or.us/COG/COG_breifhis.htm, 1.

10. Keisling, *Oregon Blue Book, 1999–2000.*

11. Becky Waldrop, "Valley Schools Feel Squeezed by Tax Changes," *Corvallis Gazette Times,* September 3, 2000.

12. Waldrop, "Valley Schools"; Brent Steel, Bruce Weber, and Karen Seidel, "The Impact of Ballot Measure 5 on City and County Finances," Oregon Legislative Discussion Paper Series (Eugene: Bureau of Governmental Research and Service, 1991).

13. U.S. Census Bureau, "Oregon State and Local Government Finances by Government and State," http://www.census.gov.

14. U.S. Census Bureau, "Oregon State and Local Government."

15. U.S. Census Bureau, "Oregon State and Local Government."

16. Michelle Cole, "County Asks to Shrink Monument Drastically," *Oregonian,* July 17, 2001, A1.

17. Oregon Revised Statutes 190.010.

13. FISCAL POLICY

1. Jeff Thompson analyzes the distribution of the income tax burden in Oregon in "Clearing the Air on Tax Day: Assessing the Tax Burden in Oregon" (Silverton OR: Oregon Center for Public Policy), April 15, 2001, http://www.ocpp.org.

2. "A Surprise for Taxpayers in Some 'Low Tax' States: Minus the Federal Taxes,

They're Actually 'High Tax' States" (Washington DC: Tax Foundation, 2001), http://www.taxfoundation.org. Richard F. Winters, "The Politics of Taxing and Spending," in *Politics in the American States: A Comparative Analysis*, 7th ed., ed. Virginia Gray, Russell L. Hanson, and Herbert Jacob (Washington DC: Congressional Quarterly Press, 1999), 310.

3. Robert Gavin, "For Fifth Time, Oregon Tries to Balance Budget," *Wall Street Journal*, September 3, 2002, A6.

4. A good general source for budget information is Ted Kulongoski, *Governor's Budget: State of Oregon 2003–2005* (Salem: Oregon Department of Administrative Services, 2003); *Update: Budget Highlights, 2003–2005 Legislatively Approved Budget* (Salem: Oregon Legislative Fiscal Office, 2004), 1.

5. Bill Graves, "Progress Board Prospects Uncertain," *Oregonian*, October 8, 2002, B5; Erin Hoover Barnett, "Budget Cuts Said to Erode Foundation of Social Services," *Oregonian*, October 6, 2002, B1. A discussion of how authorization is related to appropriations in Congress can be found in Aaron Wildavsky and Naomi Caiden, *The New Politics of the Budgetary Process*, 3d ed. (New York: Longman Press, 1997), 6–14.

6. Kiesling, *Oregon Blue Book, 1999–2000*.

7. James Mayer and Erin Hoover Barnett, "Budget Would Add Cuts, Not Taxes," *Oregonian*, April 18, 2003, A1; "Oregonians Make a Painful Choice," *Oregonian*, January 29, 2003, B10; Harry Esteve, "New anti-tax leader rises from ashes of measure," *Oregonian*, February 15, 2004.

8. Anne O'M. Bowman and Richard Kearney, *State and Local Government*, 5th ed. (Boston: Houghton Mifflin, 2002), 362, 371; James J. Gosling, *Budgetary Politics in American Governments*, 2d ed. (New York: Garland Publishing, 1997), 80–82.

9. PERS Board, *Annual Report for the Public Employees Retirement System, 2000*, Salem, 2000; James Mayer, "PERS Bills Clear Governor, Head to Court," *Oregonian*, May 10, 2003, A1.

10. Mayer, "PERS Bills," A1; James Mayer, "PERS reform case opens at state high court," *Oregonian*, July 31, 2004.

11. Kulongoski, *Governor's Budget*, C23.

12. Information for this section is compiled from many sources, including Bowman and Kearney, *State and Local Government*; Gosling, *Budgetary Politics*; Winters, "Politics"; Robert S. Lorch, *State and Local Politics*, 6th ed. (New York: Prentice Hall, 2001, 322–31; Tobert Tannerwald, "Are State and Local Revenue Systems Obsolete?" *New England Economic Review* (July/August 2001): 27–44; William Oakland and William Testa, "State-Local Business Taxation and the Benefits Principle," *Economic Perspectives* 20 (January/February 1996): 2–20; Thomas

D. Lynch, *Public Budgeting in America* (Englewood Cliffs NJ: Prentice Hall, 1990), 296–311; Robin W. Broadway and David E. Wildavsin, *Public Sector Economics*, 2d ed. (New York: Little and Brown, 1984), 225–28.

13. Harry Bodine, "Sponsor of Measure 5 Says Tax Relief Coming," *Oregonian*, November 19, 1991, B2.

14. Gail Kinsey Hill, "Oregon 'Tax Shift' Ignites Hot Election Year Debate," *Oregonian*, August 31, 1992, A1; Steve Mayes, "Home Values Soar in County," *Oregonian*, June 25, 1991, A1.

15. Bill Graves and Steven Carter, "Oregon Schools: Treading Water," *Oregonian*, September 1, 1996, A1; Oregon Legislative Fiscal Office, *Budget Highlights: Legislatively Approved Budget, 1993–1995*, Salem, 1993, 2–3.

16. Information regarding the impacts of Measure 50 is drawn from Oregon Legislative Revenue Office, *Oregon's Property Tax System*, Salem, 1999. A more generalized description of its workings and effects can be found in Harry Bodine and Brent Hunsberger, "How Does Measure 50 Affect Your Property-Tax Bill?" *Oregonian*, September 25, 1997; James Mayer, "Measure 50 Didn't Force Major Cuts," *Oregonian*, December 26, 1997, A1.

17. Oregon Legislative Revenue Office, *Research Report 1–01*, Salem, January 8, 2001; Paul Warner, Oregon legislative revenue officer, telephone interview with Mark Henkels, September 23, 2002; Oregon Legislative Revenue Office, *Research Report #1–0: School Finance*, Salem, December 6, 2000.

18. Tannerwald, "State and Local," 27–44; Oakland and Testa, "Business Taxation," 2–20.

19. Martha Brannigan, "Repeal of Florida 5% Service Tax Caps Controversy Other States Viewed Warily," *Wall Street Journal*, December 11, 1987, 1.

20. Winters, "Politics," 316–17.

21. Oregon Legislative Revenue Office, *Research Report 1–01: Income Taxes*, Salem, September 20, 2000.

22. Oregon Department of Administrative Services, *Oregon 2003–2005 Tax Expenditure Report*, Salem, 2003, 147–48.

23. Administrative Services, *Tax Expenditure Report*, 5.

24. Oregon Legislative Revenue Office, *Research Report: State Spending Limit*, Salem, December 6, 2000.

25. City of Salem, Fiscal Year Budget 2001–2002.

26. Oregon Legislative Revenue Office, *2003 Oregon Public Finance Facts*, Salem, 2003, F5.

27. Bill Graves, "Living With Measure 5," *Oregonian*, June 28, 1992, A19.

14. ENVIRONMENTAL POLICY

1. Bradbury, *Oregon Blue Book, 2001–2002*.

2. Brent Steel and Nicholas Lovrich, "An Introduction to Natural Resource Policy and the Environment: Changing Paradigms and Values," in *Public Lands Management in the West*, ed. Brent Steel (Westport CT: Praeger, 1997), 3–16.

3. Douglas Constain and James Lester, "The Environmental Movement and Congress," in *Social Movements and American Political Institutions*, ed. Anne Costain and Douglas McFarland (Lanham MD: Rowman and Littlefield 1998), 185–90.

4. Oregon Progress Board, *Oregon State of the Environment Report 2000: Statewide Summary*, Salem, 2000, 8.

5. Gifford Pinchot, *The Fight for Conservation* (New York: Doubleday, Page, 1910).

6. Robyn Eckersley, *Environmentalism and Political Theory: Toward an Ecocentric Approach* (Albany: State University of New York Press, 1992).

7. Donald Scherer and Thomas Attig, eds., *Ethics and the Environment* (Englewood Cliffs NJ: Prentice-Hall, 1983).

8. Oregon Progress Board, *Oregon State*, 8.

9. John Muir, *Selections* (New York: Library of America, 1997); Aldo Leopold, *A Sand County Almanac* (New York: Oxford University Press, 1949).

10. Thomas Kuhn, *The Structure of Scientific Revolutions* (Chicago: University of Chicago Press, 1970).

11. Riley Dunlap and Ken Van Liere, "The New Environmental Paradigm," *Journal of Environmental Education* 9 (1978): 10–19.

12. Leopold, *Sand County*.

13. Bradbury, *Oregon Blue Book, 2001–2002*.

14. Bradbury, *Oregon Blue Book, 2001–2002*.

15. Christopher Simon, "The County Supremacy Movement and Public Lands in Oregon," in *Public Lands: Management in the West*, ed. Brent Steel (New York: Praeger, 1997), 111–28.

16. Governor's Natural Resources Office, *What Is the Oregon Plan for Salmon and Watersheds?*, Salem, 1997.

17. Ronald Inglehart and Wayne Baker, "Modernization, Cultural Change, and the Persistence of Traditional Values," *American Sociological Review* 65 (2000): 19–51.

18. Alexander Mather, *Global Forest Resources* (Portland OR: Timber Press, 1990).

19. David Truman, *The Governmental Process* (New York: Knopf, 1951).

20. Brent Steel, Peter List, and Bruce Shindler, *Directory of Oregon Forest Interest Groups* (Corvallis: Extension Forestry Program, Oregon State University, 1993).

21. Resources for the Future, *The State of the States: Assessing the Capacity of States to Achieve Sustainable Development through Green Planning, 2002*. Available at http://www.rri.org/SOC_Full_Report.pdf.
22. Oregon Progress Board, *Oregon State*, 207.
23. Friends of the Earth, http://www.foe.org/cleanwater/grades/percent.html (2001).
24. Oregon Progress Board, *Oregon State*.
25. Resources for the Future, *State of the States*.

15. HEALTH POLICY

1. Penelope Lemov, "Health Care in Critical Condition," *Governing*, October 1999, 22; and "Late News," *Modern Healthcare*, September 23, 2002, 4.
2. Michael D. Reagan, *The Accidental System* (Boulder CO: Westview Press, 1999), 86–88.
3. These numbers are from the state budget for 2001, adopted in July 2001, but later cut due to reduced revenue during the 2001–2003 biennium. Oregon Legislative Revenue Office, *Budget Highlights*, Salem, July 2001.
4. Katy Muldoon, "Oregon Assesses Health Program," *Oregonian*, July 29, 1994. 1.
5. Quoted by Michael Abramowitz, "Oregon Blazes a Trail," *Washington Post*, June 9, 1992, health section, 12.
6. Kitzhaber defended and explained his position at the time in the article "Who'll Live? Who'll Die? Who'll Pay?" *Oregonian*, November 27, 1987, B1.
7. See Michael Specter, "Oregon Legislators Face Up to the Hard Job of Playing God," *Washington Post National Weekly*, February 15, 1988, 33.
8. Quoted by Abramowitz, "Oregon Blazes a Trail," 14.
9. Timothy Egan, "Oregon Lists Illnesses by Priority To See Who Gets Medicaid Care," *New York Times*, May 3, 1990, 1.
10. Michael Specter, "Plan Covers All Needy But Not All Ailments," *Washington Post*, July 1, 1991, 1.
11. For broader consideration of rationing, see Robert H. Blank, *Rationing Medicine* (New York: Columbia University Press, 1988).
12. Quoted by Abramowitz, "Oregon Blazes a Trail," 13.
13. Oregon Medical Association, "Survey of Public Opinion," Princeton, Gallup poll, February 1991.
14. Roberta Ulrich, "State Health Care Plan Rejected," *Oregonian*, August 4, 1992, 1.
15. Robert Pear, "Plan to Ration Health Care Is Rejected by Government," *New York Times*, August 4, 1992, 6.

16. See Norman Ornstein, Andrew Kohut, and Larry McCarthy, *The People, the Press and Politics* (Boston: Addison-Wesley, 1988), particularly 13–17; E. J. Dionne Jr., "Survey of Electorate Finds Weak Political Parties and Conflicts Over Change," *New York Times*, October 1, 1987, 14.

17. Quoted by Jeff Mapes, "Denny Smith: Health Plan May Be Killed," *Oregonian*, June 29, 1994, B1.

18. Jeff Mapes, "Denny Smith: health plan may be killed," *Oregonian*, June 29, 1994, D3.

19. James W. Fiscus and Donna McMahon, "Oregon Health-Rationing Plan Draws National, Industry Interest," *Oregonian*, April 24, 1991, B5.

20. Marilyn Werber Serafini, "Up Against ERISA," *National Journal*, February 11, 1995, 349–52.

21. Bob Young, "Marlboro's Man," *Willamette Week*, July 31, 1996, 1.

22. Mark Nelson, chief campaign consultant for the tobacco industry, presentation at Oregon State University, November 4, 1996.

23. Patrick O'Neill, "Health Plan Has Growing Pains," *Oregonian*, February 14, 1997, C1.

24. Steve Suo, "Qutub Seeks Health Plan Savings," *Oregonian*, February 5, 1999, 1.

25. Don Colburn, "Proposal Brings More People into Health Plan," *Oregonian*, October 26, 2001, C1.

26. Bruce Weber and Monica Fisher, *Oregon's Fiscal Choices: Historical Context and Long-Term Implications* (Corvallis: Program for Governmental Research & Education, Oregon State University, January 1997), 1.

27. Theodore Marmor, *The Politics of Medicare* (New York: Aldine, 1973); Paul Starr, *The Social Transformation of American Medicine* (New York: Basic Books, 1982), 237–89.

16. SOCIAL ISSUES

1. Theodore J. Lowi, "American Business, Public Policy, Case-Studies, and Political Theory," *World Politics* 16 (July 1964): 677–715; Theodore J. Lowi, "Four Systems of Policy, Politics, and Choice," *Public Administration Review* 32 (July/August 1972): 298–310.

2. Raymond Tatalovich and Byron W. Daynes, eds., *Moral Controversies in American Politics: Cases in Social Regulatory Policy*, with foreword by Theodore J. Lowi (Armonk NY: M. E. Sharpe, 1988).

3. For further analysis of the initiative process, see Council of State Governments, *Book of the States 1998–1999* (Lexington KY: Council of State Governments, 1998); Thomas E. Cronin, *Direct Democracy: The Politics of Initiative, Referendum, and Recall* (Cambridge: Harvard University Press, 1989); David S. Broder,

Democracy Derailed: Initiative Campaigns and the Power of Money (New York: Harcourt, 2000).

4. The OCA has worked diligently to prevent gay rights as well. See William M. Lunch, "Oregon: Identity and Politics in the Northwest," in *God at the Grass Roots: The Christian Right in the 1994 Elections*, ed. Mark J. Rozell and Clyde Wilcox (Lanham MD: Rowman & Littlefield, 1995).

5. From http://www.ncsl.org.

6. Brady Adams, Senate president, written interview with author, December 14, 1999; Lynn Snodgrass, House speaker, written interview with author, December 14, 1999; Maura Roche, M&R Strategic Services, interview with author, September 14, 1999.

7. Lon Mabon, Oregon Citizens Alliance, interview with author, April 28, 1998.

8. From http://www.vote-smart.org.

9. Lisa Grace Lednicer, "House Will Take Up Bills on Abortion, Gay Rights," *Oregonian*, May 31, 1999, E1.

10. Steve Suo, "Speaker's Measure of Success Is Her Own," *Oregonian*, July 4, 1999, A1.

11. Lednicer, "House Will Take Up Bills."

12. Lisa Grace Lednicer, "Making a First-Term Impression," *Oregonian*, July 25, 1999, D1.

13. Representative Kenneth Mannix, interview with author, September 22, 1999.

14. Roche interview, September 14, 1999.

15. Representative Bill Witt, interview with author, September 30, 1999.

16. Lisa Horowitz, Oregon NARAL, interview with author, April 28, 1998; Roche interview, September 14, 1999.

17. Lisa Grace Lednicer, "House Speaker Delays Abortion Bill Hearing," *Oregonian*, June 30, 1999, D5; Suo, "Speaker's Measure."

18. Lednicer, "House Speaker."

19. Witt interview, September 30, 1999.

20. Michael Barone and Grant Ujifusa with Richard E. Cohen and Charles E. Cook Jr., *Almanac of American Politics 2000* (Washington DC: National Journal, 1999).

21. Witt interview, September 30, 1999.

22. Gayle Atteberry, Oregon Right to Life, interview with author, May 14, 1998.

23. Lou Beres, Christian Coalition, interview with author, May 13, 1998.

24. Ralph Reed, *Active Faith* (New York: Free Press, 1996).

25. Mannix interview, September 22, 1999.

26. Witt interview, September 30, 1999.

27. Suo, "Speaker's Measure."

28. Senator Eileen Qutub, telephone interview with author, October 13, 1999.

17. EDUCATION POLICY

1. *Public Survey of State and Local Government Issues in Oregon*, (Corvallis: Program for Local Government Research and Education, Oregon State University, 1992 to 2000). Also available at http://osu.orst.edu/dept/pgre/.

2. Betsy Hammond, "Kulongoski Slams His Own School Spending Plan," *Oregonian*, April 11, 2003.

3. Julia Silverman, "Teachers' Unions, Sizemore in Court," *Salem Statesman Journal*, September 12, 2002.

4. Clive S. Thomas, "Interest Groups and Lobbying," in *Politics and Public Policy in the Contemporary American West*, ed. Clive S. Thomas (Albuquerque: University of New Mexico Press, 1991).

5. Oregon Teacher Standards and Practices Commission, http://www.tspc.state.or.us/.

6. Richard Vedder, *Money for Nothing? An Analysis of the Oregon Quality Education Model* (Portland: Cascade Policy Institute, 2000).

7. To many rural school districts, as well as districts with traditionally poor finances, the equalization of school funding was a blessing. These districts are now better supported than they were under the old locally dominated system. But most children in Oregon attend schools in the large districts, including Portland and Eugene, which have absorbed significant budget reductions during the same period.

8. William M. Lunch, "Oregon: Identity and Politics," in *God at the Grass Roots*, 227–51.

9. Karen Armstrong, *The Battle for God* (New York: Random House/Ballantine, 2000), 309–16.

10. One of the authors of this chapter was in Salem during the 1991 legislative session and interviewed a number of the home schooling parents when they came to the capitol for lobbying days.

11. Armstrong, *Battle*, 315.

12. Oregon Department of Education, "Education's Priorities and Operations," http://www.ode.state.or.us/.

13. Bruce Weber, Brent Steel, and Robert Mason, *Measure 5: What Did Voters Really Want?*, legislative discussion paper (Corvallis: Rural Policy Research Group, Oregon State University, University of Oregon, and Oregon Economic Development Department, 1991); Brent Steel, Bruce Weber and Karen Seidel,

The Impact of Ballot Measure 5 on County and City Government Finances, legislative discussion paper (Corvallis: Rural Policy Research Group, Oregon State University, University of Oregon, and Oregon Economic Development Department, 1991).

14. Oregon Department of Education, http://www.ode.state.or.us/.

15. James Mayer, "Comparisons among Taxpayers Are Complex, Not Always Informative," *Oregonian*, July 19, 2002, A10. Mayer argues that one should be careful making comparisons without controlling for income and population size.

16. Budget and Fiscal Policies Division, Oregon University System, *Resident and Nonresident Undergraduate Tuition and Fee Rates*, Salem, 2002.

17. Community Colleges Workforce Development, *Revenue and Expenditure Report*, Salem, 2002, available at http://www.workforce.state.or.us/stateboard.

18. Oregon University System Institutional Research Services, *Fall 2000 Enrollment Records*, Salem, 2000, available at http://www.ous.edu/irs/graybook00.

19. Oregon State University Extension Service, "A Portrait of Poverty in Oregon," http://eesc.orst.edu/agcomwebfile/edmat/html/em/em8743/.

20. Cover letter to Governor Kitzhaber and Superintendent Bunn from Quality Education Commission, *Quality Education Model 2000*, Salem, December 2000.

18. OREGON IN PERSPECTIVE

1. Harry Esteve, "Witt's Compromise Spending Plan Could Burst Deadlock, Boost Career," *Oregonian*, September 5, 2002, A1; Harry Esteve, "Legislators Place Tax Increase on the Ballot," *Oregonian*, September 18, 2002, A1; James Mayer, "Lawmakers' Deal Spares Schools More Big Cuts," *Oregonian*, September 19, 2002, A1.

2. Jeff Mapes, "Kulongoski Favors Tax as Best of Bad Options," *Oregonian*, October 11, 2002, A1.

3. James Mayer and Steve Esteve, "Once More, It's Much Less for State Budget Forecast," *Oregonian*, May 16, 2002, A1; Charles E. Beggs, "Lawmakers end longest session," *Associate Press State and Local Wire*, August 23, 2003; David Steves, "Oregon governor seeks to ease sharp budget cuts forced by tax-hike rejection," *Register Guard*, February 6, 2004.

4. "Gumming Up the Body Politic," *Oregonian*, September 25, 2000, E8.

5. George C. Hough Jr., "Oregon's Changing Demographics 2000" (paper presented at the 2000 Summer Legislative Leadership Institute, Monmouth OR, July 26–28, 2000).

For Further Reading

REFERENCE WORKS

There are several good general reference books on Oregon. The most comprehensive is the *Oregon Blue Book* (Salem OR: Secretary of State), which is published every two years by the secretary of state. The *Blue Book* is the official guide to Oregon government, providing information on all levels and branches of government, as well as general information on the state. The most recent *Blue Book* is available online at http://bluebook.state.or.us/. Written in encyclopedic form, Connie Battaile's *The Oregon Book: Information A to Z* (Newport OR: Saddle Mountain Press, 1998) includes more than thirty-five hundred entries on Oregon, including ones dealing with government, history, and economics. Another good reference work is Lewis A. McArthur's *Oregon Geographic Names* (Portland: Oregon Historical Society Press, 1992).

HISTORY AND CULTURE

Several good histories are available on Oregon. Perhaps the best general history is Gordon B. Dodds's *Oregon: A Bicentennial History* (New York: W. W. Norton, 1977). Along with providing background on the development of the state, it devotes considerable attention to the state's politics. Other good histories include Dodds's *The American Northwest: A History of Oregon and Washington* (Arlington Heights IL: Forum Press, 1986), Dorothy O. Johansen's *Empire of the Columbia*, 2d ed. (New York, Harper & Row, 1977), and David Alan Johnson's *Founding the Far West: California, Oregon, and Nevada, 1840–1890* (Berkeley: University of California Press, 1992). Johnson's book pays particular attention to the writers of the state's constitution. Terence O'Donnell provides a short but sweeping overview of Oregon's early history with a strong emphasis on its culture in *That Balance So Rare* (Portland: Oregon Historical Society Press, 1997). O'Donnell's book includes a useful timeline of Oregon events up to the 1990s.

There are several valuable books that analyze particular periods in Oregon's past. Peter G. Boag's *Environment and Experience: Settlement Culture in Nineteenth-Century Oregon* (Berkeley: University of California Press, 1992) provides an excellent cultural and environmental history of frontier life in Oregon. Robert J. Loewenberg's *Equality on the Oregon Frontier: Jason Lee and the Methodist Mission, 1834–43* (Seattle: University of Washington Press, 1976) offers an analysis of the mixture of religion, economics, and politics of Oregon's early Protestant missionaries and settlers. Richard Neuberger provides a valuable picture of Oregon from the mid-1930s to the 1950s in his collection of essays *They Never Go Back To Pocatello: The Selected Essays of Richard Neuberger* (Portland: Oregon Historical Society Press, 1988). During that period, Neuberger was considered Oregon's leading journalist. He eventually entered politics, rising to the office of U.S. senator.

The history of the Progressive movement in Oregon is less well documented. The two most detailed works are PhD dissertations. They are Warren Marion Blankenship's "Progressives and the Progressive Party in Oregon, 1906–1916" (University of Oregon, 1966), and Tony Howard Evans's "Oregon Progressive Reform, 1902–1914" (University of California, Berkeley, 1966).

Some information on the Progressive movement can be found in E. Kimbark MacColl's *The Shaping of a City: Business and Politics in Portland, Oregon, 1885–1915* (Portland OR: Georgian Press, 1976), which traces the early history of Oregon's largest city. The book devotes considerable attention to the political corruption that helped spur the Progressive movement in the state. A subsequent book by MacColl, *The Growth of a City: Power and Politics in Portland, Oregon, 1915–1950* (Portland OR: Georgian Press, 1979), covers Portland's history up to the 1950s. Carl Abbott's *Portland: Planning, Politics and Growth in a Twentieth-Century City* (Lincoln: University of Nebraska Press, 1983) offers a superb history of Portland politics from the Lewis and Clark Exposition in 1905 through the early 1980s. Another good book on Portland is Jewel Beck Lansing's *Portland: People, Politics, and Power, 1851–2001* (Corvallis: Oregon State University Press, 2003).

GOVERNMENT AND POLITICS

There are two books that provide a general overview of Oregon's political system. Bill Mainwaring's *Government, Oregon-Style* (Salem OR: Westridge Press, 1999) provides a straightforward, if brief (eighty-seven pages), description of the state's political system. Thomas L. Mason's *Governing Oregon: An Inside Look at Politics in One American State* (Dubuque IA: Kendall/Hunt, 1994) was written by a former state legislator and includes many personal insights on Oregon politics. Information on how local governments work in Oregon can be found in the League of Oregon Cities' *Handbook for Oregon City Councilors* (Salem: League of Oregon Cities, 2000).

The best historical overview of political parties in Oregon is Robert E. Burton's *Democrats of Oregon: The Pattern of Minority Politics: 1900–1956* (Eugene: University of Oregon Books, 1970). While the title suggests the book focuses on Democrats, it gives a good overview of the state's politics during that period. More contemporary information on parties can be found in Susan A. Banducci and Jeffrey A. Karp's essay "Oregon" in *State Party Profiles: A 50-State Guide to Development, Organization, and Resources* (Washington DC: Congressional Quarterly Press, 1997), 265–72, edited by Andrew M. Appleton and Daniel S. Ward. Pam Ferrara and David Buchanan's *The Almanac of Oregon Politics*, 2d ed. (Philomath: The Almanac of Oregon Politics, 1994) presents a straightforward summary of the electoral history of Oregon state legislative districts from 1972 to 1994. This book gives the reader a strong sense of the importance of local geography in Oregon's legislative elections.

The number of books on other aspects of Oregon's political system is limited, but there are a few that focus on specific topics. Richard J. Ellis's *Democratic Delusions: The Initiative Process in America* (Lawrence: University Press of Kansas, 2002) examines the use of the initiative process in the nation, with particular attention devoted to Oregon. Harman Zeigler and Michael Baer's *Lobbying: Interaction and Influence in American State Legislature* (Belmont CA: Wadsworth, 1969) is now a bit dated, but it does provide good insight into interest group lobbying in Oregon. Douglas Heider and David Dietz provide a session-by-session history of Oregon's legislature from before statehood through 1991 in *Legislative Perspectives: A 150-Year History of the Oregon Legislature from 1843 to 1993* (Portland: Oregon Historical Society Press, 1995). *Adventures in Politics: We Go to the Legislature* (New York: Oxford University Press, 1954), written by

Richard Neuberger, is a collection of essays on Oregon politics in the early 1950s. Finally, Richard B. Webb's "A Formal Model of Oregon's Budgetary Process" (PhD diss., University of Oregon, 1977) is one of the few works focusing specifically on Oregon's budget process.

RACE, ETHNICITY, AND GENDER

Studies on race, ethnicity, and gender provide additional insight into Oregon's culture and politics. Particular attention has been focused on the position of Indians in Oregon's history and into modern times. One fine early effort is Erna Gunther's *Indian Life on the Northwest Coast of North America As Seen by the Early Explorers and Fur Traders during the Last Decades of the Eighteenth Century* (Chicago: University of Chicago Press, 1972). Gunther's work reconstructs the societies of Northwest Native American peoples at the time of European contact and first settlement. Roberta Ulrich's *Empty Nets: Indians, Dams, and the Columbia* (Corvallis: Oregon State University Press, 1999) chronicles the efforts of Indian tribes to protect their fishing rights along the Columbia River, and ultimately their way of life. The book also provides valuable insight into tribal government, treaty rights, and related issues. Carolyn N. Long's *Religious Freedom and Indian Rights: The Case of Oregon v. Smith* (Lawrence: University Press of Kansas, 2000) analyzes the important First Amendment court case concerning the rights of Klamath Indians to practice their religion without government interference.

There is a scattering of works on other groups. *Nosotros: The Hispanic People of Oregon* (Portland: The Oregon Council of the Humanities, 1995), edited by Erasmo Gamboa and Carolyn M. Buan, is a collection of essays that traces the complex history of Latinos in Oregon from 1500s to today. Elizabeth McLagan's *A Peculiar Paradise: A History of Blacks in Oregon, 1788–1940* (Portland OR: The Georgian Press, 1980) provides an account of African Americans in Oregon. Linda Tamura's *The Hood River Issei: An Oral History of Japanese Settlers in Oregon's Hood River Valley* (Urbana: University of Illinois Press, 1993) examines the contributions of Japanese immigrants to Oregon's early development, as well as the injustices they faced in the wake of Pearl Harbor. Jean M. Ward and Elaine A. Maveety have put together a collection of the writings by Oregon's leading suffragist in *"Yours for Liberty": Selections from Abigail Scott Duniway's Suffrage Newspaper* (Corvallis: Oregon State University Press, 2000). Finally, *Experiences in a Promised Land: Essays in Pacific Northwest History* (Seattle: University of Washington Press, 1986), edited by G. Thomas Edwards and Carlos A.

Schwantes, offers a collection of essays on women, racial minorities, and radical groups in the history of the region.

CONTEMPORARY POLICY CONCERNS

A number of books provide more detailed information about some of the major policy issues debated in Oregon. For example, among the books focusing on the Oregon Health Plan are *Five States That Could Not Wait: Lessons for Health Reform from Florida, Hawaii, Minnesota, Oregon, and Vermont* (New York: Health Affairs Milbank Memorial Fund, 1994), edited by Daniel M. Fox and John K. Iglehart; *The New Politics of State Health Policy* (Lawrence: University Press of Kansas, 2001), by Robert B. Hackey and David A. Rochefort; and *Rationing America's Medical Care: The Oregon Plan and Beyond* (Washington DC: Brookings, 1992), edited by Martin A. Strosberg, Joshua M. Wiener, Robert Baker, and I. Alan Fein. Oregon's assisted suicide law have been the subject of at least two books: *Dying Right: The Death with Dignity Movement* (New York: Routledge, 2001), by Daniel Hillyard and John Dombrink, and *Assisted Suicide: Finding Common Ground* (Bloomington: Indiana University Press, 2001), edited by Lois Snyder and Arthur L. Caplan.

There are a number of good books on natural resource policy in Oregon. Kai Lee's *Compass and Gyroscope* (Washington DC : Island Press, 1995) examines the conflict between hydropower generation and fish habitat in the Columbia River. Jim Lichatowich's *Salmon without Rivers: A History of the Pacific Salmon Crisis* (Washington DC: Island Press, 1999) offers a well-researched examination of the decline of salmon in the Pacific Northwest over the past 150 years. William Robbins's *Landscapes of Promise: The Oregon Story, 1800–1940* (Seattle: University of Washington Press, 1997) provides a history of how extraction industries created the economic and political structure of Oregon. Finally, Carl Abbott, Deborah Howe, and Sy Adler review the progress of Oregon's pioneering effort in land-use planning in *Planning the Oregon Way: A Twenty-Year Evaluation* (Corvallis: Oregon State University Press, 1994).

PERSONALITIES

There are several detailed biographies on leading political actors in Oregon. Biographies of former U.S. senators are among the most common. Steve Neal's *McNary of Oregon: A Political Biography* (Portland: Western Imprints, 1985) offers a biography of Senator Charles McNary, one of the nation's leading Progressive Republicans from 1920s to the 1940s. Mason Drukman's *Wayne Morse: A Political Biography* (Portland: Oregon Historical Society Press, 1997) is a recent work on one of Oregon's most important national figures from the 1940s through the 1960s. Mark Kirchmeier's *Packwood: The Public and Private Life from Acclaim to Outrage* (San Francisco CA: HarperCollins West, 1995) traces the life of Senator Bob Packwood from his early years through the sexual misconduct scandal that drove him from office. Mark O. Hatfield and Diane N. Solomon's *Against the Grain: Reflections of a Rebel Republican* (Ashland OR: White Cloud Press, 2000) is an autobiography of the former Oregon governor and U.S. senator.

Several Oregon governors have also been the focus of biographies. Gary Murrell's *Iron Pants: Oregon's Anti-New Deal Governor, Charles Henry Martin* (Pullman: Washington State University Press, 2000) tells about the conservative Republican governor during the 1930s. In *An Editor for Oregon: Charles A. Sprague and the Politics of Change* (Corvallis: Oregon State University Press, 1998), Floyd J. McKay offers a biography of the influential Salem newspaper editor and the person who would succeed Martin as governor. Brent Walth's *Fire at Eden's Gate: Tom McCall and the Oregon Story* (Portland: Oregon Historical Society, 1994) is a detailed biography of Oregon's progressive Republican governor.

DATA SOURCES AND GOVERNMENT DOCUMENTS

Material on the Web

Some of the best data available on Oregon can be accessed on the Internet. Data include election histories, campaign finance reports, state legislative records, and the governor's budget. Here are some of the most valuable Web sites:

Election Data

The Elections Division in the secretary of state's office provides material on a wide variety of topics, including state election laws, party registration figures, a log of recent initiatives and referenda, and past election results, through its official Web site (http://www.sos.state.or.us/elections/elechp htm). The site also provides a searchable database on campaign finance in state elections.

Legislation and Laws

Information on the Oregon Legislative Assembly can be found on the legislature's official Web site, at http://www.leg.state.or.us/. The site provides information on individual legislators, the legislative process, measure histories, session statistics, and other related topics. A searchable index of all the laws passed by the Legislative Assembly is available online at http://www.leg.state.or.us/ors/home.html. Oregon's constitution can be found at http://bluebook.state.or.us/state/constitution/constitution.htm.

Court Action and Legal Opinions

The Web site for the Oregon Department of Justice (http://www.doj.state.or. us/) includes information on the department's role in the state, as well as a database on opinions rendered by the attorney general. The Web site for the Oregon Judicial Department provides the opinions of the Supreme Court, Court of Appeals, and Tax Court, along with general information on the court system. This Web site can be found at http://www.ojd.state.or.us/.

Government Finance

The Legislative Fiscal Office and Legislative Revenue Office regularly conduct research on issues related to government spending and taxes in Oregon. Many of their reports can be found at http://www.leg.state.or.us/budget_tax/home.htm. The Oregon Budget and Management Division develops the governor's budget and oversees budget-related issues. The office's Web site (http://www.bam.das.state.or.us) provides links to the governor's budget and to legislative action.

Government Performance

Information on Oregon's efforts to measure government performance can be found online at the Oregon Progress Board Web site (http://www.econ.state. or.us/opb/). The site includes data on the performance of both state and county governments.

Economy and Demographics

The Oregon Office of Economic Analysis serves as the main forecasting unit for the state of Oregon, producing the state's economic and revenue forecasts, as well as other reports. Several of the office's reports, including the economic forecasts, are available online at http://www.oea.das.state.or.us/. The Population Research Center at Portland State University is the official source for all population information for the state. The center produces a variety of reports on social, economic, and demographic trends both for the state and for local governments, many of which are available at www.upa.pdx.edu/CPRC/.

Public Opinion

The only regularly conducted public opinion poll in Oregon is one that is administered every two years by the Program for Governmental Research and Education at Oregon State University. The poll focuses on voter understanding of and attitude toward government programs and taxation. Some of the survey results are available at the program's Web site (http://oregonstate.edu/Dept/pol_sci/pgre). The Oregon Progress Board conducts a social survey of Oregon residents every two years as well, tracking trends in economic well-being, health care, and other social issues. The results of the survey can be found at the Progress Board's Web page listed above.

Local Concerns

The University of Oregon Library contains a detailed bibliography of sources to find data and other information on local areas in Oregon. The library's Web site provides links to statistics on agricultural, economic, educational, environmental, welfare, and other issues. The site is located at www.libweb.uoregon.edu/govdocs/localdat.html.

Newspapers

The largest newspaper in the state is the *Oregonian*, which provides a good source of information on politics and government in the state, as well as other news. The *Salem Statesman Journal* also devotes considerable attention to state politics. It provides hometown coverage of the events in the state capitol. Another source is the *Eugene Register-Guard*. The Oregon State Library provides a searchable index to these three newspapers, as well as several smaller ones. The index is available online at http://db.osl.state.or.us/orind1.htm.

Other Sources

As in most states, the state government in Oregon produces a variety of reports and publications on state activities, not all of which are available online. These publications are made available to the public at libraries throughout the state. There are currently twelve full depository libraries in Oregon, which receive copies of all state publications that are deposited with the State Library. There are another fifteen libraries that receive the state's core publications. The depository libraries house, among other works, the state criminal code, the *House Journal* and *Senate Journal*, which provide the official records of House and Senate action, and the complete version of the governor's budget. The Oregon State Library Web site (http://www.osl.state.or.us/home/techserv/cordocs.html) includes a list of the major public documents it distributes to these libraries. In some cases, the listing provides a link to an online version of the document.

Two other sources also provide important documents. First, the Oregon State Archives maintains all the formal records of the state, including those for state agencies, the legislature, and the U.S. Census. The archives also maintains a selection of county-level records. Second, the Oregon Historical Society has an extensive research holding that includes a broad collection of both primary and secondary research materials. These materials include book manuscripts and serials, a broad selection of newspapers from across the state, historical records, maps, personal and business papers, architectural drawings, and original artifacts.

Contributors

JOE BOWERSOX

Joe Bowersox is associate professor of politics at Willamette University, where he teaches courses in environmental politics, policy, and law. Bowersox received his PhD in political science from the University of Wisconsin–Madison in 1995. His publications include articles on Oregon water policy, forest policy, and environmental political theory. He is coauthor and coeditor with John Martin Gillroy of *The Moral Austerity of Environmental Policy* *(2002)*, and with Karen Arabas, *Forest Futures: Science, Politics, and Policy for the Next Century* (2004).

RICHARD A. CLUCAS

Richard A. Clucas is associate professor of political science at Portland State University. He received his PhD from the University of California at Santa Barbara in 1990. He is the author of *The Speaker's Electoral Connection: Willie Brown and the California Assembly* (1995) and *The Encyclopedia of American Political Reform* (1996). He is the editor of *Readings and Cases in State and Local Politics* (2005) and the general editor of ABC-CLIO's reference set on state government.

RUSS DONDERO

Russ Dondero has been a professor in the Department of Politics and Government, Pacific University, Forest Grove, Oregon, since 1974. He received an MA and PhD from the University of Minnesota. He is a recognized expert and analyst of Oregon politics. He teaches courses in American politics. He is also the founder and coordinator of Pacific University's annual Tom McCall Forum.

E. D. DOVER

E. D. Dover is professor of political science, public policy, and administration at Western Oregon University. Dover has a BA in political science, an MA in public administration, and an MA in communication from the University of Wyoming. He received his PhD in political science from the University of Colorado in 1985. Dover is the author of four books on American parties: *Party Activists and Interest Groups* (1985), *Presidential Elections in the Television Age: 1960–1992* (1994), *The Presidential Election of 1996: Clinton's Incumbency and Television* (1998), and *Missed Opportunity: Gore, Incumbency and Television in Election 2000* (2002).

RICHARD J. ELLIS

Richard J. Ellis is Mark O. Hatfield Professor of Politics at Willamette University in Salem, Oregon. His research and teaching focuses on American political culture and political development, the American presidency, and the initiative and referendum. His books include *American Political Cultures* (1993), *The Dark Side of the Left: Illiberal Egalitarianism in America* (1998), *Founding the American Presidency* (1999), and, most recently, *Democratic Delusions: The Initiative Process in America* (2002).

JAMES C. FOSTER

James C. Foster is professor of political science at Oregon State University, Cascades. He regularly teaches courses on constitutional law, administrative law, gender and law, and American political thought. He has published articles on legal education, book chapters on affirmative action and equality debates, edited *Governing Through Courts*, and coauthored the two-volume *Constitutional Law: Cases in Context*.

MARK HENKELS

Mark Henkels is professor of political science and public policy and administration at Western Oregon University. He has taught state and local government and a wide variety of policy-oriented courses at Western Oregon

University since 1988. He has supervised interns serving in scores of state and local government and nonprofit agencies. His research interests include local environmental activism, the impact of direct democracy in the states, and patterns of state budgeting. His PhD in political science comes from the University of Utah.

ALANA S. JEYDEL

Alana S. Jeydel is an assistant professor at Oregon State University. She received her PhD from American University and has taught at North Carolina State University in Raleigh, the State University of New York at Oneonta and York College of Pennsylvania. Her research interests include social movements, women in Congress, and legislative leadership.

DENISE LACH

Denise Lach is codirector of the Center for Water and Environmental Sustainability (CWEST) at Oregon State University. Her research and publications focus on issues raised by individuals and organizations dealing with environmental problems, including the use of scientific information, the role of stakeholders, and the significance of citizen involvement in decision making. She received a BS in English/Education from the University of Minnesota (1976) and an MS (1988) and PhD (1992) in sociology from the University of Oregon.

WILLIAM LUNCH

William Lunch is professor and chair of political science at Oregon State University. He is also the Political Analyst for Oregon Public Broadcasting. He regularly broadcasts political analysis on OPB radio of Oregon and is an occasional analyst on Northwest regional political developments for National Public Radio. His PhD is from the University of California, Berkeley; in 1987, the University of California Press published his book, *The Nationalization of American Politics*.

JERRY F. MEDLER

Jerry F. Medler is an associate professor emeritus of political science at the University of Oregon. Medler has published articles on the Oregon governor, the politics of land-use planning, and the role of the media in environmental policy. Undergraduate courses taught include elections and campaigns, mass media and U.S. politics, and coastal resources management policy.

JIM MOORE

Jim Moore has been watching Oregon politics for over thirty years. On the faculty of the University of Portland from 1990 to 2001, he has also been a political analyst for Portland television and radio stations. He is currently a political consultant and serves as the political analyst for KPDX Fox 49 television, and KINK radio in Portland.

DOUGLAS F. MORGAN

Douglas F. Morgan is the director of the Executive Leadership Institute and a professor of public administration in the Mark Hatfield School of Government at Portland State University. He received his PhD in political science from the University of Chicago in 1971. His research has been published in such journals as *Public Administration Review*, *Administrative Theory and Praxis*, and *Administration and Society*.

MELODY ROSE

Melody Rose is an associate professor of political science in the Mark Hatfield School of Government at Portland State University. She received her PhD from Cornell University in 1997. She is the author of several articles on the impact of divided government on social policy. Her teaching interests include party politics, the presidency, and women and public policy.

BRENT S. STEEL

Brent S. Steel is professor of political science and director of the Master of Public Policy program at Oregon State University, Corvallis. He received his PhD in political science from Washington State University in 1984. He is the editor of *Public Lands Management in the West* (1997), coeditor of *Global Environmental Policy and Administration* (1999), and coauthor of three books including *Citizens, Political Communication, and Interest Groups: Environmental Organizations in Canada and the United States* (1992); *Political Culture and Public Policy in Canada and the United States: Only a Border Apart?* (2000); and *Environmental Politics and Policy: A Comparative Perspective* (2002).

Index

In the Politics and Governments of the American States series

Alabama Government and Politics
By James D. Thomas and William H. Stewart

Alaska Politics and Government
By Gerald A. McBeath and Thomas A. Morehouse

Arizona Politics and Government: The Quest for Autonomy, Democracy, and Development
By David R. Berman

Arkansas Politics and Government, second edition
By Diane D. Blair and Jay Barth

Colorado Politics and Government: Governing the Centennial State
By Thomas E. Cronin and Robert D. Loevy

Hawai'i Politics and Government: An American State in a Pacific World
By Richard C. Pratt with Zachary Smith

Illinois Politics and Government: The Expanding Metropolitan Frontier
By Samuel K. Gove and James D. Nowlan

Kentucky Politics and Government: Do We Stand United?
By Penny M. Miller

Maine Politics and Government
By Kenneth T. Palmer, G. Thomas Taylor, and Marcus A. LiBrizzi

Michigan Politics and Government: Facing Change in a Complex State
By William P. Browne and Kenneth VerBurg

Minnesota Politics and Government
By Daniel J. Elazar, Virginia Gray, and Wyman Spano

Mississippi Government and Politics: Modernizers versus Traditionalists
By Dale Krane and Stephen D. Shaffer

Nebraska Government and Politics
Edited by Robert D. Miewald

Nevada Politics and Government: Conservatism in an Open Society
By Don W. Driggs and Leonard E. Goodall

New Jersey Politics and Government: Suburban Politics Comes of Age, second edition
By Barbara G. Salmore and Stephen A. Salmore

New York Politics and Government: Competition and Compassion
By Sarah F. Liebschutz, with Robert W. Bailey, Jeffrey M. Stonecash,
Jane Shapiro Zacek, and Joseph F. Zimmerman

North Carolina Government and Politics
By Jack D. Fleer

Oklahoma Politics and Policies: Governing the Sooner State
By David R. Morgan, Robert E. England, and George G. Humphreys

Oregon Politics and Government: Progressives versus Conservative Populists
By Richard A. Clucas, Mark Henkels, and Brent S. Steel

Rhode Island Politics and Government
By Maureen Moakley and Elmer Cornwel

South Carolina Politics and Government
By Cole Blease Graham Jr. and William V. Moore

West Virginia Politics and Government
By Richard A. Brisbin Jr., Robert Jay Dilger,
Allan S. Hammock, and Christopher Z. Mooney

Wisconsin Politics and Government: America's Laboratory of Democracy
By James K. Conant